AID TO RUSSIA 1941-1946

STRATEGY, DIPLOMACY, THE ORIGINS OF THE COLD WAR

Contemporary American
History Series
William E. Leuchtenburg,
General Editor

Aid to Russia
1941 - 1946

STRATEGY, DIPLOMACY, THE ORIGINS OF THE COLD WAR

George C. Herring, Jr.

COLUMBIA UNIVERSITY PRESS

NEW YORK AND LONDON

George C. Herring, Jr. is Associate
Professor of History at the University
of Kentucky.

Library of Congress Cataloging in Publication Data

Herring, George C., Jr.   1936–
  Aid to Russia, 1941–1946.

  (Contemporary American history series)
  Bibliography: p. 343–354
  1. Lend-lease operations (1941–1945)
  2. United States—Foreign relations—Russia.
  3. Russia—Foreign relations—United States.
  I. Title.
D753.2.R9H47   338.91′47′0973   72-10545
ISBN 0-231-03336-2 (cloth)
ISBN 0-231-08348-3 (paperback)

To My Mother and to the
Memory of My Father

ACKNOWLEDGMENTS

It is a pleasure at the completion of a project such as this to look back and acknowledge with gratitude the many debts incurred over the years of research and writing. A generous fellowship endowed by the Stettinius Fund, Inc., enabled me to begin research on the diplomacy of lend-lease while I was a graduate student at the University of Virginia. A grant from the Ohio University Research Committee made possible a summer of research in Washington, and grants from the University of Kentucky Research Foundation facilitated numerous additional research trips, gave me a summer free for writing, and assisted in the preparation of a final manuscript.

Numerous libraries and government repositories provided invaluable assistance in the location of documents. The staffs of the National Archives, the Franklin D. Roosevelt Library, and the University of Virginia Library were particularly helpful in this regard. Dr. Robert W. Coakley of the Office of the Chief of Military History generously shared with me his great knowledge of lend-lease and of War Department and U.S. Army records. The late E. Taylor Parks and Dr. Arthur Kogan of the Department of State Historical Office answered my many queries on the availability and location of diplomatic records.

Writers of contemporary history can learn much from participants in the events they study, and I am especially indebted to Professor John N. Hazard of the Columbia University School of Law, who not only provided me with recollections of his experiences with lend-lease to Russia but also made available to me some of his personal papers and carefully read my final manuscript. Mr. Willis C. Armstrong, formerly of the USSR Branch of the Foreign Economic Administration, provided detailed and most helpful responses to my questions, and along with Professor Hazard helped to fill gaps in the written record.

Professor Edward E. Younger of the University of Virginia originally suggested that I undertake this study, and I sincerely hope that he will be pleased with the result. Professor John L. Gaddis of Ohio University read the manuscript and made many helpful suggestions. My former colleague, Professor Alonzo L. Hamby of Ohio University, rendered invaluable advice during the years we shared an office in Bentley Hall and perceptively criticized the final draft. Professor William E. Leuchtenburg, the general editor of this series, encouraged my work from the outset and patiently assisted me thereafter, offering countless suggestions on research and writing and detailed criticism of every page of manuscript. Only those who have had the good fortune of working with him can fully appreciate the benefits derived from his wise and friendly counsel.

Finally, I thank Bernard Gronert of the Columbia University Press for his cooperation and assistance, and Dorothy Leathers for typing the manuscript. Most important, I thank my wife Nancy, who prodded when I was lazy, tolerated my frequent periods of preoccupation, and took care of John and Lisa while daddy was away on trips or at the office writing. Her loving encouragement and help made it all much easier.

                                    GEORGE C. HERRING, JR.
Lexington, Kentucky
August, 1972

CONTENTS

INTRODUCTION

During the Second World War, the United States furnished the Soviet Union more than 17,000,000 tons of supplies valued at over $10 billion. This massive program of military assistance occupied a central place in the wartime relations between the two nations. The failure of the United States to render effective assistance to the Russians in the first years of the war intensified an already deep Soviet distrust of the Western powers, and for a time threatened the existence of the alliance. By the end of 1943, however, lendlease to the USSR had reached substantial proportions and it became a symbol of the spirit of allied cooperation encour-

aged by the leaders of both the United States and the Soviet
Union. Stalin himself paid glowing tribute to the American
contribution to Soviet military victories. Numerous commentators, both Russian and American, expressed their belief that lend-lease had helped to promote a mutual trust
and understanding that could be extended into the postwar
era. To give substance to these hopes, officials in both nations developed plans for American aid to assist Russia's reconstruction from the devastation of war.[1]

The dreams of wartime began to fade even before the battles had ended, however, and were soon replaced by
disillusionment, growing bitterness, and mutual antagonism.
Military collaboration had only covered over, not removed,
the long legacy of suspicion and hostility between the two
nations, and the efforts of the leaders of the Grand Alliance
to resolve fundamental—perhaps irreconcilable—disputes
over postwar objectives came to naught. The defeat of the
enemy in 1945 removed the most binding tie that had held
the allies together. Within two years after the day of victory,
Soviet-American hostility had deepened into that conflict
known as the Cold War. The abrupt termination of lend-
lease assistance at the end of the war and the quick breakdown of negotiations on a postwar loan contributed to the
rising conflict and symbolized the transition from alliance to
enmity.

"Inevitably," Robert A. Divine has written, "the Cold
War cast its shadow over the historiography of World War
II."[2] Economic assistance, which had been so important in
the wartime relationship, became an issue of great controversy in historical accounts of the development and breakdown of the Grand Alliance. Within three years after the
end of the war, Soviet government spokesmen and official
historians began to minimize the importance of lend-lease in
the triumph over Nazi Germany. As early as February, 1948,
the trade union newspaper *Trud* observed that the arms received from the United States during the war were "by far
poorer in quality" than Russian-made weapons. Subsequent
Russian accounts of World War II either played down or ig-

nored altogether the role of American assistance. An official history of the *Economy of the USSR During World War II* by Nikolai A. Voznesensky, Chief of the State Planning Commission, conceded that the United States had provided aid to the Soviet Union, but estimated that it had amounted to only 4 percent of domestic production and stressed that most of it had arrived late in the war after the defeat of Germany had been assured by the "brilliant victories of Soviet arms."

By 1949, Russian attacks on lend-lease had become more bitter. A Soviet review dismissed as "ridiculous" suggestions that American aid had played a significant part in the war. Writers resurrected old charges that "ruling circles" in the United States had deliberately held back assistance to their ally in 1942 and 1943 to weaken its postwar position and to insure their own dominance over the peace settlement. Lend-lease was not a "weapon of victory," as Americans believed, but a device by which U.S. "monopolists" made "fabulous riches" at the expense of suffering people and a "many-edged weapon of American imperialism" employed ruthlessly in the quest for world domination.[3]

As the Russians deflated the volume and importance of lend-lease, Americans inflated it. The illusion spread that the United States had provided the bulk of the USSR's war supplies and insured its survival of the Nazi invasion.[4] More significant, as the Cold War gripped the United States in the late forties and early fifties, frustrated and anxious Americans sought scapegoats for the rise of the communist menace. A group of right-wing postwar revisionists found in President Franklin D. Roosevelt's wartime "appeasement" of the Soviet Union the primary cause of the Cold War. Either through ignorance, stupidity, or treachery, it was alleged, Roosevelt had fought the war and conducted American diplomacy in a manner that insured the postwar expansion of communism.

These revisionists singled out lend-lease as one of the major articles in their indictment of Roosevelt's leadership. The President had extended aid to Stalin in 1941 unconditionally, without requiring political commitments that might have limited Soviet ambitions, thus losing that "precious moment when the Russian armies were being driven back like cattle before Hitler's onrushing legions, when Stalin lacked everything save men."[5] Throughout the war, Roosevelt had lavished gifts upon the ungrateful Russians, not only depriving the United States and its other allies of essential equipment, but also contributing to the creation of that "monstrous military power that would cast a lengthening shadow over Europe and Asia throughout the following decades."[6] In 1949 one disgruntled former lend-lease official even issued sensational accusations that Roosevelt and his pro-communist advisers had given the Russians the raw materials and technical information necessary to produce an atomic bomb.[7]

Congressional investigations proved these most extreme charges without foundation, but criticism of the President's lend-lease policies persisted and received backing from prominent scholars. The distinguished diplomatic historian, Thomas A. Bailey, doubted that Roosevelt could have secured meaningful political commitments from Stalin in return for economic assistance, but he contended nonetheless that FDR's handling of lend-lease was lacking in astuteness and mischievous in its results. Roosevelt, Bailey asserted, "appears to have concluded that if we were to give the Soviets all they wanted, generously and without demur, they might be weaned away from their dangerous ideas of world revolution and co-operate wholeheartedly in the common enterprise of building a better tomorrow." It was a "gigantic gamble," according to the historian, and it failed. The President's attempts to conciliate the Russians not only "weakened us but further inspired mistrust in the Kremlin."[8]

Like Bailey, the career diplomat, historian, and expert on the Soviet Union, George F. Kennan, conceded that Roosevelt could not have extracted political concessions from Stalin as *quid pro quo* for lend-lease, and given the conditions under which the war was fought, Kennan doubted that the United States could have done much to prevent Soviet expansion into Eastern Europe. But in his influential interpretation of *American Diplomacy, 1900–1950,* he questioned the wisdom of the administration's policies on aid to Russia in the later stages of the war. There was "no adequate justification for continuing a program of lavish and almost indiscriminate aid to the Soviet Union at a time when there was increasing reason to doubt whether her purposes in Eastern Europe, aside from the defeat of Germany, would be ones which we Americans could approve and sponsor." [9]

This highly critical interpretation of Roosevelt's handling of aid to Russia has persisted in some quarters to the present. Indeed, the fullest and most recent scholarly study concludes that the story of American lend-lease to the USSR constitutes a "narrative of unfettered aid to a suspicious ally, of a Red Army given mobility that made it an incredible striking force, and of a shattered nation that received unquestionably valuable industrial potential to spark her reconstruction, all with virtually no attempt to credit her allies in any more than a grudging way." [10]

The persistence of such views reflects more the staying power of traditional Cold War assumptions than present concerns, however, for in the last decade the gradual thaw in Soviet-American relations and the massive disillusionment in the United States resulting from the war in Vietnam have combined to produce dramatic changes in interpretations of wartime and postwar diplomacy. New revisionists, deeply influenced by the profound changes within the Soviet bloc and by American policies in Southeast Asia, have turned conventional interpretations of the Cold War on their head, shifting responsibility from the USSR to the United States. They view Stalin as a cautious conservative and a staunch nationalist, dedicated to promoting the traditional interests of the Russian state rather than to fomenting world revolution. They regard his attempts to establish a sphere of influence in Eastern Europe as natural and legitimate because of the chronic weakness and instability of that region and its strategic importance as a gateway to Russia. On the other hand, they argue that the persistent efforts of the United

States to dislodge the USSR from Eastern Europe and to deprive her of the fruits of victory provoked an aggressive Soviet response and initiated the Cold War.[11]

The new revisionists diverge when interpreting the sources of America's provocative policies. Moderates stress the change in leadership in 1945 from a conciliatory and sympathetic Roosevelt to a doctrinaire and aggressive Harry S. Truman as the turning point in Soviet-American relations. The more radical revisionists contend that American Cold War policies resulted inevitably from a capitalist drive for domination of the world economy.[12] Moderates and radicals agree, however, that, at least from 1945 on, the United States employed its economic resources ruthlessly and relentlessly to prevent the Soviet Union from consolidating its control over Eastern Europe. The Truman administration drastically reduced lend-lease at V-E Day to coerce the USSR into conforming with American postwar aims. The United States abruptly terminated all lend-lease shipments at V-J Day to force the Russians (and indeed other nations) to request credits for reconstruction to which it could attach harsh political and economic concessions. Unsuccessful in forcing the Soviet Union to surrender, American diplomats then denied her aid in the immediate postwar period, forcing her to rely on her own resources for the arduous job of relief and rehabilitation. In short, revisionists regard American dollar diplomacy as a significant source of Cold War conflict.[13]

The new revisionism has in the past few years set off a vigorous debate on American foreign policy during and immediately after the Second World War. Many historians have rejected both the assumptions behind and the conclusions of the revisionists. Some question their heavy stress on U. S. economic policy as a major source of friction with the USSR. Conceding that the termination of lend-lease and the handling of postwar assistance "strengthened Soviet suspicions," Arthur M. Schlesinger, Jr., has concluded that generous American aid for Russia at the end of the war would not have "made much essential difference" in the course of relations between the two nations. Nevertheless, revisionism seems to gain in force and adherents, and even a recent critic has suggested that a more liberal American policy on economic assistance might have eased postwar tensions. Thus in the twenty-six years since the end of World War II, the problem of American aid to Russia between 1941 and 1946 has remained lively and controversial.[14]

Much of the writing on this subject suffers from serious weaknesses, however. Few studies deal with the problem in any depth, and most have not taken advantage of the abundance of archival and manuscript sources that has become available to scholars only in recent years. As Divine has observed, moreover, most of the writing on wartime and postwar diplomacy reflects an obvious preoccupation with the Cold War. Interpretations have been highly colored by the emotions and prejudices of the times. Authors have ignored the context in which major decisions were made; they have failed to judge the diplomacy of the period on its own terms. Finally, both the revisionists of the forties and those of the sixties and seventies share an implicit acceptance of what D. W. Brogan has termed the "illusion of American omnipotence." They assume that the United States had the capacity to prevent the Cold War. They argue that different policies on economic assistance alone might have averted or at least limited the conflict that developed after 1945.

The study that follows considers in detail American aid to the USSR from 1941 to 1946 and attempts to assess its importance in Soviet-American relations during and immediately after World War II. It focuses on the evolution of U. S. policies for lend-lease and aid for Russian reconstruction; explores the assumptions upon which American policy makers acted and the ends they sought to achieve through the use of foreign aid; and examines the influences at work in specific policy decisions and the manner in which policies were implemented. It rests on the fundamental premise that the diplomacy of global war was an infinitely complicated process involving many different forces which were rarely in harmony and often in conflict.

American diplomatists, especially those of World War II, have often been accused of ignoring the Clausewitzian dictum that war is a continuation of diplomacy by other means. This study will show, however, that U. S. policy makers were keenly aware of the potential political value of economic assistance to the USSR and that throughout the period they vigorously debated the tactics that should be employed to make it an effective instrument of diplomacy. This debate forms a central issue in the making of American policy toward Russia during these years; it reveals much about American attitudes toward the Soviet Union and about the goals and instruments of U. S. policy.

Aid policies were not established in a vacuum, however, and a study of the major wartime decisions must take into account the strategic context in which they were made. Immediate military demands as well as long-range strategic goals often dictated policy; in the case of the USSR, logistics set very strict limitations on the scope and volume of the assistance provided. Military exigencies did not always compete with political objectives; but in certain instances they did, and decisions had to be made and priorities established. Analysis of these cases tells much about the nature of American wartime diplomacy.

Domestic politics also affected foreign aid, sometimes decisively. Those responsible for handling assistance for the USSR had to consider the deep-seated suspicions Americans had long entertained toward the Soviet Union and communism. More important, they had to take into account the political implications of foreign aid itself. Lend-lease represented a sharp departure from past American practices in foreign relations. Americans valued its importance as an instrument of war, but because of its novelty and the expense it involved they always regarded it with a suspicious eye. It depended upon annual appropriations from Congress. Throughout the war it remained a potentially volatile political issue, and could not be kept out of partisan politics.

Aid for reconstruction presented even more difficult political problems. Thoughtful and articulate observers repeat-

edly stressed that the United States must avoid a repetition
of the economic mistakes of World War I, but this did not
reflect a general understanding of the degree of destruction
and economic dislocation wrought by World War II or acceptance of a general commitment to provide massive and
generous aid for rehabilitation. On the contrary, there was
broad disagreement about the nature and scope of America's
role in the postwar world economy, and considerable opposition to programs or proposals that involved spending large
sums of money. Those responsible for making policy could
ignore these considerations only at their own peril.

This is a study then of the interaction of strategic, diplomatic, and political influences in the shaping of American
policy for aid to Russia from 1941 to 1946. It attempts to dis-
cern the specific objectives American diplomats hoped to
achieve through the use of economic assistance, to show how
they handled lend-lease and aid for Russian reconstruction,
and to evaluate the effects of their policies on the diplomatic
relations between the United States and the USSR. In a
broader vein, it seeks to contribute to an understanding of
the sources, goals, and methods of American diplomacy during and immediately after the Second World War and to assess the utility and limitations of economic assistance as an
instrument of coalition warfare and foreign policy.

AID TO RUSSIA
1941 - 1946

STRATEGY, DIPLOMACY,
THE ORIGINS OF THE
COLD WAR

Chapter 1

"TO WALK WITH THE DEVIL"

THE DECISION TO AID RUSSIA, JUNE - NOVEMBER, 1941

ON JUNE 22, 1941, THE ANNIVERSARY OF NAPOLEON'S INVASION OF RUSSIA, Hitler attacked the Soviet Union along a two-thousand-mile front from the Arctic to the Ukraine and caught the USSR completely unprepared. The *Luftwaffe* destroyed Russian air units in the west on the first day of the war. Breaking through Soviet lines, the *Wehrmacht* encircled defending forces, inflicted huge losses, and took thousands of prisoners. The Nazis advanced rapidly during the early weeks of the war, overrunning the Baltic States and approaching Leningrad, driving to Smolensk, and moving close to Kiev. German propagandists boasted that the war was won.

From the beginning, it was apparent that Russia's survival might depend upon assistance from other nations then resisting Hitler, nations which in the past had opposed Soviet communism with as much vigor as Nazism. Great Britain responded immediately. In a dramatic broadcast on the night of June 22, Prime Minister Winston S. Churchill welcomed the Soviet Union into the anti-Hitler coalition and called upon the British people to put aside past differences with the USSR. "We shall give whatever help we can to Russia and the Russian people," Churchill pledged, and "we shall appeal to our friends and allies in every part of the world to take the same course, and pursue it, as we shall faithfully and steadfastly to the end." [1]

Churchill directed his final appeal toward the United States and President Franklin D. Roosevelt. By June, 1941, America had abandoned the position of neutrality assumed upon the outbreak of war in 1939. The swift advance of Hitler's troops across the continent of Europe to the English Channel in the spring and summer of 1940 had awakened Americans to the German menace, weakened traditional isolationist assumptions that Europe's wars did not concern the United States, and aroused growing support for aid to Britain. Roosevelt had responded on June 10, 1940, by promising to extend to "opponents of force the material resources of this nation." But the President and the American people harbored a deep aversion to involvement in the war, and in succeeding months Roosevelt had moved very slowly in implementing his promise. As embattled Britain girded for the anticipated invasion, the administration worked cautiously within the "cash-and-carry" limitations imposed by the Neutrality Act of 1939 to assist the British in placing orders for millions of dollars worth of war supplies with American firms. In September, after four months of deliberation, the President agreed to give Churchill fifty obsolete destroyers in return for the right to construct and maintain military and naval bases on eight British possessions in the Caribbean.[2]

The perilous state of British finances compelled Roosevelt to act more forcefully in December, 1940. Churchill frankly advised that the United Kingdom could not fight on without greater quantities of American supplies, and warned that its dwindling dollar resources would soon make cash purchases impossible. The President responded with lend-lease, an ingenious measure that bypassed the Neutrality Act by conferring upon him sweeping powers to "sell, transfer, exchange, lease, lend, or otherwise dispose of" any item to any nation whose defense he deemed vital to the security of the United

States. The terms of transfer would be set by the President, either payment in kind or in property or "any other direct or indirect benefit." Offering lend-lease to the American people, Roosevelt stressed the importance "from a selfish point of view of American defense, that we should do everything to help the British Empire defend itself," and explained the necessity of getting rid of the "silly, foolish old dollar sign." He spoke in grave terms of "an emergency as serious as war itself," and called upon the United States to become the "great arsenal of democracy." [3]

The lend-lease proposal sparked a great debate in American foreign policy, a debate, Roosevelt later remarked, that was argued "in every newspaper, on every wave length— over every cracker barrel in all the land." A vocal minority of hard-core isolationists, mostly Republicans, opposed lend-lease vigorously. Certain that the war was not America's concern and that Hitler did not threaten the United States, they denounced lend-lease as a provocative and dangerous measure that would inevitably drag the nation into war and would destroy democracy at home by conferring dictatorial powers on the President. Some isolationists reluctantly accepted the need for aid to Britain, but they rejected lend-lease as a dangerous departure from neutrality and instead proposed the more conventional method of loans. In contrast, a small minority of interventionists viewed the war as a death struggle between totalitarianism and democracy and argued that American intervention was necessary to defeat Hitler. They supported lend-lease, but pressed for even more decisive action to aid Britain. The great majority of Americans were more cautious. Fearing the German threat, they were willing to risk war to insure a British victory. But they still hoped this could be achieved without American troops, and they supported lend-lease as a means to that end.[4]

After a long and often stormy debate, Congress passed the Lend-Lease Act on March 10, 1941, by large and partisan majorities. Contemporary observers attached great significance to the decision. In London, *The Economist* cited it as a "Declaration of Interdependence," and the New York *Times* hailed the death of isolationism in the United States. Isolationists agreed. "We have torn up 150 years of traditional American foreign policy," Senator Arthur Vandenberg of Michigan lamented. "We have tossed Washington's Farewell Address in the discard. We have thrown ourselves squarely into the power politics and power wars of Europe, Asia and Africa. We have taken the first step upon a course from which we can never hereafter retreat." [5]

The Lend-Lease Act unequivocally committed the United States to provide all possible assistance to Britain. But it did not resolve the ultimate question of intervention. Isolationists accepted their defeat bitterly. They did not surrender, however, and in succeeding weeks stepped up their battle against deeper involvement in the conflict. They warned that the administration would next attempt to convoy supplies across the Atlantic, a step that was certain to provoke German retaliation, and reminded the President that, despite the majorities supporting lend-lease, the American people were united on only one point: "that we shall not fight another war on foreign soil." [6]

The isolationist warning distorted popular feelings, but it did contain an element of truth. Most Americans regarded Germany as an enemy and supported all-out aid to Britain even though it involved risks. But they were reluctant to accept the logical consequences of their own attitudes, and to take action that might draw them more deeply into the conflict. Roosevelt shared their hopes and fears. He was certainly aware when he conceived lend-lease that it might not be enough, that American troops might eventually be required to save Britain, and he was not entirely candid when he defended the Lend-Lease Act as a means of keeping out of war. But he sincerely hoped that intervention might yet be avoided. He realized that the United States was not prepared to fight, either physically or emotionally, and though he was anxious to assist the British, he was equally anxious to avoid steps that might lead to hostilities with Germany.[7]

Consequently, the President did not follow up lend-lease

with bold measures. His more belligerent advisers pressed for convoys, warning that Hitler's U-boat campaign in the Atlantic would render lend-lease useless. But Roosevelt hesitated, agreeing only to establish patrols in the North Atlantic to report the presence of submarines to British vessels and justifying this step on defensive grounds. Even when the public responded favorably to his May 27 address declaring an unlimited national emergency and affirming emphatically that supplies *would* be delivered to the United Kingdom, the President refused to convoy British merchant ships. Thus, the historian Robert A. Divine has written, "as the war in Europe approached its climax with the German invasion of Russia in June, 1941, the United States appeared to be drifting aimlessly." [8]

Barbarossa introduced another difficult issue into the already complicated political equation. Isolationists saw new hope for building support against intervention and responded jubilantly. Ex-President Herbert Hoover declared that the entry of communist Russia into the conflict made a "gargantuan jest" of the argument that the war was a struggle between totalitarianism and democracy. General Robert E. Wood, president of the isolationist pressure group, America First, asserted that it should settle once and for all the "interventionist argument here at home. The war party can hardly ask the American people to take up arms behind the Red flag of Stalin." [9] Hitler's preoccupation with the Soviet Union relieved the danger of a German invasion of the British Isles and removed any threat from the Western Hemisphere. "Now we can just let Joe Stalin and the other dictators fight it out," Senator Burton K. Wheeler, Montana Democrat and leading isolationist, exulted. Isolationists agreed that American aid for Russia was unthinkable. It would not only be immoral, Hoover observed, but it would also be bad policy for the United States to help Stalin fasten the "grip of communism on Russia" and to extend it over the world. General Wood questioned whether the United States could continue to aid Britain without some definite assurance that "everything we send will not be relayed to Stalin in accordance with Mr. Churchill's pledge." [10]

Most interventionists did not attempt to gloss over ideological differences with the USSR. They conceded that the war was being fought between the two "most dangerous international brigands of modern times." But they urged Americans to view the war realistically, to recognize that Germany, not Russia, threatened American security, and that the United States must not relax its efforts to counter that threat.[11]

Interventionists did not, however, recommend direct aid to Russia. They were aware that there was very little the United States could do, at least in the beginning, to assist the Soviet Union. Most of all, they feared that proposals to extend aid to Russia would confuse the American people and set back efforts to help Britain. "It would not be easy," the Washington *Post* commented, to "convince them [the American people] that aid to the Soviet Union is in precisely the same category of self-helpfulness as aid to Britain." [12]

The interventionist assessment accurately gauged public reaction to the Russo-German war. The American people overwhelmingly preferred a Russian victory, but they did not approve aid to the USSR. Traditional suspicions of communism, reinforced by the propaganda of Roman Catholics and patriotic societies, and fresh memories of the "rape" of Poland in 1939 and the attack on Finland in 1940, prevented any outpouring of sympathy for the Soviet Union after the German attack. Americans preferred a Russian victory because they considered Hitler the greatest menace to their own safety, but they did not feel the same mutuality of interests with the USSR they felt with Great Britain and they did not favor extending lend-lease. A Gallup poll of June 24, 1941, reported that only 35 percent of those questioned endorsed aid to the Soviet Union on the same basis as aid to Britain, while 54 percent opposed it and 11 percent expressed no opinion.[13]

Within the United States government, the military vigorously resisted shipment of supplies to Russia. Secretary of War Henry L. Stimson, an ardent interventionist, looked upon the new war as an "almost providential occurrence," relieving pressure on Britain and providing an unexpected opportunity to win the battle of the North Atlantic. Military intelligence predicted that Germany would triumph within three months at most, and warned that aid to the USSR would be wasted or even wind up in German hands. Stimson reported to President Roosevelt the nearly unanimous opinion of army strategists that instead of diverting supplies to the USSR the United States should use the respite to push "with the utmost vigor our movements in the Atlantic theater of operations." [14]

Others among the President's inner circle disagreed. Secretary of the Interior Harold Ickes and Secretary of State Cordell Hull contended that the United States was committed to support any nation fighting Germany. But the strongest endorsement for aid to the USSR came from Joseph E. Davies, a close personal friend of Roosevelt since the Wilson campaign of 1912 and an ardent Russophile. Liberals had protested in 1936 when the President had appointed Davies, a millionaire and president of one of Washington's most exclusive clubs, as ambassador to communist Russia. But Davies, who described himself as a "corporation attorney with a liberal outlook," surprised his critics. He took a deep interest in Russian agriculture, industry, and art. He consistently presented a favorable picture of the Soviet experiment to U. S. officials and to the American public, even defending Stalin's purges of 1938. His views on the USSR were usually uncritical and sometimes naive—he once stated that Stalin was fully committed to "altruistic concepts." Unlike many Americans, however, he was not blinded by hatred and distrust of communist ideology. He erred in refusing to concede any ideological bases for the Kremlin's actions; but he correctly perceived the strong nationalist element in Stalin's foreign policy, predicting the Nazi-Soviet pact of 1939. Retired from public life in 1941, Davies maintained valuable contacts with the Russian embassy in Washington and considerable influence with the White House.

In the days after the German invasion, the former ambassador took upon himself the mission of dispelling American "prejudices and misinformation" about the Soviet Union and building support for lend-lease. During his ambassadorship, he had repeatedly advised skeptical Washington officials that the Red Army was a potent military force, and upon learning of the German attack he immediately told reporters that Russian resistance would "amaze and surprise the world." Rejecting the argument that communism threatened the United States, he argued that it was "just plain common sense" to assist a nation fighting Germany. In late June and July, he was a constant visitor at the State Department and White House, repeating again and again his conviction that the USSR would hold out and urging timely assistance, regardless of ideological differences.[15]

Roosevelt inclined toward Davies' arguments, but he was not free to implement his old friend's proposals. He "feared the possibility of Communist expansion far less than the fact of fascist aggression . . . ," James MacGregor Burns has written. He rejected the gloomy forecasts of the army, and he may have hoped that the dramatic change in the war would make possible the defeat of Germany without American intervention. He shared Churchill's view that the United States should do everything it could to prevent a German victory in Russia. But the political situation in the United States and the domestic response to Barbarossa required him to move cautiously. At a press conference on June 24, he indicated that the United States would give the USSR as much aid as possible, but he went on to stress that it would be quite difficult to do anything immediately— Russian requests would be of such character "that you can't just go around to Mr. Garfinckel's and fill the order and take it away with you"—and he emphasized that aid to Britain still had top priority. Roosevelt carefully sidestepped questions whether the assistance would come under lend-lease.[16]

That same day, the administration began to take cautious

steps to prepare the way for future aid to the Soviet Union. The Treasury Department released $39 million in Russian assets frozen under a general order of June 14 applying to all European nations. The next day, the White House announced that the Neutrality Act would not be applied to the Russo-German war, leaving Soviet ports open to American shipping. Within a week, conversations began in Moscow and Washington on military assistance, and on June 30, the Soviet ambassador in the United States, Constantine Oumansky, presented the State Department a formal request for $1,836,507,823 worth of aircraft, guns, ammunition, and industrial equipment.[17]

Roosevelt responded deliberately and quietly to the request. On July 10, he met with Oumansky and told him the United States would do what it could to fill the orders. He then directed his subordinates to try to meet Russia's most urgent needs before October 1. If the Red Army could hold out until that date, he speculated, the onset of winter would halt military operations until spring.[18]

Approval of the Russian requests immediately raised the question of finances. Roosevelt and his advisers realized that the USSR did not have sufficient cash resources to finance a long-term program of assistance. But lend-lease was out of the question. The first appropriation of $7 billion was nearly exhausted, and the administration would soon have to go before Congress for additional funds. Isolationists had already introduced resolutions excluding Russia from lend-lease, and the President feared a premature move could imperil the appropriation and even threaten the entire program.[19]

Avoiding any step that might provoke a domestic reaction, the administration at the same time arranged temporary expedients to finance shipments. Public statements minimized the size and importance of Russian requests and conveyed the impression that the Soviet government had ample cash to pay for them. Behind the scenes, Roosevelt authorized the Treasury Department to purchase Russian gold and directed the Secretary of Commerce and Federal Loan Administrator,

Jesse H. Jones, to open negotiations for purchases of strategic raw materials, the proceeds from each to cover the cost of war supplies. The discussions moved slowly, however, and the Russian aid program got off to a slow start. During the entire month of July exports to the USSR amounted to only $6.5 million.[20]

Harry Hopkins' visit to Moscow in late July and early August stirred Washington to more forceful action. A friendly reporter accurately described Hopkins in the summer of 1941 as the "second most influential man in America." Roosevelt appreciated the former social worker's unswerving loyalty and respected his ability to penetrate quickly to the heart of a problem—Churchill once dubbed him "Lord Root of the Matter"—and to get things done. Hopkins shared the President's concern with the German threat and his commitment to aid Britain. And in the tense months before Pearl Harbor he served as Roosevelt's "eyes and ears," providing him with intelligence from a variety of sources, and his "do man," who with "unquestioning loyalty and a slashing contempt for red tape goes out to put his chief's ideas into action." [21]

Hopkins was in London in July, 1941, preparing for an upcoming conference between Roosevelt and Churchill when he conceived the idea of a trip to the USSR. Concerned with the lack of reliable intelligence on the war and with the pervasive pessimism in Washington and London regarding Russia's ability to resist, he concluded that first-hand information was essential. Direct communication might also boost Stalin's morale, Hopkins advised the President, and would indicate to the Russians in an "unmistakable way that we mean business on a long-term supply job." Roosevelt approved the suggestion and immediately cabled Stalin to treat Hopkins "with the same identical confidence you would feel if you were talking to me." [22]

Wearing a grey homburg borrowed from Churchill and flying in the tail-section of a PBY Catalina transferred to the Royal Air Force under lend-lease, Hopkins arrived in Archangel on July 26. After being treated to a sumptuous dinner by local dignitaries, he flew on to Moscow and began a series of conferences with Stalin in the Kremlin on July 30. The Russian leader discussed the war openly and candidly. He admitted that his armies were inferior to the Germans, but he counted on winter to slow their offensive and he expressed "great confidence that the line during the winter months would be in front of Moscow, Kiev, and Leningrad." He discussed Russian war production and predicted that the Red Army would face the Germans at full strength by May, 1942. Stalin pressed Hopkins for immediate shipment of urgently needed supplies, especially guns, and requested long-range commitments of high octane gasoline, aluminum for aircraft construction, and tanks. "Give us anti-aircraft guns and the aluminum," he stated emphatically at one point, and "we can fight on for three or four years." [23]

Hopkins left Moscow on August 1, deeply impressed by Stalin's optimism. The discussions proved conclusively to him that reports of an imminent Russian collapse were unfounded, and Stalin's requests confirmed that he was planning for a long war. From this point on, Roosevelt and Churchill ignored predictions of disaster on the Eastern front, stepped up their efforts to get immediate help to Stalin, and began to lay plans for massive long-range assistance.

Actually, Stalin was much more pessimistic than he dared admit to Hopkins,[24] and in August the Russian position worsened. The Germans continued to inflict staggering losses on the Red Army; by the middle of August they had taken most of the Ukraine and by early September they threatened Leningrad. Events in the USSR moved rapidly, Russian supply officials in the United States protested, but action on their requests for supplies had come very slowly.

From the outset, aid to the USSR had run up against difficult problems. Confusion and inertia in a bureaucracy not organized for war inhibited effective handling of Soviet orders, and the inability or unwillingness of the Russians to provide precise specifications for items requested complicated the procedure. Most important, the American economy was not producing war materials in quantities sufficient to meet the needs of United States' rearmament and foreign requests. As the Red Army defended the lines in front of Leningrad, Smolensk, and Kiev, and the British fought in North Africa and in the skies above England, the United States Army held maneuvers at Fort Bragg, North Carolina, in which small trucks simulated tanks and troop carriers. Anxious citizens contributed pots and pans, hair curlers, and ice cream dippers to relieve a drastic shortage of aluminum. The army was short of all types of guns, was just beginning to receive medium tanks from assembly plants, and would not have adequate stocks of ammunition until December, 1942.[25]

Facing the near impossible task of readying their forces for war, the military watched with horror as the British and then the Russians began to lay claim to large portions of already inadequate supplies. The Chairman of the United States Maritime Commission, Admiral Emory S. Land, sarcastically complained to Roosevelt that if the United States was not careful, it would wake up one morning to find the White House en route to England with the Washington Monument being used as a steering oar. Secretary of War Stimson stated the army's position more directly. "I am the only man in the whole government," he protested, "that is responsible for the difficult decision of whether we can give up planes or other munitions with safety to our own defense. All of these other people are just hell-bent to satisfy a passing impulse or emotion to help out some other nation that is fighting on our side and they have no responsibility over whether or not our own army and our own forces are going to be left unarmed or not." When the Russians presented the War Department urgent requests for aircraft, they were told that the planes could not be provided without stripping the defenses of the United States.[26]

On August 1, Roosevelt acted vigorously to combat the administrative inefficiency and military footdragging. He lectured his cabinet for forty-five minutes, accusing them, especially Stimson, of giving the Russians the runaround and ordering that top priority be given to their requests. "I am sick and tired of hearing that they are going to get this and they are going to get that," Secretary of the Treasury Morgenthau recalled his saying. "Whatever we are going to give them has to be over there by the first of October, and the only answer I want to hear is that it is under way." He ordered Stimson to send the aircraft immediately, even though there were none to replace them. "Get the planes right off with a bang next week." [27]

When Morgenthau commented that with Hopkins out of town no one had the influence to get action, Roosevelt indicated that he would put one of the best administrators in Washington in charge of expediting Russian aid. The following day, he appointed Wayne Coy of the Office of Emergency Management with a ringing directive: "Please get out the list, and please, with my full authority, use a heavy hand —act as a burr under the saddle and get things moving." [28]

Armed with the President's orders, Coy went to work immediately. In some cases, he could accomplish little: the Russians had requested, for example, a volume of tank armor plate that would have absorbed the entire American output for the next twenty-four months. But persistent pressure applied throughout the supply apparatus produced notable results. Coy went directly to Stimson to secure the aircraft Roosevelt had promised the Russians. When the army protested that they were needed to train pilots in Texas, he acidly reminded them that the war was not being fought in Texas. Stimson reluctantly gave in and within two days released two hundred planes for delivery. Coy also persuaded the British to transfer from their stocks 1,000 tons of toluol (used in the production of aviation gasoline). He located 1,200 tons of aluminum and had it rushed to New York for immediate shipment, and he secured promises from American manufacturers to make available 173 machine tools by the end of the year. In all, during the two weeks Roosevelt was away at the Atlantic Conference, he got two ships loaded and dispatched for Russia plus commitments of additional material for later delivery.[29]

His victory did not, however, end the civilian-military conflict over disposition of supplies. On August 18, the President approved additional Russian requests for over $145 million of military equipment. Army Chief of Staff George C. Marshall agreed to token releases of bombs and submachine guns, but insisted that shortages prevented shipment of anything else. Marshall protested that ambassador Oumansky would "take everything we own if we submit to his criticism," and insisted that any additional supplies would have to come from allotments for Great Britain.[30]

On August 30, Roosevelt intervened again. He advised Stimson and Secretary of the Navy Frank Knox: "I deem it to be of paramount importance for the safety and security of America that all reasonable munitions help be provided for Russia, not only immediately, but as long as she continues to fight the Axis powers effectively." Again responding to Presidential pressure, the War Department substantially upped its offerings to Russia, although in many categories they still remained far below requests.[31]

At the same time, the President began to develop plans for expanded long-range assistance to the USSR. To establish Russian requirements and to coordinate Anglo-American production and allocation of supplies, Roosevelt and Churchill, with Stalin's agreement, had arranged a three-power conference to meet in Moscow in September. Hopkins was ill and unable to undertake another wearing mission, so he selected W. Averell Harriman, then "Lend-Lease Expediter" in London, to head the American delegation. Son of the great railroad builder, Harriman was himself a highly successful businessman. His labor policies as chairman of the board of Union Pacific Railroad had won him a reputation as a liberal. In contrast to most of his fellow industrialists, he had supported and worked with the New Deal, first with the National Recovery Administration and later as a member of the Business Advisory Council of the Department of Commerce. He had also established close relationships with the President and Hopkins and had been derided by anti-New Deal businessmen as one of Hopkins' "tame millionaires." From 1939 to 1941, he served in the industrial mobilization program. A tireless worker and devoted public servant, described by George F. Kennan as a man of "monumental and unchallengeable integrity," Harriman held the complete confidence of his superiors and the deep admiration of his subordinates. His closeness to Roosevelt and Hopkins, his experience with lend-lease, and his knowledge of British supply capabilities ideally qualified him to head the Moscow mission.[32]

In the weeks that followed, the administration prepared carefully for the upcoming conference. To assist Harriman, Hopkins selected a group of civilian and military officials with experience in supply matters, most of whom were known to be sympathetic to the Russians. Harriman and Hopkins conducted a series of exhausting discussions to determine the quantities of supplies that might be pledged to the USSR, and on August 30, Roosevelt directed the Secretaries of War and Navy to draw up long-range programs allocating available material to meet British, Russian, and American needs.[33]

The Harriman mission arrived in London on September 15 and began a series of preparatory discussions with the British delegation, headed by Lord Beaverbrook, Churchill's Minister of Supply. The Americans quickly encountered difficulties with their British counterparts who were now alarmed that expanded aid to Russia would cut down significantly the volume of supplies they might expect to receive from the United States. However, after a week of heated conferences and some compromise on both sides, the delegates hammered out a program to offer the Russians.[34]

The Anglo-American mission proceeded on to Archangel, and there boarded Soviet aircraft for the flight to Moscow. The reception accorded the visitors clearly reflected the anxious atmosphere prevailing in the USSR in the autumn of 1941. When the pilots strayed from their course they were fired upon by nervous air defenses around the capital. But when the delegation arrived safely in Moscow on September 28 they received a uniquely cordial welcome. No one in the party could recall a previous occasion since the revolution when the Soviet government had flown the flags and played the national anthems of foreign dignitaries.[35]

For the next four days, British and American officials met with Stalin and his economic and military advisers against a background of steady anti-aircraft fire. The strains of war obviously affected the Russian leader's mood. Although he maintained a friendly disposition during most of the conferences, he was at times brusque, and expressed great impatience and annoyance when Harriman and Beaverbrook attempted to explain why certain requests could not be granted. But when the United States and Britain presented their final offerings on September 30, Stalin made no "effort to conceal his enthusiasm." "It was my impression," Harriman reported to Washington, "that he was satisfied that Great Britain and America meant business." [36]

On October 1, 1941, delegates to the Moscow Conference signed a confidential protocol listing in detail the items and quantities of supplies the United States and Britain would make available before June 30, 1942. In several vital categories, commitments fell far below Russian requests: 1,100 tanks a month had been requested, only five hundred per month had been promised; 2,000 anti-tank guns and anti-aircraft guns monthly had been requested, an over-all total of 5,000 pledged. But the entire program was substantial, the United States alone committing itself to more than 1,500,000 tons, and it represented a great sacrifice considering the limited stocks then available. To compensate for deficiencies in military supplies and to demonstrate good faith, Harriman and Beaverbrook had agreed to go beyond the London program in providing raw materials and other non-military supplies.[37]

American offerings in the Moscow Protocol totaled over $1 billion and immediately reopened the problem of finances. Indeed, Roosevelt's stopgap methods of financing had already run into trouble before the Moscow conference. On August 15, Morgenthau had advanced the USSR $10 million against future deliveries of gold, but negotiations with Federal Loan Administrator Jones for purchases of raw materials had produced no agreement. The Russians had exhausted their own limited dollar resources, and on September 4, Oumansky, somehow forgetting that it had never been offered, lamented to Secretary Hull that he had made the "mistake of his life" in refusing lend-lease. Ardent supporters of aid within the administration shared the ambassador's concern. The United States had made a commitment, Hopkins complained to Morgenthau on September 23, and "Now, by god, we can't deliver on it. . . . It's just god damned discouraging." [38]

Popular backing for the Soviet Union had increased significantly during July and August. A Gallup poll of August 5 reported that 70 percent of those sampled favored the sale of war supplies to the USSR, and another poll in September revealed that 49 percent approved the extension of credits. Interventionists who had initially expressed reservations came out openly and forcefully behind aid to Russia in August. In many important areas, opposition was breaking down. Even that bastion of anti-communism in the United States, the American Federation of Labor, endorsed the provision of all possible supplies to Stalin to help defeat the "Nazi war machine." And at its boisterous annual convention in Milwaukee, the American Legion voted down a resolution opposing assistance for the Russians amidst shouts of "To Hell with Hitler," and roundly booed Senator Bennett Champ Clark of Missouri, a leading isolationist and one of the Legion's seventeen original founders.[39]

Despite these encouraging developments, Roosevelt still hesitated to extend lend-lease to the Russians. Although a majority of Americans endorsed the sale of war supplies or the extension of credits to the USSR, the Gallup poll of August 5 revealed an equal division on lend-lease, 38 percent for and 39 percent against. Isolationists in Congress continued to attack the Soviet Union and introduced new resolutions barring it from lend-lease. With the appropriation still pending, the President delayed. He explained to Oumansky on September 11 the "extreme difficulty" facing him because of the "prejudice or hostility to Russia and the unpopularity of Russia among large groups in this country who exercise great political power in Congress."[40]

Thus the administration again fell back on expedients. Roosevelt ordered Jones to make available to Soviet officials $100 million against future purchases of raw materials, and Morgenthau provided an additional $50 million against future shipments of gold. Hopkins frankly advised that the Russians could not count on lend-lease in the near future, and he told U.S. officials that the administration would have to "lay pretty low" on the matter until after the appropriation had passed Congress.[41]

The President prepared carefully for the impending battle. He attempted to disarm Catholic opposition by securing a statement from Pope Pius XII making a careful distinction between aid to the Soviet Union and aid to communism, and then pushed the point by revealing a Nazi plan to abolish all organized religion. To make lend-lease more palatable to congressional conservatives, he appointed a former industrialist and chairman of the board of U. S. Steel, Edward R. Stettinius, Jr., as lend-lease administrator, ostensibly replacing Hopkins, whose reputation as a careless spender was certain to arouse opposition. The lend-lease appropriation was lumped in with appropriations for the Tennessee Valley Authority, the Army, Navy, and Coast Guard, on the assumption that a lot of congressmen would vote for a "general catch-all" when they would not vote for lend-lease, and Democrats were advised to vote for the bill as a matter of party policy.[42]

The President obscured his ultimate goal to avoid a full-fledged debate on lend-lease to the Soviet Union. In meetings with congressional leaders, he denied any immediate intention of extending lend-lease to the Russians, implying that they could continue to pay cash for supplies for the indefinite future. But he stressed that exclusion from funds under the appropriation would be a terrible blow to Soviet morale, and he insisted that the uncertainties of the war demanded that he should not have "his hands tied in any way."

Administration officials testifying before congressional committees reiterated this position again and again, and Democratic congressmen took the same position in the debate on the floor.[43]

The strategy succeeded brilliantly. Extreme isolationists attacked the idea of lend-lease to Russia, and Representative Robert Rich, Pennsylvania Republican, introduced the first of several amendments in the House making the USSR ineligible for funds under the appropriation. But the administration held Democrats in line. And when Republican John Taber of New York, a long-time power on the Appropriations Committee and an inveterate foe of Roosevelt, conceded that although he had no use for communism he nevertheless felt it would be inadvisable to deny the President authority to handle war supplies as the military advised, it was clear that the amendment had no chance of passage. The House voted down the Rich amendment and other similar amendments by overwhelming majorities. The USSR was scarcely mentioned in Senate hearings and debates. The bill passed both houses on October 24, and was signed by Roosevelt four days later.[44]

In view of his earlier statements to Congress, the President would probably have preferred to delay indefinitely placing Russia under lend-lease; but by the time the appropriation bill passed, it was evident that he could hold off no longer. On October 29, Harriman delivered his final report on the Moscow Conference. He indicated that American commitments in the supply protocol totaled over $1 billion. He emphasized that effective use could be made of the supplies, that the continuation of the Soviet Union "as an active belligerent is of paramount importance, and that every effort should be made to assist her and assist her promptly." But, he warned, the Russians would not be able to finance the full program by themselves, and the use of lend-lease funds should be authorized at the "earliest moment possible."[45]

Events on the Eastern front reinforced Harriman's warnings. On September 30, Hitler had launched operation "Typhoon," the "final offensive" against Moscow. Again he caught the Red Army off guard and the Germans penetrated deep behind Soviet lines. When advance Panzer units broke through to within fifty miles of Moscow, panic seized the capital. The diplomatic corps was evacuated to Kuibyshev on October 15; the following day—the "great skedaddle" of October 16—hundreds of government officials, party leaders, even secret police, fled Moscow, burning and looting as they departed. On October 20, Stalin proclaimed a state of siege and set civilians to work strengthening fortifications outside the half-deserted city. Ten days later the Russian leader broadcast an emotional appeal to his people to rally in defense of "Holy Russia." [46]

Roosevelt responded to these events immediately and decisively. On October 30, he cabled Stalin that he had approved the commitments to Russia in the Moscow Protocol and had authorized their financing under lend-lease. Still cautious as far as the American people were concerned, however, the President established a unique arrangement to make lend-lease to Russia more acceptable, offering Stalin a $1 billion credit, bearing no interest and with repayment not to begin until five years after the war. Stalin quickly accepted the offer, and on November 7, 1941, the twenty-fourth anniversary of the Bolshevik Revolution, the administration officially announced the extension of lend-lease to the Soviet Union.[47]

The decision evoked surprisingly little opposition. The Chicago *Tribune* warned that American money would now be used by communists to "further their revolutionary designs" in the United States, and some critics charged that the administration had deliberately deceived the American people to get the lend-lease appropriation passed. More striking, however, was the silence of many isolationists—even Senator Wheeler "declined to comment"—and the resignation if not enthusiasm with which most Americans accepted the decision.[48]

The exigencies of war explain this reaction. By November, 1941, the United States was a belligerent in everything but name. On October 31, U-boats torpedoed and sank the destroyer *Reuben James* in the North Atlantic, and on November 7, the Senate repealed sections of the Neutrality Act forbidding the arming of merchant ships and the carrying of cargo into belligerent ports (the House had taken similar action on October 17). The U. S. Navy was engaged in undeclared warfare with Germany. Tensions with Japan rose steadily, and war seemed likely if not imminent.

The Russians were fighting a common enemy, and the stubborn determination with which they defended the homeland called forth increasing admiration in the United States. American images of the USSR had already begun to shift perceptibly. Stalin himself, *Time* remarked, once regarded as a "sort of unwashed Genghis Khan with blood dripping from his fingertips," had come to seem "increasingly benign," even a "nice old gentleman." Many Americans, to be sure, continued to regard Soviet communism with profound suspicion and dislike. But, *Fortune* pollsters observed, they did not allow their distrust of communism to "soften appreciably their attitude toward Hitler. . . ." An October *Fortune* poll showed that 21.9 percent were prepared to accept the Soviet Union as a full partner with England in the fight against Germany, 51.4 percent would work with and aid Russia as long as it would help defeat the Nazis, and only 13.5 percent opposed giving any assistance or encouragement. Representative Clifton Woodrum, Virginia Democrat, probably expressed the sentiments of the majority when he opened the October lend-lease debate with a Rumanian proverb: "It is permitted to walk with the devil until the bridge is crossed." [49]

Regardless of their politics, many Americans agreed that their fate could depend upon events in Russia. Interventionists who felt U. S. entry into the war was necessary realized that the fall of the Soviet Union would weaken the allied cause immeasurably. Those who still hoped that Hitler could be defeated without intervention recognized that victory on the Eastern front was essential. Even isolationists, who did not consider Germany a threat, were aware that continued Russian resistance was the last hope of avoiding direct involvement. "Aid to Russia was a price many of them seemed willing to pay," Raymond Dawson has concluded, "if it would help stave off the far greater evil of American belligerency." Thus by November 1, 1941, Roosevelt had committed the United States to all-out aid to the USSR and had won broad popular support for that decision.[50]

In the atmosphere of disillusionment that followed the Second World War, conservative critics leveled bitter attacks against the decision to extend lend-lease to the USSR. Arguing that Hitler could not have defeated Stalin under any circumstances, they contended that the United States would have done better to remain aloof from the conflict and allow the two giants to destroy each other. U. S. aid not only insured a Soviet triumph but also facilitated the rise of the USSR as a great and menacing power.

This argument oversimplifies an infinitely complex problem. It seems entirely possible in retrospect that Germany might not have been able to defeat Russia and that, if it had, the burdens of governing a large, alien, and hostile territory might in the long run have weakened rather than strengthened it. But American neutrality in the Russo-German war involved risks that seemed at the time too great to shoulder. Had Hitler won a decisive victory in 1941 or 1942—and this seemed quite possible at the time—the short-term consequences could have been catastrophic. The Germans would have secured vast quantities of food and raw materials to strengthen their already formidable war machine, the Near East and Africa would have been left vulnerable to Nazi penetration, and Japan would have been given a free hand in the Far East. The psychological impact on other nations resisting Hitler would have been enormous, and the world balance of power would have shifted against Britain and the United States.

Aid to the Soviet Union afforded both immediate and long-term advantages. With Hitler in control of much of Europe and threatening the United Kingdom and America still unready for war, Roosevelt and Churchill had much to gain by helping Stalin, thereby tying down German arms and limiting Germany's capacity to strike elsewhere. Only a prophet could have foreseen the almost miraculous recovery of the USSR at a time when her weakness most impressed outside observers. Even if her rise to postwar power had been predictable, the fact remains that if the Red Army had defeated the Nazis without external assistance, the United States would have had less influence over the Kremlin after the war and would have faced greater hostility.

Roosevelt therefore reached the correct decision, and he handled the delicate issue of aid to Russia with consummate skill. He made clear his intention to support Stalin, but he wisely avoided large, dramatic commitments that could not have been fulfilled and that would have aroused powerful domestic opposition. While quietly providing maximum immediate aid and formulating plans for long-range assistance, he allowed time for popular support to increase and himself subtly contributed to its development.

His easy victory in Congress might suggest that he could have acted sooner and more decisively. But this would be a tenuous judgment. Political backing for Russia mounted only slowly and reached the safe stage in October, in large part because of events in the North Atlantic. The President's control of Congress was at best uncertain in August and September, as demonstrated by the narrow vote on renewal of selective service. The overwhelming vote against denying lend-lease to the USSR therefore reflected a changing American attitude toward the war. It was also testimony to Roosevelt's astute handling of a potentially explosive issue. He had won a significant victory; but the problem of getting effective aid to the Soviet Union would offer an even greater challenge to his leadership.

Chapter 2

"EXACTLY WHAT THEY WANT"

THE UNCONDITIONAL AID POLICY, SEPTEMBER–DECEMBER, 1941

EVEN BEFORE BARBAROSSA, DISCUSSIONS HAD BEGUN WITHIN THE Roosevelt administration on the most effective methods that might be employed if military necessity demanded close collaboration with the Russians. The debate would continue throughout the war, and the issues it raised represent one of the most important problems in the study of America's wartime relations with the USSR. Involved were complex questions of Soviet objectives and methods, the possibilities of establishing a successful working relationship with the Russians in war and peace, and the means by which American interests might best be protected. One of the most important problems was whether the United States might secure more from its relationship with the USSR by extending economic assistance unconditionally or by attaching political strings.

When intelligence reports indicated clearly in June, 1941, that Germany planned to invade the Soviet Union, the State Department immediately set down its position on the prospects for cooperation with Russia and the methods by which it could best be achieved. Its proposals reflected a legacy of suspicion and antagonism dating from the Bolshevik Revolution. Americans had feared the Soviet Union's avowed objective of fomenting world revolution, and resented its crude efforts to encourage unrest in other nations. The Russian government's refusal to honor Tsarist debts and agreements made with Western powers in the 1920s reinforced suspicions, and when the United States finally abandoned its policy of non-recognition in 1933, the State Department sought to secure concessions in return. But the department's frustrating and largely unsuccessful efforts to implement the Roosevelt-Litvinov Agreements gave rise to strong convictions, as one official put it, that "no action or policy should be based upon the word of the Kremlin however solemnly pledged." The long and tedious arguments that accompanied even minor negotiations, the restrictions placed upon American diplomats in the USSR, and the constant obstructions they met in attempting to perform their duties convinced most State Department officials that it was impossible to establish normal and friendly relations with the Russians.[1]

Soviet foreign policy from 1939 to 1941 deepened distrust. Stalin's "appeasement" of Germany strengthened the impression that the Kremlin was unprincipled, and the attacks on Poland and Finland confirmed suspicions that Soviet expansionism was ruthless and dangerous. Recognizing the strategic importance of the USSR in Europe and Asia, the State Department had attempted to improve relations in late 1940. But the discussions achieved little; and the Russians' insistent demands for export licenses on critical war supplies at the time they were trading extensively with Germany and their efforts to secure recognition of their absorption of the Baltic States only aroused deeper antagonism among Americans.[2]

The State Department therefore confronted the prospect of future collaboration convinced that the Russians could not be trusted and that they must be handled with great caution. A policy memorandum of June 14 stressed that "day-to-day relations" should be based "so far as practicable on the principle of reciprocity." The United States should respond to any Soviet approaches with "reserve" until it was certain they were not "engaging merely in maneuvers for the purpose of obtaining unilateral concessions and advantages" for themselves. It should reject any "suggestions that we make concessions for the sake of 'improving the atmosphere of American-Soviet relations' " and should "exact a strict *quid pro quo* for anything which we are willing to give the Soviet Union." [3]

The American ambassador in Moscow, Laurence A. Steinhardt, endorsed the State Department's recommendations. Experience with the Soviet government had convinced him, the ambassador observed, that "they do not and cannot be induced to respond to customary amenities, that it is not possible to create 'international good will' with them, that they will always sacrifice the future in favor of an immediate gain, and that they are not affected by ethical or moral considerations, nor guided by the relationships which are customary between individuals of culture and breeding." The Russian psychology, Steinhardt concluded, "recognizes only firmness, power, and force, and reflects primitive instincts and reactions entirely devoid of the restraints of civilization." [4]

William C. Bullitt, ambassador to the Soviet Union from 1934 to 1936, provided additional support for a tough policy. Bullitt's views on Russia had changed radically since 1919 when as Woodrow Wilson's youthful, idealistic emissary to the Lenin government he had pressed for a sympathetic, accommodating policy and had resigned in disgust when Wilson ignored his recommendations. Bullitt had journeyed to Moscow in 1934, the first American ambassador to the USSR, with similar goals. But two years of frustrating experiences left him bitterly disillusioned. "We should not cherish for a moment," he advised Secretary Hull in 1936, "the illusion that it is possible to establish really friendly relations with the Soviet Government. . . ." After the German invasion, Bullitt warned Roosevelt of the dangers of Soviet imperialism, and counseled that, if the United States assisted Stalin without first getting from him public pledges to refrain from expansion, the United States would face a more dangerous situation at the end of the war than it had in 1918. Bullitt advised that, in return for American aid, Stalin should be required to renounce openly all territorial claims in Europe and Asia and to accept as valid and binding the Russian boundaries of August, 1939, before the invasion of Poland.[5]

Roosevelt rejected Bullitt's advice. He refused in 1941 and thereafter to attach political conditions to aid for Russia. Indeed, he went beyond this, giving lend-lease to the USSR a unique status, according it top priority over the competing demands of Britain and the United States, and exerting every effort to insure that American shipments of supplies met commitments.

In a *Life* magazine article published in 1948 under the suggestive title "How We Won the War and Lost the Peace," Bullitt purported to explain the ideas behind the President's policy. "Bill, I don't dispute your facts, they are accurate," he recalled FDR saying in 1941. "I don't dispute the logic of your reasoning. I just have a hunch that Stalin is not that kind of man. Harry [Hopkins] says he's not . . . and I think that if I give him everything I possibly can and ask nothing from him in return, noblesse oblige, he won't try to annex anything and will work with me for a world of democracy and peace." [6]

Bullitt's portrait of Roosevelt as an incredibly naive and amateurish diplomatist set the tone for a series of bitter postwar attacks on the President's handling of Russia. In the disillusionment that followed the conclusion of World War II, some intemperate critics went beyond the former ambassador, arguing that a lust for power and insatiable political ambition blinded Roosevelt to reality and led him into policies that would endanger the United States by strengthening enormously the forces of world communism. Even moderate writers agreed that the President had completely misunderstood or ignored the traditional aggressiveness of

Russia, the tenets of communist dogma, and the ruthlessness and deceitfulness of Joseph Stalin. Roosevelt, it was argued, foolishly refused to use the powerful weapon of economic assistance to force concessions from the Russians in their hour of peril. Instead, he gave them everything they requested, no strings attached, apparently believing that his generosity would create close bonds of friendship and insure postwar cooperation. It was a great gamble, the distinguished diplomatic historian Thomas A. Bailey concluded in 1950, but the "Rooseveltian policy of appeasement, as all the world knows, did not work out happily." [7]

These postwar writers accurately denoted the outlines of Roosevelt's unconditional aid policy, but they distorted the motives that determined it. The President may have agreed with former ambassador Davies that Soviet foreign policy had been basically defensive and that its primary objective was the security of the Russian state, not the expansion of communism. He certainly felt that the USSR had ample reason for its deep suspicion of the West, and he seems to have believed that if the United States could prove to Stalin that it could be trusted the chances of postwar collaboration would be improved. But the unconditional aid policy stemmed more from the immediate and urgent requirements of war than from Roosevelt's hopes for the future. It cannot be understood apart from the context of 1941, the desperate conditions on the Russian front and the enormous difficulties limiting effective aid to the USSR.

For the Soviet Union, *Newsweek* commented on October 20, 1941, it was "the hour of supreme trial." To be sure, the Nazi offensive against Moscow had stalled. Russian defenses had stiffened, and heavy mud slowed German motorized units and fouled logistics. When Stalin addressed a celebration of the revolution on November 7, Moscow was safe. But the over-all situation remained critical. Hitler's armies occupied much of the Ukraine. They had taken Kiev, its capital, Kharkov, its most important industrial city, and the Donets Basin, which produced all of its coal and most of its steel and power. In early September, the Germans had laid siege to Leningrad, and for the next two months Nazi aircraft and artillery pounded it relentlessly, systematically following the Fuehrer's orders to "raze the City of Petersburg from the face of the earth." On November 8, the besieging armies tightened the noose, cutting off the last supply route from Moscow. Leningrad, birthplace of the Bolshevik revolution, center of much of the USSR's most specialized industry, faced the onset of winter isolated from the rest of the nation, with only two weeks' food supply, its population facing certain doom.[8]

In all sectors, the Russian people endured horrible suffering. Nazi aircraft and tanks leveled hundreds of towns and villages. Occupying troops treated the civilian population without mercy, deporting thousands to Germany for slave labor, leaving others to die of starvation, and ruthlessly exterminating Jews and Communist party members. In Kiev, the Gestapo murdered more than 100,000 Jews. An estimated half of Kharkov's population of 700,000 "disappeared" during the period of German rule. The ordeal of the people of Leningrad has become legendary. From October, 1941, they were without fuel and power and were subjected to constant air raids and shelling. City officials were forced to cut daily allotments of food below the subsistence level. Desperate people murdered for ration cards and attempted to survive on unimaginable food substitutes: breads made from cellulose and cotton fiber, soups produced from carpenter's glue that had been scraped off the walls, horrible smelling jellies derived from sheep guts and calves skins. In November, 1941, the first month of the "starvation winter," more than 11,000 Leningraders perished—you "just stepped over corpses in the street and on the stairs," a survivor later recalled. The numbers would rise, and it has been estimated that more than one million died of hunger in the siege.[9]

German successes severely crippled the military capacity of the nation. The invading armies occupied territory that contained about 40 percent of the prewar population of the USSR. They had inflicted devastating losses on the Red Army and had taken hundreds of thousands of prisoners, as many as 200,000 at Kiev alone. Thus within five months after the start of the war, the Soviet Union faced a drastic manpower shortage. Underequipped at the outset, the Red Army suffered tremendous losses of supplies in the first weeks of the war. Major industrial areas were occupied by the Germans or destroyed by the Russians in retreat. The evacuation of heavy industry to the Urals ranks as one of the greatest feats of the war, but the process of evacuation itself disrupted manufacturing for months. Total industrial output dropped by more than one half from June to November, and in certain critical areas, the decline was greater. Aircraft production fell to one quarter of prewar figures and ball-bearing production to 5 percent. Soviet agriculture also suffered heavily. Territory occupied by the Germans in November, 1941, had accounted for 38 percent of Russia's prewar cereal output and 84 percent of its sugar.[10]

The perilous conditions on the Eastern front in October and November, 1941, underscored in the minds of Washington officials the urgency of getting help to the Russians. Fully committed to the defeat of Germany, President Roosevelt realistically perceived that the ability of the USSR to survive the Nazi invasion and fight on might determine the outcome of the war. But the immediate prospects were not encouraging. The fall of Moscow or Leningrad could be a crushing blow to Russian morale. The loss of the fertile Ukraine and the dislocation of industry made the Soviet Union dependent upon outside help for many essential supplies. The President realized that the extent to which the United States came through on the pledges made at Moscow might determine whether the Red Army could hold out through the winter.

Roosevelt and his advisers also felt that the provision of effective aid to the USSR was necessary to bind Stalin into a solid coalition against Hitler. The President appreciated the Kremlin's deep mistrust of the West, and recognized that it was grounded not only in Marxist ideology but also in the unfriendly policies pursued by Western nations since the revolution. He may have shared Davies' belief that Soviet fears of a Western betrayal had been instrumental in the decision to make a deal with Germany in 1939. He certainly agreed with Davies' observation that Stalin might again be tempted to come to terms with Hitler if he became convinced that "further resistance was hopeless because the United States and Britain either could not or did not deliver them the goods to do the fighting." On the other hand, as Harriman stressed, if the United States and Britain could meet the supply schedules set up in the Moscow protocol and could maintain close personal contact with Stalin, "the suspicion that has existed between the Soviet Government and our two governments might well be eradicated." [11]

But it was not easy to translate these intentions into effective action. Throughout 1941, U. S. war production lagged behind the steadily rising demands of the United States, Britain, and Russia. Vital raw materials remained in short supply, and the administration had not established a workable system of priorities to govern the use of available stocks. In the uncertain atmosphere of non-belligerency, industry hesitated to convert plants to the manufacture of war materials, and the President had not taken decisive measures to curtail civilian consumption. He had set up a number of emergency agencies to coordinate preparedness, but they were crippled by bureaucratic warfare between New Dealers and dollar-a-year men and by the lack of clearcut directives from above.[12]

In August and September, the administration had taken important steps to speed up industrial mobilization. Roosevelt created yet another agency, the Supply Priorities and Allocation Board, which in the months before Pearl Harbor finally effected a satisfactory means of setting priorities. More important, he ordered his civilian and military advisers to draw up a comprehensive study indicating the degree of economic expansion necessary to defeat Germany. The result of this survey, the Victory Program, revealed that, at its present rate of growth, American war production would not surpass that of Britain and Canada until the end of 1942, and indicated that the volume would at least have to be doubled to insure adequate quantities of supplies. The harsh statistics enumerated in the Victory Program shook many administration officials out of their complacency and produced intensified attempts to expand production and to employ all available resources more efficiently. But the full impact would not be felt until much later. At the time Russia was placed under lend-lease and for many months thereafter, shortages of steel, aluminum, and finished munitions hindered fulfillment of protocol commitments.[13]

The establishment of machinery to process lend-lease orders also required much time and experimentation. Before approving requests, officials had to determine whether items were available and in what quantities, whether they were eligible for transfer under lend-lease, and most important, whether they were needed most by the requesting country, another ally, or the United States. Once a request was approved, the item would have to be located in current stocks or priorities would have to be secured for raw materials and production ordered. The process involved the activities of numerous agencies, required staggering amounts of paperwork, and created countless administrative problems.

Roosevelt had refused to establish a single agency to handle the entire lend-lease operation. To insure his own personal control over it, he delegated to Hopkins authority for approving requisitions and allocating funds, and left with the War, Navy, Agriculture, and Treasury Departments responsibility for procuring supplies. The early procedures for handling applications for aid were extremely cumbersome. Requisitions went through a maze of offices—sixteen in the War Department alone—before approval, and each one had to be signed by the President before procurement could begin. In August, an average of ninety days was required to process an order, and it took many more weeks before priorities could be secured and items could be produced, purchased, and readied for shipment.[14]

The lend-lease program thus got off to a very slow start. "If we are to be honest with ourselves," John Maynard Keynes of the British Treasury complained in August, "we must admit that the switch over from cash purchase to Lend-Lease has retarded the war effort by six months." The arsenal of democracy, columnist Raymond Clapper acidly observed in September, was still a "popgun arsenal." [15]

In the late summer of 1941, Roosevelt attempted to simplify and expedite lend-lease procedures. To spare Hopkins the burdens of administrative detail and conserve his limited energy for policy, the President on August 28, 1941 named Stettinius, another of Hopkins' "tame millionaires," as Lend-Lease Administrator, making him responsible for supervising the processing of requisitions and for record-keeping. To eliminate the White House bottleneck, Roosevelt on September 16 increased Stettinius' authority, empowering him to approve requisitions and to allocate funds up to $300 million. After gradually expanding the Lend-Lease Administrator's power in succeeding weeks, the President on October 28 established the Office of Lend-Lease Administration, with Stettinius as head, and delegated to him full responsibility for exercising the powers conferred by the Lend-Lease Act.[16]

Stettinius attacked his job under anything but ideal conditions. He hastily assembled a staff in an unfinished apartment building on Virginia Avenue. "Beaverboard partitions daubed with white paint separate offices," the New York *Times* reported. "There are few doors for rooms. Electric phone and signal wires are strung badly everywhere. File cabinets appear hastily thrown into place. Corridors are thronged with earnest young men and women, some with a just-out-of-college look on their faces." On the wall of a conference room hung a single poster with the warning: "Time is Short." [17]

Working individually and together, OLLA and the procurement agencies gradually speeded up the processing of lend-lease requests. But it took many months to clear up the backlog of orders, and until long after the United States entered the war, the procedure remained inefficient. Duplication of effort between OLLA and the other agencies created tension and confusion. Civil-military conflict continued, the military deeply resenting civilian control over the allocation of war materials, and civilians annoyed with the constant delay in procurement of munitions for lend-lease countries. Men worked impossible hours under the most trying conditions, and tempers became strained.[18]

Russian supply officials in the United States compounded the difficulties. Sent to America to secure supplies, they realized that the fate of their country, their own careers, perhaps even their lives, depended upon their ability to carry out orders. They were, Dean Acheson has recalled, "clumsy and difficult. Not daring to depart in the smallest particular from their instructions, they had no flexibility, no feel for the possible." They failed to adhere to standard American specifications, and long delays resulted as OLLA attempted to work out modifications. Representatives of Amtorg, the Russian trading corporation in the United States, refused to take responsibility for changing specifications, even when it was impossible to meet the original request. Amtorg haggled incessantly over prices, demanded the right to inspect factories, insisted on warranties for defective parts, and flooded the desks of OLLA officials with requests for items not included in protocol lists. Frequently, after Americans had made frantic efforts to secure items, the Russians would suddenly indicate that they were no longer needed.[19]

Their suspiciousness and secretiveness annoyed those U. S. officials with whom they came into contact. American motives, John Hazard of OLLA has written, "were presumed to be those of the capitalists and not those of genuine friends seeking to help the USSR as one member of a family will help another." If the United States had to depart from supply schedules because of unanticipated difficulties, the Russians immediately suspected foul play and agreed to the changes only with the greatest reluctance. At the same time, they refused to divulge any information about Soviet production capabilities, military operations, and supply requirements. "They are keeping a veil of secrecy about all of their movements," Stimson complained in November, and it is "awfully difficult to help people who do that." [20]

The tactless manner in which Soviet officials dealt with

their American counterparts produced more friction. Their requests usually came in the form of demands. "They simply walked in, all of them sober-faced, never cracked a smile, smart as they could be," Secretary of Agriculture Claude Wickard recalled. "They said, 'Here is what we want.' And they'd just sit there. There wasn't much negotiation to it." They showed gratitude for assistance only after being told frankly by one American that occasional expressions of thanks might help their cause. They exerted unrelenting pressure on American officials from the top to the lower levels of the bureaucracy. "Nothing was more characteristic of Russian conduct in Washington in those years than constant and vigorous needling," Willis C. Armstrong, also of OLLA, would write. Ambassador Oumansky's abrasiveness especially provoked Americans. Secretary Hull described him as "insulting in his manner and speech." Stimson was more outspoken. Oumansky, he wrote in his diary, was "nothing but a crook." [21]

Soviet officials naturally attempted to exploit the confusion within the American bureaucracy. When their requests were rejected by one agency, they proceeded with dispatch to another and resubmitted them. "The Russians are all over town!" was a common saying among U. S. supply officials in the winter of 1941 and after. On occasion, they went directly to the White House where they usually received a sympathetic hearing and got action. Often they used their position with Roosevelt and Hopkins to intimidate lesser officials. "On any protest we made," an Air Force colonel later recalled, "they would respond 'Your President has ordered you to send us those airplanes. Now don't tell me that you can change your President's order, because we know better.'" The Soviet representatives were under tremendous pressure from Moscow and their desperate attempts to get supplies are quite understandable. But their heavy-handed manners and their stubborn insistence on fulfilling the letter of each agreement created much ill will in Washington and placed additional strains on a U. S. supply apparatus already atrophied by inertia and bound up in red tape.[22]

Roosevelt and Hopkins quickly perceived the obstacles

standing in the way of aid to Russia, and they designed the unconditional aid policy to insure maximum shipments to the USSR under the most adverse conditions. The administration was not ignorant of the potential power of lend-lease as an instrument of diplomacy. Indeed the State Department had begun to use it as early as the summer of 1941, attempting to extract from the British commitments to reduce postwar tariffs in return for economic assistance. But the President concluded that it would be self-defeating to demand political concessions from the Russians. He frankly admitted to Bullitt that commitments from Stalin would not be "worth having," that while the Russian leader might make certain promises to secure American aid he would most likely break them later if it suited him. More important, attaching political strings would delay the provision of urgently needed military supplies to the nation then bearing the burden of the struggle against a common enemy. It would intensify Soviet suspicions of the West and thereby jeopardize the overriding goal of building a unified coalition against Hitler. Secretary Hull rejected proposals from congressmen that the Russians be required to settle the old debt question before they could receive lend-lease. Aid to the USSR, the secretary advised one senator, "is deemed to be in the interest of our own national defense." The policy of the United States, Harriman advised the American delegates to the Moscow Conference, would be to "give and give and give, with no expectation of any return, with no thought of a quid pro quo." [23]

Roosevelt and Hopkins attached so much importance to the Moscow protocol that they gave it a special status within the lend-lease program. They made most of the major policy decisions themselves, and established a separate division in OLLA, reporting directly to Stettinius and through him to the White House, to administer the protocol. The arrangement concluded at Moscow, which gave the Russians the opportunity to negotiate on the quantities and types of supplies to be given and which was regarded as a firm commitment by the U. S. and Britain, was itself unique. By

October, 1941, lend-lease officials had begun to compile semi-annual or annual programs for each nation. But they regarded these only as general guidelines for planning and not as definite promises. The usual lend-lease schedule was always subject to modification when changes in the availability of supplies or shipping or in the strategic situation might force adjustments of priorities for competing demands.[24]

Harriman and Beaverbrook had agreed before going to Moscow, however, that a precise offer would give greater encouragement to the beleagured Russians, and the protocol negotiated there listed specific quantities of supplies to be delivered before June 30, 1942. The agreement contained several escape clauses, but the United States and Britain would come to regard it as a binding obligation, limited only by the availability of shipping. The protocol was "our Bible," Harold Macmillan, then a junior official in the British Ministry of Supply, would later recall. "We were pledged to carry it out with scrupulous and literal devotion." The Moscow agreement thus gave the Russians significant advantages that other lend-lease nations did not share.[25]

The administration made other exceptions to speed up aid to the Soviet Union. To evaluate most accurately competing requirements and to insure that lend-lease was not abused, all nations had been required to justify their requests for supplies by furnishing detailed information proving their need for each item and their capacity to use it against the enemy. But this condition was not applied to Russian orders. It was doubtful whether the Kremlin could provide such information because of the dislocation of industry and the confused state of economic planning after the German invasion. The Soviet penchant for secrecy made it unlikely that the data, if available, would be shared. The President therefore decided that attempts to require the Russians to support their requests would only irritate them and hold up shipments. They were asked to state a "purpose" for items requested, and the army and navy examined these statements to determine whether they seemed legitimate. But the USSR was not made to file the elaborate supporting information demanded of other nations. Secretaries Stimson and Knox complained that without justifications it was impossible to weigh accurately Russian needs against competing claims, but their protests were ignored.[26]

Roosevelt also laid down strict rules for those Americans coming into frequent contact with Soviet officials in Washington. Aware that antagonism against the Russians could hinder aid to the USSR, he insisted that his subordinates be patient and understanding, that they meet their Soviet counterparts more than halfway and avoid getting angry with them no matter how difficult it might be. The White House went out of its way to reassure a suspicious Russian Embassy that delays in shipments had resulted primarily from the lack of time for adequate planning and not from indifference to its needs. Harriman warned the State Department to stop pressing the USSR to grant American engineers and technicians visas to assist in the construction of a refinery for aviation gasoline. Such attempts, he advised, would only arouse Russian fears and "would not help in building confidence." OLLA conceded that Amtorg's demands to negotiate on prices for supplies were unreasonable. But its stated policy was to avoid displeasing the Russians for if their desires were not considered the aid program might fail. In the beginning, Harriman advised Stettinius, we "ought to do exactly what they want." [27]

To insure that all the elements of this policy were followed in Moscow and in Washington, the administration named to key posts trusted individuals who were known to be sympathetic toward the Russians. General James H. Burns, an army ordnance expert, coordinated Soviet supply operations in Washington. After graduating from West Point, Burns had earned a reputation as a brilliant administrator for his work in the War Department during World War I, and he had held a variety of administrative positions since. A genial Irishman, with a solid jaw and twinkling eyes, the general knew his way around Washington and had contacts with all the "right people." He had worked closely with Hopkins, as coordinator of British and French munitions purchases in the United States in 1940 and as his top assistant in the early days of lend-lease. Burns had had no experience dealing with the Russians prior to the summer of 1941. But he was devoted to his chief and he would become one of the most zealous advocates of all-out aid to the USSR and one of the most ardent defenders of the unconditional aid policy.[28]

Colonel Philip Faymonville, like Burns a West Pointer and a career ordnance officer, was made special lend-lease representative in the Soviet Union. Unlike Burns, Faymonville was a retiring, scholarly individual with a gift for languages and a deep interest in history, music, and art. While on duty in the Philippines, he had developed fluency in Russian, and he was a natural choice as staff officer for the American Expeditionary Force sent to Siberia in 1918. After serving as military attaché in Tokyo, Faymonville returned in 1926 to the United States, where for the next seven years he attended various army schools, took night courses in Russian literature and world communism, and served for a brief period as senior military aide to President Roosevelt. When the U. S. Embassy was opened in Moscow in 1934 he was appointed military attaché and he remained in that post until 1939. During this period, he traveled extensively over the USSR and established numerous close and friendly contacts with Red Army officers and civilians. His "small bachelor apartment in the American Embassy Building became one of the few places in Moscow where foreigners could meet Russian officers, musicians, professors, actors and scientists at informal social gatherings." [29]

Known by his fellow officers as "the Bolshevik," Faymonville was a controversial figure long before his appointment as lend-lease representative in the Soviet Union. His reports as military attaché had emphasized the military powers of the Red Army, a view quite out of line with official thinking in the War Department. In the summer of 1941 he had been one of the few military men in Washington to predict that Russia would survive the German invasion. The accuracy of his prognosis and his contacts with the Red Army made him an attractive figure to the President and Hopkins. Ambassador Bullitt and the State Department's East European specialist Loy Henderson, both of whom had served with him in Moscow during the thirties, protested that he was too sympathetic to the Russians. General Marshall admonished Hopkins that the colonel had been "almost defiant of regulations" in dealing with a Russian military mission in Washington in July. But Roosevelt and Hopkins ignored these warnings, sending Faymonville to oversee lend-lease operations in the Soviet Union and giving him great latitude in his position. The appointment symbolized the administration's commitment to a generous, understanding policy toward the USSR.[30]

In November, 1941, the President also gave lend-lease to Russia a special priority that would prevail throughout the war. The need to meet monthly protocol schedules and shipping dates took precedence over everything else. If supplies were available and were required for protocol lists, they were set aside for the Russians under absolute priority over the competing demands of Britain and the United States.[31]

Roosevelt placed the full power and prestige of his office squarely behind his promises to Stalin. When bottlenecks threatened to hold back shipments he intervened personally. He exerted steady pressure on the War and Navy Departments to meet obligations, and on occasion lend-lease officials aroused Hopkins from sleep or the sickbed to go to the army and force Stimson to release supplies for the Russians. As a result of all of these measures, the administration was able to secure a substantial volume of supplies for the USSR in November, 1941.[32]

But the shipping crisis—the single greatest problem in 1941 and after—left the United States behind protocol schedules from the outset. The Moscow agreement placed with the Russians primary responsibility for shipping; the United States and Britain bound themselves only to make the supplies available. To assist them, OLLA authorized on November 13 the use of lend-lease funds to arm and repair Soviet vessels in U. S. ports. Harriman and Beaverbrook realized, however, that the Russian merchant marine was too small to take on the entire burden of delivery, and they agreed to provide as many ships as possible to handle protocol supplies.[33]

A drastic shortage of shipping limited their ability to help. In the fall of 1941, crews in American shipyards from Portland, Oregon, to Bath, Maine, worked in three shifts, twenty-four hours a day, six days a week, and on September 28, "Liberty Fleet Day," fourteen merchant vessels slid down the ways in Atlantic, Pacific, and Gulf ports, the greatest mass launching since World War I. That same day, the U. S. Maritime Commission announced a gigantic construction program which aimed for the completion of two ships a day until the end of 1943. But this vast expansion of American shipbuilding could not begin to fill the huge gaps left by the Battle of the Atlantic. German U-boats destroyed about 5 million tons of British shipping in 1941, more than twice the combined output of British and American shipyards.[34]

The long and hazardous supply routes to the Soviet Union strained the limited shipping available. The north Russian ports of Murmansk and Archangel were nearest to the United States—still over 4,600 miles distant—and because these ports were closest to the war zones in their country, the Russians insisted that the bulk of supplies be shipped by this route. In September, the Royal Navy instituted convoys from Iceland along the Norwegian coast to Archangel and during the winter months the convoys moved through successfully under cover of darkness. But the great distance to north Russia, and the long "turnaround period" required large numbers of ships to meet monthly schedules, and ice, heavy seas, and harassment from German U-boats and aircraft slowed the passage of the convoys and threatened heavy losses.[35]

An alternative route by the Pacific required the transport of supplies from American west coast ports more than 4,500 miles to Vladivostok, and since the distance from port to war zone was several times that from Archangel the route was not extensively used in 1941. To safeguard a southern route to the USSR, the British and Russians had jointly occupied Iran in August, 1941, and in September the United States had dispatched a military mission to assist the British in expanding transport facilities in the Persian Gulf. But the distance from New York to the gulf was over 12,000 miles, Iranian ports were too primitive to handle large volumes of supplies, and the narrow roads and single-track railways linking gulf ports with the Caspian Sea and southern Russia were poorly maintained and frequently impassable. Stettinius aptly described the development of a major supply route through Iran as a "task of enormous dimensions." The work just got underway in 1941, and it would be many months before the route could handle a significant volume of supplies.[36]

Thus, within days after the extension of lend-lease to Russia, the administration would confront the transportation crisis that would stymie its efforts to meet protocol obligations until the end of 1943. Initial surveys estimated that shipping was available to move only about two fifths of the supplies scheduled for delivery during the month of November. Despite this pessimistic appraisal, Hopkins ordered OLLA to find the necessary ships. When the Maritime Commission argued that docking facilities in Archangel were inadequate to handle even the small number of vessels available for November and December, he directed them to provide the tonnage and leave the rest to Russian ingenuity.[37]

The results of these activities did not satisfy the Russians, who again faced the possibility of military disaster. On November 16, the Germans launched another offensive against Moscow. Within a week they had advanced to within fifteen miles of the capital, from where Nazi generals later recalled viewing the spires of the Kremlin through their fieldglasses. On November 19, the Soviet Embassy protested to the State Department that the shipping situation could "be described only as catastrophic. . . ." Three days later, the Embassy addressed another complaint to OLLA, pointing out that, although ten vessels had been promised for October, only five had been provided and one had not been seaworthy, and while thirty-one ships had been promised for November, only seven had been made available by the twenty-first of the month. Cargo requiring fifteen to seventeen ships was presently lying in U. S. ports, inadequately protected against weather, theft, and sabotage. The situation was "critical." [38]

The Russian protest stirred immediate action in Washington. When General Burns advised Stettinius that the Maritime Commission was not exerting itself to provide ships for the Russians, Stettinius took the matter directly to the White House. Roosevelt immediately ordered Admiral Land to make available sufficient ships for the protocol subject only to "insurmountable physical limitations." Land responded that it would not be "humanly possible" to secure, load, and dispatch the ninety-eight ships requested by the Russians by the end of December—only half this number could be furnished. The Lend-Lease Administrator warned that forty-nine must be the "absolute minimum," and everything possible should be done to increase the tonnage. To expedite aircraft shipments, Roosevelt even toyed with the idea of transporting planes to the Persian Gulf by aircraft carrier. He reluctantly accepted the Navy's objections that no carriers could be spared and agreed to send the planes by merchant ship. "OK," he penciled on a memo to Hopkins, "but say to them from me: Hurry, Hurry, Hurry!" [39]

By the first of December, Soviet-American relations had reached a state of crisis. Stettinius told Hopkins on November 28 that failure to live up to the Moscow agreement would have "very serious repercussions," and several days later he remarked to Burns that there was "no more pressing matter facing us than the whole shipping problem." The difficulties became public on December 3, when the New York *Times* columnist Arthur Krock reported that the administration had fallen "far, far short" of its commitments and that the Russians were most displeased. Roosevelt's Press Secretary, Stephen Early, admitted in a subsequent news conference that the United States was not meeting it obligations to the USSR, but he hastened to add that there had been no change in policy. The President was determined to keep his word.[40]

Stettinius attacked the shipping problem without stint from November 27 to December 6, and achieved significant results, dispatching over $11,500,000 worth of supplies in that week alone. By December 6, OLLA had received assurances of shipping to bring protocol schedules up to date by the end of the month. But the Japanese attack on Pearl Harbor nullified this progress. "Throughout the U. S. military structure," Army historians have written, "the shock of war was violent." The War Department was caught about three months short of completing its rearmament program, and suddenly it faced the reality of a two-front war. The army immediately imposed an embargo on all lend-lease shipments, called back ships just underway to England and Russia, and hastily unloaded aircraft, guns, and ammunition for reshipment to Hawaii and the Philippines.[41]

The total embargo on lend-lease lasted only twenty-four hours, but, Stettinius advised Burns, it "completely upset" the Russian aid program. Shipping schedules were thrown off, ports were hopelessly congested, and throughout the entire supply mechanism the confusion was "just perfectly unbelievable." American entry into the war left the United States far behind its protocol commitments with little hope that the deficits could be soon made up. American exports to Russia from June 22 through December 6 totaled more than 350,000 tons and were valued at over $65,000,000. But most of this relatively small volume comprised orders submitted before the Russians were placed under lend-lease. One of Hopkins' aides valued actual protocol shipments at less than $500,000, and Harriman estimated that, as of December 24, the United States had shipped only 25 percent of the tonnage pledged.[42]

Because of the haste with which these supplies had been readied for shipment, many items arrived in the USSR unfit for use. Defective generators had been installed in a number of P-40 fighters, and spare parts and instructions for operation had been left out. Similar defects and omissions plagued subsequent deliveries, and at the end of 1941 the Russians reported that thirty-five of two hundred and twenty-eight P-40's were out of commission and the remainder were operating without generators. The American military attaché in Russia advised Washington in November that the Russians considered U. S. planes "unfit and unsafe for use at the front." American prestige was suffering, he warned, and the issue was becoming significant politically.[43]

By December 7, the Russian military situation had improved substantially. The USSR had scored its most significant victory over German arms by recapturing Rostov-on-the-Don, the gateway to the Caucasus, on November 29. A small Russian detachment gallantly held off a furious assault against Sebastopol in the Crimea. Most important, the Red Army had again stopped Hitler's offensive against Moscow, and had launched a counteroffensive against German positions around the capital on December 6.[44]

The great victories of November swelled Russian pride and insured the nation's survival through the winter. But the Germans still occupied huge portions of Soviet territory, and though their troops were for the moment in retreat they remained a powerful fighting force. The USSR still badly needed aid from the West, and Soviet officials made no attempt to hide their displeasure at the small volume of supplies received from the United States.

The events of November and December, 1941, confirm in retrospect the wisdom of Franklin Roosevelt's unconditional aid policy. In giving lend-lease to Russia a unique status and top priority, FDR was not acting from naiveté nor from a blind and innocent faith that Stalin, if treated generously, would respond in kind. He was concerned above all with the immediate problems of the war, and he demonstrated astuteness and realism in dealing with these problems. He wisely ignored the protests of the military that Russian requests could not be properly evaluated unless they were supported by the "justifications" required of other nations. Shortages of supplies and shipping insured that the Soviets would have to give top priority to their most urgent needs and that they would not abuse the unconditional aid policy. He realized that the Russians were difficult to deal with, but he did not attempt to change their ways. Rather he asked Americans to understand their sensitivities and to be sympathetic toward their plight in the interest of promoting common goals.

The President was aware of the risks in his policy, but he acted upon the greater risk of a German victory in the USSR. He recognized that political commitments extracted in 1941 would be of little value years later in different circumstances. He may have feared that the proud and sensitive Stalin would reject American aid rather than make binding promises to the United States. In any event, he perceived correctly that the attachment of political conditions would delay aid to Russia when it had to be expedited, and would increase Soviet suspicions when they had to be overcome. At a time when inefficiency, confusion, and shortages stymied the Russian aid program, Roosevelt realistically avoided creating further and more difficult problems.

Yet, despite the unconditional aid policy, the special status and top priority given the Russian protocol, and the President's vigorous action to speed up shipments, American aid to the USSR in the early months of the war had been insubstantial and unsatisfactory, and had not won the confidence of the Russians. U. S. entry into the war would provide an even sterner test for the President's attempts to bring the Soviet Union into a tight alliance against Hitler.

Chapter 3

PEARL HARBOR TO STALINGRAD

"NOTHING WOULD BE WORSE THAN TO HAVE THE RUSSIANS COLLAPSE"

DURING THE SECOND WORLD WAR,
THE MILITARY HISTORIAN
J. F. C. Fuller has written, God "marched with the biggest
industries rather than with the biggest battalions." The
highly mechanized armies of that war consumed huge volumes of food, fuel, and munitions, and military operations
depended on the availability of vital supplies in sufficient
quantity, at the right place, and at the appropriate time.
Without the sinews of war, the morale of armies and civilian
populations would diminish, and statesmen might be
tempted by the lure of a negotiated peace.[1]

As supplymaster of the Grand Alliance, Franklin D. Roosevelt was primarily responsible for allocating the output of
American industry among the various members of the coalition. The role would have been fraught with difficulties
under any circumstances, but it was especially perilous in
1942, when American industry was not producing to full capacity, when shipping was still in short supply, and when allied armies retreated before the enemy on three fronts.
American diplomacy in 1942 was, in large measure, lend-

lease diplomacy. Its principal objective was to distribute supplies in the manner best calculated to contain Axis offensives and to hold the alliance together for the anticipated counteroffensive. Its implementation required not only expert knowledge of strategy and logistics, but also an acute sensitivity to the political and psychological needs of the allies.

This was especially true in the case of the USSR, the ally bearing much of the burden of defense against the Axis and a nation still deeply suspicious of the West. Failure to provide adequate assistance would inhibit its capacity to fight, discourage its will to resist, and increase its already pervasive suspicions. It might, as the President recognized, encourage Stalin to strike a bargain with the enemy. On the other hand, the needs of the other allies and of the United States itself could not be ignored. Supplying the Soviet Union entailed grave risks and heavy costs, and it would be self-defeating to strip American arsenals and to squander limited shipping to assist Russia if by doing so the capacity of the western allies to hold the defensive and to mount an offensive was thereby limited. The principal task of lend-lease diplomacy during 1942 was, therefore, to strike a balance between these competing demands without impairing the military effectiveness or the political cohesiveness of the alliance.

From Pearl Harbor to the epic battle of Stalingrad, Roosevelt's diplomacy met constant challenges and encountered repeated frustration. The first challenge came from the U. S. military. American entry into the war naturally produced immediate and intense demands for a change in the supply priorities established before Pearl Harbor. The Japanese navy controlled the seas from Hawaii to the Bay of Bengal, and from Wake Island to Singapore, superior Japanese invading forces fell upon hopelessly outmanned American and British garrisons. Unprepared and immediately thrown back upon the defensive, the U. S. Army and Navy desperately searched for guns, ammunition, aircraft, and shipping to reinforce their beleagured outposts. "We must run a rake through the United States," Air Force Chief of Staff General H. H. Arnold advised his staff on December 10, "gathering up every combat plane and fill[ing] up every pursuit group." [2]

The army lifted its total embargo of lend-lease shipments on December 8, and began to release supplies for the allies. But on December 10, John J. McCloy, Assistant Secretary of War in charge of procurement and lend-lease, advised OLLA that no aircraft or ammunition could be spared for lend-lease before the end of the month, and an army general curtly advised Stettinius to stop pressing for supplies. "We have got to go slow, and we just can't be bothered with people demanding this and that." General Marshall informed the President in mid-December that diversions from lend-lease programs would only be temporary, but they were "imperative," and suggested that Russian protocol commitments could not be resumed in full until February 1; both Marshall and Stimson agreed that the protocol would have to be revised in view of expanded American requirements. Stettinius was left the unpleasant task of telling the Russians they would not get everything promised them.[3]

When Prime Minister Churchill arrived in Washington on December 22 to confer with Roosevelt, pressures on the military had mounted. The hopeful spirit of the Christmas season, the code name "Arcadia" given the conference, the optimism exuded by both men could not conceal the grim realities of the war in the Pacific. The small American detachment on Wake Island fell on Christmas Eve, and Japanese invaders drove toward Manila from three sides. Britain conceded the loss of Hong Kong.

But looming disaster in the Far East did not alter the basic strategy adopted by the United States and Britain in 1941. At Arcadia, Roosevelt and Churchill reaffirmed the agreement to concentrate maximum force against Hitler and to hold Japan in defensive operations until the defeat of Germany was assured. The USSR occupied an essential place in their plans. As Churchill pondered the war aboard the H. M. S. *Duke of York* en route to the United States, the Red

Army's counteroffensive had forced the Germans into retreat
from Moscow along snowy roads littered with hundreds of
crippled Nazi vehicles. "Hitler's failure and losses in Russia
are the prime fact in the war at this time," the Prime Minister wrote on December 16. "Instead of what was imagined to
be a swift and easy victory, it [Germany] has now to face the
shock of a winter of slaughter and expenditure of fuel and
equipment on the largest scale." It was up to the United
States and Britain to send "without fail and punctually, the
supplies we have promised. In this way alone shall we hold
our influence over Stalin and be able to weave the mighty
Russian effort into the general texture of the war." [4]

Roosevelt shared Churchill's appraisal of the importance
of the Russian front and the necessity of meeting supply
commitments. At the very time the War Department was
stripping ships of guns and planes originally intended for
the USSR, the President casually advised the Soviet Ambassador, Maxim Litvinov, that the Russians would get everything promised them. When lend-lease officials warned that
presidential intervention would be necessary to establish a
greater "sense of urgency" among Americans regarding Russian aid, Roosevelt immediately set down clear, firm guidelines. Rejecting the army's proposals to revise the protocol
and to delay resumption of full shipments until February 1,
he simply ordered that the protocol be reestablished by January 1, and that existing deficiencies be made up by April 1.
Amendments had to be approved by him and would be com-
pensated by increased volumes of other items. "The whole
Russian program is so vital to our interests," he concluded,
"I know that only the gravest consideration will lead you to
recommend our withholding longer the munitions our Government has promised the U. S. S. R." [5]

Roosevelt and Churchill again emphasized the importance
of aid to Russia at a conference with the British and American Chiefs of Staff on January 12. When General Marshall
proposed the immediate dispatch of a convoy of reinforce-
ments to the Far East, even though it would necessitate a 30
percent reduction in shipments to Russia for the next four

months, the President at first casually remarked that the plan sounded good. But Churchill expressed strong reservations (the Russians would "probably yell like hell and they are inflicting heavy casualties on Nazi troops"), and Roosevelt agreed that "there might be unfortunate repercussions in Russia if at the very time they are pinched as at present we let them down." Hopkins then remarked that the proposed cutback involved only seven vessels per month and that it ought to be possible to find that many. The conferees decided that shipments to Russia must not be reduced and Hopkins immediately directed Admiral Land to come up with the extra ships.[6]

During the month after the United States entered the war, the army and navy did manage to secure a measure of control over the allocation of military supplies. To coordinate more effectively the distribution of munitions among all the allied nations, Roosevelt and Churchill agreed at Arcadia to establish a Combined Munitions Assignment Board, a committee made up of representatives of the armed services of both nations and responsible to the Combined Chiefs of Staff. Harry Hopkins served as chairman of the MAB, and his presence insured ultimate civilian authority over its decisions. But the creation of the board transferred from a civilian agency, OLLA, to a military body the primary responsibility for drawing up and implementing lend-lease munitions' programs.[7]

This change in procedure would in time vastly increase the military's power over lend-lease. But it did not affect the handling of aid to Russia. At Arcadia, Roosevelt and Churchill tacitly agreed that the protocol should retain its unique status. The volume of supplies to be provided the Soviet Union would, as in the past, be determined in tripartite negotiations. The MAB would have only limited influence in these negotiations, and it could not alter the decisions resulting from them. Thus the Arcadia Conference maintained the unique procedure for aid to Russia and reaffirmed its top priority.[8]

In the weeks after Arcadia, the administration concentrated on a much more difficult problem, making up the steadily widening deficit in protocol shipments. Deliveries of supplies had amounted to only about 25 percent of commitments by December 7, and Pearl Harbor had done inestimable damage. The temporary embargo disrupted shipping schedules, diversion of supplies and vessels left large gaps that could not be made up easily, and the disorder in American ports following the declaration of war made it extremely difficult to establish new schedules.[9]

By mid-January, shipments lagged far behind promises, and the Russians began to protest vigorously. In Moscow, Commissar Anastas I. Mikoyan stressed to General Faymonville that the success of the Red Army's winter counteroffensive hinged on American supplies, but to date the record had been lamentable: 705 tanks promised, only sixteen received, 600 planes promised, only eighty-five delivered. The Red Army had an immediate and urgent need for all supplies listed in the protocol, and the only hope of preventing the escape of German armies from around Moscow was to make up the shortages at once.[10]

Stettinius quickly brought these protests to the attention of the President, informing him that inadequate shipping was the primary cause of the failures and suggesting that pressure be brought upon Admiral Land. That same day, FDR complained to the admiral that he was "terribly disturbed" that ample shipping had not been found for Russia, and ordered him to give the matter his immediate personal attention. The United States had made a firm commitment to the USSR, he asserted, and "we simply cannot go back on it. You simply must find some ships that can be diverted at once for this Russian business." Hopkins advised Faymonville at the same time that everything possible would be done to bring protocol schedules up to date.[11]

A month produced negligible results, and on February 16, the Russians took their case directly to the White House. Tactfully, but forcefully, General Alexander Repin, head of the Russian military mission in the United States, complained that delivery of supplies had been "very slow," with quantities far below protocol figures. The number of ships assigned the Russians had been inadequate, the crews unreliable, and the docking facilities poor. American tanks and planes already in the Soviet Union were inoperative for lack of ammunition and spare parts. Thanking the President for previous assistance, Repin urged him to take the steps necessary to "speed up the supplying of my country with military equipment and strategic raw materials so urgently needed for continuation of the victorious struggle against our common enemies." [12]

Stettinius and Morgenthau verified the accuracy of the Russian complaints, and Roosevelt was acutely aware of their implications. "I do not want to be in the same position as the English [he confided to Morgenthau on March 11.] The English promised the Russians two divisions. They failed. They promised them help in the Caucasus. They failed. Every promise the English have made to the Russians, they have fallen down on. . . . The only reason we stand so well with the Russians is that up to date we have kept our promises. . . ." He left no doubt of the importance he attached to aid to Russia. "I would go out and take the stuff off the shelves of the stores," he told Morgenthau, "and pay them any price necessary, and put it in a truck and rush it to the boat. . . . Nothing would be worse than to have the Russians collapse." [13]

Roosevelt's homey affirmation overlooked the enormous practical problems that still plagued the protocol. The Russians themselves were at least partly to blame. Certain that they would have to repay the $1 billion credit under which lend-lease was being financed, they continued to haggle over prices, attempting to get the most supplies for the least amount of money. They submitted their specifications late, and persisted in placing what Stettinius called "Tiffany specifications," requests for non-standard types of steel and other raw materials that could be produced only by special order and with considerable delay. Adjustment and modification of these specifications required hours of work, and then the Russians were reluctant to accept changes. William Batt of the War Production Board accurately described the specifications problem as a "hideous mess." [14]

Americans had to share with the Russians responsibility for the breakdown of the aid program. The War Production Board had not given priority to Soviet requests for steel and the material was simply not available. The military naturally continued to resist raids on their precious stocks, despite the President's directive of December 28, and expressed great irritation at the insistent complaints of the Russians and their refusal to recognize the existence of shortages and the demands of the United States.[15]

The main problem, everyone agreed, was shipping. Despite shortages of tanks, aircraft, and steel, supplies were piling up in east coast ports awaiting shipment to the USSR. In late January the Russians were assured of forty-five ships as a "firm commitment," and then only twenty-six could be made available. Admiral Land defended himself as best he could. "We haven't got enough ships. . . . I have known it for some time. . . . We have never lived up to our promises; and, as far as I can see, we are probably unlikely to live up to them with exactitude. The repair yards are 300 percent overloaded. The sinkings are going faster than the buildings, and there are a thousand other excuses that are not worthwhile even to go into. . . ." Even when vessels were available, snarls in the railroad yards prevented expeditious loading.[16]

"We are turning the town upside down to get supplies for Russia," Hopkins wrote Harriman, as he, Stettinius, and Morgenthau attacked these problems. In response to American urging, the Russians appointed on February 25 a Purchasing Commission in the United States, headed by a general and admiral, and with broad authority to handle details of supply procurement. The ability of the commission to negotiate on specifications and other matters without having to refer everything back to Moscow greatly simplified processing of the protocols. Replacement of the civilian mission, Amtorg, with a military mission better geared to wartime purchasing eliminated much of the delay that had resulted from negotiations on prices.[17]

To make the Russians less price-conscious and to place Russian aid on an equal basis with that of Britain, the administration terminated in late February the credit arrangement established in October, 1941, and put the protocol on a straight lend-lease basis. At the same time, the Treasury and War Departments created special sections to work out expeditiously the backlog of specifications that had accumulated. Morgenthau worked to find the steel necessary to make up commitments, and Stettinius pressed the War Department to release military equipment. "As you are aware," he wrote McCloy on February 24, "the relations between this Government and the Soviet Government have been constantly disturbed by the failure of this Government to meet its commitments, and I feel that you would agree with me that a deficiency in tanks at this time would create a most unfortunate situation." Stettinius also prodded Admiral Land to release sufficient ships to bring the Russian program up to date by the end of March.[18]

Incipient conflicts with the Russians over military strategy and postwar political objectives gave an added sense of urgency to the supply problem. Stalin had indicated early in the war that he desired from his allies, in addition to maximum shipments of supplies, the immediate establishment of a second front in Europe and recognition of Russia's frontiers before the German invasion of June 22, 1941. Lack of shipping and battle-ready troops made it impossible for the United States and Britain to undertake an early invasion of the continent. Acquiescence in Stalin's territorial demands, which included the Baltic States of Lithuania, Latvia, and Esthonia, posed an equally difficult problem. Secretary of State Hull objected to any political agreements or secret treaties, especially if they violated the principle of self-determination, and at least partly in deference to American protests, Churchill agreed in December, 1941, to postpone political discussions until later.[19]

During the early months of 1942, however, as Russian complaints about supply deliveries and the second front mounted, the British began to weaken. Unwilling to risk a premature assault on Europe and unable to provide supplies in quantities promised, Churchill on March 7 reversed his earlier opposition to political discussions and requested from Roosevelt a free hand to negotiate with Stalin, warning that it was essential to reach an agreement before the Germans launched their spring offensive. The British ambassador, Lord Halifax, advised Under Secretary of State Sumner Welles that his country must conclude a treaty with Stalin as a "political substitute for material military assistance," warning that a break with the Soviet Union could cause the fall of the Churchill government and its replacement by a "frankly Communist, pro-Moscow" government.[20]

The specter of a "red" Britain failed to sway the State Department. Welles condemned the British argument as "not only indefensible from every moral standpoint, but likewise extraordinarily stupid." Assistant Secretary of State Adolf A. Berle warned of a "Baltic Munich." Hull advised Roosevelt that giving in to Stalin's demands might improve relations with Russia temporarily, but it would be a dangerous precedent and would only encourage him to demand more in the future. Recognition of Russian control over the Baltic states would be a blatant violation of the Atlantic Charter. The Secretary insisted that the test of American "good faith" should be the "degree of determination which we show loyally to carry out our promises to aid the Soviet Government with equipment and supplies." [21]

Although he did not commit himself openly to Hull's proposed use of economic aid as a substitute for political concessions, Roosevelt appears to have accepted the strategy in principle. He was more flexible on the Baltic issue than the State Department, recognizing that the United States could do little to prevent Stalin from taking these nations. But he fully appreciated the dilemma created by the Russian leader's demands. He told his cabinet in March that agreement to Soviet absorption of the Baltic states might lead to demands for more land, perhaps for parts of Poland. He feared that it would also awaken popular memories of the secret treaties of World War I and arouse American opinion against the USSR. Failure to meet Soviet conditions, on the other hand, would increase tensions with an ally at a critical point in the war. Anxious to defer discussions of political problems until the end of the war, the President advised the cabinet that shipments to Russia had to be expedited and a new protocol with substantial increases offered to Stalin as soon as possible in order to provide tangible evidence of "good faith."[22]

Roosevelt had political as well as military concerns in mind, therefore, when in mid-March he gave absolute top priority to aid to the Soviet Union. On March 17, he ordered that "all material promised under the protocol be released for shipment at the earliest possible date regardless of the effect of these shipments on any other part of our war program." On the same day, he directed Admiral Land to find sufficient ships for Russia "regardless of all other considerations." Hopkins left no doubt of the President's intent. The protocol, he stressed, "must be completed in preference to any other phase of our war program."[23]

Roosevelt's dramatic orders came at a time of stunning defeats in the Far East. From January to March, 1942, Japan had swept across the Pacific and Southeast Asia with such speed, Robert Sherwood has recalled, that the "pins on the walls of map rooms in Washington and London were usually far out of date." Singapore had fallen on February 15, an event described by Churchill as "the greatest disaster to British arms which our history records." By mid-March, Japanese forces had completed the conquest of Malaya, Java, and Borneo, landed on New Guinea, and occupied Rangoon. For weeks, American and Filipino troops isolated on the Bataan peninsula had valiantly held off the invaders. Without food, clothing, and drugs, exhausted from disease and malnutrition, they could not hold out much longer, and on March 17 their commanding general, Douglas MacArthur, arrived in Australia to begin preparations for developing the next line of defense in the Pacific.[24]

The President sustained the "Russia first" policy in the spring of 1942 against mounting pressures to avenge the defeats in the Far East. He ignored cries of "Pacific First" from conservative politicians and editors at home. Even after the surrender of Bataan and Corregidor sealed the fall of the Philippines, he resisted demands from the U. S. Navy, General MacArthur, and a nervous Australian government to upgrade the strategic importance of the Pacific theater. "In the matter of grand strategy," he advised MacArthur in May, "I find it difficult this Spring and Summer to get away from the simple fact that the Russian armies are killing more Axis personnel and destroying more Axis materiel than all the other twenty-five United Nations put together. Therefore, it has seemed wholly logical to support the great Russian effort in 1942 by seeking to get all munitions to them that we possibly can. . . ." Hopkins informed reporters at an off-the-record briefing that aid to Russia "is without question the most important task for the moment." [25]

Roosevelt's forceful orders of March 17 and the groundwork already laid by Hopkins, Morgenthau, and Stettinius produced striking results. The army released for the USSR all light tanks consigned to American forces for March and to Britain for April. Trucks and planes were made available in quantities only slightly below schedules, and Russia was given the entire American output of field telephone wire in January and 90 percent of that for February and March. By the end of April, deficiencies remained only in anti-tank and anti-aircraft guns. The March 17 directive also broke open the shipping bottleneck. Seventy-nine freighters cleared American ports for the USSR in April, and to make up all remaining shortages in the protocol, the President ordered that fifty ships per month should be scheduled for North Russian ports until the end of November.[26]

This tremendous expansion of American exports to the Soviet Union and the completion by the U. S. Army of plans for the opening of a second front in Europe in late 1942 or early 1943 seemed to offer a means out of the dilemma created by Stalin's political demands. Roosevelt's invitation to Stalin in late March to send his Foreign Minister, Molotov, to Washington was not intended to imply a direct *quid pro quo.* There seems little doubt, however, that the President hoped the provision of increased supplies and the promise of a second front might entice the Russian to soften or abandon altogether his territorial demands and at least would insure that political disputes would not disrupt the alliance.[27]

Stalin, still attempting to get the best deal possible, rejected Roosevelt's proposal to dispatch Molotov to Washington immediately; instead he sent him to London to negotiate the long-delayed treaty with Britain. But military disasters in the southern sector of the Russian front weakened Stalin's hand. While Molotov was in London, the Germans routed a Red Army assault on Kerch in the Crimea and decimated three armies attempting to liberate Kharkov. These catastrophes cost the USSR heavily in men and equipment, left southern Russia vulnerable to an anticipated German summer offensive, and rendered it more than ever dependent upon Western help. Consequently, when the British continued to resist Soviet political terms for the alliance, Stalin, aware that American military support was essential, suddenly ordered Molotov to accept a treaty without territorial provisions and to proceed on to the United States.[28]

The Russian foreign minister arrived in Washington on May 29, protected by elaborate security measures, traveling under the pseudonym "Mr. Brown," and prepared to extract from the United States definite commitments on the second front and increased shipments of supplies. By this time, however, unanticipated developments had cut the bases from under Roosevelt's diplomacy and left him in an extremely embarrassing position, unable to make the sort of promises the Russians desired. Instead of smoothing over the nascent conflicts in the alliance, the Molotov discussions opened a fissure that would widen dangerously in the months to come.

An unusual combination of events in the North Atlantic in March and April had produced the most serious challenge to Roosevelt's diplomacy. In February, Hitler began to mass surface ships, U-boats, and aircraft in Norway to disrupt the convoys to North Russia. Weather worked in his favor. Unusually heavy ice masses slowed the passage of merchant ships and forced them to hug the Norwegian coast where in the perpetual daylight of the Arctic spring they were easy prey for submarines and dive-bombers. Losses on the Murmansk run mounted in April, and the burden of defending the convoys strained the resources of the Royal Navy. Late in the month Churchill reluctantly decided to limit operations to three convoys every two months each comprised of twenty-five to thirty-five ships.[29]

Roosevelt acquiesced, and the administration hurriedly adjusted production programs and shipping schedules. Deliveries to the Persian Gulf were increased to the maximum, but the still very limited capacity of the ports and the transportation network into the Soviet Union left this route inadequate to compensate for reduction of the northern convoys. Ships originally assigned to Russia were diverted to other uses, and the administration urged the Russians to designate priorities for protocol items to insure the most effective use of available shipping.[30]

Churchill's decision to cut back the convoys dashed hopes that protocol shipments could be brought up to date by the end of May and insured that the deficits would continue to grow larger. At the same time, army and navy strategists concluded that because of the shortage of merchant vessels a second front could not be accomplished without a substantial reduction in proposed supply commitments to the USSR during the period from June, 1942, to June, 1943.[31]

Thus Molotov, who had journeyed to Washington to secure unequivocal pledges for the opening of a second front and for increased shipments of supplies was disappointed on both counts. The Soviet Foreign Minister brought with him four special requests for lend-lease assistance. The most important, a proposal that the United States send one convoy a month to Archangel, reflected obvious Russian disenchantment with British operations in the North Atlantic. The administration rejected it out of hand, on grounds that the convoys could be executed most effectively in concert with Great Britain. It also turned down, because of the lack of supplies and shipping, Molotov's requests for increased deliveries of two different types of aircraft. The President and Hopkins agreed only to send three thousand trucks monthly to the Persian Gulf.[32]

Roosevelt could offer only qualified assurances of a second front in 1942, and he emphasized that it would be impossible unless the Russians would agree to a reduction in shipments of supplies from 4.1 million to 2.5 million tons during the period from June, 1942, to July, 1943. He attempted to soften the blow by pointing out that the reduction would consist entirely of raw materials and industrial equipment. But it would have to be made to release the shipping necessary to invade Europe. The Russians "could not have their cake and eat it too." [33]

Molotov did manage to secure Roosevelt's agreement to an equivocal statement that "full understanding was reached with regard to the urgent task of creating a Second Front in Europe in 1942." Interpreting this as a firm commitment, he conveniently ignored the qualifications in the President's earlier promises. Thus, although his special requests for supplies had been turned down and he had been put on notice that the opening of a second front would require substantial reduction in supply deliveries, the Foreign Minister told Davies that he was leaving Washington much happier than when he arrived and that he was "entirely satisfied" with the results of the talks.[34]

Molotov's happiness was only transitory, however, for shortly after he returned to Moscow Churchill arrived in Washington to talk Roosevelt out of an early invasion of Europe. The Prime Minister, who had never been enthusiastic about the operation, argued forcibly that the limited invasion the allies were capable of executing in 1942 would have little effect on the Russian front, that it would be extremely risky, perhaps even disastrous, and he doubted whether sufficient landing craft were available to undertake it. He proposed instead an assault on North Africa to help secure the allied position in the Middle East.

Roosevelt might have resisted Churchill's arguments had it not been for the fall of Tobruk on June 21. The capitulation of this symbol of British resistance threatened a complete collapse in the Mediterranean with the loss of vital oil supplies and the Suez Canal and posed the possibility of a union of triumphant German and Japanese forces. The catastrophe also represented a grave political crisis for the Prime Minister, who faced a vote of censure in Parliament on his return to London.[35]

Churchill's peril, which for the moment overshadowed the war in Russia, probably determined the President's decision to support the North African landing. He was also anxious to get American troops into action somewhere in 1942, and he rationalized the decision on grounds that it would help encourage the Russians. Yet he must have realized that it could not make up for the European landing Stalin so urgently desired.

In the meantime, disaster had struck the northern convoys. On June 27, PQ17, consisting of thirty-four merchant vessels, sailed from Iceland escorted by a destroyer force with Anglo-American cruisers in immediate support. As the convoy neared Bear Island off the Norwegian coast, the Admiralty learned that the Germans were dispatching a large force of surface ships, including the dreaded *Tirpitz,* for the attack. Unwilling to risk the small force of cruisers against superior German firepower, the Admiralty ordered them to withdraw and, to minimize losses, ordered the destroyers to disperse. Misinterpreting the orders, the destroyer escort withdrew with the cruisers. "The scattered, defenceless convoy," Churchill later wrote, "now fell an easy prey to the marauding aircraft and U-boats." Twenty-three of the thirty-four ships were sunk, carrying to the bottom more than 130,000 tons of supplies.[36]

The dismal fate of PQ 17 forced the Admiralty to make hard decisions. During July, sinkings in the North Atlantic had reached unprecedented figures. In the week July 7 to 14 alone, the allies had lost 400,000 tons, and if losses continued at that rate, sinkings would exceed construction by $2\frac{1}{2}$ to 1. Unwilling to risk continued heavy losses on the Murmansk run, the Admiralty in mid-July suspended the convoys indefinitely, at least until the melting of the ice and the passage of perpetual daylight should lower the risks of operations.[37]

The first protocol expired on June 30, 1942, several weeks before the indefinite suspension of the convoys. Considering all the obstacles confronting aid to Russia, the American performance was not unimpressive. The United States shipped 1,273,600 tons of supplies during the first protocol period, roughly 80 percent of its original commitment at the Moscow Conference. Deliveries of jeeps, chemicals (including TNT), and clothing actually exceeded promises, while shipments of tanks fell only slightly short. These figures by themselves, however, provide a misleading picture. Over 300,000 tons of supplies were lost at sea during the period October, 1941, to July, 1942, and with the suspension of convoys, an additional 129,000 tons of cargo intended for Russia were unloaded in the United Kingdom and diverted to other uses. In certain critical areas, American shipments fell far short of protocol schedules. Deliveries of planes comprised about two thirds of promises, guns less than one tenth, and trucks, less than one half. As late as September, 1942, OLLA had furnished only about 85 percent of the materials promised in the first protocol, with the main shortage in industrial equipment and machine tools.[38]

The shipping crisis, which was primarily responsible for the first protocol deficits, also delayed completion of the second protocol. After plans for a second front in 1942 had been postponed, Roosevelt ceased pressing the Russians to accept reductions in shipments. The United States offered the USSR over 8,000,000 tons of supplies for the period July 1, 1942, to June 30, 1943, and requested that they select 4,400,000 tons to be sent to North Russian ports. No sooner had the Russians accepted this arrangement than the British Admiralty had suspended the convoys, and it became clear that even the 4,400,000 tons could not be delivered. On July 29, U. S. officials urged the Russians to accept a readjustment of production and shipping schedules to prevent the accumulation of large surplus stocks. They refused, however, and though shipments continued the protocol remained unsigned and the delay became an additional source of friction.[39]

The deficiencies under the first protocol, the delays in the second protocol, the decision regarding the second front, and suspension of the northern convoys came as bitter blows to the USSR. Militarily, the perilous winter of 1941 had given way to the "Black Summer" of 1942. The Red Army's winter counteroffensive had failed to achieve its objective of smashing all German forces between Moscow and Smolensk, and in June German armies were still entrenched within eighty miles of the capital. The situation was even more critical in the south. The defeats at Kerch and Kharkov had been followed by the fall of Sebastopol, which had held out against siege since October, 1941. Then on June 28, Hitler launched a major offensive aimed at Stalingrad and the oil fields of the Caucasus. Within a month, the Nazis had retaken Rostov and sped toward the Caucasus; by early August, they had crossed the Don and were driving toward Stalingrad.[40]

Again thrown back on the defensive, with no hope of relief and with both allies far behind in their supply deliveries, the Russians reacted angrily. Davies found Ambassador Litvinov "sore, suspicious and resentful," and complaining that the Russians were doing the fighting while the other allies were doing the "global planning." Ambassador William H. Standley reported from Moscow that Soviet protests had become "more and more bitter and sarcastic" as shipments of supplies had fallen farther and farther behind schedule. When Churchill informed Stalin of the decisions to terminate the convoys and to invade North Africa, he received a reply he accurately described as "rough and surly," which stated "in the most emphatic manner that the Soviet Government cannot acquiesce in the postponement of a second front in Europe until 1943." [41]

The Russians refused to admit the formidable obstacles facing the United States and Britain. Stalin remarked to Standley in April that the only real hindrance was the unwillingness of American contractors to accept Russian orders. He blamed the PQ 17 fiasco upon the Royal Navy's incompetence, he refused to accept the Admiralty's excuses for terminating shipments to Murmansk, and he told Churchill that "with good will and readiness to fulfill the contracted obligations these convoys could be regularly undertaken and heavy losses could be inflicted on the enemy." The Soviet press accused the British of stopping the convoys so they could keep for themselves what rightfully belonged to Russia.[42]

The Russians denounced their capitalist allies for conspiring against them, frequently insinuating that they were sending the USSR only enough aid to keep her fighting, with the obvious intention of allowing Germany and the Soviet Union to destroy each other. When Churchill went personally to the Kremlin in August, Stalin, according to Harriman, spoke "with a degree of bluntness almost amounting to insult," "caustically" denouncing the allies' failure to support him, and advising Churchill that he could not win wars if he was afraid of the Germans and unwilling to take risks.[43]

Roosevelt urged Churchill to be understanding. "We have got always to bear in mind the personality of our Ally and the very difficult and dangerous situation that confronts him," he wrote. "No one can be expected to approach the war from a world point of view whose country has been invaded. I think we should try to put ourselves in his place." He attempted to reassure the Soviet premier as best he could, advising him through an intermediary that if the Russians would assign priorities to their requests and show the United States how to deliver them, there was almost no limit to what could be provided. In a personal message to Stalin after Churchill had departed from Moscow, FDR expressed American appreciation for the "magnificent resistance" put up by the Red Army, and again promised that the United States was "coming as quickly and as strongly to your assistance as we possibly can." [44]

Promises meant little to Stalin and the Russians. Even as Roosevelt wrote, German tanks had broken through to the Volga north of Stalingrad, cutting off all access to the city except by barge from the east. By September 1, the Nazis had advanced to the foothills of the Caucasus. At a dinner for the touring Wendell Willkie, Stalin expressed great disappointment at the paucity of aid received from his allies, and complained that supplies received were often older types unsatisfactory for use at the front.[45]

Russian relations with the West reached the point of crisis in October, 1942, when Churchill again suspended the northern convoys after a brief resumption in September had resulted in heavy losses. The Red Army fought savagely in and around Stalingrad, but the German advance continued and on October 14, the city was nearly lost. Bitterness against the allies mounted. *Pravda* published vicious cartoons, accusing the British of cowardice and of collaboration with the Nazis. In a much publicized letter to Associated Press correspondent Henry Cassidy, Stalin complained that Western assistance to Russia was of "little effect" and demanded a "complete and timely fulfillment by the allies of their obligations." When Churchill advised Stalin of the decision to terminate the convoys, he replied only with a curt "Thank you." Communications with the Russian leader then lapsed into an ominous silence.[46]

Throughout the anxious weeks of Stalingrad, Roosevelt remained calm and optimistic. When Churchill expressed deep concern at the abrupt termination of communications from Stalin, the President attempted to encourage him. "Having come to the conclusion that the Russians do not use speech for the same purposes that we do," he advised the Prime Minister, "I am not unduly disturbed about the responses or lack of them that we have received from Moscow. I feel very certain that the Russians are going to hold throughout this winter."

Roosevelt's optimism did not, however, produce any complacency about aid to Russia. On the contrary, he cabled Churchill, "We must be able to prove to Stalin that we have carried out obligations one hundred per cent and we must therefore proceed vigorously with our plans for supplying them. . . ."[47] With the fate of Stalingrad in doubt and Russia's relations with the West at their lowest point, he worked vigorously in October and November to repair the crisis in confidence. Shipping remained the principal problem. On October 2, FDR reaffirmed the high priority already given to aid to the USSR. The convoys again suspended, he instructed his aides to "make every effort to utilize to the maximum the supply routes that may be available to us." He immediately scheduled increased shipments of raw materials and foodstuffs by the Pacific to Vladivostok, and gave top priority to expanding drastically the capacity of Persian Gulf ports and modernizing the rail and truck routes into Trans-Caucasia. On October 6, he put into effect long-delayed plans to ferry aircraft to Fairbanks, Alaska, from whence they would be flown by Russian pilots into Siberia. The administration even ordered studies of the feasibility of transporting supplies to the USSR via the Bering Sea.[48]

To compensate for supply deficiencies, Roosevelt attempted to expedite projects of special importance. The Russians badly needed tires for military vehicles, but a severe rubber shortage prevented the United States from meeting their needs. OLLA therefore proposed to ship to the USSR machinery and equipment from an unused Ford Motor Company plant in River Rouge, Michigan, which would be reassembled in Russia and would produce one million tires per year with Russian rubber. On October 13, the President directed William Jeffers, Administrator of the Rubber Committee of the War Production Board, to begin procurement on the tire plant immediately.[49]

To break the deadlock on the second protocol, Hopkins advised that planning proceed as though nothing had happened. The United States retreated a step from its initial position, agreeing that production schedules would not be changed but still reserving the right to divert to other uses items that could not be shipped. General Burns devised a compromise agreement stating Russian objections to the original Anglo-American offerings and indicating British and American intentions to do everything possible to meet them. On October 6, allied representatives signed the second protocol in Washington, the United States and Britain offering to make available to Russia, 4,400,000 tons of supplies before June 30, 1943, and to provide as much shipping as possible to deliver the tonnage.[50]

The Russians never agreed in principle to accept reductions from the original protocol figure. But Stalin, realistically perceiving that the United States and Britain could not send everything promised, made clear his most important needs in personal communications with Roosevelt and Churchill. He would forego shipments of tanks, guns, and ammunition to make possible delivery of increased quantities of aircraft, aluminum, and food. Frankly admitting in a cable of October 7 that the situation at Stalingrad had deteriorated, the Russian leader blamed it primarily on a shortage of airplanes. The Germans, he advised, had gained two-to-one air superiority in the south and experience had shown that the "bravest troops are helpless unless protected against air attack." The need for food was equally serious. Germany occupied 42 percent of prewar land under cultivation, most able-bodied men had been drafted into the army, and agricultural machinery and draft animals had been requisitioned for military use. Russian food production had declined sharply, and famine threatened many cities. Stalin therefore asked Roosevelt for delivery of five hundred fighter planes per month, for two million tons of wheat within the next year, and for as much food as could be spared.[51]

Roosevelt went to work immediately on Stalin's request, but at every turn he encountered frustration. The President himself conceded that the U. S. could not possibly provide Russia with five hundred fighter planes per month, but he passed on Stalin's cable to General Marshall with the notation that it was "very desirous that at least one hundred additional aircraft be sent the Russians monthly." The Joint Chiefs of Staff opposed even the limited recommendations of the White House, however, insisting that they could not go above the current protocol levels of two hundred planes a month without seriously jeopardizing the North African invasion. Roosevelt could therefore inform Stalin only that he had ordered a drastic increase in production of fighters in order to make possible increased future deliveries to the USSR. In addition, the President as a substitute directed the immediate implementation of operation VELVET, a plan to dispatch an Anglo-American bomber force to operate under Russian command in the Caucasus. He continued to press the chiefs of staff for additional aircraft, and in late 1942 secured the release of two hundred transport planes for delivery to the Soviet Union.[52]

Roosevelt readily acceded to Stalin's appeals for vastly expanded deliveries of foodstuffs and trucks, but the persistent problem of transportation obstructed implementation of his promises. Inadequate shipping prevented the expeditious dispatch of men and materials to develop the Persian Gulf supply network. In the meantime, the United States had sent to Iran more vessels than could be unloaded and, ironically, congestion in the ports discouraged the allocation of ships carrying the men and equipment to relieve this congestion. Operations in the gulf remained far behind schedule, and would not reach the target capacity of 200,000 tons monthly until September, 1943. Poor planning and bad weather slowed the development of the Alaska-Siberia air ferry route, which did not achieve its goal of 142 aircraft per month until April, 1943.[53]

Plans to expand deliveries of food via the Pacific ran up against equally serious problems. This route had been used only slightly prior to the fall of 1942, but since the Japanese permitted neutral ships carrying non-munitions to pass through their waters, the administration hoped to send to Vladivostok on Russian vessels the bulk of the food supplies promised Stalin. The USSR did not have available sufficient tonnage, however, and the U. S. was unable to transfer to Soviet registry the twenty freighters requested by Stalin. Major west coast ports were already glutted with men and supplies moving to support American operations in the Far East, and the ports of Portland, Oregon, and Tacoma, Washington, which were assigned to the Russians could not handle the huge volume of cargo suddenly thrust upon them.[54]

The administration could do little to develop the Pacific supply route in 1942. Fifteen American ships were transferred to the Soviet flag in November and December, and additional port space was given the Russians in Seattle and San Francisco. But these steps brought no immediate improvement. The sudden transfer of tons of supplies into the Pacific Northwest clogged railroad lines and ports, and the Russians complicated matters by constantly shifting priorities on items they wanted delivered. The Pacific was no more able than the Persian Gulf to take up the slack left by termination of the northern convoys.[55]

The Soviet government itself undercut several projects to which Roosevelt had attached great importance. Twice Russian officials changed specifications on the building that would house the tire factory, each time forcing modification of the plant design. The equipment was not delivered until the end of 1943, and the factory was still not in operation at the end of the war. Stalin delayed a month before accepting Roosevelt's offer of project VELVET, and by the time an Anglo-American air mission had arrived in Moscow to complete preparations for establishing the bomber force, the Russian leader had changed his mind about its usefulness. After several inconclusive meetings, Soviet air officials advised the allied mission that they would welcome the bombers but did not want British and American crews. Washington and London regarded the Soviet move as a poorly disguised attempt to increase allocations of aircraft, and since it gutted the principal purpose of the plan, to promote active cooperation between allied military units, they rejected it out of hand.[56]

Administrative difficulties in Washington continued to hold back aid to Russia. Responsibility for the protocol was scattered among hundreds of offices. The White House established broad policies, the State Department negotiated agreements. OLLA compiled programs and handled requests for protocol items, the War Production Board set priorities, the War, Navy, Treasury, and Agriculture Departments were responsible for purchasing, and the War Shipping Administration (successor to the Maritime Commission) allocated shipping. The system inevitably bred confusion. Agencies and offices worked at cross-purposes, and there was no means of coordinating the entire operation.

The Russians had occasionally used the loose organization to their advantage, but by October, 1942, they were protesting the disorder. Konstantin I. Lukashev, chairman of the Russian Purchasing Commission in the United States, advised Hazard in a "very informal, friendly" conversation that the frequent reorganization of agencies handling lend-lease and the constant shifting of personnel within those agencies had made effective planning extremely difficult. He regretted that many individuals had taken it upon themselves to nullify the President's directives on aid to the USSR and that there was no single agency or person that could command all the offices dealing with the protocol.[57]

Stettinius reported Lukashev's complaints to Hopkins in a conference several days later and himself stressed that implementation of the protocol had become terribly confused for lack of central direction. Roosevelt and Hopkins responded on October 30 by establishing a President's Soviet Protocol Committee, with Hopkins as chairman and General Burns as executive officer and composed of representatives of every department and agency involved in planning and implementing the protocols. The PSPC institutionalized the unique status already given to aid to Russia, and its establishment reflected the President's determination to expedite the program and to maintain tight personal control over its implementation. Under Hopkins' direction, the committee established policies on Russian aid, set priorities outside the regular lend-lease procedure, and exerted pressure on the departments and agencies to meet protocol schedules.[58]

By the end of November, the tide of battle at Stalingrad had begun to turn. On November 19, Stalin launched a daring counteroffensive, and within four days the Red Army had encircled the German besiegers in Stalingrad. The Russians held off a German force sent to relieve Stalingrad from the south, and by the end of December had driven it back one hundred and twenty miles.

The United States made only a limited contribution to this most significant of battles. Roosevelt's moves of October and November would bring great gains in Soviet supply by the end of 1943. Establishment of the Protocol Committee insured a degree of centralized planning and execution that had been sadly missing before. Expansion of the Persian Gulf and Pacific supply routes would make possible a vast increase in shipments within the next twelve months. But during the most critical days of Stalingrad, the United States fell far behind its protocol commitments. By the end of November, it had shipped only 840,000 out of a scheduled 1,608,000 tons.[59]

In fact, knowledgeable officials in Washington admitted that American assistance had not been decisive in Russian campaigns through Stalingrad. The United States had provided large quantities of some very significant items that the Russians could not produce for themselves. From November, 1941, to December, 1942, 400,000 miles of field telephone wire were shipped to the USSR, and without this wire communications might not have been maintained along the front. Losses of livestock during 1941 created a severe shortage of leather, making it impossible for Russian factories to produce boots in sufficient quantities to protect Red Army soldiers from the Russian winter. The United States again helped meet the shortage, sending 10,500 tons of leather under the first protocol and four million pairs of boots in 1941 and 1942. American steel, aluminum, and copper went into the construction of guns, tanks, and aircraft, and contributed to the miraculous resurgence of Soviet industry.[60]

But American shipments of guns, tanks, and planes up to the summer of 1943 were small compared to Russian production and did not meet Russia's needs. Most of the tanks were light and medium types which could not stand up against heavier German models. Until large numbers of P-39 Airacobras began to roll off American assembly lines in late

1943, the aircraft sent the USSR were not only few in number but inferior to Russian fighters and not extensively used. By OLLA's admission, the United States sent only an "infinitesimal" quantity of artillery. Thus while the U. S. was able to fill important gaps in Soviet production and American aid undoubtedly gave the Russians a psychological boost in 1941, lend-lease military equipment played only a small part in Soviet operations through Stalingrad.[61]

There is only one thing worse than fighting a war with allies, Winston Churchill is said to have remarked, and that is fighting without them. The stormy history of the Grand Alliance in 1942 reveals the truth of Churchill's observation and underscores the perils of coalition warfare. It was a year of military reversal and frustration, of broken promises and disappointment, of deep political tension. Historians will long debate the merits of Roosevelt's decision to delay the second front and to postpone as long as possible a showdown over Stalin's territorial demands. But it is not even debatable that the allies' failure to invade Europe in 1942 and their refusal to agree to a treaty with political provisions severely damaged the tenuous relationship with the USSR during the year of its greatest trial.

Without the second front and a political alliance, lend-lease became the most important link between the Western allies and the USSR and the ultimate test of good faith. Although shipments of supplies during the period to Stalingrad never met Russian expectations, Roosevelt still employed this instrument of coalition warfare to the best possible advantage. Wisely, he refused to bend to the demands of his military advisers that American requirements be taken care of first. Recognizing that the Russian front remained the key to allied strategy, he continued to give top priority to lend-lease to Russia and exerted persistent pressure on his subordinates to make good American promises to Stalin. Yet he did not allow the Russian program to jeopardize other operations. And ever sensitive to the needs and political requirements of all the allies, he acquiesced when the hard-pressed British could not go on with the convoys, even though he knew the backlash that would follow.

When the inevitable bitter reaction came from Moscow, the President did not allow it to affect his judgment. He remained calm and understanding and sympathetic. And in the anxious weeks of Stalingrad, he attempted to do everything he could to meet Russia's most urgent supply requirements and to convince Stalin of his good faith and desire to help. Some of his acts were little more than symbolic; the effect of others would not be felt for many months. Yet in sum they show his abiding concern for the fate of an ally and reveal his staunch determination to do something to help. Primarily because of Roosevelt's leadership, Americans put tremendous energy into the Russian aid program in 1942. To Roosevelt, Soviet victories provided sufficient return. Other Americans expected more, however, and when their expectations were not met they began to question the President's policies.

Chapter 4

"IN WARTIME DIPLOMACY MUST GO BY THE BOARDS"

ADMIRAL STANDLEY AND UNCONDITIONAL AID

ON MARCH 8, 1943, A GROUP OF AMERI-
CAN WAR CORRESPONDENTS GATHERED
informally in the library of Spasso House, the residence of the
U. S. ambassador in Moscow. The ambassador, former Chief of
Naval Operations William H. Standley, had just returned to
the capital from Kuibyshev, and the reporters had come to
welcome him back and to look for news. The admiral's initial statements offered little excitement. He spoke of his long
train ride, of the weather and living conditions in Kuibyshev. None of the newsmen bothered to take notes. Then
one of them casually posed a question: "We're sending
quite a lot of stuff over here, aren't we, Mr. Ambassador?"
In answer, the *Colliers'* writer Quentin Reynolds later
wrote, Standley "dropped a bomb that exploded in that com-
fortable library and was heard all over the world." "You
know, boys," he began, choosing his words carefully, "since
I've been here, I've been looking for evidence that the Russians are getting a lot of material help from the British and
us . . . but I've yet to find any evidence of that fact. The
Russian authorities seem to want to cover up the fact that

they are receiving outside help. Apparently they want their people to believe that the Red Army is fighting this war alone." [1]

When advised that the ambassador's statement was for the record, the excited correspondents rushed two blocks to the subway, then to the Foreign Office, where to the shock of Soviet censors they placed Standley's words on cable. The following day, newspapers across the United States headlined the story, and in Congress, where the lend-lease act was being considered for renewal, the Standley statement consumed most of the day's debate. For a brief period, the ambassador appeared to have sparked a major political crisis for the Roosevelt administration and a diplomatic incident of serious proportions. [2]

After the tumult had subsided, Americans tended to dismiss the incident as nothing more than a "tempest in a teapot," the indiscretion of an intensely patriotic and outspoken man. In fact, it represented much more than that. Standley was openly challenging the administration's policies for handling aid to Russia. Aware that Americans, both individually and collectively, had expended great energy to get supplies to the USSR and had tried to cooperate as closely as possible in the common task of defeating the enemy, the ambassador had been deeply antagonized by the Russian response. The Soviet government had made only grudging acknowledgment of American aid; more often than not, it had given the impression that little had been received and had implied that the allies were deliberately holding back. In addition, Soviet officials had reacted coolly to his requests for help and in a variety of ways had obstructed his tasks.

An ardent advocate of full cooperation with Russia during wartime and after, Standley concluded that if this goal were to be realized American policy must change. The United States should provide all possible assistance, but it should require the Russians to reciprocate, and should use its aid to insure that they did. Having failed to convince Roosevelt in personal conversations of the merits of his views, he expressed them openly, in hopes of proving they would work.

His statement of March, 1943, set off a debate on the unconditional aid policy that would last the remainder of the war.

Standley had gone to Moscow as ambassador in April, 1942, without prior diplomatic experience but with a long and distinguished career in the U.S. Navy behind him. After graduating from the Naval Academy, he had served with the Asiatic Fleet during the Philippine insurrection. By 1933, he had risen to admiral and was appointed Chief of Naval Operations. He retired from active duty in 1937, but several years later answered the President's call to return to Washington and assist in the industrial mobilization program.[3]

Roosevelt appears to have selected the admiral for the embassy in Moscow on the basis of their close personal friendship and because of Standley's experience with the supply problems that loomed largest in Russian-American relations during 1942. The two men had known each other since World War I, when Standley was superintendent at the Naval Academy and Roosevelt Assistant Secretary of the Navy. They shared a common interest in ships and the sea, and during the 1930s Standley had been quite successful in pushing the President's "big-navy" program through a penurious Congress. An ardent interventionist during the early years of World War II—he had advocated an American declaration of war on Germany as early as June, 1940–Standley had provided vocal support for Roosevelt's policy of aid to Britain and Russia. His long experience in the Navy, his work with the Office of Production Management, and his participation in the Harriman mission to Russia in 1941 provided excellent background for the principal task of his ambassadorship, the expedition of aid to the Soviet Union.[4]

The admiral attached great importance to his mission. "I had imagined that my job would be a very busy one," he later recalled, "Ambassador in the capital of an important ally in the middle of a great war." He arrived in his post "full of good will" for the Russian people and most anxious to establish closer military collaboration between the two nations. It was not long, however, before he became deeply disillusioned. Sixty-nine years old, he was not well suited for the rigorous conditions of wartime Russia, and in letters to friends he repeatedly complained of the "personal discomforts" he suffered. An open, gregarious individual, he chafed under the isolation imposed upon foreign diplomats by the Soviet government, and he resented the constant presence of GPU officers around him. He was in the USSR nearly a month before he finally secured an audience with Stalin, and his every representation to Soviet authorities met with frustrating delay. "It seems that is our chronic condition here," he lamented to a State Department official, "always expecting and waiting for something to happen and when that does or does not happen something else is expected." [5]

To relieve the boredom, Standley finally constructed a golf driving range in the backyard of his temporary residence at Kuibyshev. But he could find no such easy solution to his problems in dealing with the Soviet authorities. The ambassador's persistent efforts to promote cooperation between the two allies got nowhere. The Russians' secretiveness, their adamant refusal to exchange intelligence about the German army and its weapons and to allow American observers at the front annoyed him greatly. Whether attempting to spread the American way of life to the Russian people by showing Disney films, trying to look after the needs of American bomber crews forced down over Siberia and interned in the USSR, to improve air travel and mail deliveries between the United States and Russia, to insure that relief supplies got through to the Polish army, or even to speed up supply deliveries to the Russians, he encountered the same response—procrastination and obstruction. He protested to Secretary Hull in July, 1942, that he had been "continually subjected to delays, interference, and indifference on the part of subordinate Soviet officials" who seemed to be making an "almost studied effort" to thwart his work. At the same time, the Russians' constant complaints about American supply failures and postponement of the second front and their insinuations that the United States was not doing all it could to assist the USSR offended his sense of fairness and his intense nationalism. [6]

Thoroughly frustrated by Russian inaction, Standley soon began to question the administration's policy of dealing with the Russians on their own terms. A blunt, outspoken individual, more accustomed to the manners of the quarterdeck than those of diplomatic councils, the ambassador believed that the United States should present its complaints directly to the Russians and demand a change. He later recalled that he got nowhere if he approached Soviet officials as a "veritable Casper Milquetoast humbly asking for favors." "I came to believe in standing up to them, in being forceful and demanding, in making what promises I was told to make and trying my best to keep them, but also in insisting that they keep their promises to us. . . . I had no hesitancy in speaking in a blunt, pointed and salty sailorman fashion." [7]

Standley regarded lend-lease as a potentially powerful bargaining weapon. But he found himself without any influence in determining lend-lease policies and with little information regarding lend-lease decisions. Since the beginning of the aid program, the Roosevelt administration had determined to accept all Soviet requests at face value and had attempted to provide the maximum assistance with no strings attached. General Faymonville, the chief of the U.S. lend-lease mission in Moscow, was an enthusiastic, indeed zealous, advocate of the unconditional aid policy, and to the great annoyance of the ambassador he usually operated independently of the embassy, forwarding Russian requests for supplies directly to OLLA or to Hopkins in Washington and seldom bothering to inform Standley of his actions. [8]

Roosevelt's habit of sending numerous unofficial envoys to Moscow further irritated Standley. The administration seldom told him the purpose of their visits, and once in Moscow they often bypassed him in dealing with the Russians. He soon began to fear that his position had been so undermined that he could not deal effectively with his Russian counterparts. [9]

Outraged at his treatment by both Russians and Americans, Standley journeyed to Washington in October, 1942, ostensibly to deliver an important message from Stalin but in fact to get clearcut orders forcing Faymonville under the authority of the embassy and to try to alter the President's handling of aid to Russia. At one conference, he challenged the unconditional policy directly. "Stop acting like a Santa Claus, Chief!" he recalled advising Roosevelt. "And let's get something from Stalin in return. Faymonville agrees to give them everything in the world they ask for, from a darning needle to a tire factory, which they won't have operating ten years after the war. My advice is to treat Stalin like an adult, keep any promises we make to him, but insist that he keep his promises, too. And if he doesn't make good within a reasonable time, hold out on him until he does. The Soviets will take advantage of any other course of action." [10]

Roosevelt and Hopkins finally gave Standley a directive extending his control over Faymonville's lend-lease mission, but they politely ignored his views on dealing with Russia. His suggestions were, at the very least, untimely. The battle of Stalingrad was then reaching a decisive stage, and the United States was far behind in its protocol commitments. American relations with the USSR were "bad," Hopkins lamented to Davies, and Stalin was "sore." At this very time, the administration was desperately searching for some means to repair the crisis in confidence, and it did not seriously consider Standley's proposal. At the first meeting of the President's Soviet Protocol Committee on November 25, Hopkins conceded that the Russians were difficult to deal with and that the United States was doing for them what it was not doing for the other allies. The unconditional aid policy had been established with some misgivings, Hopkins admitted, but it would be continued and should not be brought up for further consideration. The Russians might be on the verge of a major victory and it was now more important than ever to do everything possible to expedite shipment of supplies.[11]

A week later, General Burns sent to Hopkins a memorandum on Russian-American relations that was probably intended as an answer to Standley and that Robert Sherwood has called "an excellent statement of Hopkins' own views on the subject of relations with the Soviet Union." Next to

Great Britain, Burns stressed, the USSR was the most important nation to the United States. Russian assistance would be
needed not only to win the war but to build a secure peace.
It was therefore vital that the United States be "so helpful
and friendly to her" that she would continue to fight on
until the defeat of Germany, assist in the war against
Japan, and "willingly join us in establishing a sound peace
and mutually beneficial relations in the post-war world." The
United States could develop this friendship by "doing everything possible in a generous but not lavish way to help Russia," and by sending her supplies "to the limit of shipping
possibilities." Taking a slam at Standley, Burns advised sending to the USSR as ambassador a man of "top rank as to national standing, vision, ability and willingness to serve the
country first." The Soviet Union should be treated as one of
the three "foremost powers in the world." The administration should establish a firm policy of treating the USSR as a
"real friend," and only those individuals who were loyal to
this principle should be assigned to Russian posts.[12]

   Burns's memo was not distributed or designated as official
policy, but the views expressed therein seem to reflect the
administration's strategy. The President was determined to
do everything possible to meet his obligations and to convince Stalin of his good faith. He was only too aware of the
problems in transporting supplies to the USSR, and he felt
that the unconditional aid policy was essential to insure
maximum performance under adverse conditions. To attach
conditions to aid, as Standley suggested, would increase Soviet suspicions at a time when they were already pronounced. It would also delay assistance to Russia at one of
the most crucial periods of the war. Thus the administration
continued the established policy in hopes that it would
make possible a substantial contribution to the war and
would help to establish the basis for a lasting friendship.

   In the months after Standley's trip to Washington, the allied military position improved dramatically. The Red
Army's November counteroffensive produced a major victory

at Stalingrad, and by late January it was wiping out the remnants of German resistance. Anglo-American armies were
preparing their final compaign to destroy German power in
North Africa. The United States had secured naval suprem-
acy over the Japanese, and was ready to begin the long advance across the Pacific to the home islands. The supply situation too had begun to get better. Churchill reinstituted the
northern convoys in December, 1942, and thirty-nine ships
cleared American ports carrying a record volume of 243,000
tons.[13]

Roosevelt and Churchill met with their chiefs of staff at
Casablanca in an atmosphere of hope in late January. Their
optimism was tempered, however, by persisting doubts
about Russia's future relationship with the West. At Casablanca, the Americans and British again agreed to defer the
invasion of France, this time possibly until 1944, in favor of
a 1943 invasion of Sicily. Postponement of the second front
insured that aid to Russia, from both a military and political
standpoint, must retain its top priority. But here too grave
uncertainties remained. The allies could not risk excessive
losses to get supplies to the USSR, and the Combined Chiefs
of Staff finally established a shipping program to bring the
protocol up to date by the end of 1943, provided that losses
on the Murmansk run could be held to not more than 2.4
percent per month. If they exceeded that figure, the convoys
would again have to be suspended.[14]

Roosevelt and Churchill clearly recognized the possible
impact of their Casablanca decisions on Stalin, and sought to
soften the blow as much as possible. They advised him only
in the vaguest terms of their decision regarding the second
front, holding out at least a dim hope that it might still be
accomplished in 1943. A cable of January 25 informed the
Russian that the allies would "spare no exertion to send you
material assistance by every available route," but significantly omitted a qualifying clause in earlier drafts: "it would
be no more in your interest than ours to do so at a cost
which would cripple our capacity to relieve pressure on you

by continuing an intensified offensive on our part." To help assuage Stalin's doubts, they also agreed at Casablanca on the unconditional surrender formula.[15]

But in the weeks after Casablanca, military reversals on several fronts and persistent supply problems increased concern in the West about future relations with Russia. In mid-February, Hitler had briefly retaken the initiative on the Eastern front, recapturing Kharkov and again applying heavy pressure on the Red Army. Germany had badly beaten American armies at Faid and Kasserine Passes, and the Anglo-American offensive in North Africa ground to a standstill. In February, another record volume of supplies, 342,000 tons, left American ports for the USSR. But it was already clear that this volume could not be maintained. Continued congestion in Persian Gulf ports forced a drastic cutback in ships and tonnage scheduled for March. And as the daylight hours lengthened in the Arctic region in early March, the British Admiralty again began to fear renewed German attacks on the convoys.[16]

By early March, Russia's relations with the West had grown more and more uncertain. Stalin was not put off by Roosevelt's and Churchill's equivocation, and began to raise embarrassing questions about the date of the second front. He expressed great perturbation about the slowdown of operations in North Africa, and he was certain to respond angrily if the convoys were again terminated. There were, Sherwood has recalled, "more and more questions from Moscow and very few indications of cordiality." Rumors of a separate peace between Russia and Germany abounded in Washington. The situation, according to Davies, was "tense and dangerous." With Soviet-American relations at one of their lowest points during the entire war, Admiral Standley once again challenged Roosevelt's policies, this time openly, setting off an incident that threatened for a time to have enormous repercussions.[17]

The ambassador had become greatly annoyed with the Soviet government's refusal to credit the allies for the assistance they had rendered. During the first months of the

Russo-German war, probably for the purpose of boosting morale at home, the Soviet press had given considerable attention to allied aid. *Pravda, Izvestia,* and *Red Star* had quoted American production statistics with satisfaction, printed pictures of U. S. and British weapons on the way to the front, and faithfully reported the supply agreements concluded among the three nations. Both the degree and the enthusiasm of the reporting declined noticeably in the first half of 1942. After the second front failed to materialize, information on lend-lease virtually disappeared from the press, and Soviet leaders complained openly about the inadequacy of the material and military support they were receiving. Fighting for their very survival, the Russians understandably found it hard to comprehend why their allies were not doing more. Their disappointment with supply deliveries and with delays in the second front far outweighed any gratitude they might have felt for the help actually received.[18]

But Standley, who had borne personally the brunt of Russian complaints, and who realized how hard the government in Washington was trying to get assistance to the USSR, found the Kremlin's attitude intolerable. Stalin's letter to Henry Cassidy in October, 1942, had especially vexed him. It was, he wrote later, a "cruel blow! I knew the sacrifices our Armed Forces and our citizens were making to send war materials and other supplies to Russia; I knew better than most men the terrible toll in ships and seamen that the Murmansk convoy route was taking." The ambassador concluded that the Soviet government was deliberately "attempting to conceal from the Russian people the nature and extent of the aid which the British and American people were giving so generously to the Russian Armed Forces and the Russian people." [19]

By January, 1943, the State Department shared some of Standley's concerns, for lend-lease was again becoming an important political issue. Throughout 1942, the aid program had enjoyed broad popular support. Even in February, when the military situation in the Far East was especially grim, a large majority of Americans favored sending increased supplies to Britain, Russia, and China. A Gallup poll of January, 1943, indicated that 80 percent of those questioned approved the lend-lease program, and that 90 percent accepted increased shipments of food to Britain and Russia even if it required rationing in the United States. Americans, in short, were wise enough to appreciate that the shipment of supplies abroad would help speed the day of victory and save American lives.[20]

In fact, the major criticism leveled against the Roosevelt administration in 1942 was that it was not doing enough for the allies. Commenting in July on the latest lend-lease report, the *Wall Street Journal* warned that the program "totters on the verge of failure;" as far as battles then underway were concerned, "all aid now leaving these shores will arrive, like the last convoys to Tobruk, just in time to be too late." Several months later, the *Nation* observed that the figures in the President's *Sixth Report to Congress on Lend-Lease Operations* should "cure any complacency about the aid we are furnishing our allies." Authorization of funds was "astronomical, but actual exports are puny." Liberals were especially concerned with the failure to provide more effective assistance to Russia, and hinted that the generals and dollar-a-year men in the administration were sabotaging the program, "finding every reason to keep it [material] at home or to disperse it on twenty battle fronts all over the world while the crucial front which may decide the war was left for months with only part of our promises fulfilled." [21]

Conservatives, long critical of the administration for sending supplies to Britain and Russia while American forces in the Pacific lacked all types of equipment, broadened their attacks in early 1943, reviving old anti-New Deal charges of waste, inefficiency, and corruption, and playing on the domestic shortages just beginning to hit Americans. The Hearst press accused the administration of sending beer to the British at the expense of American taxpayers, and of "wholesale shipment of American industrial plants to Russia at a time when Americans are being held down to the absolute necessities of life." The Republican party had won a major victory in the election of 1942, and when Congress convened in early 1943, with renewal of lend-lease one of the first items to be considered, columnists reported that the Republicans were "unlimbering their blunderbusses" for an impending battle to weaken the President's powers over lend-lease and to secure greater congressional control over expenditures.[22]

Vividly recalling the lend-lease battle in 1941, Roosevelt cautioned Stettinius that he would probably be in for a "terrific grueling" on the hill. The administration was confident the authorization would be extended, but it feared a long and possibly divisive debate, and it wanted to demonstrate convincingly that aid to the allies had been substantial and that it had been put to effective use. The State Department therefore asked Ambassador Standley in late January to try to secure statements from Russian officials indicating that American supplies had made an important contribution to Russian campaigns.[23]

The admiral immediately contacted Molotov and directed his military attachés to go to their opposite numbers in search of the requested information. But, he wrote later, all they got was the "usual Russian runaround." Stalin's Red Army Day order of February 23 omitted any mention of lend-lease supplies from the United States and Britain, and complained that in the absence of a second front the USSR was "bearing the whole brunt of the war." The Russian leader's statement aroused considerable criticism in the American press and further incensed Standley. Then several weeks later, when the ambassador learned that the American Communist Party was getting credit for relief supplies sent from the United States by charitable organizations, he determined to join the issue directly. "During war time," he once observed, "diplomacy must go by the boards. The truth is the only kind of diplomacy worth a damn. . . ."[24]

Thus, at his impromptu press conference on March 8, Standley accused the Soviet government of deliberately concealing from its people the existence of American aid. Referring to the current debate in Washington on lend-lease, he remarked that the Congress was a "big-hearted, generous body of men, who will go to great lengths to help a friend, if they know that their efforts are really helpful. . . ." But without such knowledge, he added, they might "take the opposite tack." He reported his own inability to discover evidence that U. S. supplies were actually being used by the Red Army, and concluded with great emphasis: "It's not fair —the American people are giving millions to help the Russian people and yet the Russian people do not know where the supplies are coming from." [25]

His comments, he recalled some years later, hit the headlines of American newspapers like a "bombshell." Coming one day after a much publicized speech by Vice-President Henry A. Wallace warning that the United States must not "double-cross" the USSR, they set off a brief but potentially explosive debate on Soviet-American relations. Isolationists and Russophobes attempted to arouse latent American suspicions of the Soviet Union. The Chicago *Tribune* headlined its story "REDS HIDE OUR AID," charged that Americans were being misled into giving millions of dollars worth of supplies to an unappreciative recipient, and even hinted that lend-lease might be stopped. On the other side, liberals accused the State Department of hatching an anti-Soviet conspiracy, and demanded Standley's resignation.[26]

The press printed Standley's charges on the day the lend-lease bill came before the House of Representatives for debate, and in Stettinius' words, they "created quite a stir." Isolationist Republican Hamilton Fish of New York praised the ambassador's courage and frankness, and demanded that the administration issue an unequivocal statement denying or verifying his accusations. Privately, Representative John Vorys, Ohio Republican and a leading critic of the administration's handling of lend-lease, expressed hope that Standley's statement might win support for an amendment he planned to offer requiring a thorough, continuing investigation of the entire lend-lease operation.[27]

The administration responded quickly. At a press conference, Acting Secretary of State Sumner Welles refused comment until he had seen a full text of the statement, but emphasized that Standley had not consulted the department before acting and expressed confidence that he had not intended to raise doubts about the trust and understanding that existed between the two allies. Stettinius hurriedly got up material for Senator Tom Connally and Representative Sol Bloom, floor leaders for the lend-lease bill, to prove that large quantities of supplies had been sent to Russia, were being used effectively in combat, and were appreciated by the Russians. In the Senate debate, Connally expressed grave concern that "any incident might be provoked at this time which would in anywise cause any friction or unpleasantness between Russia and the United States." Regardless of what the ambassador might say, he continued, the people of the United States and the Congress would "not be deterred in going ahead with the reenactment of lend-lease and in continuing to supply to Russia every available ounce of material and food necessary to the winning of the war." [28]

Although it caused a brief flurry of excitement in Congress and the country, the Standley statement had no effect on the lend-lease bill. Congressmen of all political persuasions agreed that lend-lease was an essential instrument of war and that delay of its renewal could have serious military and political consequences. The bill passed both houses after only brief debate, with no amendments, and by overwhelming majorities (82 to 0 in the Senate; 407 to 6 in the House). Even the old isolationists, Burton K. Wheeler, Gerald P. Nye, and Robert Reynolds, voted for the bill because, Wheeler explained, "we are at war, and because the bill is a war measure." [29]

Russophobes attempted to prolong the debate, to raise questions about the Kremlin's future intentions, and to build support for a tougher American policy. *Catholic World* praised Standley's bluntness as the "answer to a patriot's prayer," protested the lack of cooperation the USSR had shown its allies, and denounced its lack of gratitude for American aid. Continued appeasement, the editor warned, could only lead to another war. Standley had done well to reveal the facts, "let the hush-hush diplomats say what they will." [30]

Such warnings had little effect on an American public whose attitudes were being conditioned by the realities of war. Pollsters noted throughout these years the persistence of a "strong undercurrent of suspicion" of the USSR and a marked uneasiness about Stalin's postwar aims, especially in Eastern Europe. But the alliance with the Soviet Union had produced significant changes. Warmth toward the Russian people had grown slowly during the dark days of 1942 and had blossomed into enthusiastic admiration and cordiality after the victory of Stalingrad. In some instances it reached the verge of euphoria, as with a *Life* reporter who early in 1943 described the Russians as "one hell of a people," who "look like Americans, dress like Americans, and think like Americans." Opinion analysts also noted the growth of more tolerant attitudes toward the Soviet government and toward communism, which "graduated from something despicable in and of itself, to a system which we dislike but which we will tolerate in Russia because the Russians like it." Most important, the war had convinced a majority of Americans that the United States and the USSR shared common interests at present and in the future. American commentary on the Soviet Union during the war years tended to be uncritical and was often marked by wishful thinking, but it would be wrong to exaggerate either the degree or the solidity of popular optimism about the prospects of Soviet-American relations. In fact, opinion was suspended in a delicate balance between fear and hope, with events themselves to determine which side would ultimately win out. [31]

Nevertheless, in 1943 most Americans were not inclined to be distracted from the immediate task at hand. Many agreed with Representative Luther Johnson of Texas that it was "unwise, when we are engaged in war, to make faces at our allies." Most major newspapers dismissed the Standley incident as a "tempest in a teapot." It is not "the amount of publicity which is given Lend-Lease aid nor even whether the Russians are deeply grateful that counts," the Washington *Post* reasoned pragmatically. "To the extent that our aid to Russia enables that country to do greater damage to the common foe, we are helping ourselves." Concerned primarily with defeating the Axis and impressed by the Red Army's recent triumphs, Americans were not overly perturbed about Russia's alleged ingratitude or lack of cooperation.[32]

The administration was no doubt relieved at the mild domestic reaction to the Standley incident, but its principal concern was the possible impact of the statement on Soviet-American relations. Davies was startled when he heard the ambassador's words reported over the short-wave radio, and he could not understand Standley's actions. "Even if the criticism of the Soviet Government was justified," he recorded in his diary, "obviously it should not have been handled in this way." Hopkins remarked that relations with the Soviet Union were "bad enough" before "Standley pulled this boner"; now they were "critical and had very serious possibilities." Roosevelt told Davies and Hopkins that Standley had "messed things up" by speaking "out of turn" and that his usefulness had ended. He would have to be brought home as soon as possible without making it appear to be a recall. Stalin would not trust him, and there were many urgent matters to be taken up with the Russian leader.[33]

Standley's statement did annoy and antagonize Soviet officials. According to the British news correspondent, Alexander Werth, it "shocked and pained many Russians, who thought it callous and in poor taste." "We've lost millions of people," Werth overheard one official remark, "and they want us to crawl on our knees because they send us spam." The Soviet ambassador, Maxim Litvinov, was "indignant and resentful," and privately denounced Standley's actions as a "disservice to the joint war effort" and a "serious violation of diplomatic conduct." Former ambassador Oumansky later complained to Davies that Standley's scolding of the Russians in the "public square" had breached "every rule that should be employed among friends," and *War and the Working Class* condemned the ambassador's remark as a blatant falsehood.[34]

Whatever their true feelings, however, Soviet leaders went out of their way to prevent the incident from disturbing relations with the United States. Litvinov immediately brought to Welles' attention a long list showing instances where American aid had been mentioned in *Pravda* and *Red Star*. At a Washington luncheon celebrating the second anniversary of the passage of the Lend-Lease Act, Litvinov broadcast over all American radio networks a statement expressing Russia's deep appreciation for American aid. On March 15, *Pravda* devoted half its foreign news section to a full report of lend-lease aid received from the United States, and Standley reported to Washington that within a week of his statement a "veritable rash" of comment poured forth from Soviet officials and the press reporting in detail information about lend-lease shipments and expressing gratitude. The USSR was just as anxious as the United States to prevent the incident from getting out of control and hereafter it was careful to pay its respects to American aid with regularity.[35]

The affair blew over quickly without any repercussions. Standley would even argue that his actions had produced beneficial results. Whatever "the character of my remarks from the standpoint of diplomatic technique," he wrote proudly to a State Department associate, "the aftermath here has been good." He advised Secretary Hull that his statement might help to place "our relations with Russia on a more realistic basis" and thereby contribute to "closer understanding and good will now and in the postwar period." There was some truth in the ambassador's argument. At least the Russians became more sensitive to American opinion, and this would be a great boon to the Roosevelt administration in 1944 and 1945 when it faced mounting criticism of lend-lease at home.[36]

Nevertheless, the ambassador's statement embarrassed the administration politically and diplomatically. Roosevelt and Hopkins felt quite correctly that Standley's provocative charges, issued during a most delicate period in Soviet-American relations without clearance by the State Department, had been untimely, impolitic, and potentially dangerous.

The administration delivered no official rebuke to the admiral, but it immediately began a quiet search for his successor.[37]

Two days after his press conference, Standley sought to take advantage of the opening, warning Roosevelt and Hull that the United States could not deal successfully with the Russians on anything but a "bargaining basis." The policy of acceding freely to Soviet requests with no strings attached, he advised, seemed to "arouse suspicions of our motives in the Oriental mind rather than to build confidence." The Russians, he complained, were withholding from their allies vital military information about German weapons and tactics that would be of great assistance to the United States. They had ignored numerous American requests for help and for information, and had persistently delayed responding to American inquiries about their use of lend-lease. Objecting vigorously to what he called the Russian tactic of "minimum collaboration," Standley asked permission to take the problem up directly with Stalin.[38]

The administration again rejected Standley's recommendations as untimely. The allied advance in North Africa had slowed to a halt, and plans for the second front were still uncertain. The Germans had once more concentrated extensive forces in Norway to disrupt allied shipping, and again in March Churchill was forced to suspend the convoys until September to conserve shipping for the invasion of Sicily, thus insuring that the second protocol would not be completed by July 1. Instead of the sixty-four vessels scheduled to sail to North Russia in the first half of 1943, only thirty-six actually departed, and twenty-nine of these were unloaded in England. Persian Gulf ports remained so jammed that shipments had to be cut back far below schedules to allow time to clear up the backlog. Deliveries to Vladivostok were increased above the Casablanca schedule, but were still inadequate to compensate for termination of the convoys.[39]

The Russian military position had improved significantly by the spring of 1943. In the south, advancing Red Army forces had driven the Germans back beyond Rostov and the

Donets River, and in the north more than two hundred and fifty miles west of Moscow. But these changes did not result in an immediate improvement of Soviet relations with the West. Stalin was undoubtedly concerned that Hitler still might be able to stabilize a front and mount another offensive. Large chunks of territory remained to be liberated. It would have been natural, as Adam Ulam has suggested, for the suspicious premier to conclude that the allies would slacken their efforts to assist him after the victory at Stalingrad, and he was probably influenced by the rumors of a separate peace that became endemic in 1943.[40]

Thus he continued to react angrily to bad news from Washington and London. He protested that the allies did not push the North African offensive more vigorously and warned that the invasion of Sicily could not replace a second front in France. Uncertain statements about a cross channel invasion aroused "grave anxiety in me," he wrote Churchill, "about which I feel I cannot be silent." When advised of cessation of the convoys, he objected heatedly to the "catastrophic diminution of supplies of arms and military raw materials," correctly predicting that the alternative routes could not possibly make up the losses.[41]

With allied relations with Russia still tense and uncertain, and Stalin's correspondence increasingly bitter, Roosevelt flatly rejected Standley's proposal to demand greater cooperation. "We are inclined to believe," Hull advised the ambassador, that "it would not be opportune just now when Stalin is undoubtedly preoccupied with the critical military situation to endeavor to enter into a discussion with him of the character proposed." Six weeks later, Standley asked Roosevelt to accept his resignation.[42]

The administration's rejection of Standley's proposals did not close the debate on policies toward Russia. On the contrary, the ambassador seems to have expressed the growing disenchantment of an increasing number of American officials with the Russians and with the unconditional aid policy. "Many of my friends here, both British and American, seniors and juniors," Harriman cabled Hopkins from London in mid-March, "are secretly pleased at the way Standley spoke out in Moscow, even if this was an indiscretion. The feeling is growing here that we will build trouble for the future if we allow ourselves to be kicked around by the Russians." The ambassador's frankness encouraged others to state their views, and in the spring and early summer of 1943, numerous Americans began to question the administration's handling of lend-lease to the USSR.[43]

Harriman himself was among the first to speak up. Even before the Standley incident, in late February, 1943, he had advised Roosevelt and Hopkins to back British attempts to condition resumption of the northern convoys on Soviet agreement to allow the establishment of British air units in North Russia. Returning to Washington in April, Harriman challenged the policy of granting all Russian requests for assistance with no questions asked. He expressed himself as "unalterably opposed" to approving shipment of long-range industrial equipment that might not be operational until after the war. Critical materials and shipping space would be wasted without any significant effect on American relations with the USSR. "At all events," he argued, "we cannot allay suspicion of twenty-five years making by gestures of a minor character. My experience is that the Russians are brutally and bluntly frank with us and we can well afford to be equally so." [44]

Harriman shared these views with top officials in OLLA, and in June they too began to express doubts about the President's lend-lease policies. The Deputy Lend-Lease Administrator, Bernhard Knollenberg, advised Stettinius that the major defect in lend-lease operations was the lack of information concerning the efficiency and good faith with which the Russians were using American equipment. "The time has come," he observed, "when the United States ought to insist on being permitted to inform itself of the administration of lend-lease supplies in Russia. There is no longer any valid reason why Russia should be exempted from reasonable inquiry in the field which we insist upon in the case of other countries receiving large amounts of lend-lease aid."

Stettinius expressed general agreement with these views, advising Hopkins several days later that he feared the Russians might be taking advantage of American generosity. "It may be," he commented, "that the Russian AA priority has been overplayed in Washington—necessary at first, but now in many cases a firm, hardboiled attitude is needed." [45]

The army had reached the same conclusion much earlier. A War Department memorandum of January 23, 1943, advised that the United States should continue to furnish all possible aid to the Soviet Union "provided—and provided only—that Russia cooperates with us and takes us into her confidence. The time is appropriate for us to start some straight-from-the-shoulder talk with Mr. Joseph Stalin." [46]

The special priority Roosevelt had given aid to Russia in 1941, requiring that supplies be procured to meet protocol schedules whether or not shipping was immediately available, had for a long time impeded the army's efforts to equip its own divisions for battle. During periods when the northern convoys were not sailing, supplies intended for Russia began to accumulate in American ports. Army officials complained in December, 1942, that more than 400,000 tons of steel had been set aside awaiting shipment to the USSR at a time when steel shortages were crippling other supply programs, and that thousands of trucks had to be scrapped because shipping was not available and storage facilities were inadequate.[47]

This arrangement was intolerable to the army when supplies were still short in all theaters, and it was made more so by the Russians' refusal to cooperate. The army saw great advantage to be gained by sending observers to the Russian front to get first-hand information on German equipment and tactics. In addition, since the beginning of the war army officials had wished to establish close exchange of intelligence with the Russians. But the Soviet government had resisted every American initiative. On occasion, it would allow select officials—usually those in a position to expedite requests for supplies—to visit the front. But it refused to permit regular observers and rejected proposals of American military and naval attachés to establish regular exchanges of intelligence.[48]

As frustrations with the Russians increased, the army began to urge changes in lend-lease policy. In April, Under Secretary of War Robert P. Patterson proposed to Hopkins that the special priority for aid to Russia be ended and that protocol commitments should henceforth be limited to estimated available shipping, with provision for diversion to other needs if these estimates exceeded capabilities. At the same time, he strongly urged the insertion of a clause in the third Soviet protocol giving U. S. military attachés in Moscow the same privileges of visit and information accorded Russians in the United States.[49]

The administration did take measures in the spring of 1943 to prevent shipment of industrial equipment that would take more than eighteen months to put into operation, but it adamantly resisted all other proposals to alter policies for aid to the USSR. Hopkins and the Protocol Committee persuaded the British to withdraw a proposed clause to be inserted in the third protocol requiring the Russians to allow the establishment of air bases for the RAF around Murmansk. They sustained the original priority for lend-lease to the USSR despite the cost and waste it entailed, and they again ruled against trying to secure any *quid pro quo*. The protocols had been designed not only to get the maximum assistance to the Soviet Union, the committee advised Patterson, but also to "secure the confidence" of its government so that it would be more likely after the defeat of Germany "to assist in the defeat of Japan and in the negotiation of a sound peace." Those officials who had worked on the previous protocols had discovered, moreover, that "the Soviets are very difficult to deal with on a bargaining basis" and that they responded "most satisfactorily in performing their share of an understanding when a generous offer is made that does not force them to bargain." [50]

The question of "full cooperation" with Russia flared up again during Joseph Davies' visit to Moscow in May, 1943. Deeply concerned by the state of Soviet-American relations,

Roosevelt had dispatched the former ambassador on a very delicate mission, to try to arrange a personal meeting between himself and Stalin. At an off-the-record press conference on May 21, American war correspondents, who were well-informed on Russia's refusal to share intelligence with the United States and who felt, according to Quentin Reynolds, that Soviet-American collaboration should be a two-way street, asked Davies if he had broached this problem with Stalin. Davies replied tartly that he had not and that the Russians were providing the United States all the information it needed.[51]

Davies' less than candid response did not satisfy the reporters, who retorted that they had been advised differently by top U. S. military leaders. According to Admiral Standley, a "protracted and exceedingly bitter controversy" followed, Davies insinuating that the newsmen were not acting in the best interest of their country by criticizing the Russians. "The atmosphere of the conference was very strained and hostile," Standley reported to Secretary Hull, "and on several occasions I feared that some untoward incident might arise." [52]

The confrontation in Moscow prompted further discussions within the administration on policies toward the Soviet Union. General James H. Burns, Executive Officer of the Protocol Committee, had been in Moscow at the time of Davies' visit. Upon his return to Washington, he defended established policies, cautioning OLLA officials that it was futile to challenge the Russians' three-hundred-year tradition of "not giving out information." Nor did he have any illusion that the Soviets would allow American officials to come to the front to oversee lend-lease operations. "They aren't going to let people go in and run Russia," he advised. "They are going to figure that out themselves. You have to trust them, and they will do a very good job." [53]

A draft memorandum, written around May 28, 1943, obviously in response to the Davies incident, further elaborated on administration policy. Like the Burns memorandum of December, 1942, it emphasized that friendship with the USSR was of vital importance to the United States during the war and in the peace to follow. This friendship could best be achieved by a policy of understanding, frankness, generosity, and sincerity, and by a spirit of courtesy in dealing with all Russians—"in other words a genuine Good Neighbor Policy." Americans must appreciate the tremendous sacrifices Russia had made in the war; they must recognize that U. S. aid was going to the Soviet Union to help her defeat the enemy and not "for minor purposes of getting information from her which she is reluctant to give." [54]

A raging feud within the American embassy in Moscow soon compelled the administration to take drastic action to implement the principles embodied in the memorandum. The military and naval attachés, who were close to Admiral Standley and in general shared his views toward Russia, had for months been engaged in a bitter, personal conflict with General Faymonville. Davies advised the President upon returning from his visit with Stalin that conditions in the embassy were so bad something must be done, and during the summer of 1943 the hassle leaked out to the press. Intolerant of political squabbles within its own ranks and embarrassed by the publicity given the feud, the army decided to recall both Faymonville and the attaché, General Joseph Michella. Davies attempted to spare Faymonville on grounds that the Russians "trusted him," but the army refused to budge, recalling both men, reducing them in rank, and sending Faymonville to an ordnance depot in Texarkana, Arkansas. The administration seized this opening to reorganize and alter the functions of its military representatives in Moscow. The post of attaché, whose recognized duty was to secure information about the nation in which it was located, was abolished in the USSR. In its place, the administration established a United States Military Mission charged with the broader responsibility of coordinating Soviet-American military operations. General Marshall made clear to the chief of the new mission, General John R. Deane, that he was not to attempt to pry intelligence from the Russians.[55]

The administration's continued need for Russian support

and the prevailing uncertainties in Soviet-American relations determined the President's decision to stand by the unconditional aid policy. Although the military situation on all fronts had improved substantially, the United States still needed a total Russian commitment to conduct operations against Germany, and wanted Russian participation to shorten the war against Japan. More important, as the most critical stage of the war passed in early 1943, postwar problems inevitably surfaced, and the enigma of Russia dominated early discussions of the peace. Roosevelt clearly realized, according to an "informed" journalist, that defeat of the Axis in Europe would leave the Soviet Union "the only first-rate military power on the continent." The question at the heart of postwar planning was "what use the Kremlin proposed making of such power." Roosevelt and British Foreign Secretary Anthony Eden agreed in the spring of 1943 that Stalin would continue to demand his 1941 frontiers, including the Baltic States and Poland's eastern territory, and admitted that there was little they could do to prevent his making these claims good. Anxieties about Poland mounted in April when Stalin broke relations with the Polish government-in-exile in London.[56]

The future in war and peace depended upon Russia. But Roosevelt was aware in the early summer of 1943 that he had yet to win Stalin's confidence. By July, the United States had shipped only 70 percent of the tonnage promised in the second protocol. Again in May, Roosevelt and Churchill postponed the second front, this time until 1944. The President felt that he had much to ask of the Russians, but still little to give.[57]

Events in May and June underscored the continued delicacy of Russia's relations with the West. Stalin, too, was conscious of his need for American help. The Russian mood following Stalingrad had been one of exultation, and there had been rash predictions that the Germans could be defeated by the end of the year with or without outside assistance. But the German recapture of Kharkov in March, a move facilitated by the transfer of substantial troops from the West, reminded the Russians that while ultimate victory seemed certain Anglo-American support was essential to limit the price. As a lull set in on the entire front in the late spring of 1943, the Russians, remembering vividly the assaults of 1941 and 1942, nervously awaited the German summer offensive. Rumors of a separate peace and uncertainty regarding the allies' position on postwar issues heightened anxieties.[58]

Russia's attitude toward the West in May and June reflected these concerns. In sharp contrast to 1942, public statements of Russian officials and the Soviet press adopted an increasingly warm tone toward the United States and Britain. Stalin's May Day order of 1943 praised in the most exuberant tones the allied victory in North Africa and the "valiant Anglo-American airmen" who were delivering "smashing blows" against the enemy. The press devoted detailed attention to reports of allied operations and to statements of their leaders. On June 9, 1943, the anniversary of the Russian-American lend-lease agreement, Molotov hailed the vital role played by lend-lease in the war and indicated that the lend-lease operation provided a solid basis for Russian-American cooperation after the war. *Pravda* commented that the Russian people not only knew about lend-lease but highly valued "the support coming from the great Republic beyond the ocean." [59]

These changes in the official line at least in part reflected a sincere appreciation for the growing contribution of the allies to the defeat of the enemy. Perhaps more, they betrayed Stalin's realization of his continued dependence on the Western allies. Significantly, as Alexander Werth has pointed out, the most extravagant statements of praise for the United States and Britain came immediately after Russia's break with the Polish exile government and on the eve of the German summer offensive.[60]

But the warmth and friendship were still subject to immediate change. When in June Churchill informed Stalin of postponement of the second front until 1944, the Russian sent back an angry cable charging the allies with deception and bad faith. "Your decision," he advised Roosevelt, "creates exceptional difficulties for the Soviet Union which, straining all its resources for the past two years, has been engaged against the main forces of Germany and her satellites, and leaves the Soviet Army, which is fighting not only for its country, but also for its allies, to do the job alone, almost single-handed, against an enemy that is still very strong and formidable." The problem, Stalin advised Churchill in a cable of June 24, is "not just the disappointment of the Soviet Government, but the preservation of its confidence in its Allies, a confidence which is being subjected to severe stress." Stalin recalled Litvinov from Washington and Maisky from London. There was, Sherwood noted, "an atmosphere alarmingly reminiscent of that which had preceded the Molotov-Ribbentrop Pact of August, 1939, and the fears of a separate Russo-German armistice were revived." [61]

Even before these ominous developments had taken place, Admiral Standley had submitted his resignation as ambassador to the Soviet Union. In poor health, he felt he could not withstand the rigors of another Russian winter. More important, his service in Moscow had been unrewarding and even humiliating. The administration had rarely consulted him on policy decisions, frequently left him uninformed of important negotiations, and consistently rejected or ignored his recommendations. The President's reliance on personal emissaries had embarrassed and infuriated him, and when he learned in May that Davies was coming to meet personally with Stalin he determined to resign. At Roosevelt's insistence, he remained in Moscow during the summer of 1943 and returned to the United States in October. [62]

Despite his own personal sense of failure, many of the admiral's contemporaries found much to praise in his diplomacy. He became something of a hero to those who feared Roosevelt was coddling the Russians, and his bluntness and candor, best demonstrated by the March, 1943, statement, appealed to those people who had long distrusted the polish and evasive rhetoric of traditional diplomacy. The ambassador, Quentin Reynolds wrote admiringly, possessed the same "rugged and uncompromising honesty the pioneers must have had." "He was first of all an American," Walter Kerr added, "and he believed the truth never hurt anyone." Attacking Roosevelt's diplomacy for its softness and neglect of American interests, Senator Richard Russell of Georgia singled out Standley as the type of "two-fisted diplomat" who could best "create respect and genuine good will" for the United States. "The old type of kid-glove diplomacy does not have any place in today's international dealings," the senator declared. "Everyone can understand men like Admiral Standley who speak bluntly their minds." [63]

By the time Standley returned home, Russian-American relations had improved considerably, and some observers credited the ambassador with the change. "In Moscow," Kerr wrote, "we thought Standley's frankness had cleared the atmosphere and we saw repeated evidence of closer relations from then on." Even the New York *Times,* which had roundly criticized Standley's statement in March, praised him warmly at the time of his resignation. The Russians "found he was talking their language and liked it," the *Times* editorialized. Since that time Soviet-American relations had been less one-sided, and the ambassador had constructed a solid "foundation upon which his successors can build." [64]

Such appraisals exaggerated the effectiveness of Standley's diplomacy. One can only sympathize with his impossible situation and with the frustrations that provoked his calculated indiscretion. Still his accusations against the Soviet government were badly timed and missed the mark. Himself a proud man, the admiral forgot that other peoples also had pride. Rightly concerned that the Russians did not appreciate American efforts, he failed to understand the anxiety of a nation that had suffered so much and that felt, rightly or wrongly, that it had been let down by its allies. The point was not whether the Russians appreciated American help or whether they publicized it but whether they used it effectively in battle. And in asking for Russia's acknowledgment of American generosity, the admiral neglected to consider that lend-lease was an act not of altruism but of calculated self-interest.

Coming at a most delicate stage in the evolution of the wartime alliance, Standley's statement could have disturbed Russian-American relations. That it did not is testimony to the restraint exercised by both governments, a restraint required by the exigencies of warfare. The ambassador and those who praised him correctly noted some improvement in Russian-American relations after the summer of 1943, but incorrectly traced it to Standley's toughness and candor. The increasingly warm tone in official Russian statements masked a considerable underlying distrust, and reflected at once a recognition of dependency and the military successes just beginning to develop from that dependency.

Standley and his aides in Moscow had good reason to be annoyed at their treatment by Russian authorities, but they were naive in thinking that lend-lease could be used as a bargaining instrument to promote the illusive goal of "full cooperation." In some cases, the cooperation they sought was basically symbolic. General Marshall himself admitted that while intelligence about the German army would have been useful it would not have changed American tactics significantly. In every instance, the quest for cooperation ran up against a deeply ingrained tradition. It might have been incomprehensible to Americans, but it existed and no amount of aid could have broken it down.[65]

President Roosevelt did not share his ambassador's annoyance with the Russians and rejected as unsound Standley's proposed strategy for dealing with them. He took a much more relaxed and broadminded view of the Kremlin's alleged ingratitude. He conceded to a group of journalists in September, 1943, that the Russians did not "throw their hats up in the air over aid we give them." But, he added, that "doesn't mean they lack in appreciation"; that was just their "way." Whether or not the President agreed with Burns's contention that generosity rather than bargaining would best promote friendship and cooperation, he recognized that since the United States had consistently fallen short of its protocol commitments lend-lease furnished only a weak instrument of pressure. More important, he perceived that assistance to the USSR had one overriding purpose—to defeat the enemy—and he wisely refrained from introducing new problems into an already strained and uncertain relationship.[66]

In retrospect, Standley appears a well-intentioned but ineffectual diplomat. Ignored by both Washington and Moscow during most of his tenure in the Soviet Union, he created a brief splash in both capitals in March, 1943, but he had no lasting effect on wartime diplomacy. He is significant because he reflected that disdain for traditional diplomacy so pervasive among Americans, and because he was one of the first officials to express disenchantment with the Russians and to advocate changes in American policies. His protests were stifled and his proposals turned down in 1943. But in 1944 and after, as the nature of the war changed and political problems assumed a greater importance in the alliance, Standley's successors in Moscow, with more tact and discretion, would express similar fears and advocate similar changes in policy.

Chapter 5

HARRIMAN AND DEANE

"A FIRM BUT FRIENDLY *QUID PRO QUO* APPROACH"

IN 1941 W. AVERELL HARRIMAN HAD BEEN ONE OF THE ORIGINATORS AND MOST outspoken advocates of unconditional aid for Russia. Harriman had begun to question the policy in 1943, and his views continued to change after his appointment as ambassador to Russia in October, 1943. By 1944 he, along with his aide General John R. Deane, had become a forceful proponent of what he called "a firm but friendly *quid pro quo* approach." Harriman's shifting attitudes toward aid to the USSR reflect the profound changes taking place in the allied military position after mid-1943, and the simultaneous reappraisal among many American officials of the appropriate place of lend-lease in this new and very different phase of the struggle against the Axis. More important, Harriman's proposals for altering the unconditional aid policy were based on a growing concern about Russian-American relations in the postwar world, on a fear that Roosevelt's policies had misled the Russians regarding American intentions, and on a conviction that lend-lease might be used effectively to exact political concessions from the Soviet government.

The Roosevelt administration had conceived the unconditional aid policy to meet certain specific and very urgent needs. The demands of military strategy and the necessity of overcoming the Soviet leadership's old suspicions of the West required that the United States do everything possible to increase the Soviet Union's capacity to resist the Nazi onslaught and to convince her leaders of American good faith. With Britain on the defensive and the United States not in the war, lend-lease offered the only tangible assistance available. The difficulties in procuring and shipping supplies and the problems of dealing with the secretive and suspicious Russians had required special measures to expedite lend-lease to the USSR. The continuing crisis in Soviet-American relations during 1942 and 1943 provided ample reason for maintaining the unconditional aid policy.

By early 1944, however, the conditions which had given rise to the policy had changed radically or disappeared altogether. During the summer of 1943, the allies reversed the direction of the war in Europe. Within two weeks in July, the Red Army shattered Hitler's summer offensive against the Kursk salient, mounted a major counteroffensive of its own, and quickly penetrated deep behind German lines. The Reich was never able to regain the initiative on the Eastern front, and after Kursk the Red Army began its relentless sweep westward toward Berlin. On August 5, Moscow celebrated with fireworks and booming cannon the liberation of Orel, the first major city retaken from the Nazis. The victory salutes would be heard again and again in the months ahead. By the end of 1943, two thirds of Soviet territory had been liberated, and completion of the task was set for early 1944.[1]

During the same period, Anglo-American armies drove the enemy from the Mediterranean. By early summer, they had destroyed the last remnants of German resistance in North Africa. Allied forces invaded Sicily in July, completed their conquest by mid-August, and followed up with assaults against the Italian mainland in early September. On September 8, Italy surrendered.

Military successes helped to lessen the suspicion and antagonism that had pervaded the Grand Alliance in 1942 and 1943. A spirit of harmony and cautious optimism characterized the first meeting of the Big Three at Teheran in November. The Western allies gave categorical assurances that France would be invaded in May, 1944; Stalin agreed to launch a simultaneous offensive to prevent the movement of German troops to the west, and promised to enter the war against Japan after Germany was defeated.

Cautious moves toward postwar cooperation paralleled the growing military collaboration among the allies. At the Moscow Conference of Foreign Ministers in October, the United States, Britain, and the Soviet Union agreed to a broad statement of principles affirming their intention to work together to settle postwar problems and to establish effective machinery to preserve the peace. Roosevelt, Churchill, and Stalin continued discussions of political issues at Teheran, and although no formal agreements were concluded they left the conference encouraged that a solid basis for cooperation existed. Teheran ushered in a period of relative harmony that would last until after D-Day.[2]

Lend-lease contributed mightily to the military victories and to the growth of unity within the alliance. By the time of Teheran, the Roosevelt administration had overcome most of the obstacles that had limited shipments in the first years of the war. Some critical items would remain scarce throughout 1944 and 1945, but by mid-1943 American war production had reached enormous proportions. Tons of munitions and civilian supplies poured forth from fields and factories across the nation, and in 1944 the United States produced 44 percent of the arms output of all belligerent nations. The U-boat would remain a nuisance, but it would no longer hamper allied logistics. By 1943 the construction of merchant vessels exceeded losses by five to one; the Mediterranean was opened to allied shipping; and "hunter-killer" groups of submarines, aircraft, and surface vessels relentlessly searched out and destroyed enemy raiders, clearing the North Atlantic for Liberty ships. The intensification of Pacific campaigns and the rising demands of occupation forces across the globe combined to produce another transportation crisis in December, 1944, but until that time shipping was adequate to support essential operations.[3]

Resolution of the shipping and supply problems and the development of more effective machinery for handling foreign orders made possible a vast expansion of shipments to the allies. Lend-lease exports, which had totaled less than $5 billion in 1942, rose to more than $11 billion in 1944. The expedient of 1941, a source of much disappointment and dissension in 1942, became in 1943 and 1944 a vital instrument of coalition warfare and a tangible manifestation of allied cooperation.

In the last months of 1943, lend-lease to the USSR swelled to record proportions. Deliveries via the Pacific to Vladivostok increased tremendously by September, and even before this date the Persian Gulf route finally reached its target capacity. Reporting on one of the most remarkable achievements of the war, a New York *Times* correspondent marveled in the spring of 1943 how British and American engineers had transformed the "Persian plains and plateaus into a vast conveyor belt" bearing tons of supplies from Gulf ports to delivery points in Southern Russia. The U. S. Army had dredged new harbors, constructed docks, and installed modern unloading equipment, and ports which had handled only 7,000 tons annually before the war absorbed over 200,000 tons monthly by mid-1943. Modern assembly lines in the port areas discharged trucks and armored cars at the rate of one every four minutes. Engineers and firemen from the Erie, New York Central, and Pennsylvania railroads drove supply trains across the Iranian desert and over the steep grades and hairpin turns of the northern mountains, "1400 miles of the roughest, toughest railroading to be found anywhere in the world." Iranians and Americans "jockeyed" huge trucks from Abadan and Basra into the Caucasus, in heats up to 120 degrees and over roads so dusty the drivers had to be equipped with respirators.[4]

By August and September, 1943, the Pacific and Persian

Gulf routes together handled over 500,000 tons of supplies. With the resumption of the northern convoys in November, shipments to the USSR totaled a record 569,000 tons, and in December and January exceeded 600,000. Deliveries fell off slightly in February, March, and April, 1944, because of the strain on supplies and shipping from final preparations for the invasion of France, but in May they again exceeded 500,000 tons and remained consistently at that level for the following year. Shipments during the third protocol period (July 1, 1943 to June 30, 1944) totaled over 6,000,000 tons, more than double the volume delivered under the second protocol and 30 percent *above* commitments.[5]

By 1944, lend-lease was contributing significantly to Soviet war production and military operations. American raw materials, machine tools, and industrial equipment played an important part in the reconstruction of Soviet industry during the last years of the war, and by Stalin's own admission, about two thirds of all major industrial enterprise had been rebuilt with equipment or technical assistance from the United States. Steel rails, locomotives, and flatcars assisted the movement of supplies from industrial centers to the front. A special type of coal similar to Russian grades and located in Arkansas mines fired the boilers of factories and power plants. The General Electric and Westinghouse corporations developed especially for the USSR "power trains," generators mounted on flatcars that could be moved from area to area as need required and that helped compensate for power losses resulting from the destruction of the Dnieper Dam and other vital sources.[6]

Lend-lease clothing and foods helped protect Red Army soldiers from cold and hunger. The Russians advanced westward in boots especially designed to provide maximum protection against melting ice and snow and mass-produced in the United States under processes created by a Russian expatriate and former chief of the tsar's boot factories. American fats and oils provided an estimated half of the Red Army's requirements in 1943 and 1944, and a lend-lease official reported from the front in July, 1944, that Russian soldiers

were "almost unanimous" in praise of American fat back
which they ate in various forms, "sometimes just slicing it on
a strip of bread." The Lend-Lease Administration pioneered
the development of concentrated and dehydrated foods to
help avert a critical food shortage in the USSR and to save
vital shipping space. Packing plants in the Middle West prepared thousands of cans of "Tushonka," a pork product sea-
soned with bay leaves according to a Russian formula. American food processers invented new methods of dehydrating
eggs, fruits, and vegetables, and even produced dehydrated
Borscht in packages no bigger than a box of safety matches.
Foodstuffs comprised almost one third the tonnage of the
third protocol and contributed significantly to the diet of
soldiers and factory workers.[7]

By the summer of 1943, American military equipment was
much in evidence on the Russian front. "I saw Airacobra,
Kittyhawk and Tomahawk fighters in service at an airport
outside Moscow," AP correspondent Henry Cassidy reported. "I saw American medium and light M-3 tanks, Ma-
thildas and Valentines, being turned over to Red Army bri-
gades behind the front. I rode in jeeps at an artillery camp. I
saw a Cossack unit using American field telephones in
maneuvers." American guns still made up only a small per-
centage of those in use, and the Russians never found U. S.
tanks adaptable. But Soviet pilots increasingly respected
American aircraft, and especially admired the speed, diving
capacity, and durability of the P-39 Airacobra, affectionately
calling it "cobrushka," which roughly translated means
"Dear Little Cobra." [8]

Contemporary observers and military historians agree that
vehicles and automotive equipment represented the most
important American contribution to the Russian victory. On
a rare visit to the front in mid-1944, General John R. Deane
reported that he "encountered American trucks everywhere," and on the same tour General Sidney Spalding estimated that American trucks accounted for about half the au-
tomobile transportation he saw. Russian officers and men
lavished praise on U. S. vehicles and especially liked the Stu-

debaker truck. "Their eyes lit up everytime they mentioned 'Studybackers,'" Deane remarked, and a Russian general bluntly told Spalding: "We love the Studebaker." The Russians also employed American motorcycles extensively, and developed a special fondness for that precocious World War II baby, the jeep, which they called "Ooeelees" (for Willys) and which adapted well to the rough Russian roads. American vehicles contributed greatly to the "new look" of the Red Army after Stalingrad, Alexander Werth later wrote, and a historian of the Russo-German war has added that lend-lease put the Red Army Infantry "on wheels for the first time in its history." Army officers candidly admitted to Harriman in the summer of 1944 that they could not have advanced so rapidly without American trucks.[9]

From his own observations, Werth concluded that the Red Army "unquestionably appreciated the help from the West—whether in the form of Airacobras, Kittyhawks, Dodges, jeeps, spam, army boots, or medicines." A New York *Times* correspondent visiting the Ukranian front in 1944 found "abundant signs of the part that United States supplies are playing in the Red Army's success," and among officers and men alike a "ready appreciation" for them. A Soviet general told Deane and Spalding that American supplies "had come to the rescue," and added that if a piece of equipment was American the Russians assumed it had been perfected and had to take a look at it. Even the Russian people, who were not well informed about American aid, knew of it and expressed their gratitude. Deane later wrote that Harriman was regarded outside Moscow as the father of lend-lease to Russia, and wherever he went he was "received with great acclaim." After a visit to Murmansk and Archangel in April, 1944, Harriman told a press conference, "Everyone in the North—civilians and military alike—expressed appreciation for the direct assistance that United States equipment has been to them and for the volume of supplies which they had seen passing through the ports and going south to the Red Army and Russian people."[10]

Russian gratitude was naturally tempered by a fierce and

justifiable pride in the accomplishments of the Soviet Union. A woman munitions plant worker commented to the *Saturday Evening Post* correspondent, Edgar Snow: "Your help is good and we thank you for it. But fighting for yourself is better than letting other people fight for you." The Soviet press always emphasized that Russian resistance in 1941 and 1942 had made possible the success of allied strategy, and many articles in *Pravda* and *Izvestia* reported glowingly on Russian industrial achievements without giving any indication that they had been facilitated by assistance from the allies.[11]

Soviet publicity for lend-lease carefully balanced the exigencies of diplomacy against the requirements of domestic politics and ideology. After the Standley incident, the press regularly acknowledged the receipt of supplies from the United States. But the Kremlin was reluctant to advertise among the Russian people the great accomplishments of American industry or to give too much attention to the contribution of allied aid to Soviet military success. Russian newspapers therefore usually confined their reports to condensed summaries of U. S. press releases and relegated these items to the back pages. *Pravda* and *Izvestia* editorialized on lend-lease only rarely, and according to Frederick Barghoorn, who served in the U. S. Embassy in Moscow during the war, party agitators throughout the USSR attempted to play down its importance and political workers at the front even tried to dampen the enthusiasm of the army for American supplies.[12]

Yet what seems most striking in retrospect is the warmth of the official tone in 1944 and early 1945. The public complaints of the first years of the war were not heard, and during the peak of Soviet-American friendship from Teheran to D-Day, Russian authorities gave considerable publicity to lend-lease and went out of their way to express their gratitude for it. In a statement on the twenty-sixth anniversary of the revolution, Stalin declared that allied assistance had "considerably facilitated the successes of our summer campaign," and in an editorial on the tenth anniversary of the establishment of diplomatic relations between the two nations, *Pravda* noted that the Soviet people "highly value the moral and material aid which the United States has given." At Teheran, Stalin toasted American aircraft production, without which the war would have been lost, and hailed the "great leadership" of President Roosevelt in producing supplies and delivering them to Russia. In April, 1944, *Red Star* devoted a third of a page to American achievements as the "arsenal of democracy" and Stalin's Red Army Day Order of 1944 credited lend-lease for much of his armies' recent accomplishments. On the eve of D-Day, Moscow displayed bright posters depicting allied supplies being landed in Russia and bearing quotations from Stalin's May Day Order.[13]

Soviet expressions of gratitude reached their height of cordiality on the second anniversary of the Russian-American lend-lease agreement, June 11, 1944. Molotov, according to Ambassador Harriman, was "fulsome in his praise of American industry and of the contribution lend-lease has made to Soviet military achievements." Editorials in *Pravda, Izvestia,* and *Red Star* hailed the growing collaboration between Russia and her allies, and displayed prominently a lengthy report issued by the Commissariat of Foreign Trade on aid furnished the USSR during the war.[14]

By the beginning of 1944, therefore, lend-lease to the USSR had entered a new phase. The Roosevelt administration had overcome most of the problems that had so limited the aid program at the outset, and shipments had increased substantially. There was no longer any question about the will or the capacity of the United States to provide effective military assistance. Russian complaints about the quantities of supply deliveries ceased, and unabashed enthusiasm about the quality of American equipment replaced the angry protests against earlier defective shipments. Soviet officials gratefully acknowledged the contribution of lend-lease to their victories and voiced their conviction that it had made possible a closer collaboration in war and had laid a solid foundation for postwar friendship.

In these radically changed circumstances of 1944, American officials began to question the continued necessity of the unique aid policies established for Russia in the dark days of 1941. Indeed, in 1943, the administration had begun to adapt its general lend-lease policies to the new conditions. With American troops taking on a greater burden of the fighting in Europe and assuming the major role in the war against Japan, U. S. Army officers, determined to look after their own needs first and perhaps resentful that the requirements of the allies had been given top priority at the beginning of the war, applied increasingly stringent criteria to foreign requests for aid. Policies established in 1943 stipulated that items would be approved for shipment only if the Joint Chiefs of Staff deemed them essential for approved operations and if they could not be produced by the requesting country.[15]

As the sense of urgency of 1941 and 1942 receded and the flow of American supplies abroad mounted, civilian and military supply officials became increasingly sensitive to the domestic political implications of lend-lease. Americans appreciated the aid program's contribution to the war—the New York *Times* aptly labeled it the "kingpin of our whole war effort"—and gave it solid if not enthusiastic support. By the summer of 1943, however, a potentially dangerous opposition had developed. Industrialists and foreign traders accepted lend-lease as an essential war measure, but complained that it had led to an "unwarranted encroachment" on private enterprise and demanded the return of trade to normal commercial channels as soon as possible. Conservative newspapers and anti-New Deal congressmen attacked Roosevelt for administering the program inefficiently and wastefully, protesting that the American taxpayers' dollars were being squandered on such luxuries as bugles and drums for the British Army and electric fans for "perspiring officials of His Majesty's Government in the Middle East." Critics of the administration held lend-lease responsible for growing domestic shortages of foodstuffs. And conservatives warned that it might even become part of a millennial New

Deal scheme for postwar reconstruction. Senator Hugh Butler, Nebraska Republican, denounced it as the "most colossal dole of all times," and predicted that it was only the "opening handout of what will finally become a world-wide W. P. A." [16]

The opposition picked up strength in October, 1943, when five senators, headed by the powerful Georgian Richard Russell, returned to Washington from a tour of the war fronts. Vocally supported by a small coalition of Southern Democrats and isolationist Republicans, the Russell group opened fire on the administration for its careless neglect of American interests throughout the world. They charged the President with amassing an astronomical debt and dangerously depleting American resources by spreading lend-lease across the world with a "prodigal hand" and by failing to demand anything in return from the allies. The senators warned that the United States was once again playing the role of "global sucker," allowing the British to use American supplies to secure commercial and political advantages at the expense of the United States. They demanded the establishment of a "realistic and tough-minded policy," executed by "two-fisted diplomats," to insure that the allies did not abuse American generosity and to force them to provide raw materials and access to bases in return for American assistance.[17]

Roosevelt professed not to take his critics seriously. "Washington seethes over the latest scandal," he wrote sarcastically to a friend. "The five Cook's Tourists from the Senate who marched up a hill and then marched down again." He advised a group of journalists in an off-the-record briefing that the senators' remarks had attracted much more attention abroad than at home, and noted that Senator Russell had privately admitted that the critical features of his report had been blown out of proportion to their real importance.[18]

Nevertheless, the President could not ignore these signs of political trouble. Conservatives in the House and Senate had already succeeded in wrecking a number of old New Deal programs, and in 1943 had destroyed the National Resources

Planning Board, a plan designed by liberals to deal with the problems of postwar reconversion. Already on the defensive in domestic policy, the administration handled its foreign policy with extreme care. For months, Roosevelt and Hull had attempted to delay congressional discussion of postwar issues for fear that open debates might produce an isolationist reaction that would threaten allied unity and undermine domestic support for the war. By October, however, intense pressure from internationalist groups and from individual congressmen had forced them to give way, and on October 13, two days after Russell issued his charges against lendlease, the Senate Foreign Relations Committee began study of the Connally Resolution, committing the United States to join with the other allies to prevent future wars.[19]

Although the Connally Resolution easily passed the Senate on November 5, the events of October, 1943, underscored the need for caution in the administration of lendlease. The Russell attacks had attracted widespread attention and produced demands for a searching investigation of the aid program. The Senate Appropriations Committee made clear it was through voting "blank check and lump sum" appropriations, and warned that henceforth it was going to be a "tough job to get money out of Congress." Isolationists had linked the administration's alleged careless dispensation of foreign aid with its grand and dangerous designs for the postwar world, and although they had failed to defeat the Connally resolution they indicated that they would attempt to exploit the two issues to defeat a fourth term for Roosevelt. With an election approaching, the war to be won, and the peace to be established, the administration had to render lend-lease invulnerable to conservative and isolationist charges of waste, inefficiency, and neglect of American interests.[20]

In the early fall of 1943, the President made several key personnel changes and drastically reorganized a number of executive agencies with an eye to neutralizing conservative opposition in Congress. Under pressure from Secretary Hull, he reluctantly accepted the resignation of Sumner Welles as

Under Secretary of State. On September 25 he appointed in Welles's place Edward R. Stettinius, Jr., who as Lend-Lease Administrator had established an excellent working relationship with Congress and had won accolades from conservatives for his handling of the aid program. In the aftermath of the bitter feud between Vice-President Henry Wallace and Secretary of Commerce Jesse Jones, a much publicized and embarrassing struggle between liberals and conservatives for control of the administration's economic foreign policy, the President completely revamped the administrative machinery for economic warfare. On the same day he appointed Stettinius to replace Welles, Roosevelt announced the merger of OLLA and twenty other agencies into a new Foreign Economic Administration which would be responsible for lend-lease, relief operations in liberated areas, preclusive buying of strategic raw materials, and export and import controls.[21]

The President named Leo T. Crowley to head the new agency. A self-made man who had started out as a grocery boy in Milton Junction, Wisconsin, Crowley had risen to wealth and power in that state's banking and utilities, and had secured a position of influence within the Democratic party. His work stabilizing Wisconsin's banks during the depression had attracted him to Roosevelt, who had brought him to Washington in 1934 to head the Federal Deposit Insurance Corporation. In time, he would gain a reputation as one of Washington's most effective administrators and would become one of the President's most valued trouble-shooters. A handsome, silver-haired bachelor who shunned Washington society and "cultivated obscurity," Crowley's modest tastes and puritanical personal habits reflected his conservatism on most political and economic issues. Since the first years of the New Deal, he was regarded, along with his friends Jesse Jones and Joseph P. Kennedy, as a power in the conservative faction of Roosevelt's inner circle and a "restraining hand" on Hopkins and the "big spenders." At least from the standpoint of domestic politics, he was an ideal choice for the FEA. He was a Catholic. He had close ties with conservative congressmen of both parties. As Dean Acheson has noted, he understood "very well Talleyrand's admonition, 'Above all, no zeal,' " and he could be counted upon to pursue cautious policies that would not provoke domestic opposition.[22]

Crowley's FEA and military supply officials tightened up considerably the handling of lend-lease in 1943 and 1944. They examined requests with increasing care and required more detailed justifications to make certain that only supplies absolutely essential for military operations were approved. FEA gradually cut back the list of items eligible for shipment, removing such controversial commodities as tobacco and butter for civilian consumption, and required the British to expand their shipments of raw materials to the United States under reverse lend-lease. The army and FEA took special pains to insure that the allies did not use lend-lease to secure economic or commercial advantage at the expense of the United States, rejecting requests for industrial equipment that might not be operational before the war ended and attempting to prevent the allies from retransferring American supplies to other nations for their own political benefit.[23]

The new policies led to pronounced reductions in lend-lease shipments. Even before D-Day, the army began reducing the flow of munitions to the United Kingdom, and in the second half of 1944 the dollar value of these shipments declined by one fourth. In early 1944, FEA cut back British civilian supply requirements by $300 million. These measures helped the administration to defend its program before Congress, and in the spring of 1944 lend-lease was again renewed for one year by large majorities. The opposition could not be eliminated, however, and until the end of the war domestic politics played an increasingly important part in the shaping of lend-lease policies.[24]

Because of its status outside regular lend-lease procedures, the Soviet aid program was not affected by the changes in policy instituted in 1943 and by the resultant cutbacks. The volume of supplies to be provided Russia was still determined by multilateral negotiations rather than by the unilateral decisions of American supply agencies. The United States continued to accept Russian requests for assistance at face value, without requiring justifications. It continued to regard protocol figures as binding obligations, and continued to provide the maximum supplies that could be procured and shipped, even exceeding protocol schedules when possible.

Significantly, the domestic critics of lend-lease had said little about aid to the USSR. The isolation of the Eastern front prevented the leakage of any evidence that Soviet officials might have abused the lend-lease authority. Many Americans agreed, moreover, that the Russian people had paid the highest price of any allied nation in suffering, lives, and devastation of their country, that they had made vital contributions to the defeat of the enemy, and that they deserved any aid rendered.[25]

Some U. S. officials recognized, however, that the unique policies established for aid to the USSR left the administration especially vulnerable to political attack. Stettinius' 1944 bestseller, *Lend-Lease: Weapon for Victory,* frankly admitted that the United States knew little about how the Russians used American supplies and that it had not required from them the same sort of information demanded of other nations. But the administration had carefully avoided publicizing the special arrangements it had designed to expedite aid to Russia, and usually gave the impression that Soviet aid was handled like other programs. Revelation of the full story of the unconditional aid policy might in the politically charged atmosphere of 1944 have set off a storm in Congress.[26]

A growing number of American officials argued that in the vastly changed circumstances of 1944 the unconditional aid policy was not only unnecessary but potentially dangerous. The period of greatest crisis had passed, and it was no longer essential to treat the Russians differently from other nations. The policy offered no means of insuring that all supplies requested by the Russians were essential for military operations. It allowed possible waste of critical supplies, and was susceptible to abuses that if publicized could have profound political repercussions.

Concrete evidence began appearing in 1943 to support these vague fears. Increasingly large orders for industrial equipment suggested that the Russians might be trying to use lend-lease for purposes of postwar reconstruction. Indications that the USSR was transferring to Iran supplies similar to those received under lend-lease aroused concern that they might be promoting their own political influence with the use of American equipment. Thus, by early 1944, a number of American officials began to propose changes to bring the Russian aid program into line with general lend-lease policies. As in 1943, the most vigorous criticism of unconditional aid came from the U. S. Embassy in Moscow.[27]

To smooth relations with the Russians and to end the squabbling that had torn the embassy apart, the administration in September, 1943, had reorganized the structure and shuffled the staff of its diplomatic and military mission in the Soviet capital. The President had named a trusted aide, Harriman, to replace Standley as ambassador. The army had recalled Faymonville, and the Joint Chiefs of Staff had abolished the posts of military and naval attaché. In their stead, a U. S. Military Mission had been created and placed under the direct authority of the ambassador. General John R. Deane, formerly a secretary to the Combined Chiefs of Staff, was named to head the military mission. General Sidney P. Spalding, who had worked with General Burns on the Protocol Committee, replaced Faymonville as lend-lease representative.[28]

The new American mission was not unfriendly to Russia and all of its members agreed upon the strategic importance of maintaining a steady flow of supplies to the Red Army. Spalding was every bit as zealous as Faymonville in support of aid to the USSR, and Deane, like Standley before him, recalled arriving at his new post "prepared to be lavish in my recommendations for the delivery of American supplies." Harriman had questioned some features of Roosevelt's policy in 1943, but during his tenure in Moscow he vigorously backed the provision of all supplies necessary for military operations.[29]

After several months in the Soviet Union, however, both Harriman and Deane began to see positive dangers in the prevailing policy. Quite by accident, Deane learned in January, 1944, of one instance in which the Russians had not put to effective use supplies desperately needed for other operations. Experiencing difficulties installing American diesel engines in their own patrol craft, Soviet navy officials had called upon the military mission for technical assistance. The U. S. Navy officer sent to help found to his horror that of the ninety engines thus far lend-leased to Russia only three had been installed, hulls were available for only an additional forty-five, and forty-two were deteriorating from rust. At the same time, the Russians had requested fifty engines to be delivered in 1944.[30]

This particular type of engine was also used in the landing craft that formed the backbone of amphibious operations in Europe and the Pacific. Shortages had long held back the invasion of Europe and waste could not be afforded. The discovery of this example of waste caused Deane to wonder whether the Russians might have overordered other supplies. He requested from Soviet Commissar for Foreign Trade Anastas I. Mikoyan information that might help to justify Soviet requests for other items in short supply, and was shocked by the Commissar's angry retort that he could get anything he wanted, without explanation, simply by going directly to Washington.[31]

Consequently, on January 16, Deane requested from General Marshall the authority to insist that the Russians provide justifications for their requests for items in short supply in the United States. Ambassador Harriman firmly supported the general's proposal. Now that the period of military crisis was over, he cabled Hopkins, there was no reason why Soviet authorities should not be required to justify their orders for scarce supplies. The initiation of such a procedure would force them to examine their requirements more carefully and would insure that precious items were not wasted. It would not, according to Harriman, adversely affect Russian-American relations. Indeed, he predicted, if the United States demonstrated firmness, the Russians would "respect us more." [32]

The Harriman and Deane cables reopened in Washington the debate that had accompanied the institution of the unconditional aid policy. Secretary Stimson and the War Department had opposed the President's 1941 decision to accept Russian requests at face value. Having already introduced in 1943 more rigid standards for approving lend-lease shipments to other nations, the War Department and the Joint Chiefs of Staff enthusiastically endorsed the recommendations submitted by Harriman and Deane as a means of establishing tighter control over aid to the USSR. Secretary of the Navy Frank Knox, who had also objected to the original policy and who had been greatly annoyed by the Russians' misuse of marine diesel engines, also approved the suggestion. In a personal communication to the President, Knox went one step beyond Deane, urging that the Soviet government be required to furnish complete, detailed justifications for *all* supplies they ordered.[33]

The President's Soviet Protocol Committee staunchly defended established policies. The committee's chairman, Hopkins, and its executive officer, General Burns, were both seriously ill at this time, but their top assistants, Isador Lubin and General John York, advanced a variety of arguments against the Harriman-Deane proposal. Mistakenly believing that Deane was requesting authority to review all Soviet requirements, Lubin and York maintained that the military mission had neither the staff nor the data necessary to undertake such an enormous task. At the same time, they minimized the danger of continuing to accept Russian orders without requiring justifications. Deane had cited only one example of Soviet misuse of supplies, and they doubted that this was sufficient to justify a change in policy. Shipping limitations had in the past always compelled the Russians to order only those supplies they needed most urgently, and would continue in the future to provide a safeguard against stockpiling of lend-lease materials.[34]

More important, Lubin and York foresaw serious repercussions if the United States modified its lend-lease policies. Lubin feared, with reason, that there were many officers in the army and navy who would attempt to use the revision in policy to reduce military assistance to the USSR. York advised the Joint Chiefs of Staff that General Burns was "heartsick" when he learned of Deane's cable, and he warned them that a change in policy might undermine Burns's attempts to promote through lend-lease a spirit of trust and friendship in Soviet-American relations. Since 1941, he observed, the administration had assumed that Soviet officials had acted in good faith and had ordered only those supplies that were required for military operations. This policy had contributed to the steady improvement of relations with the USSR. Its sudden reversal would suggest to the Russians that the United States no longer considered their needs important and would imply a lack of trust in their word. In any event, York concluded, the change proposed by Deane would probably not meet the need for which it was designed. The Soviet government might do without American aid rather than abandon its aversion to divulging secret information. "It is rather late for us to be insisting on a change in this policy of theirs," York concluded, "without inciting their bitter resentment."[35]

After extended discussions within the administration, the President accepted the Protocol Committee's recommendations. General York urged Deane and Harriman to submit to him any additional evidence of Soviet stockpiling or misuse of supplies and assured them that officials in Washington would act promptly to limit further shipments of items not essential for operations. Roosevelt advised Knox that the navy should carefully review Soviet needs for diesel engines before delivering any more to the USSR. But no change in policy was instituted.[36]

The Protocol Committee's response did not satisfy Harriman. He immediately advised Washington that he had not wanted to make final decisions on all Russian requests, but only to examine more carefully specific orders that American officials in Moscow or in Washington had doubts about. He questioned the view that shipping would continue to limit the volume of aid to the Russians, and warned that unless the United States began to "get at least some knowledge of the purposes for which they are using our shipments we lay ourselves wide open to just criticism at home." Admitting that the United States could never expect to establish with the USSR the sort of frank and open relationship it enjoyed with Great Britain, he nevertheless thought it "desirable to attempt to break down Russian traditional reluctance to give reasonable information." Soviet officials made a practice of considering American requests for cooperation "on the basis of reciprocity," he continued, and the United States would be well advised to act in a similar fashion. "We may wish to recommend that in respect to some specific items Soviet requests be held up until the Soviets take action on U. S. requests of a related character." [37]

The administration again rejected Harriman's proposals, repeating the argument that shipping "for some time to come would remain the limiting factor in our program of aid for the USSR." In fact, difficulties in navigating the Pacific in winter and a recurrent shortage of merchant vessels resulting from mobilization for D-Day had forced cutbacks in aid to Russia, and shipments during February, March, and April dropped to the lowest volume since June, 1943.

But Roosevelt and his advisers were motivated by other considerations as well. Since the beginning of the war, the President had handled aid to Russia with the greatest care and had resisted any changes in the unconditional aid policy. Like the Protocol Committee, he may have felt that lend-lease had contributed to the growing cordiality in Soviet-American relations after Teheran. Unlike Harriman and Deane, he did not believe that the changed conditions of the war either required or permitted a change in policy. On the contrary, he persisted in his conviction that Russia had to be handled with great delicacy, and he was reluctant to take any step, however small, that might set back the steady improvement in relations or upset future military collaboration in Europe and the Far East.[38]

Harriman and Deane acquiesced in the decision, and during the spring and summer of 1944 offered no further recommendations for changes in policy. But in August and September they reopened the issue. This time their warnings took on a distinct tone of urgency and the emphasis of their proposals changed. In January they had stressed the military importance of preventing waste of supplies and the domestic political consequences of allowing the Russians to abuse the unconditional aid policy. In the autumn of 1944, they urged changes to prevent a deterioration of Soviet-American relations and to promote the achievement of America's postwar political objectives.

These changes in tone and emphasis reflected the experiences of Harriman and Deane in Moscow during the spring and summer, and the growing importance of political questions in Soviet-American relations after the allied summer offensives brought victory over Germany in sight. Officially, at least, the period after D-Day was marked by great warmth. But Americans in Moscow did not find this spirit carried over into their day-to-day relations with the Soviet government. Their isolation remained as complete as in the first years of the war. "It accorded poorly not only with the outward facade of wartime cordiality and collaboration among allies which the Western powers, at any rate, were endeavoring to maintain, but also with the intimate feelings of many of us serving there," the Second Secretary of the U. S. Embassy, George F. Kennan, later wrote. "We were sincerely moved by the sufferings of the Russian people as well as by the heroism and patience they were showing in the face of wartime adversity. We wished them nothing but well. It was doubly hard, in these circumstances, to find ourselves treated as though we were the bearers of some species of the plague." [39]

During their first six months in the USSR, Harriman and Deane achieved remarkable success furthering Soviet-American military cooperation. They extracted from the Russians a considerable amount of intelligence, improved radio communications between the two nations, negotiated exchanges of weather data, and even secured Russian agreement to the establishment of American air bases in the Ukraine for shuttle bombing operations against Germany.

But each of these agreements was accomplished only after months of tedious negotiations and frustrating delays, and the Russians usually demanded maximum concessions in return. With each agreement the Americans' patience wore thinner, and when in the summer of 1944 Harriman and Deane began to attempt to secure Russian cooperation for operations against Japan, they met steadfast resistance from a government still anxious to maintain a strict neutrality.[40]

The Russian attitude annoyed Deane greatly, and he wearied of the procrastination and constant haggling. Harriman shared Deane's impatience and frustration. But the direction of Soviet foreign policy in the late summer of 1944 alarmed him even more. The most volatile issue was Poland, rapidly becoming a major test case for allied cooperation. For months, the Polish exile government in London and the USSR had been at a standoff over the questions of postwar boundaries and the composition of the government of liberated Poland. President Roosevelt recognized that the Poles' demands were probably unattainable; he regarded the Soviet position with some sympathy and realized that their military power would in time give them the capacity to settle the dispute on their own terms. But because of the important bloc of Polish-American voters in the United States and because of the American commitment to self-determination of peoples, the President wanted to prevent Russian absorption of Poland. Throughout 1943 and 1944, the United States attempted to reconcile the Soviet demand for security and the ambitions of the London Poles by arranging a compromise on the boundary dispute and working out an agreement insuring independence for postwar Poland. It would prove to be a futile undertaking, but as late as July, 1944, even after Stalin had announced the formation of a Polish Committee on National Liberation, Harriman remained confident of ultimate success.[41]

The Warsaw uprising in late July severely jolted the ambassador's hopes. Stalin had ample strategic and logistic grounds for not crossing the Vistula to aid the Polish underground. But his angry denunciation of the Poles' "adventurism" seemed to Harriman and other Westerners to betray a callous disregard for human life. And his adamant refusal to allow the British and Americans to fly across Russian lines to deliver supplies to the underground appeared to the ambassador to be politically motivated. Kennan recalled Harriman and Deane returning to Spasso House after an unsuccessful meeting with Molotov "shattered by the experience," and Harriman cabled Washington that for the first time since he had been in Moscow, he was "gravely concerned" by the attitude of the Russian government, whose refusal to assist the Poles seemed to be based upon "ruthless political considerations." [42]

Kennan thought the Warsaw episode should have been made the occasion for a "full-fledged and realistic political showdown with the Soviet leaders: when they should have been confronted with the choice between changing their policy completely and agreeing to collaborate in the establishment of truly independent countries in Eastern Europe or forfeiting Western-Allied support and sponsorship for the remaining phases of their war effort." [43]

Harriman did not go this far, but he too in the days after the Warsaw uprising began to express grave apprehension about the future of Soviet-American relations and to advocate a searching reevaluation of U. S. policies. "Now that the end of the war is in sight," he cabled Hopkins on September 10 "our relations with the Soviets have taken a startling turn evident during the last two months." American requests for cooperation in the European and Pacific wars had been held up "with complete indifference to our interests," and the Russians had shown an "unwillingness even to discuss pressing problems." At the same time, Soviet demands on the United States were becoming "more insistent." [44]

The pattern of Russian foreign policy disturbed the ambassador even more. "The Soviets' indifference to world opinion regarding their unbending policy toward Poland and ruthless attitude toward the uprising in Warsaw are best described by Molotov's statement that the Soviets would judge their friends by those that accept their policies," he wrote. In a later cable to the State Department, Harriman predicted that, in the interest of security, the Soviet Union would attempt to dominate Poland and to establish a sphere of influence in the Balkans and Eastern Europe. He admitted that American interests in the area were not large. "What frightens me," he added, "is that when a country begins to extend its influence by strong arm methods beyond its borders under the guise of security it is difficult to see how a line can be drawn. If the policy is accepted that the Soviet Union has a right to penetrate her immediate neighbors . . . penetration of the next immediate neighbors becomes at a certain time equally logical." [45]

Harriman advocated a change in American policy to head off the dangerous trend in Soviet actions. He reported a growing conviction that the Russians had "misinterpreted our generous attitude toward them as a sign of weakness, and acceptance of their policies." The time had arrived when "we must make clear what we expect of them as the price of our good will. Unless we take issue with the present policy there is every indication the Soviet Union will become a world bully wherever our interests are involved."

The ambassador did not approve "drastic" changes, but suggested the adoption of a "firm but friendly *quid pro quo* attitude." Admitting that Russian leaders had little understanding of the West and were "unduly sensitive and suspicious" of British and American motives, he recommended: "In general, we should be understanding of their sensitivity, meet them much more than half way, encourage them and support them whenever we can, and yet oppose them promptly with the greatest of firmness where we see them going wrong." It should be made plain to them that "their failure to conform to our concepts will affect our willingness to cooperate with them. . . . They should be made promptly to feel specific results from our displeasure." And on matters that "are vital to us and on which we can find no compromise . . . I believe we should make them understand patiently but firmly that we cannot accept their point of view and that we are prepared to take the consequences if they adhere to their position." [46]

Economic aid occupied a prominent place in Harriman's "firm but friendly *quid pro quo*" approach. He did not advocate drastic cutbacks in the shipment of essential military supplies. "As you know," he cabled Hopkins on September 3, "I have consistently recommended, and still do, maximum shipments in the immediate future." But he, along with Deane, again emphasized that the Russians should be made to justify their requests for items in short supply. And the United States should secure a *quid pro quo* for any shipments that did not contribute directly to military operations. "I am satisfied," the ambassador warned Hopkins, "that the only way we can induce them to give sympathetic consideration to our legitimate requests is to make them feel their negative attitude will affect our willingness to cooperate with them on matters that have no immediate effect on the war." [47]

During these same weeks, Harriman and Deane, without authorization from Washington, began to adopt a "somewhat firmer and more uncompromising policy" toward the Russians. Deane bluntly advised the Red Army General Staff that its repeated failure to consider American requests had created the impression that the Russians did not wish to cooperate, and warned that this might influence "our previous all-out desire to assist Russia, particularly in the allocation of items not needed for the war." Shortly afterward, Harriman reported to Hull that the Red Army had made "more quick and favorable decisions" than "for months previous." The ambassador reiterated his conviction that greater cooperation might be expected from the "general adoption" of a firmer policy.[48]

In Washington, General Henry H. Arnold, chief of the Army Air Force, vigorously supported Harriman's and Deane's recommendations. Arnold advised Hopkins that the American policy of generosity toward the Russians had not "paid off," and warned that a "stiffer attitude towards our Soviet friends may be more productive in furthering our own interests. Conceivably, the Soviets, who have a reputation for being tough realists, may be more inclined to play with us if we adopt a policy matching their own." Specifically, the general recommended that in the future the United States should not furnish the Russians any supplies above protocol schedules without securing concessions to advance American interests in the European and Far Eastern wars.[49]

The proposals of Harriman, Deane, and Arnold did not lead to a general reassessment of American policies toward Russia. The White House turned down Harriman's request to return to Washington immediately for consultations with the President, and neither Hopkins nor the State Department responded to his suggestions for a firmer policy. In a brief reply to Arnold, Hopkins offered the only clue to the administration's thinking at this period. Rejecting the general's advice, Hopkins explained that because of the top-secret discussions then taking place in Moscow on Russian entry into the war against Japan, "I think we better let that lie as it is for the present." Apparently concerned that any change in the handling of lend-lease might upset future military collaboration with Russia, the President and Hopkins did not seriously consider the recommendations of Deane, Harriman, and Arnold.[50]

The success of the October negotiations probably confirmed in Hopkins' mind the wisdom of his caution. Stalin agreed to enter the war against Japan three months after the defeat of Germany, and to pursue the strategic objectives outlined by the American Chiefs of Staff. He assented to the establishment of U. S. air bases in Russia's Maritime Provinces, to the use of Petropavlovsk as a naval base, and to proceeding at once with joint planning for operations. In return, the United States promised to ship an additional 1,000,000 tons of supplies for Russian campaigns in the Far East.[51]

The United States did not participate directly in the simultaneous political discussions between Churchill and Stalin, and refused to approve the sphere of influence arrangement agreed upon by them. But the Americans, like the British, seem to have been greatly encouraged by the meeting. Even Harriman, who had been so pessimistic just weeks before, was reassured by the "exceedingly cordial" atmosphere of the talks and by Stalin's "friendly and conciliatory attitude." "All three Allies," Herbert Feis has written, "thought much good had come out of the Churchill visit to Moscow. It was judged that the stress over many political situations in Europe—actual and prospective—had been eased, and dangers of dissension lessened." [52]

Despite the improvement in Soviet-American relations, Harriman remained convinced that American lend-lease policy should be changed. In Washington in early November to report on the Churchill-Stalin talks, he advised the Protocol Committee that the time had come to establish a "give and take" relationship with the USSR.[53]

Within several weeks, Deane would reiterate the recommendation in even stronger language. After the successful October negotiations, the general had anticipated expeditious joint planning for Far Eastern operations. But, he later recorded, the "days passed and nothing happened." When pressed for action, the Russian General Staff responded curtly that American proposals were "under consideration." [54]

Thoroughly disillusioned, Deane dispatched a blistering cable to General Marshall on December 2. "Everyone will agree on the importance of collaboration with Russia—now and in the future," the general observed. But, he added, "it won't be worth a hoot unless it is based on mutual respect and made to work both ways." When the Red Army was "back on its heels," it was necessary to provide the maximum assistance with no questions asked. The military situation had long since changed, but American policy had not adapted. "We still meet their requests to the limit of our ability, and they meet ours to the minimum that will keep us sweet." Deane was convinced that this approach would not work. "Gratitude cannot be banked in the Soviet Union. Each transaction is complete in itself without regard to past favors. The party of the second part is either a shrewd trader to be admired or a sucker to be despised."

The general did not despair for the future. He felt that Russia and the United States had few conflicting interests, and he regarded the individual Russian as a most "likeable person." But he was convinced that if Russian-American cooperation were to be made a reality, U. S. policy must change. The United States should continue to provide all possible assistance but should make the Russians justify those requests whose need was not apparent. In cases where aid did not contribute directly to winning the war, "we should insist on a *quid pro quo*." The institution of this policy might at first provoke a strong reaction from the Russians. But Deane concluded, "I feel certain that we must be tougher if we are to gain their respect and be able to work with them in the future." [55]

Deane did not propose drastic or unreasonable changes in lend-lease policy. Neither he nor Harriman approved sharp cutbacks in aid to the USSR or the rejection of any legitimate Soviet requests for military assistance. Rather they attempted by requiring the Russians to furnish justifications for items in short supply to bring the protocols into line with other lend-lease programs, to insure that available supplies were put to most effective use, and to make certain that the lend-lease authority was not abused.

The "firm but friendly *quid pro quo* approach" held out the possibility of important advantages for the United States. It would have provided safeguards to insure that American interests were protected in the dispensation of economic assistance. It would have strengthened the bargaining position of U. S. representatives in Moscow, making it possible for them to negotiate more forcefully with Soviet officials on proposals for military collaboration. Harriman and Deane correctly saw that gratitude could not be banked in the Soviet Union, and that the unconditional aid policy had created among the Russians the conviction that they could get anything they wanted from the United States if they pressed hard enough. A change in policy might have produced limited military and political concessions and might have forced Soviet officials to be more respectful of the desires of the United States.

It would not, however, have affected the broader outlines of Soviet foreign policy, especially toward Eastern Europe. Stalin had made clear since the beginning of the war that the postwar security of the USSR required the establishment of a ring of "friendly" states around its periphery. He never deviated from that goal, and he would not have sacrificed it for any amount of assistance. In addition, the military situation in December, 1944, had immeasurably strengthened the Russian hand. The Red Army had already liberated Yugoslavia, Bulgaria, Rumania, and half of Poland, and stood poised east of Warsaw for the final thrust into Germany. At the same time, the German counteroffensive in the Ardennes had repulsed the American drive eastward, set back the strategic timetable by more than a month, and imposed a severe strain on U. S. resources in manpower and supplies.

Thus the proposal to employ economic aid as a means of forcing the Russians to conform to American standards was neither practicable nor realistic. By the end of 1944, the Red Army was in a position to dictate the political settlements in most of Eastern Europe and economic pressure would have been of no use whatever. Victory over Germany still required close military cooperation among the allies, and American strategists were especially anxious that the Russians renew their own offensive with the greatest vigor to prevent Germany from sending additional troops to the West.

Roosevelt perceived all these factors clearly. He explained to a group of senators on January 11, 1945, that the Russians had the power in Eastern Europe and there was little he could do to change this. Economic aid, he argued, did not "constitute a bargaining weapon of any strength," because the only instrument available was lend-lease and to cut it back would hurt the United States as much as it hurt the Russians. He also feared that an attempt to use economic pressure for political ends might jeopardize military cooperation at a time when it was "obviously impossible" to break with the Russians.[56]

The President never seriously considered altering lend-lease policies as proposed by Harriman and Deane. He recognized the dangers in continuing unconditional aid, but he apparently felt they were insignificant compared to the risks. Harriman and Deane had not produced evidence of extensive Soviet overstocking. Indeed, the ambassador informed the Protocol Committee in May, 1944, and again in November that in general he was "much impressed" by Russian use of American assistance and that he had found no evidence that lend-lease industrial equipment had gone into stockpiles. In any event, the shipping crisis of late 1944 had reduced aid to Russia to the lowest level in almost a year.

On the other hand, changes in lend-lease policy did involve distinct dangers. The President still had much to ask of the Russians. The U. S. military considered Russian participation in the war against Japan essential to insure a speedy victory and to minimize American losses. Roosevelt was intent upon securing full Soviet participation in the proposed United Nations' Organization, which, as he told the senators, offered the best hope of softening Russian policy in Eastern Europe. In a sense, the President was now a captive of his own earlier decisions. Having once adopted a unique policy for aid to Russia, he evidently felt that he could not alter this policy without risking a break in the tenuous relationship he had built with Stalin and thereby jeopardizing the immediate goals he deemed most vital.[57]

The administration did not, therefore, officially respond to Deane's cable of December 2, and a Presidential memorandum of January 5, stressing that aid to Russia was still a "matter of utmost importance" and that the United States must continue to provide the "maximum amount of supplies which can be delivered to her ports," implied that lend-lease policy would not change. In late February, the Protocol Committee explicitly rejected Harriman's proposal that Russian requests for petroleum be held back until the Soviet government satisfied American demands for the establishment of a tripartite commission to administer Rumanian petroleum resources. "For nearly 4 years," the committee advised the ambassador, the United States had "followed a policy laid down by the President and Mr. Hopkins which precludes a barter basis with respect to Lend-Lease for the achievement of political or diplomatic ends." The Russians had been informed that every effort would be made to meet their requests for petroleum, and it "may be presumed that military plans may be seriously delayed by failure to deliver." [58]

Thus Harriman and Deane's vigorous efforts of 1944 did not produce changes in the handling of lend-lease. But they were not without effect. The Protocol Committee's cable to Harriman on March 3 suggested that modifications might be introduced when the fourth protocol expired, and assistance to Russia under the fifth protocol might be "related to major military and political objectives." More important, many of Roosevelt's leading advisers had been converted to the Harriman-Deane assumptions by January, 1945, and they began to apply these assumptions to the related and extremely complex question of aid for Russian reconstruction.[59]

Chapter 6

THE ONLY "CONCRETE BARGAINING LEVER"

AID FOR RUSSIAN RECONSTRUCTION

ON JANUARY 3, 1945, THE SOVIET COMMISSAR FOR FOREIGN AFFAIRS, Vyacheslav Molotov, presented to Ambassador Harriman an aide mémoire containing a Russian request for a $6 billion loan for postwar reconstruction. Along with a similar proposal by Secretary of the Treasury Henry Morgenthau for a $10 billion loan on most liberal terms, Molotov's note posed the issue whether the generous, unconditional policy Roosevelt had established for lend-lease during the war should be extended into the peace. The American response to the Molotov request and the Morgenthau recommendations makes clear that by January, 1945, significant new influences were shaping U.S. attitudes and policies toward aid for the USSR.

Domestic politics, which had played little part in determining policies for lend-lease to the Soviet Union, from the very beginning placed sharp limitations on the handling of aid for reconstruction. Americans accepted lend-lease as a necessity required by the exigencies of war. But they still regarded foreign aid as a costly and novel undertaking, and they were willing to accept only limited obligations for postwar rehabilitation. In 1944 and 1945, moreover, that keen appreciation of self-interest which had provided the underpinning for domestic support of lend-lease began to erode. The approach of victory in Europe produced rising demands for an end to swollen wartime budgets and a return to fiscal normalcy. The eruption of political disputes within the alliance in late 1944 made Americans less sympathetic toward the urgent needs of all allied nations for U. S. support. Roosevelt was so sensitive to these domestic pressures in the last months of his Presidency that he refused to raise openly the question of aid for reconstruction lest a hostile reaction jeopardize his broader foreign policy aims. At least in part because of these inhibitions, the administration was in no position to respond positively to the proposals advanced by Molotov and Morgenthau.

More important, by the beginning of 1945, the attitudes of American policy makers toward aid to the USSR had undergone important changes. In 1943 and 1944, when discussions on assistance for rehabilitation had begun, most Washington officials looked upon it primarily as a means of stimulating American commerce and of demonstrating good will toward the Russian people. By January, 1945, however, most of Roosevelt's top advisers shared Harriman's alarm about Soviet policies in Eastern Europe. They also agreed with the ambassador that economic assistance provided one of the few instruments available to the United States to influence the direction of Stalin's foreign policy and felt that it should be used carefully to promote the postwar objectives of the United States. The President himself, even though he had adamantly refused to alter lend-lease policy, appears to have been influenced by his advisers' arguments on postwar aid. His cautious, measured response to the Molotov note indicates that he too was beginning a reappraisal of the future of Soviet-American relations and of the utility of economic assistance as an instrument of diplomacy.

Thus the discussions on postwar aid to the USSR in early 1945 represent a turning point in the wartime relations between the two allies. From this point on, U. S. officials would be forced to calculate carefully the domestic political implications of their handling of economic assistance. Increasingly they would look upon aid as a weapon to force the USSR to come to terms rather than as a means of buying good will.

Even before the United States entered the war, the State Department had begun to consider the problems of postwar relief and reconstruction. The pace of study quickened in January, 1942, after the Russians submitted a formal proposal for the establishment of a United Nations' relief organization, but throughout that year and into the next the President remained preoccupied with the war and the discussions proceeded without any guidance from above. Nevertheless, the millennial public statements of Vice-President Henry A. Wallace and Under Secretary of State Sumner Welles, calling for an active and presumably massive American commitment to repair war damage and assure freedom from want throughout the world, focused considerable public attention on the issue and conveyed the impression that the administration was planning a gigantic program for reconstruction and even contemplating postwar extension of lend-lease.[1]

In fact, OLLA had in 1942 prepared an amendment to the Lend-Lease Act making possible its use for reconstruction, but when the President began to set forth his own ideas in mid-1943, they proved to be considerably more modest. In June, he approved American participation in the proposed United Nations Relief and Rehabilitation Administration, an organization which despite its imposing title was designed to provide only direct relief to war-devastated areas. In October, he agreed to a formula for financing UNRRA's work by an outlay of 1 percent of the national income of participating nations, $2.1 billion for the United States. At the same time, he firmly rejected the use of lend-lease as an instrument for postwar reconstruction, insisting that it must cease with hostilities and that any additional aid must be provided through loans or credits.[2]

Roosevelt's decision to adopt a cautious, limited program

for rehabilitation reflected in part a miscalculation of the extent of war damage and of the degree to which the conflict had disrupted the world economy. From the beginning, the administration grossly underestimated the needs for reconstruction. Acheson has aptly labeled early discussions on the problem "preparations for an unknown world," and indeed in 1941 a British official had suggested that much of the burden of relief might be assumed by charitable organizations. Visions had advanced beyond this by late 1943, but they were still far from reality. A State Department report conceded that the needs for reconstruction would be "large," but added that loans "with some provision for repayment will be sufficient for most areas and will be the best way to do the job." In fact, as Acheson has recently pointed out, "UNRRA would have done its work and passed away before we were to know what 'rehabilitation' really required from us." [3]

In any event, in the conservative atmosphere of 1943, administration officials felt certain that Congress would not approve extension of lend-lease into the postwar period. Industrialists and foreign traders had already put themselves solidly on record against it, and the mounting opposition to lend-lease in Congress underscored the need for caution. Consevatives had sneered at Wallace's alleged promises of a "quart of milk for every Hottentot" and condemned his proposed "giveaway" of American wealth, and the powerful Republican, Senator Arthur Vandenberg of Michigan, denounced the administration's initial draft of UNRRA as an instrument making possible the pledge of "our total resources to whatever illimitable scheme for relief and rehabilitation all around the world our New Deal crystal gazers might desire to pursue. . . ." [4] The administration would not make public until November, 1944, its decision to end lend-lease with the war, but one year earlier it committed itself to a conservative program for postwar assistance.

With the plan outlined and the critical period of the war past, the United States in October, 1943, opened informal discussions with the USSR on postwar economic problems.

Secretary of State Hull took with him to the Moscow Conference of Foreign Ministers a memorandum expressing the desire of the American people to "cooperate fully in the rehabilitation of war damage in the U.S.S.R.," and recommending the opening of formal discussions as soon as possible. While Hull was in Moscow, Donald Nelson, former head of the War Production Board, engaged in unofficial talks with Stalin and other Soviet officials on the prospects of postwar trade between the two nations. Harriman continued these talks with Molotov and Mikoyan after the conclusion of the Moscow Conference, and he and President Roosevelt discussed the problem en route to the Big Three meeting at Teheran. The crowded agenda of the conference did not leave time for conversations on reconstruction but, upon departing Teheran, Roosevelt advised Harriman to express to Stalin his regrets for not taking up the matter and authorized the ambassador to continue his talks with the Russians. From this point on, the question of American aid for reconstruction occupied an important, if not central, place in Soviet-American relations.[5]

The administration's interest in providing postwar credits to the USSR reflected in part a genuine sympathy for the suffering of the Russian people and a humanitarian impulse to assist them in the reconstruction of their ravaged country. Americans also recognized, as General Burns had pointed out in December, 1942, that the provision to Russia of "very substantial credits on easy terms to finance her post-war rehabilitation" offered a means of furthering Soviet-American cooperation in war and peace.[6]

In addition, U. S. officials saw important practical advantages to be derived from postwar aid to Russia. Haunted by what the historian William A. Williams has termed the "nightmare of depression," they recognized that the New Deal had only partially healed America's economic malaise and that the especially critical problem of unemployment had been solved by the conversion of the economy to war production. Fearing the return of large-scale unemployment once the war ended, many economists, publicists, and gov-

ernment officials looked upon an expanding foreign trade as
one principal means of averting a postwar economic crisis.[7]

Estimates on the prospects of postwar Soviet-American
trade varied sharply. The State Department's Eastern European division took a pessimistic outlook. Admitting that
Russia's needs for reconstruction would be "overwhelming,"
it concluded on the basis of prewar trade figures that the
Russian and American economies were not complementary
and that the USSR produced very few goods that could be
exported to the United States to provide the purchasing
power to underwrite large orders of American equipment.[8]

But most Washington officials did not share this caution.
Nelson, Harry Dexter White of the Treasury Department,
and Lauchlin Currie of FEA argued that war damage in the
Soviet Union had created a huge demand for American industrial equipment. Currie, basing his estimate on the annual volume of lend-lease shipments of industrial supplies,
predicted that the United States might be able to export as
much as $1 billion per year in the postwar period, and
White estimated that Russia might be able to absorb a total
as high as $10 billion. White also noted that American sup-
plies of raw materials had been dangerously depleted during
the war, and that the Russians had large stocks of man-
ganese, tungsten, mica, graphite, chrome, mercury, copper,
and iron ore that could be exported to the United States and
would provide the basis for financing a substantial postwar
trade. Nelson predicted a "great future" for Soviet-American
commerce, and Currie described its potentiality as "enormous." [9]

Soviet officials encouraged American hopes. Stalin told
Nelson in October, 1943, that the Russians liked American
products and wished to import substantial quantities of locomotives, railroad equipment, machine tools, and other industrial equipment. Molotov and Mikoyan repeated the
same advice to Harriman, and *War and the Working Class*
observed that the Soviet Union offered for the United States
"a voluminous and stable market such as most likely no
other customer would ever be. The state and character of

our trade considerably enlighten the organization of mutual economic relations and free the exporters from the risk of loss of their investments due, possibly to the bankruptcy of their customers, which often happens among private concerns." These same sources made clear, however, that "the size and structure" of Soviet imports would "depend considerably upon the size and conditions" of the credits offered.[10]

Initial discussions on these questions revealed broad differences between Soviet and American positions and within the United States government itself. In early February, 1944, Mikoyan suggested to Harriman an initial credit of $1 billion, at 1½ percent, to run for twenty-five years with repayment beginning in the sixteenth year. The State Department's Eastern European Division doubted that the Russians could handle a credit larger than $200 million and suggested an amortization period of ten to twenty years. Harriman proposed an initial credit of $500 million, at an interest rate of between 2 and 3 percent, to be amortized over a period of twenty-five to thirty years. Currie was much more optimistic, recommending a loan of $1 billion at 3 percent, and the Treasury Department exceeded his generosity with a recommendation for $5 billion at 2.1 percent.[11]

Before these differences could be reconciled, the administration had to confront the hard realities of domestic politics. The only existing agency with authority to grant foreign credits was the Export-Import Bank, originally chartered as a government corporation in 1934 to finance the trade with Russia that was expected to flow from the Roosevelt-Litvinov Agreements. By early 1944, the bank's capital was virtually exhausted, and in any event the Johnson Act of 1934 forbade the bank from extending loans to those nations, including the Soviet Union, that were in default on their obligations to the United States.[12]

Thus the administration had no instrument at hand to extend postwar credits to Russia, and before a concrete offer could be made it would have to ask Congress to repeal the restrictive provisions of the Johnson Act and expand the lending authority of the Export-Import Bank. With an election only months away, the President hesitated to open a potentially explosive issue, and while several government agencies continued to study the problem, Hull advised Harriman on February 8 to inform the Soviet authorities that although the United States was "disposed to assist them in every way possible in this matter we cannot at this time indicate either the amount or the exact nature of these long-term financial arrangements." [13]

In the meantime, Oscar Cox, General Counsel of the Foreign Economic Administration and one of the authors of the original Lend-Lease Act of 1941, came up with an ingenious means of providing stopgap assistance to the Russians until the legal authority could be obtained from Congress to underwrite a comprehensive program of postwar assistance. Cox's idea resulted from the dilemma created by requests for $300 million worth of industrial and capital goods which Soviet officials had submitted in late 1943 as a supplement to their third protocol requirements.

The Russians insisted that all of the equipment was necessary for war production and therefore justifiable under lend-lease. American supply officials recognized, however, that much of it would have a long life and might be of value for years after the war ended. Without justifications or detailed knowledge of the Soviet economy, there was no way to be certain that the Russians were not taking advantage of the lend-lease mechanism to secure supplies they needed for postwar reconstruction. On the other hand, no one could predict with certainty when the war would end, and it was important to put into procurement any items that were necessary for military operations. The Protocol Committee feared that rejection of Russian orders for industrial equipment might have an adverse effect on Soviet-American relations. Yet if the requests were approved and the war ended before the items were shipped, the United States might be left with a large volume of unexportable surpluses that could not be absorbed in the domestic market.[14]

After intensive study, Cox discovered a means of resolving

all of these problems and at the same time providing a mechanism to give the Russians some transitional assistance between the end of lend-lease and the beginning of a long-range program of aid for reconstruction. Section 3 (c) of the Lend-Lease Act provided that supplies under contract to lend-lease nations could be delivered until July 1, 1947. Cox therefore proposed that the Russians be invited to submit requests for industrial equipment that might have a postwar as well as a wartime use. Those items that were actually shipped before the end of hostilities would be financed under lend-lease; those contracted for but not shipped would be paid for on credits to be arranged under authority of section 3 (c).[15]

The 3 (c) device offered numerous advantages. Supplies could be procured more rapidly under the lend-lease program than through normal purchasing procedures. The Russians would be assured maximum deliveries of industrial equipment. The administration would not have to fear political repercussions and would not have to secure new legislation from Congress. If the war should end suddenly, the United States would be protected against the possibility of an undeliverable surplus. Cox further suggested that, once the $300,000,000 program had been completed, the Soviets might be encouraged to submit requests for additional industrial supplies that could be justified as essential for military use but that would also make possible a "big start" toward postwar reconstruction.[16]

Most U. S. officials approved Cox's proposal as an acceptable expedient for dealing with a difficult problem, but several dissenters protested that the administration should act more decisively. The Treasury Department favored going to Congress at once to secure authorization for a $10 billion loan for the USSR. A dramatic move of this sort, treasury officials argued, would reassure business and labor that the administration was taking action to combat postwar unemployment and economic stagnation. An arrangement with the Soviet government for repayment in raw materials would help to build up America's dwindling stock of precious resources. Most important, a loan of this magnitude would give the President a "powerful lever" to help shape postwar political and economic settlements.[17]

More vigorous protests came from Ambassador Harriman in Moscow. Harriman endorsed the 3 (c) idea in principle, but he warned Washington that it was nothing more than a "stopgap and does not meet the issue." The United States must move ahead immediately and formulate a larger, long-range program to assist Soviet recovery. Delay could seriously affect America's postwar economic readjustment. American businessmen might lose their competitive advantage in trade with Russia; negotiation of an agreement would require much time and should be completed and in effect before the end of the war so that Russian orders could be put into production immediately to "cushion the shock" of reconversion. An early agreement on postwar aid would also give hope to the Russian people and would insure the Soviet Union's maximum contribution to the war by allowing the release of reserves of manpower and supplies for the last phases of operations. In the absence of such an agreement, Soviet officials might, moreover, begin to doubt the sincerity of American offers to help.[18]

But Harriman pressed for immediate action primarily on grounds of diplomatic strategy. Most officials in Washington regarded postwar aid as a means of assuring Soviet authorities of American good will. But the ambassador, from the very beginning of the discussions, had stressed the "importance of credits in our overall relations with the Soviet Government," and the bargaining power they provided the United States to achieve its postwar political objectives. At this stage of the war (February, 1944), Harriman appears to have been convinced that Stalin and his advisers were not set on dominating adjoining nations. But, he warned Washington, the expansionist spirit was still alive in some circles of the communist party, and the chaos within the satellite nations of Eastern Europe and the Balkans that would follow liberation from German rule might create pressures for Russian absorption. Economic assistance, Harriman pointed out to

Secretary Hull, offered "one of the most effective weapons at our disposal to influence European political events in the direction we desire and to avoid the development of a sphere of influence of the Soviet Union over Eastern Europe and the Balkans." Provision of aid to the liberated satellites would blunt the appeals of the communists, contribute to the establishment of sound economic conditions under a democratic form of government, and reduce internal pressures for joining the USSR. By the same token, a generous offer of aid for Russian reconstruction might encourage and strengthen the position of those Soviet leaders who wanted to concentrate on domestic problems after the war.[19]

Thus, the ambassador concluded, economic assistance offered the United States "one of our principal practical levers for influencing political action compatible with our principles." It should be used carefully and withheld if "individual countries do not conform to our standards." But if it was to be "of real value in our overall relations with the Soviet Government, as a benefit which they can obtain from us if they play the international game with us in accordance with our standards we must have a well forged instrument to offer them. Vague promises excite Soviet suspicions whereas a precise program offered to them (but always kept within our control thru the approval of each transaction) will in my judgment be of definite value."[20]

Harriman therefore regarded aid for Russian reconstruction as important not only to hasten the conclusion of the war and to smooth American reconversion to peacetime production but also as a powerful weapon to promote America's postwar objectives, especially the prevention of a Soviet sphere of influence in Eastern Europe. The 3 (c) agreement was a start in the right direction, but no substitute for more decisive action. He appreciated the domestic political problems involved, but affirmed that the "triple-barrelled advantages to us which I describe may furnish ammunition and ideas for dealing with political problems at home in obtaining effective legislation."[21]

Both the Treasury Department and Harriman offered

powerful arguments for immediate measures, but the political climate in Washington in February and March, 1944, was not congenial to bold new initiatives. On the contrary, the early interdepartmental discussions on postwar assistance for the USSR took place against a background of increasingly bitter conflict between the administration and Congress. The coming elections and uncertainty whether Roosevelt would seek a fourth term intensified the usual friction between Capitol Hill and the While House, and the easing of the military crisis encouraged restive congressmen to become more assertive. Republicans and Southern Democrats joined forces in January to emasculate a bill sponsored by the President simplifying voting procedures for servicemen in national elections. Roosevelt labeled the new bill a "fraud" and would later refuse to sign it. In February, the Senate gutted the administration's tax program and the President vetoed its substitute measure. Interpreting Roosevelt's angry and sarcastic veto message as a direct attack on legislative prerogatives, congressmen of all political persuasions proceeded defiantly to pass the tax bill over his veto.[22]

Foreign policy issues were not immune from the executive-legislative dispute. The House and Senate approved American participation in UNRRA in February, but only after attaching restrictive amendments to the authorization. Senator Vandenberg warned Acheson, moreover, that his colleagues were not as enthusiastic about UNRRA as the substantial majority vote would seem to indicate. "There is tremendous latent 'suspicion' of this entire enterprise in the Senate," he observed, and UNRRA would have to be administered "strictly and rigidly within the 'specifications' which have been laid down." [23]

Congress renewed lend-lease for an additional year in the spring of 1944 by large majorities, but the tone of the debate rather than the size of the vote impressed many observers. None of the members questioned the necessity of continuing lend-lease, but a growing number expressed protests over the administration's handling of the program and voiced grave suspicions about its postwar intentions. Isolationists disseminated sordid tales of the unparalleled waste and extravagance allegedly accompanying the use of lend-lease funds; they complained bitterly that the allies were taking advantage of American generosity and doing nothing for the United States in return. Republicans and conservative Democrats warned that the President's reckless spending, of which lend-lease was only one example, would plunge the nation straight into economic disaster if it was not checked by Congress, and demanded that the allies be required to replenish exhausted American stocks of raw materials and furnish bases for postwar use. Members of both parties suspected that the administration might misuse the broad authority conveyed in the Lend-Lease Act, and combined to enact an amendment forbidding the President from entering any agreements or incurring any obligations under the act except in "accordance with established constitutional procedures." British observers saw in the debates on lend-lease portents of a resurgent nationalism in the United States, and the Louisville *Courier-Journal* detected isolationist "straws in the wind." Enough was said in the debates, the columnist Arthur Krock warned, "to support the conclusion that the most enlightened statesmanship will be needed to complete the lend-lease chapter in an atmosphere worthy of its great contribution to the war against the axis." [24]

With Congress in open revolt against the administration's domestic proposals and increasingly suspicious of its foreign policy, the President apparently preferred to pass up the possible advantages noted by Harriman and the Treasury Department rather than incur the risks of opening up the issue of postwar aid for Russia in an election year. The State Department advised Harriman on March 7 only that it was considering the "timing" of asking Congress to repeal the Johnson Act and to expand the capital of the Export-Import Bank. Lend-lease officials secured from congressional leaders informal approval of the 3 (c) device in the late summer of 1944, but the administration would go no further. Not until January, 1945, after the election was safely past, did the President recommend authorization for additional measures and even then he did not place these recommendations high on his list of legislative priorities.[25]

While the question of long-term aid remained in abeyance, the State Department and FEA proceeded to work out the terms of the 3 (c) agreement. The American offer included two classes of supplies. Industrial equipment necessary for Soviet war production and which could be shipped within a reasonable time after approval (roughly eighteen months) would be financed under lend-lease if delivered before the end of the war and under a 3 (c) credit afterward. Equipment which required an "unusually long time to produce" and with a "long period of expected usefulness" would be provided on credit regardless of when shipped. The agreement fixed a flexible interest rate for both classes of supplies based on the rate the United States paid for its own debt (2.1 percent in March, 1944) plus ⅛ of 1 percent and which would go up or down with the American rate. Payments on the credit would begin after three years and would extend over a twenty-year amortization period.[26]

The State Department presented the proposal to the Soviet Embassy in May, 1944, and formal negotiations opened in Washington in July. From that time until mid-September, an American group, headed by Assistant Secretary of State Dean Acheson, and a Russian group, headed by Vice Commissar for Foreign Trade M. S. Stepanov, met almost daily in an effort to work out mutually acceptable terms. The negotiations, Acheson has recently recalled, were conducted in the "almost unbearable heat" of a corner room in the old State Department building, and against the background of suspicion and antagonism produced by the Warsaw uprising. "Even the heat of our room," the Assistant Secretary has written, "could not warm the chill between allies into cordiality." [27]

As Harriman had earlier predicted, the Russians proved to be "tough traders." Stepanov immediately objected that the interest rate was too high—the USSR could not pay more than 2 percent—and that the period of grace before payments began and the amortization period were too short.

He insisted that his government be given the right to cancel orders right up to day of shipment at no cost to itself, and that it be given the authority to determine what supplies might be included in the two classes provided for in the agreement.[28]

For days, Acheson writes, "the meetings went on with exactly the same points, often in the same words, made by each side." Americans worked out a cancellation clause satisfactory to the Russians and formulated an acceptable means of categorizing supplies. But differences on the terms of the credit could not be resolved. The United States changed its original interest proposal to a flat rate of 2½ percent, then reduced it to 2⅜ percent, and extended the period of grace to nine years. Stepanov responded by asking a return to the sliding scale but insisting that the rate should never go above 2⅜ percent. He asked that the amortization period be extended to thirty-four years, demanded price reductions of as much as 20 percent on certain items, and insisted that the United States commit itself to ship all supplies included in the agreement.[29]

Acheson stood firm. He stressed to the Russians that Congress would not approve the lower interest rate, and warned them that unless an agreement were concluded soon their requests could not be placed in procurement under the Lend-Lease Act. But his gentle efforts to persuade his Russian counterparts accomplished nothing. Stepanov asked the Americans to consider the "special factors" of the credit and to make further concessions in the "general spirit of the lend-lease agreements." He and his advisers were not moved by Acheson's argument that Congress would not approve an agreement more favorable to the USSR. Betraying a profound ignorance of American politics, one Soviet official remarked that the American people were so responsive to Russia's role in the war that they would not criticize "special concessions" to her. He added that American businessmen, both Republicans and Democrats, were so anxious to insure a substantial postwar trade with the Soviet Union that they would eagerly accept a sacrifice in interest rates. Reports in the press that the United States was negotiating with Britain for postwar lend-lease, although inaccurate and vigorously denied by the State Department, probably encouraged the Russian determination to hold out for better terms.[30]

Thus the impasse continued, and even when Acheson, displaying an increasing firmness, warned that unless the Russians demonstrated a greater willingness to compromise the entire arrangement might fall through Stepanov was not swayed. He and his associates seemed confident that once the two sides had clearly outlined their points of agreement and disagreement, the "highest people" would step in and break the deadlock.[31]

The Treasury advised further concessions to the Russians, but the FEA and State Department objected. On August 30, Ambassador Harriman, thoroughly alarmed by the Warsaw incident and by the lack of cooperation shown by Soviet officials in Moscow and already shaping his *"quid pro quo* approach" on lend-lease, advised the State Department that as a "matter of principle" no further concessions should be made in the 3 (c) negotiations. Acheson reached the same conclusion at about the same time. After carefully surveying the Soviet responses to his various proposals and interpreting their informal remarks to American officials, he determined that they were not interested in concluding an agreement but would continue to haggle and procrastinate to force the United States to meet their terms.[32]

On September 14, therefore, the American negotiators firmly presented their final offer, advising Stepanov to secure from Moscow instructions to sign it in Washington or to return home to get the approval of his superiors. Acheson again warned that a decision must be reached promptly. Orders for industrial equipment could not be placed under lend-lease too near the end of the war. If the agreement were not satisfactory, some other arrangement which would require legislation from Congress must be found. Nothing further was heard from the Russians, however, and shortly afterward Stepanov departed Washington without signing the agreement.[33]

The 3 (c) discussions significantly influenced the future course of Soviet-American economic relations. Cox had originally conceived the arrangement in response to some especially difficult Russian requests for supplies, and had hoped by rendering a liberal interpretation to the Lend-Lease Act to insure the provision of all possible wartime assistance to the USSR, to get her started on the process of reconstruction, and to advance Russian-American economic cooperation. In fact, the inability of the negotiators to reach an agreement in the fall of 1944 would eventually render the device inoperable. And the stance taken by Soviet officials during the discussions convinced the State Department and FEA that the firmer position already advocated by Harriman should be assumed in all subsequent economic discussions with the Russians. The Soviet government seemed confident that the United States needed postwar markets so desperately that it would in time willingly make a deal on almost any terms. A growing number of Roosevelt's advisers began to feel that it was urgent, from the standpoint of diplomatic tactics, to destroy this illusion.

Molotov's detailed proposals for transitional and postwar aid, presented to Harriman on January 3, reinforced American suspicions that the Russians felt they were bargaining from a position of strength and were determined to hold out for a better deal. The Soviet note, which Harriman described as "extraordinary in form and substance," attempted to lump together the 3 (c) arrangement with a larger program of assistance for reconstruction, both to be financed under a generous credit. Molotov obligingly indicated that the USSR would be willing to help relieve the United States of its postwar surplus by placing orders for up to $6 billion worth of industrial equipment. Russia would pay for the supplies with a long-term credit, to run for thirty years, at an interest rate of 2 $\frac{1}{4}$ percent with payments to begin at the end of nine years. The commissar also requested a 20 percent discount on all orders placed before the end of the war, and in presenting his requests hinted that the future development of Soviet-American relations should have a "solid economic basis." [34]

The Soviet note met a cool response in Washington. Only Secretary of the Treasury Morgenthau favored a loan as large and interest rates as low as those proposed by Molotov. Morgenthau had never shared the State Department's old suspicions of the USSR. Although he had been disgusted by the invasion of Finland in 1940, his extreme hatred for Nazi Germany in time brought him to the realization that a rapprochement with Stalin might be desirable. With the President's blessings, he worked hard in 1940 and 1941 to smooth over Soviet-American discord, and after the German invasion of Russia he became one of the most ardent promoters of aid to the USSR within the administration. Like many Americans, the Secretary of the Treasury subsequently developed a great admiration for Russian military feats: "They're doing such a magnificent job in the war . . . ," he remarked in 1944, "that I've got a weak spot for them." He was convinced, moreover, that the interests of the two nations did not clash and that collaboration in the economic as well as the political realm was essential for a peaceful and prosperous postwar world.[35]

Morgenthau's personal experiences with Soviet diplomats confirmed his belief that postwar friendship could be made a reality. Undoubtedly because of his own commitment to expediting the Russian aid program, he had got along well with the Soviet Purchasing Commission and even with the difficult Oumansky. At the Bretton Woods Conference in the summer of 1944, he had conducted extensive discussions with Stepanov on the U. S. proposals for the establishment of international agencies to stabilize currencies and to make loans for reconstruction and development. He found the Russians to be tough and often stubborn negotiators, and he was annoyed by their habit of referring every matter back to Moscow for a decision. Nevertheless, he had tried patiently to persuade them of his own earnest desire for closer collaboration between the two nations. While standing firm on substantive matters he considered vital to the success of his proposals, he had at the same time evinced a willingness to make concessions on specific questions that bothered the Russians. And throughout the discussions, he promised to use his own influence to secure substantial postwar assistance for the USSR. He succeeded in getting Soviet acceptance of his plans. He left the conference convinced, as he informed the President, that the Russians desired to "collaborate fully with the United States," and certain that the tactics he had employed were best calculated to attain this end.[36]

Aware that Roosevelt was soon to meet personally with Stalin, Morgenthau on January 1, 1945, advised the President that a liberal and concrete program of aid for reconstruction would "contribute a great deal toward ironing out many of the difficulties we have been having with the Russians." Nine days later, he forwarded to the White House a memorandum proposing a $10 billion loan bearing only 2 percent interest. In subsequent discussions with the State Department, he complained that the 3 (c) negotiations had failed because of the American tendency to "bargain and bicker" rather than to offer the Russians a "clearcut, very favorable proposal" which they could consider a "concrete gesture of our good will." He recommended a new 3 (c) agreement for the same volume of supplies but without any interest, and repeated his suggestion for a $10 billion credit to "assure the Soviet Government of our determination to cooperate with them and break down any suspicions the Soviet authorities may have in regard to our future actions." Morgenthau's proposals and the Molotov note raised the fundamental question in January, 1945, whether the liberal, conciliatory policy the administration had employed with lend-lease since 1941 would be applied to postwar assistance as well.[37]

The Secretary of the Treasury's own previous actions insured that his recommendations would encounter vigorous opposition within the Roosevelt cabinet. In the autumn of 1944, he had taken a leading role in shaping the administration's foreign policy, and at the Quebec Conference in September, he had secured the agreement of Roosevelt and Churchill to his own proposals for the postwar treatment of Germany and for lend-lease to the United Kingdom during the war against Japan. The State and War Departments bitterly resented Morgenthau's intrusion into their own domains and opposed his punitive policies for Germany. In the weeks after Quebec, the secretary had become the center of a stormy and often highly personal struggle for the control of American foreign policy. The battle raged into January, and the emotions it generated undoubtedly influenced the response of other members of the cabinet to Morgenthau's proposals for postwar aid to the USSR.[38]

The domestic political situation in January, 1945, was even less favorable to the type of proposals advanced by Morgenthau than it had been in the winter and spring of 1944. On the contrary, increasing evidence of Soviet interference in the internal affairs of Poland and Rumania and British suppression of a revolution in Greece in December, 1944, had provoked in the United States a widespread popular disillusionment with the allies and set off the most vocal attacks on the administration's handling of foreign policy since before Pearl Harbor. *Time* reported in January, 1945, that a "clamor of criticism" against Roosevelt's diplomacy had now "swelled into an outraged chorus." Liberals and conservatives alike deplored the British and Russian reversion to power politics and old-fashioned imperialism, and placed much of the blame on an administration which had not used its enormous power to back up the ideals enunciated in the Alantic Charter. Public opinion polls taken in December indicated a significant rise in popular distrust of the allies, especially the British, and an alarming decline of confidence in the President's conduct of foreign affairs.[39]

The outburst of public indignation seemed to confirm Roosevelt's persisting fears of a postwar isolationist reaction and posed serious challenges to his principal goal of committing the United States to an active and positive role in shaping postwar settlements. A group of Roman Catholic archbishops visited the State Department on December 13 and warned that although they approved American membership in an international organization they were reluctant to come out openly for it as long as the administration tolerated Soviet interference in Poland. Throughout December and January, numerous congressmen went to the White House and the State Department to protest the allies betrayal of U. S. war aims and the ineffectiveness of American foreign policy. Senator Vandenberg, fast becoming the Republican party's leading spokesman on foreign affairs, demanded that the President issue an unequivocal statement whether he intended to give Stalin a free hand in Poland. Senators Harold Burton, Joseph Ball, Lister Hill, and Carl Hatch, who had spearheaded a bipartisan drive for U. S. participation in an international organization, warned in January that the Senate might bind the President's hands by stating in advance the type of peace settlement it would approve. The journalist Allen Drury reported a "growing disillusionment and uncertainty on the Hill" when Congress convened in January, and Roosevelt's attempts to head it off were less than successful. Drury observed that the foreign policy sections of the President's annual message had "fallen flat," and that his attacks on "perfectionism," which many regarded as an ill-disguised effort to prepare the nation for the compromises he would have to make, had "soured the idealists, confirmed the isolationists, and disturbed the middle of the roaders." [40]

Shocked by events in Greece and Eastern Europe, the American nation and Congress were not in a mood in January, 1945, to back a generous program of postwar aid. A poll taken in December, 1944, revealed that 70 percent of those questioned felt that the allies should repay the lend-lease debt in full. Critics lamented that the "tens of billions of dollars" that "we are showering upon our allies does not seem to be building up any particular amount of good will for us abroad but is becoming an increasingly serious source of bitterness, jealousy, suspicion and bad feeling." Congressmen protested that the British had used American supplies to maintain their domination over Greece and that the Russians were using American money to construct a satellite in

Poland. Organs of Roman Catholic opinion, even Democratic newspapers, demanded that the United States stop underwriting Soviet imperalism and use its economic leverage to force the Russians to conform with American principles.[41]

Alarmed over the rising national debt, fearful that America's resources were being exhausted, and suspicious of the "big spenders" in the New Deal, conservatives in Congress were increasing their pressures on the administration to cut back the massive wartime expenditures as soon as possible and to limit postwar budgets. In their view, the nation simply could not afford to pour out billions of dollars worth of assistance to other nations. "We have a rich country," Senator Vandenberg advised a friend, "but it is not rich enough to permit us to support the world." Conservatives agreed, moreover, that the United States should concentrate its attention on its own economic problems at home—which Vandenberg predicted would be "by far the most serious economic problems ever confronted by any country in the history of the earth"—rather than to attempt the hopeless and thankless task of trying to rebuild the world. And they were certain that the solution of America's reconversion problems would demand a return to fiscal orthodoxy, with reduced taxes and government expenditures, a balanced budget, and the dismantling of controls over the economy.[42]

Periodic reports in the press during 1944 that the administration planned to use lend-lease for reconstruction evoked vigorous protests from congressional leaders. Vandenberg stated emphatically that the lend-lease program had to be confined "absolutely to the military operations of this war" and that it must not extend "1 minute or $1 into the postwar period." Senator Tom Connally, chairman of the Foreign Relations Committee, agreed that Congress never intended lend-lease "to serve any purpose except to aid in the military operations in carrying on this war." [43]

Democratic and Republican leaders conceded the need for relief in the immediate postwar period, which presumably would be taken care of by UNRRA, and they generally favored a limited program of credits to assist postwar reconstruction and stimulate American trade. But they insisted that any proposals for credits would have to be submitted to Congress for separate consideration, and conservatives made clear that the administration's recommendations would be subjected to close scrutiny. Vandenberg stressed that American participation in reconstruction should be on a "strictly business basis . . . ," and that any credits granted should be "*sound* credits and not a mere bookkeeping device by which we find ourselves ultimately paying for our own exports (as in 1920–1928)." Senator Robert Taft of Ohio would estimate that the total of postwar reconstruction credits to all nations should run to no more than $6 billion.[44]

The Roosevelt administration perceived the depth of congressional sentiment on matters relating to foreign aid and in late 1944 adjusted its policies accordingly. The President had never intended to extend lend-lease into the postwar period, but at Quebec in September, 1944, he had temporarily accepted an indirect method of using lend-lease for reconstruction, agreeing informally to furnish the British with a volume of supplies during the war against Japan well above their essential military requirements to assist their reconversion to a peacetime economy. On the advice of his cabinet, however, Roosevelt in November had backed away from his earlier stand on the grounds that the arrangements made at Quebec would create a "very serious political problem" at home. To assuage congressional fears, the administration affirmed categorically in November, 1944, and again in January, 1945, that "Lend-lease has been and will be an instrument of war; it will be liquidated with the end of the war." In January, 1945, the President recommended to Congress early repeal of the Johnson Act and an expansion of the lending authority of the Export-Import Bank, but he did not attach high priority to his request nor press Congress to take immediate action.[45]

Thus domestic politics made it difficult, if not impossible, for the administration to move ahead rapidly on Morgenthau's proposals for aid to the USSR. The President did not have authorization to grant credits to Russia and he would have been taking grave risks by making even vague promises without any assurance that Congress would back him up. Had he submitted to Congress at once a proposal for postwar credits to the USSR, moreover, he would also have incurred serious risks. The nation was in a highly suspicious mood, and pressures were mounting to reduce government expenditures and limit America's contribution to world recovery. Such a proposal might have set off a full-fledged debate on the administration's postwar foreign policy, thereby endangering relations with the USSR during a most delicate period and threatening American participation in the international organization.

The administration's rejection of Morgenthau's proposals stemmed more from considerations of diplomacy than of domestic politics, however. By January, 1945, most of Roosevelt's advisers disagreed with the assumptions upon which the Secretary of the Treasury based his recommendations. Morgenthau implied that the major obstacle to good relations between the United States and the Soviet Union was the deep suspicion which Russian leaders still harbored of their allies' intentions, and he proposed to combat it by providing the USSR a generous, unconditional program of aid for reconstruction. At one time or the other, most of the President's inner circle had shared this position, but Soviet actions in the last months of 1944 had raised growing doubts. The Kremlin's exclusion of the West from political settlements in Rumania and Poland and its apparent determination to establish compliant governments in those nations had deeply alarmed the State Department and confirmed latent suspicions that it was intent upon establishing a sphere of influence in Eastern Europe. Stalin's unilateral recognition of the Polish Committee on National Liberation on January 1, 1945, over Roosevelt's personal protests, suggested that the Russian leader placed greater importance on the accomplishment of his own selfish aims than on cooperating with the West in working out an international security system that would respect the rights and wishes of all nations and peoples.[46]

Soviet activities in Eastern Europe, combined with the
3 (c) negotiations, had convinced an increasing number of
U. S. officials, moreover, that Harriman's arguments had great
merit. The administration's generous, conciliatory policy toward the USSR since 1941 had given the Russians an impression of American weakness and had encouraged them to act
unilaterally. A broadening circle of the President's top advisers accepted Harriman's pessimistic appraisal of the future of
Soviet-American relations and supported his call for firmer
American policies.

Foreign Economic Administrator Crowley, the new Secretary of State Edward R. Stettinius, Jr., who had replaced
Cordell Hull in December, one of his top aides, Assistant
Secretary of State Will Clayton, and Secretary of War Stimson all opposed acceptance of Molotov's January 3 counter-
proposal and Morgenthau's recommendations on postwar
aid. They found numerous objections to Morgenthau's call
for a new 3 (c) agreement and to the Russian attempt to
merge lend-lease credits with postwar assistance. Crowley
argued that projects financed under lend-lease were an integral part of the war supply program and had to be kept separate from postwar assistance. Crowley, Clayton, and Stettinius felt that the United States had made the Russians a
generous offer and that Congress would not be likely to approve the more liberal terms set forth by Molotov and Morgenthau. Most important, they stressed that if the United
States now backed down and either combined the 3 (c)
agreement with postwar aid, as suggested by the Russians, or
accepted a new arrangement without interest, as proposed by
Morgenthau, it would strengthen the Russians' already deep
conviction that Americans were irresolute and desperate to
come to terms.[47]

Along with Harriman, these same individuals opposed an
immediate and unconditional offer of credits on unusually
generous terms. Harriman still backed postwar aid to the
USSR. He advised the State Department to disregard the
"unconventional nature" of Molotov's proposals, to "chalk
them up" to the Russians' "ignorance of normal business

procedures" and their "strange ideas" on how to "get the best trade." He continued to insist that credits gave the United States important bargaining power, and advised that the Russians be told that American willingness to assist their reconstruction would depend upon their "behavior in international matters." Secretary of War Stimson, who had warmly endorsed the ideas in Deane's long cable of December 2 (proposing a *quid pro quo* in return for lend-lease) and commended them to the President as "sound recommendations," also felt that credits should be conditioned on the receipt of specific military and political concessions from the Russians and on the establishment of greater "mutuality" in Soviet-American relations. Stettinius, Clayton, and the State Department argued that a definite offer of postwar aid should be delayed since credits offered the only "concrete bargaining lever" the United States had to try to resolve the many difficult problems of the peace.[48]

Stettinius managed to secure the President's assent to this position. After a cabinet meeting on January 10, FDR agreed to defer any definite offer of credits until after he had talked personally with Stalin at their upcoming meeting in the Crimea. "Well, after all," he advised the Secretary of State, "we are not having any finance people with us and I will just tell them we can't do anything until we get back to Washington." [49]

Alarmed by Roosevelt's decision for postponement, Morgenthau worked frantically the following week to try to convert the cabinet and through them the President to his own views. He advised Roosevelt's chief of staff, Admiral William D. Leahy, that the President and the State Department "were wrong and that if they wanted to get the Russians to do something they should . . . do it nice. . . . Don't drive such a hard bargain that when you come through it does not taste good." He repeated the same advice in a conversation with Stettinius, adding that the "carrot should be put before their nose when you first get there and let them know there's going to be financial aid for them while they're at war and financial aid for them when the war is over." [50]

The secretary got nowhere. At a cabinet meeting on January 19, Roosevelt again stated that it would be a "mistake" to make an offer to the Russians before the Big Three meeting began and again he affirmed that he wished to defer further discussion of the matter until after he had met with Stalin. Many considerations influenced the President's decision. His trust in Morgenthau had been badly shaken by the secretary's activities at Quebec, which had embarrassed the administration politically and provoked a near rebellion in the cabinet. He appreciated the domestic political dangers of Morgenthau's proposals. Roosevelt seems also, like the conservatives in Congress, to have questioned the capacity of the United States to underwrite a massive program of reconstruction. He was aware that a commitment to help Russia would send other nations scurrying to Washington for help. He told Stettinius on December 29 that while all the allies apparently thought the United States had unlimited wealth, in fact "we were getting at the bottom of our own well." It was time, he concluded, to "get tough and not be so liberal with our money." [51]

But Roosevelt's primary reason for delaying a commitment on postwar aid seems to have been his growing concern about the future of Soviet-American relations. On several occasions he had expressed in an off-hand manner his opinion that American economic power could be used to influence negotiations with the USSR. He may not have shared the dark forebodings of Harriman and the State Department, but he certainly wanted to test their propositions against his own personal talks with Stalin and the concrete agreements that might result from them. "I think it's very important," he told Stettinius and Morgenthau on January 10, that "we hold this back and don't give them any promises of finance until we get what we want." The administration thus rejected the Secretary of the Treasury's recommendations, deciding to delay action on aid for Russian reconstruction until at least after the Crimea Conference. On January 27, the State Department instructed the embassy in Moscow to advise the Russians once again that the United States was still studying methods of assisting them but was not yet in a position to make definite commitments.[52]

From February 4 to 11, 1945, Roosevelt, Churchill, and Stalin met at Yalta, the former Tsarist resort in the Crimea, and deliberated at length on the pressing problems of war and peace. The President succeeded in achieving two of his major objectives. Stalin unequivocally reaffirmed his promise to enter the war against Japan three months after the defeat of Germany, and the Russians stepped closer to active participation in the international organization by accepting an American compromise formula for voting in the Security Council and by reducing their demand for sixteen votes in the General Assembly. The Big Three dealt less successfully with the increasingly intractable conflicts over postwar political settlements, deferring some—notably the future of Germany—for later decision, and glossing over others with vague statements of general principle. The allies pledged themselves to follow the ideals of the Atlantic Charter in the liberated areas of Europe, to "reorganize" the existing Lublin regime in Poland on a "broader democratic basis," and to conduct "free and unfettered" elections for a new Polish government. The Yalta Conference seemed nevertheless to bring the Grand Alliance through another period of severe stress and produced renewed optimism within the Roosevelt administration.[53]

The spirit of hope that grew out of the meeting would, however, be of only short duration. Early attempts to implement the Yalta agreement on Poland got nowhere. Stalin's announcement that Molotov would not attend the upcoming conference in San Francisco shocked top administration officials and deeply pained the President. The Russian leader's angry accusations of Anglo-American treachery in negotiations involving the surrender of German troops in Italy added to the rising tension and evoked from Roosevelt the strongest words used in their personal wartime correspondence.[54]

The breakdown of Soviet-American relations in the weeks after Yalta brought forth from Harriman in Moscow increasingly urgent warnings. After weeks of frustrating negotiations on Poland and other East European questions, the ambassador reiterated in even stronger tones his conviction that American policy had encouraged Soviet intransigence and that it must change. He was certain that the Russian leaders had "considered as a sign of weakness on our part our continued generous and considerate attitude toward them in spite of their disregard of our requests for cooperation in matters of interest to us." The United States, he advised, must now adjust its policy to "make it plain" to them that they could not "expect our continued cooperation on terms laid down by them." It must be "firm and completely frank with them" and should make them "feel specifically how lack of cooperation with our legitimate demands will adversely affect their interests." [55]

The crisis of March, 1945, and Harriman's warnings reinforced the feeling already shared by many top U. S. officials that the nation must deal forcefully with Stalin's unreasonable demands and must show a greater determination to stand up to the Russians. Stimson advised Stettinius that the War Department was "stirred up" by Soviet treatment of American prisoners of war behind their lines and suggested that reprisals, possibly cutbacks in lend-lease, might be in order. "It certainly seems silly," the Secretary of War commented, "that we should go on giving them sugar when they are treating us this way." [56]

Stettinius himself was most concerned about securing Russian collaboration in the establishment of the United Nations and tended to be cautious at this stage, but many of his subordinates in the Department of State agreed with Harriman's views. The Eastern European division had long been suspicious of Soviet motives and skeptical of postwar cooperation. Under Secretary of State, Joseph C. Grew, who was acting secretary during Stettinius' long absences from Washington and who handled many policy matters while the secretary was absorbed with preparations for the San Francisco conference, was a staunch anti-communist. A Boston brahmin educated in the elitist environment of Groton and Harvard, a conservative Republican and career diplomat of the old school, Grew had always regarded communism and the USSR with profound suspicion and distaste. He opposed recognition of the Soviet Union in 1933 on ethical grounds— the United States should never "palliate, by recognition, the things Soviet Russia has done and the things it stands for" —and he was revulsed at the thought of socializing with the "Bolshies." During the late thirties he approved acquiescence in Japanese domination of northern China because it would help to contain the growth of communism in Asia; like many of his class he had been disgusted by the Nazi-Soviet pact and the attack on Finland. Soviet policies in the spring of 1945 only confirmed in his mind a distrust that had been building since 1917. [57]

The Roosevelt administration did not in the aftermath of Yalta adopt a distinct change of policy toward the USSR along the lines recommended by Harriman, but it was clearly reappraising old attitudes and policies, and its handling of the related questions of transitional and postwar economic assistance indicates a definite hardening of attitudes toward the Russians as well as the domestic political limitations under which it was forced to operate. At least up to late 1944, the United States had gone out of its way to meet Soviet requests for economic aid and had attempted to use lend-lease to conciliate the Russians. In February and March, U. S. officials stubbornly resisted Soviet demands they considered unreasonable, adopted a reserved and extremely cautious position toward long-term commitments, and looked upon economic assistance more and more as an instrument of pressure.

In early March, the State Department firmly rejected Soviet attempts to modify the terms of the 3 (c) agreement. Molotov's note of January 3 had at least tacitly rejected the final American offer of September, 1944, but in February Russian officials began pressing for the immediate procurement of the millions of dollars worth of supplies to be financed under the lend-lease credit. Arguing that the equipment was essential for military operations, that it was an integral part of the fourth protocol and that the United States was therefore obligated to provide it, they insisted that procurement begin immediately, with the terms of finance to be arranged later under the long-term credit proposed by Molotov. The State Department responded bluntly that transitional aid had to be separated from long-term assistance and that in the former case the United States had made its final offer. Acting Secretary Grew suggested that the Russians might submit requests for individual items through regular lend-lease channels, but warned that all of the equipment could not be put into procurement until they had agreed to the terms of finance.[58]

Domestic political pressures combined with the reappraisal of policies toward the USSR to produce an even tougher stance on transitional aid in late March. Since November, 1944, the White House had made clear its intention to limit lend-lease to war use and to terminate it when the war ended. But the Republicans in Congress profoundly distrusted Roosevelt, and they were determined, in Vandenberg's words, to hold the fourth term to "strict accountability" for its acts. Recurrent rumors in the press that the administration was negotiating lend-lease agreements with Britain, France, and Russia involving billions of dollars, and much of it intended for reconstruction, fed their suspicions. And when the State Department published the text of a 3 (c) agreement with France shortly after the Lend-Lease Act came up for renewal in February, 1945, the Republicans set out to plug up loopholes in the act that might permit its use for reconstruction.[59]

Defending administration policies, Leo Crowley repeatedly stated that lend-lease would be used only to prosecute the war and that programs for reconstruction would be sent to Congress for special consideration. He carefully explained that the 3 (c) agreements thus far concluded provided for supplies that were essential for military operations and required that any items shipped after the war ended would be paid for on credit.[60]

Despite Crowley's assurances, Republicans in the House

remained skeptical. Representative John Vorys of Ohio, the leader of the opposition, agreed that the French 3 (c) agreement was both "sound and provident," but expressed fear that the administration might still use the broad authority in the Lend-Lease Act to underwrite postwar reconstruction, Vorys and other Republicans on the House Foreign Affairs Committee demanded categorical guarantees that lend-lease be limited strictly to war use. With the threat of a long and angry floor fight looming, the administration in mid-March worked out with the Republican dissidents a compromise amendment to the act explicitly stating that lend-lease could not be used for reconstruction but allowing execution of the 3 (c) agreements already negotiated.[61]

The proceedings in the House along with indications that Germany was on the verge of collapse determined the administration's decision to withdraw the 3 (c) agreement offered the USSR months before. Stettinius advised Harriman on March 16 that "in view of military developments and recent discussions in Congress FEA now feels that it cannot proceed with the 3 (c) agreement in its present form. . . ." A week later Crowley and Grew advised President Roosevelt that because of "the present military situation, the initiation at this time of a program of procurement under a 3 (c) agreement of industrial plants requiring a long time to manufacture, ship and install might possibly be considered by the Congress as a use of the Lend-Lease Act for reconstruction purposes." They therefore recommended that the original offer be withdrawn and a new agreement proposed to finance those supplies already under contract but not delivered by the end of the war. Roosevelt quickly approved the recommendation, and the Russian Embassy was informed of the decision the following day. Withdrawal of the agreement meant in effect that this device would not be used for the purpose for which it was originally designed—to allow transitional aid which would contribute at least indirectly to Soviet reconstruction until a long-term program could be put into effect.[62]

At the same time it was taking a tougher position on 3 (c)

credits, the administration continued to delay action on credits for postwar rehabilitation. Roosevelt did not bring up the matter at the Yalta Conference, and after his return to Washington he did not even encourage top-level discussion of Molotov's request for $6 billion. When Crowley told the President on March 30 that a number of congressmen had expressed "emphatic" objections to a Russian loan and that it would be a "great mistake" to grant a loan until more was known about Russia's postwar policies, the President, according to the Foreign Economic Administrator, "concurred very definitely" in his views.[63]

Harriman, still anxious to exploit the bargaining power in postwar aid, advised the State Department on April 11 that the United States should continue to encourage the Russians to believe that "we are sympathetic to their reconstruction problems," and should move immediately to secure from Congress a general authority to make postwar loans. "We should not," he warned, "give the Soviets the idea that our desire to help is waning, although we should make it clear to them that our cooperation is dependent upon a reciprocal attitude of cooperation on their part." [64] FDR could not act on his ambassador's advice. The following day he would pass suddenly from the scene, and the knotty problem of postwar credits, along with a host of other unresolved issues, would be left to his successor.

Although American lend-lease policy remained unchanged at the time of Roosevelt's death, the administration's handling of other forms of aid to Russia had stiffened considerably. After making limited concessions in the 3 (c) negotiations, Acheson and the State Department had refused to go further, risking a breakdown in the negotiations rather than giving in to Russian demands. American officials rejected Soviet efforts to combine the 3 (c) device with a larger program of postwar aid, refused to procure 3(c) supplies until the terms of finance had been negotiated, and, in late March, with no agreement in sight, withdrew the offer altogether. Morgenthau's recommendations for a $10 billion loan received no support, and no action was taken on Molotov's request for a $6 billion loan.

The Russians quickly detected the change in American attitudes. In March, the Soviet ambassador to the United States, Andrei Gromyko, revealed to Joseph Davies his uneasiness with the state of Soviet-American economic relations, and complained that he had encountered hostility from Americans in discussions on the procurement of 3 (c) industrial equipment.[65] Several weeks later James Reston reported in the New York *Times* that Russian officials were "disturbed" by the Americans' refusal to provide the industrial equipment that had been offered many months before and by their failure to respond favorably to the request for a postwar loan. The Russians, Reston commented, were not impressed by official explanations that nothing could be done until the authority had been secured from Congress. In fact, they protested, "very little" had been done "to seek greater authority for getting the money." [66]

Domestic political pressures did influence the hardening of American attitudes toward postwar assistance for Russia. Roosevelt had always been hesitant to raise the potentially divisive issue of loans for reconstruction, and Congress' insistence that lend-lease must be limited exclusively to essential military supplies, when combined with the approach of V-E Day, left the administration little freedom of action in using the 3 (c) device.

But the Russians correctly perceived that more was involved. In fact, the American handling of economic issues from January to April, 1945, signified the abandonment of assumptions that had for years guided lend-lease policies. By this time most of Roosevelt's advisers agreed with Harriman and Deane that goodwill could not be banked in the Soviet Union and that the administration's generous and conciliatory attitude toward lend-lease had made the Russians more demanding rather than more cooperative. As Russian-American conflict intensified and the crisis over Eastern Europe deepened, American officials began to regard economic assistance as perhaps the last instrument available to them to alter the direction of Soviet foreign policy. They had not formulated specific proposals to translate their latent economic power into an effective instrument of diplomacy. But they were determined to stop responding liberally to Russian requests and to refrain from making future commitments until they saw more evidence of Russia's willingness to follow their lead in constructing a workable peace. Whether or not Roosevelt shared these views cannot be determined with certainty, but his delay on Russia's request for a loan and his approval of Crowley's and Grew's recommendations on the 3 (c) agreement suggest that he was moving toward the Harriman-Deane position in the weeks prior to his death.

Chapter 7

V-E DAY

THE END OF UNCONDITIONAL AID

ON THE MORNING OF MAY 7, 1945, TWENTY-FOUR HOURS BEFORE THE official announcement of Germany's surrender, the Associated Press leaked the news of the end of the European war. New Yorkers reacted wildly. Large and noisy crowds jammed Times Square and the financial district, blowing horns, staging impromptu parades, filling the "canyons between the skyscrapers with fluttering scraps of paper." Some knelt in the streets to pray; others stood five deep in the bars. Elsewhere in the United States the observance of victory was strangely quiet. Most people went about business as usual, stopping only for small programs at neighborhood centers or for private meditation in places of worship. American gratitude and hope for the future was tempered by the realization that a grim struggle against Japan still lay ahead.

Two days later the war-weary Russians celebrated Stalin's official proclamation of victory with less restraint. In Moscow, the celebration touched off a warm, spontaneous, and unprecedented demonstration of friendship toward the United States. Throughout the day, Muscovites thronged into the streets, and loudspeakers on every corner blared the Star-Spangled Banner along with the Internationale. Great crowds gathered in front of the U. S. Embassy and cheered exuberantly when the Soviet flag was planted next to the American. Every time an American passed through he was "clutched by the crowd and hurled happily into the air." Shouts of "Long live Truman!" "Long live Roosevelt's memory!" "Long live the great Americans!" echoed into the night.[1]

The end of the epic struggle against Hitler signaled the triumph of the Grand Alliance. It also removed the common need that had created the alliance and held it together through four stormy years, and the exultation of victory could not dispel the mounting suspicions among the allies. Indeed, the arrangements for the surrender of German armies and the unsuccessful efforts of allied leaders to coordinate the timing of the proclamation had been surrounded by discord and distrust. The simultaneous discussions at San Francisco had produced a dangerous deadlock. Even while "soldiers embraced and crowds cheered and mothers wept in gratitude," Herbert Feis has written, "the officials of the three countries that up to then had stayed together were becoming estranged."[2]

Just three days after V-E Day, on May 11, 1945, President Truman ordered termination of the unconditional aid policy and a cutback in lend-lease to the USSR. The following day civilian and military officials executed the order zealously, halting loadings in port and even calling back ships at sea bound for the Soviet Union. The abruptness of the change shocked and angered the Russians, and although Truman later modified his order the handling of lend-lease marks an important milestone in the transition from wartime alliance to Cold War enmity.

Months before V-E Day, U. S. supply officials had recognized that the end of hostilities against Germany would require adjustments in all lend-lease programs. Powerful economic interest groups had made clear their opposition to an indefinite continuation of large-scale shipments of assistance to the allies. Businessmen and farmers conceded that lend-lease had opened new markets that might be expanded after the war. But they could not exploit these opportunities until the government eased emergency export restrictions and made more items available for private trade. Eager to secure a jump on postwar competitors, fearful that New Dealers within the administration might attempt to use wartime controls to extend the government's authority over private enterprise, they raised louder protests as the end of the European war came into sight. In late 1944, the National Foreign Trade Council, the United States Chamber of Commerce, and the National Grange all demanded the relaxation of trade restrictions, the curtailment of lend-lease shipments, and the restoration of trade to commercial channels as soon as the military situation permitted.[3]

From late 1943 on, Congress had been increasingly concerned about mounting government expenditures and had placed relentless pressure on the administration to make reductions wherever possible. Congressmen accepted the necessity of continuing lend-lease during the war against Japan, but they insisted that it should be limited to the essential needs of the allies. Senator Harry S. Truman's influential war investigating committee stated emphatically in November, 1943, that "every effort should be made to reduce the cost to our taxpayers to a minimum, both by obtaining reverse lend-lease and by compelling the recipients of lend-lease to utilize the resources they have to a maximum before they request aid from us." "When the final accounting is made," Senator Millard Tydings of Maryland exclaimed in the summer of 1944, "we must pay the bill, and from now on the lend-lease money ought to be expended with a singleness of purpose, to shorten and win the war and for no other incidental purpose whatever." Responding to these pressures, U. S. agencies began in 1944 to reduce assistance to allied forces in the European and Middle East theaters. They planned more drastic reductions to accompany the shift to a one-front war.[4]

The United States Army and Navy found other reasons

for restricting lend-lease after V-E Day. They were determined for prestige that the war against Japan should be primarily an "American show," and they were deeply suspicious
of British and Russian aims in the Far East. As a consequence, they envisioned only a limited role for the allies in
operations against the Japanese. They wanted Russian entry
into the war to prevent the withdrawal of the Kwantung
Army from Manchuria to the home islands and they were
willing to offer the USSR the "maximum support possible
without prejudice to our main effort against Japan." But
they were less than enthusiastic about the participation of
the other allies, especially the British. They wanted to make
certain that lend-lease did not interfere with the huge supply
requirements of their own forces. They regarded strict limitations on foreign aid as one way of consigning the allies to a
peripheral role in the war.[5]

Thus, as early as May, 1944, the United States began to
plan for major changes in lend-lease after V-E Day. The
Joint Chiefs of Staff approved a policy restricting shipments
to those supplies "not available to the nations concerned and
which can be profitably employed against Japan in accordance with agreed strategy." Roosevelt approved this principle, apparently without giving it serious thought, and in late
July the Army Service Forces issued orders to halt all deliveries to Europe upon the cessation of hostilities against
Germany.[6]

The special status of the protocols exempted aid to Russia
from these instructions, but in the summer of 1944 several
agencies proposed measures to adjust the Soviet program as
well. Fourth protocol deliveries would continue through
June 30, 1945. In the late summer of 1944 it seemed possible
that Germany might collapse by the end of the year, and
there was persisting uncertainty whether the USSR might
enter the war against Japan. The State Department therefore
inserted into the protocol an escape clause providing that
the schedules were "subject to review and variation in the
event of major changes in the war situation." In September,
the FEA representative on the Protocol Committee proposed

that if the Russians were not at war with Japan when hostilities against Germany ended all shipments except those covered under the 3 (c) agreement (in the event that document had been signed) would be halted.[7]

Planning was already well advanced when on September 9, 1944, President Roosevelt intervened. By this time he had perceived broader political ramifications in post-V-E Day lend-lease policy. The British were pressing for continued large shipments during the war against Japan to help ease their desperate economic problems. Harriman and Deane were about to initiate important negotiations to determine the scope and nature of Soviet operations in the Far East and the volume of their supply requirements. The army's restrictive orders and the FEA proposal left little flexibility in handling economic aid after the defeat of Germany, and revelations of the proposed drastic reductions could have a serious effect on both the British and Russians and threaten their continued collaboration in the last stages of the war and the peace. Thus the President ordered that no department or agency should take "unilateral action" in policy planning and that the instructions already issued by the army should be "immediately withdrawn and cancelled." He promised to issue definite orders himself "at an early date." [8]

In the months that followed, however, Roosevelt did not set forth clear-cut instructions, and as V-E Day drew nearer the administration's policies for lend-lease remained shrouded in uncertainty. Assistance for the USSR presented especially difficult problems. In October, 1944, Stalin had again affirmed his intention to declare war on Japan, but he had also indicated that he could not enter the war until he had time to redeploy troops from Europe—an estimated three months. This meant that the Soviet Union would not be at war with the Japanese when the war in Europe ended. Under these circumstances, as one of Roosevelt's top advisers warned in late 1944, there would "undoubtedly be great pressure from Congress and the press to cease lend-lease." Since Stalin had insisted that his commitment be kept secret, moreover, there would be no easy way to explain the continuation of assistance to the USSR after V-E Day.[9]

Nor had the administration determined how to handle fourth protocol shipments if the European war ended before June 30, 1945. Most of the supplies included in the protocol were intended to support operations in Europe and great quantities had significant postwar value. The breakdown of the 3 (c) negotiations left no means for financing items delivered after V-E Day. Thus if the war should end well in advance of the terminal date for the protocol and the administration attempted to complete the established schedules, it would be violating the letter and spirit of the Lend-Lease Act. On the other hand, the Russians had come to regard protocol lists as binding obligations, and if the administration stopped shipments and left some protocol schedules unfulfilled it would risk alienating its ally.[10]

The volume of Soviet requirements for the war against Japan remained undefined. At the conclusion of Deane's conferences with the Russian chiefs of staff in October, 1944, the administration had approved the Milepost Program, calling for the delivery of 860,000 tons of supplies to the Far East for operations against the Japanese. No one anticipated that this would take care of all of the USSR's needs for a war that was expected to last as long as eighteen months. On January 5, 1945, Roosevelt had instructed his aides to begin preparations for a fifth protocol that would cover the period to June 30, 1946. But it was not until March, 1945, that American supply officials actually invited the Russians to submit detailed lists of the assistance they wanted for the Far Eastern war.[11]

Some U. S. officials recognized, moreover, that it would be difficult if not impossible to maintain the protocol system and the unconditional aid policy after V-E Day without risking violation of the pledges made to Congress to limit lend-lease to essential military supplies. Without justifications and more detailed information about Soviet production capacity and military plans, it was hard to determine whether items requested were necessary for military operations. Congress was increasingly sensitive to possible abuses of lend-lease in the first months of 1945, and if the administration continued to accept Russian orders at face value in a period of declining military intensity it would incur serious political risks. A change in policy, on the other hand, would most probably antagonize the Russians.

Roosevelt did nothing in the first three months of 1945 to resolve these questions or to clarify his own plans for lend-lease to the USSR after V-E Day. Preoccupied with more critical matters, exhausted from his wearing trip to the Crimea, increasingly perplexed by the rising tensions in Soviet-American relations after Yalta, he probably did not even anticipate the difficulties ahead in lend-lease policy. Hopkins, who had handled this sort of problem in the early years of the war, did not return to Washington with FDR after the conference with Stalin and when he did come back to the United States he went immediately to the Mayo Clinic for rest and treatment. The agencies responsible for lend-lease perceived many of the problems involved, but in view of the President's directive of September 9, 1944, they hesitated to take the initiative and simply waited for orders from the White House.[12]

In late March some officials began to press Roosevelt for guidance on policy. By this time U. S. and British forces had penetrated the Ruhr and crossed the Rhine, and the Red Army was preparing its final drive to Berlin. With the collapse of the Third Reich imminent, Under Secretary of War Robert P. Patterson urgently requested from the White House instructions on handling lend-lease. Roosevelt apparently endorsed Patterson's proposal to begin immediate planning, but he did not inform the War Department of his approval nor did he offer specific suggestions on policy.[13]

President Roosevelt thus bequeathed an uncertain legacy to his successor Harry S. Truman. He had indicated that the United States would support Soviet military operations in the Far East, but he had left indefinite the volume of supplies to be provided and the policies that would govern their handling. The resolution of these questions involved some difficult choices. Maintenance of the unconditional aid policy after V-E Day might provoke a reaction in Congress that would endanger backing for the President's postwar plans. Literal observance of the pledges made to Congress, on the other hand, could deepen the crisis in Soviet-American relations. The Russians had not been advised that V-E Day would bring major adjustments in policy, and after years of preferential treatment they could not be expected to accept changes gracefully.

The rush of events in Europe left the new President little time to resolve these questions. On April 11, the United States Ninth Army reached the Elbe, and two days later the Red Army launched an assault against Berlin. American and Russian troops joined hands at Torgau on April 25. On May 1, a provisional German government headed by Admiral Karl Doenitz announced the suicide of Adolf Hitler. The fall of the Reich within a little more than two weeks after the death of President Roosevelt forced a rapid decision on the future of lend-lease to the USSR.

Domestic political pressures severely restricted the new administration's freedom of action. During the last months of the Roosevelt presidency, relations between the White House and Congress had continued to deteriorate. "Not for years," James MacGregor Burns has written, "had the President's legislative fortunes seemed at such a low ebb." The Senate confirmed Henry Wallace as Secretary of Commerce, but only after a long and angry debate and after stripping the Commerce Department of its control over federal lending agencies. The Senate also gutted the administration's proposed emergency manpower bill and rejected the nomination of the liberal Aubrey Williams as head of the Rural Electrification Administration. Debates on every issue that came before the Congress in early 1945 revealed a pervasive distrust of President Roosevelt among Republicans, conservative Democrats, and even some liberals who usually supported him. The White House persisted in holding off a full-scale debate on foreign policy, but the longer it delayed the more suspicion seemed to build up. The revelation on March 29 that the United States had promised the British six votes in the United Nations, while assigning three votes apiece to itself and the USSR, raised a storm of protest. Congressmen of both parties, annoyed with the manner in which the President had handled the matter, wondered aloud what other secret deals might have passed among the allies at the Yalta meeting.[14]

During March and April, 1945, the House and Senate had considered the extension of lend-lease for another year, and the proceedings gave further evidence of the wide gap that had opened between the executive and the legislative branches. Administration officials testifying before the House Foreign Affairs Committee had time and again affirmed the President's intention to limit lend-lease to war use and to terminate it when hostilities ended. But they were unable to overcome the deep suspicions of the Republican members of the committee, and were forced to accept an amendment to the act explicitly stating that lend-lease was not to be used for relief, reconstruction, or rehabilitation.

The administration encountered even greater distrust and more opposition in the Senate. After hours of patient explanation, Foreign Economic Administrator Leo Crowley finally won the support of his close friend Senator Vandenberg, and the Foreign Relations Committee approved the amended House bill. But Vandenberg's Republican colleague, Robert A. Taft, remained dubious. The Ohioan argued that the exception in the House amendment permitting execution of the 3 (c) agreements nullified its intent. The recently concluded 3 (c) agreement with France, he contended, was in fact a postwar loan, since most of the supplies could not possibly be shipped before the war with Germany ended. The House bill would allow its implementation and the conclusion of similar deals right up to the end of the war. It would make it possible for the administration to send "indefinite amounts" of assistance abroad under the authority of the Lend-Lease Act.[15]

Taft did not oppose modest postwar loans to the allies—

he set $3 billion as an acceptable total for the first year of the peace—but he bitterly resented the administration's apparent attempt to make these loans indirectly through lend-lease, and he warned that the arrangement with France and reported agreements with Britain and Russia already far exceeded $3 billion. He did not trust President Roosevelt or the men around him. The New Deal bureaucrats, he complained, had become so used to "lavish treatment of every foreign nation as to lose all sense of values." They must recognize that they could not buy foreign good will. Their careless spending was certain to produce a runaway inflation that would be the United States' "number one enemy" in the postwar world. The Senator insisted that Congress must prevent the New Dealers from bankrupting the United States, and to accomplish that end he proposed an amendment striking out the exception in the House amendment and providing an "ironclad guarantee" that lend-lease would not be used for reconstruction.[16]

The issue of the Senate debate was not whether lend-lease should be terminated when the war ended—no one questioned that—but whether the President could be trusted to do this in good faith, and the reaction to Taft's proposal suggests the depth of suspicion that had developed. The amendment gained vocal support in the Senate, not only from isolationist Republicans William Langer, Kenneth Wherry, and Hugh Butler, but also from Joseph Ball and Harold Burton, Republicans who had given vital backing to the move to commit the United States to participation in an international organization. In the midst of the debate, Senator Vandenberg announced in favor of the Taft proposal, and he was joined by Democrats Millard Tydings of Maryland and Allen Ellender of Louisiana. "Considerable sentiment seems to be developing for the Taft proposal," Allen Drury recorded in his diary on April 9, "and one more slap in the face may be on its way to the White House." [17]

When the vote came the following day, the Senate defeated the Taft amendment by the narrowest of margins—a tie vote. The tally followed partisan lines, two Republicans joining thirty-seven Democrats against, and thirty-four Republicans, four Democrats, and one Progressive voting for. Vice-President Harry S. Truman presided over the debates and cast a tie-breaking vote against the amendment. Just two days later, Truman would succeed to the presidency, and the proceedings in Congress in March and April, especially the close vote on the Taft amendment, left an indelible impression on the new President and the men around him.[18]

Leo Crowley spent much of his time in the first months of 1945 defending lend-lease before congressional committees, and his experiences reinforced his already deep conviction that lend-lease must henceforth be limited to the bare essentials. Crowley's views on foreign aid did not differ significantly from those of the conservatives in Congress. Like Senator Vandenberg, he felt that the United States could not sustain its enormous wartime expenditures indefinitely. "It is fundamental," he advised his staff in March, "for the world to know that the United States' resources are not limitless." A self-made man, he also applied the lessons he had learned in the business world to the more complex field of international relations. The United States would commit a grave mistake, he argued, to assume too much responsibility for solving the economic problems of other nations. It would rob them of initiative and thwart the American goal of establishing a "peaceful, prosperous, democratic world." [19]

Crowley's conservatism also left him with a very narrow view of executive authority. "My long experience in government taught me," he later wrote that "Congress made the laws." As an official of the United States government, he felt it was his responsibility to execute the laws in strict conformity with the wishes of the Congress.[20]

Since becoming Foreign Economic Administrator, Crowley had handled lend-lease within rigidly prescribed specifications. Congress had designed the act, in his view, to meet only those requirements that the allies could not provide for themselves and that were essential for military operations. In 1943 and 1944, he had eliminated from lend-lease eligibility large numbers of items he felt could no longer be justified as contributing to the war and had sharply reduced shipments of civilian supplies to Great Britain. He grew even more cautious in 1945. As the end of the European war approached, he recognized that the distinction between wartime and postwar use would become increasingly blurred. He regarded it as his solemn obligation to make certain that lend-lease was not misused, and he took special pains to approve only those requests that would contribute significantly to military operations.[21]

Crowley's encounters with congressional committees in February and March, 1945, left no doubt in his mind regarding the sentiments of Congress on lend-lease and strengthened his determination to handle it with the utmost caution. After his initial sessions with the House Foreign Affairs Committee, he emphasized to his staff that the aid program must henceforth be administered with "great care" and in a "business-like manner." During the course of the hearings he made emphatic pledges that lend-lease would be restricted to necessary war supplies, and in the weeks that followed he demonstrated a single-minded determination to honor those pledges. In late April, he reduced British requests for civilian supplies during the war against Japan by more than $800,000,000, one third of the original figure, and he drastically scaled down the French 3 (c) agreement.[22]

In the first months of the Truman administration, Crowley played an important, sometimes decisive, role in establishing policies for aid to the Soviet Union. Working through Hopkins or the Protocol Committee, Roosevelt had maintained a tight control over the Soviet program, and the special status accorded the protocols left them outside regular lend-lease procedures. In April, 1945, however, Crowley quickly moved into the vacuum left by Roosevelt's death and Hopkins' absence from Washington. He concluded that the unconditional aid policy could no longer be justified, and he assisted in the drafting of a memorandum proposing drastic alterations in the handling of lend-lease to the USSR after V-E Day.[23]

Army officials also recognized that pressure from Congress

would force reductions in assistance to Russia after the end of the European war. In a series of meetings after V-E Day, members of the Joint Munitions Allocation Board, a sub-committee of the Joint Chiefs of Staff, stressed the necessity of cutting back aid to Russia so they could defend themselves before Congress when they went to secure appropriations for fiscal year 1946.[24]

Most important, the new President himself had been intimately connected with and deeply influenced by the events in Congress. As Vice-President, he had presided over the Senate debates on the Taft amendment and had cast the tie-breaking vote against it. The first bill he signed into law (on April 17, 1945) extended lend-lease for one year with explicit prohibitions against its use for reconstruction. Truman appreciated the depth of the conviction shared by both Republicans and Democrats that lend-lease must be restricted to the minimum. Like many other observers, he saw dangerous portents in the vote on the Taft amendment. The unified stand of the Republicans, the defection of several Southern Democrats, and the abstention of numerous other Democrats, if repeated in subsequent votes, could imperil his entire program.

Inexperienced in his new position, the President was especially sensitive to his dependence upon Congress. In May and June, the House and Senate would vote on important measures authorizing American participation in the Bretton Woods program, extending the Reciprocal Trade Agreements, repealing the Johnson Act, and expanding the lending authority of the Export-Import Bank. The critical vote on American participation in the United Nations organization would follow. The State Department and White House anticipated a bitter struggle and would express no more than a cautious optimism about the outcome.[25]

Truman thus recognized that if he was to win the confidence and support of the Congress he must handle lend-lease carefully. Discussing the administration's budget requests with his Budget Director Harold Smith on April 26, the President expressed a fear that the "isolationist spirit" might

at any time "break out into the open," and admonished him
to cut back the figures for lend-lease as much as possible.
'He was very clear," Smith recorded in his diary, that if the
administration attempted to stretch its authority under
lend-lease, it would be in for "a lot of trouble." [26]

The Truman administration therefore felt compelled to
act at V-E Day, and had Soviet-American relations been most
cordial at this time it would have substantially reduced
lend-lease to Russia. Shortly after the official announcement
of the German surrender, Army and FEA officials effected
huge cuts in the British and French aid programs and repos-
sessed tons of supplies awaiting shipment to those nations for
use in Europe. The suddenness and extent of the reductions
shocked the allies, but in Washington they were accepted as
necessary and inevitable and implemented routinely as only
an intensification of the gradual reductions that had been
made since before D-Day.[27]

The Russian aid program involved special problems and
required special consideration. It had not been affected by
the general cutbacks in 1944 and 1945. The shipping crisis
of late 1944 had reduced the volume of shipments to 406,000
tons in January, 1945, the lowest monthly figure since the
spring of 1944, but from February on the volume began to
increase steadily. By April shipments had reached 540,000
tons, and schedules provided for over 700,000 tons per
month in May and June. The United States had already invited the Russians to submit requests for a fifth protocol,
and negotiations had begun in March. Thus the Truman administration had to determine not only the degree to which
shipments should be reduced, but also whether the protocol
system and the unconditional aid policy should be continued.[28]

The deepening crisis over Poland significantly influenced
its decisions. In the three weeks before V-E Day, Truman
and his advisers brought toward a conclusion the reevaluation of American policy toward Russia that had begun in
late 1944. Again, W. Averell Harriman took the lead. For
weeks, Harriman had been working unsuccessfully to imple-

ment the Yalta Agreement on Poland. The Russians, determined that the new Poland should be friendly toward the Soviet Union, interpreted the vaguely worded agreement to fit their own needs, adamantly insisting that the existing Warsaw government should form the core of a new government and that it should be altered only by the addition of several members from the outside. The British and Americans, committed to self-determination for Poland, maintained that the agreement required formation of an entirely new government, composed of representatives from all political factions. The allied conferees were unable to agree even on the selection of a commission to establish the new government, and on April 3 Harriman cabled Washington that the talks had reached the "breaking point." [29]

Several days later, the ambassador dispatched to the State Department an "urgent" request to return home for consultation. The Russians' stubborn insistence upon dealing with Poland in their own way and their activities in the Balkans had convinced him that they intended to "go forward with unilateral action in the domination of their bordering states." He feared that the ambiguity of American policy in the past and America's acceptance of the admittedly vague Yalta agreements had encouraged them to act unilaterally. "We have been hopeful that the Soviets would accept our concepts," he advised Stettinius, "whereas they on their side may have expected us to accept their concepts, particularly in areas where their interests predominate." The time had come when the United States must alter its policies and make it clear to the Russian leaders that they could not have their way on every issue.[30]

Roosevelt and the State Department rejected Harriman's initial request to return to Washington, but immediately after FDR's death the ambassador again asked permission to come home. Stalin had agreed as a gesture of good will in memory of the departed President to send Molotov to the United States to visit the new President and to attend the opening of the San Francisco Conference. Harriman seized this occasion as a pretext for returning himself so that he could inform Truman of his appraisal of Russian intentions and could propose changes in policy. This time the State Department approved his request, advising him that it would be both "desirable" and "appropriate" for him to accompany the Soviet Foreign Minister to Washington.[31]

Molotov's insistence upon flying over Soviet territory via the Alaska-Siberia route enabled Harriman to arrive in the United States several days in advance of the Russian, and he used the time to good advantage. During the interval he was everywhere, consulting with top officials in the State Department, speaking with the President privately and in the company of his cabinet, meeting with the American delegation to the San Francisco Conference. Before each forum he delivered the same ominous message: the "basic and irreconcilable difference" between the Soviet Union and the United States was the former's urge to extend its own concepts "to as large an area of the world as possible." Once the Russians had seized control of the area along their borders, he warned, they would then attempt to "penetrate the next adjacent countries." Soviet control of other nations, he emphasized, did not "mean merely influence on their foreign relations but the extension of the Soviet system with secret police, extinction of freedom of speech, etc. . . . ." The United States faced nothing less than a "barbarian invasion of Europe." [32]

Still the ambassador was not pessimistic. He expressed confidence that a "workable basis" for Russian-American relations could be established. But only if the United States changed its policies! Americans must first "abandon the illusion that for the immediate future the Soviet Government was going to act in accordance with the principles which the rest of the world held in international affairs." Therefore the administration must stop going out of its way to conciliate the Russians. "Our generosity and desire to cooperate," Harriman argued, had been "misinterpreted in Moscow . . . as an indication that the Soviet Government could do anything it wished without having any trouble with the United

States." American officials must stop being afraid of the Russians and must start indicating to them their opposition to Soviet policies.[33]

He admitted that "we cannot go to war with Russia," but added that "we must do everything we can to maintain our position as strongly as possible in Eastern Europe." He insisted that the administration had "great leverage" in opposing Russian expansionism. Soviet leaders wanted to be "respected members of world society." Above all, they desperately needed American aid for reconstruction. He repeatedly emphasized that Americans must not "overestimate Soviet strength." The Red Army was an "extraordinarily effective but disorganized mass of human beings." The Russian economy was still "fantastically backward." Thus, he concluded, the United States had "nothing to lose by standing firm on issues that were of real importance to us." [34]

Harriman found a receptive audience in Washington. Even before he had arrived home, the State Department had endorsed his views, advising President Truman on April 13 that since the "Yalta Conference the Soviet Government has taken a firm and uncompromising position on nearly every major question that has arisen in our relations." Secretary of State Stettinius viewed Soviet intransigence on Poland as a major threat to the establishment of an international organization and its acceptance by the United States Senate. Under Secretary of State Joseph C. Grew, who served as Acting Secretary during much of the summer of 1945, was increasingly concerned by the Soviet menace. In meetings of the Secretary's Staff Committee on April 20 and 21, he acted as the perfect foil for Harriman, raising questions that would draw out the ambassador's views most forcibly. With each week Grew became more certain that the Soviet Union was set upon world domination. After a sleepless night on May 19, he confided in a private memorandum his gloomy prophesy: "A future war with Soviet Russia is as certain as anything in the world is certain." [35]

President Truman quickly, indeed almost instinctively, accepted the essence of Harriman's arguments. The new President had devoted his entire political career to domestic problems; he lacked an understanding of the complexities of international relations and he had no practical experience in diplomacy. During his brief tenure as Vice-President he had not been among Roosevelt's inner circle of advisers, and he had only the most limited knowledge of the background and ingredients of the diplomatic crisis he confronted. He did not perceive the depths of Russia's fears for her postwar security or the ambiguities of the Polish agreement. Soviet actions seemed to him a clear-cut case of wrong-doing. The Russians had violated international agreements and their unjustified attempts to dominate their smaller neighbors threatened principles that must form the basis for a workable peace. The United States must stand firmly against them.

Truman's sudden and unexpected accession to the Presidency and his own personality also explain his quick acceptance of Harriman's arguments and his handling of Soviet-American relations during his first months in the White House. Necessity forced him to rely upon the advisers he had inherited from Roosevelt, and the great majority of these men were convinced by April, 1945, that a change in policy toward the USSR was long overdue. As Samuel Lubell has pointed out, moreover, unlike FDR who "radiated serene self-confidence," Truman "seemed afflicted by an inner sense of inferiority." He alternated between "crafty caution and asserting himself boldly, even brashly, as if proving something to himself. His usual instinct appeared to be to play things close to his vest, but periodically he had to unbutton his vest and thump his chest." [36]

During the first weeks of his Presidency, Truman was in a "chest-thumping" mood. At his first meeting with Harriman on April 20, he stressed that he was not afraid of the Russians and repeated three times that he intended to be tough with them. He would make no concessions from "American principles or traditions" to win Stalin's favor. Conceding that the United States could not get everything it wanted, he still felt that on "important matters" it should be able to get

"85 percent." After all, he argued, the Russians "needed us more than we needed them." [37]

At a White House meeting on April 23, just hours before the President was to confront Molotov face to face, only Secretary of War Stimson and General Marshall dissented from the Harriman position. Stimson questioned whether the Russians were not "being more realistic than we were in regard to their own security," and warned that the United States "without fully understanding how seriously the Russians took this Polish question" could be "heading into very dangerous water." Marshall, confessing ignorance of the political aspects of the Polish problem, advised that, although the military situation in Europe was "secure," the Army still desired Russian entry into the war against Japan "when it would be useful to us." They could delay, he suggested, until the United States had done all the "dirty work." He agreed with Stimson that a break with Russia could be "very serious." [38]

Harriman and Deane forcefully rebutted these objections. Russian motives did not matter, Harriman pointed out. The real issue was whether the United States was to be a party to "Soviet domination of Poland." He admitted the possibility of a break, but felt that if things were handled "properly it might be avoided." Directing his attention to General Marshall, Deane advised that a firmer policy on political issues would not affect Russian participation in the war against Japan. They would enter the war as soon as they were able "irrespective of what happened in other fields." His experiences in Moscow had convinced him, moreover, that "if we are afraid of the Russians we would get nowhere and he felt that we should be firm when we were right." [39]

The President and most of his top advisers felt that the United States must get tough with the Russians. Thus far, Truman stated, the agreements had been a "one way street and that could not continue; it was now or never." Shortly afterward, the President gave evidence of the new approach. As he later told Joseph Davies, he gave Molotov the "one-two, right to the jaw," lecturing him in stern, sometimes sharp tones, and insisting that his country carry out the Yalta arrangement on Poland. The Soviet Foreign Minister, stunned by Truman's performance, responded that he had never been talked to in such manner. "Carry out your agreements and you won't get talked to like that," Truman retorted curtly.[40]

Tough talk and a refusal to compromise were not, however, the only elements of the new American stance. Even before Truman's confrontation with Molotov, administration officials had begun contemplating drastic changes in lend-lease policy. All concurred that Roosevelt's special handling of aid to Russia could no longer be justified. The war in Europe would soon end, and Harriman pointed out that the USSR would have ample production to meet most of its requirements for the war against Japan. American generosity had not bought Russian good will or promoted closer cooperation. Indeed, mounting evidence indicated that the Russians had abused American generosity, giving or selling lend-lease supplies to Iran, Poland, Rumania, and Bulgaria, and ignoring repeated American protests against such retransfers.[41]

Harriman stressed urgent need for instituting changes in aid policy. In the past, the United States had supplied the USSR liberally and with no questions asked even though it had refused to cooperate on important matters and had taken action that threatened American interests. He cited one recent example in Rumania. At the same time the Russians were "stripping" equipment from oil installations, some of them owned by American companies, and were refusing to agree to the establishment of a tripartite commission to administer Rumanian oil, they had insisted that the United States double its shipments of petroleum under lend-lease. The Roosevelt administration's approval of these demands, in Harriman's view, had been interpreted in Moscow as a sign of weakness.[42]

The ambassador had already proposed that the United States, in addition to protesting Soviet policies, must indicate its "displeasure" in a tangible way. Lend-lease, he advised the Secretary's Staff Committee, offered a "perfect case for action." The administration could emphasize its opposition to specific Russian acts by rejecting related requests for assistance. By doing so it would demonstrate that its wishes could not be flaunted without fear of reprisal.[43]

Harriman also related lend-lease to the broader objectives of American foreign policy in Europe. As early as April 4, he had warned the State Department that unless the United States was prepared to live "in a world dominated largely by Soviet influence, we must use our economic power to assist those countries that are naturally friendly to us." The economic chaos in Western Europe, the "lack of sufficient food and employment are fertile grounds for the subtle false promises of communist agents," and the restoration of sound economies offered a powerful obstacle against communist penetration. Harriman therefore recommended a reorientation of American economic policy toward "taking care of our western allies and other areas under our responsibility first, allocating to Russia what may be left." [44]

Thus by late April, 1945, two lines of argument had converged to create irresistible pressures for modifications in Russian lend-lease policy. Crowley's FEA and the army felt that adjustments had to be made to stick within the legal limits imposed by the Lend-Lease Act and to abide by the wishes of Congress. Harriman and the State Department desired changes in order to use lend-lease to influence the future direction of Soviet-American relations. On April 24, the State Department and FEA, after consultation with Harriman, drafted a memorandum for the President setting down specific recommendations to meet both these objectives. They advised that the United States should make no future binding commitments of assistance to the USSR and should not negotiate a fifth protocol. Henceforth Soviet requests should be handled like those from other nations. The United States would furnish items essential for Soviet operations in the Far East, but it must insist upon justifications and give all requests careful study to make certain that it provided no more than the "absolute minimum require-ments."[45]

The quick agreement on the types of changes to be made obscured important differences among the various individu-als and agencies that would profoundly effect the manner in which aid to Russia was handled at V-E Day. Leo Crowley was not acquainted with the issues that had produced the crisis in Soviet-American relations nor did he relate lend-lease to them. His principal aim was to restrict shipments of supplies, and he was not concerned with the possible effect of his actions on the USSR. Within the State Department and FEA, moreover, there were individuals who had long re-sented the special treatment accorded the Russians and who welcomed an opportunity to end it.

Harriman, on the other hand, was much more cautious. He wished to terminate the unconditional aid policy to indi-cate to the Russians that they could no longer count on a privileged status and to make possible the use of lend-lease as an instrument of diplomacy. But he feared that sudden and drastic changes in policy could have an undesirable ef-fect on American relations with the USSR. He stressed to the Secretary's Staff Committee that the initial change in policy must be made tactfully and quietly without bluster or threat. The United States must make clear to the Russians its continued intention to assist them while letting them know that they would have to be more respectful of Ameri-can wishes on specific issues.[46]

Harriman joined the American delegation in San Fran-cisco on April 24, and the opening sessions of the conference underscored in his mind the extreme delicacy of the Soviet-American relationship. Even before the conference had begun, Molotov had demanded that the Russian-spon-sored Polish government be permitted to participate. The Americans and British rejected his demands, and although the Soviet Foreign Minister had subsequently agreed to defer the issue to allow work on other problems to go ahead, the U. S. delegation feared that the impasse over Poland might still wreck the conference. The Red Army's arrest of sixteen non-communist Polish leaders intensified the crisis atmosphere.[47]

On May 9, Harriman met with Stettinius and other State Department officials in the Secretary's penthouse apartment at the Fairmont Hotel to consider the Polish crisis. The ambassador proposed a new American initiative to break the deadlock. After first conferring with the exiled Polish leaders in London, he would proceed immediately to Moscow for direct talks with Stalin. He felt that the Soviet leader cared more for his relations with the allies then did Molotov and that he might prefer "on balance a partially friendly Poland to a fully controlled Poland . . . at the expense of strain in his over-all relations with the United States and Britain." Harriman would attempt to impress upon Stalin the "gravity" of the Polish problem, and would suggest a new and simplified procedure for reconstituting the Polish government, combining the initial consultations with the actual appointment of members to a new government.[48]

The Harriman-Stettinius meeting took place the day after V-E Day, and the two men related the proposed changes in lend-lease policy to the Polish crisis and Harriman's plan for resolving it. They agreed that while the ambassador was making the direct approach to Stalin "no specific acts of pressure or retaliation should be suggested or even considered. . . ." Lend-lease would be modified to place aid to Russia on the same basis as other programs and to allow the shifting of top priority to Western Europe. But this should be done as gracefully as possible and "without any hint of relationship with the Polish or other political problems with the Soviet Union." Stettinius immediately advised Acting Secretary Grew that "generally in our attitude toward the Russians with respect to lend-lease and similar matters we should be firm while avoiding any implication of a threat or any indication of political bargaining." [49]

On May 10, Harriman flew back to Washington to discuss with the President his proposal for breaking the Polish deadlock and to oversee implementation of the changes in lend-lease policy. Truman enthusiastically endorsed the idea of going directly to Stalin. Shortly afterwards, the ambassador attended a meeting at the State Department of representatives of all departments and agencies involved with the Russian aid program. The participants quickly agreed that the end of the war in Europe required immediate adjustments in lend-lease to the USSR, and directed Grew and Crowley to draft a memorandum for the President's signature incorporating the principles set down by Harriman.[50]

The memorandum, completed the next day, closely followed the draft of April 24 and provided for specific changes in policy on which all U. S. officials had long agreed. Only those fourth protocol supplies necessary for Soviet operations in the Far East or to complete industrial plants already partially delivered would be shipped. There would be no fifth protocol, and both current and future supply programs would be approved on the "basis of reasonably adequate information regarding the essentiality of Soviet military supply requirements and in the light of all competing demands for supplies in the changing military situation." [51]

But the memorandum also included an additional and important phrase that would provoke a major incident in Soviet-American relations. Supplies on order for the USSR which were not required for Far Eastern operations or to complete industrial plants would be "cut off immediately as far as physically practical." If interpreted strictly, the phrase could mean but one thing, and it did not convey Harriman's intent. A War Department official who had participated in the May 10 meeting insisted that the ambassador had said nothing about "cutting off" lend-lease for Russia, and Harriman himself noted several days later that he had intended to cut off production of new supplies but not shipments of supplies already programmed.[52]

The confusion stemmed from the failure of the May 10 meeting to define precisely how the new policy would be put into effect. The conferees at the State Department had not spelled out to what extent fourth protocol supplies ready for shipment would be withheld. Nor had Harriman made clear to those involved with lend-lease the importance of avoiding rash action. Because of the need for secrecy he had not explained to the others his plan to break the deadlock over Poland; indeed he and the President had not even taken the State Department into their confidence. The meeting thus left considerable leeway to those responsible for implementing the policy, and Crowley, who took the lead in drafting the memorandum, had firm convictions on what must be done. The words "cut off immediately" clearly reflect his steadfast determination to adhere strictly to the letter of the law.

No one detected the significance of the wording. The Secretary of State's Staff Committee approved the memorandum without qualification. Secretary of War Stimson had questioned the wisdom of a firm stand on Poland, but he had long opposed the unconditional aid policy and the proposed modifications seemed to him a long overdue reform that would put the Russians on notice that "we could no longer give them everything they wanted and they must apply and justify their needs in the same way others did." [53]

That evening, Grew and Crowley presented the memorandum to President Truman. Both wanted to be sure the President fully understood the implications of the order and would back them up. Crowley predicted a sharp response from the Russians, and he "did not want them running all over town looking for help." Apparently believing that the memorandum merely restated the ideas Harriman and Stettinius had discussed with him the day before, Truman, by his own recollection, signed it without even reading it. At the same time he approved an aide mémoire to the Russian Embassy advising that the end of the European war necessitated a readjustment of the lend-lease program and indicating the basic outline of the adjustments. There was no hint in the document that supplies on hand "would be cut off immediately." [54]

Early in the morning of May 12, the subcommittee on shipping of the Protocol Committee met to plan implementation of the President's directive. A heated debate ensued.

General Charles Wesson, the FEA representative, insisted that the memorandum should be interpreted literally. He had helped draft it and he was certain that the "Government meant business." Items aboard ship that were not intended for operations in the Far East should be removed; even ships at sea containing supplies for European operations should be brought back or the committee would have to explain why. From now on the approach should be "when in doubt, hold" instead of "when in doubt, give."

Army officials disagreed, observing that this narrow interpretation would require calling back ships at sea, unloading them and sorting all the supplies removed, and then reloading those items intended for Far Eastern operations. It was the custom, they argued, that once a shipment started it continue to its destination. Deviation from this rule would not only be a breach of propriety but would also cause disorder in American ports. But General Wesson adamantly stuck to his position, and he secured the backing of General John York, the acting chairman of the Protocol Committee, who emphasized that Congress would insist upon drastic action. The Army acquiesced, and the subcommittee issued orders to officials in Atlantic and Gulf ports to cease loading supplies for the Soviet Union and to call back ships at sea bound for Russia.[55]

FEA's zealous execution of the order produced immediate reverberations in Washington. The Russian Embassy learned what had happened from its trade officials in New York before receiving the State Department's aide mémoire, and the Soviet chargé phoned Acting Secretary Grew at once for confirmation. Grew evasively admitted no knowledge of ships being turned around, and referred his caller to Assistant Secretary Clayton.[56]

In the meantime, officials in the Soviet Supply Section of FEA, certain that the subcommittee's action did not reflect the intent of the May 10 meeting, contacted Harriman and Clayton at the State Department. The ambassador and assistant secretary were shocked, and immediately got the President's permission to countermand the subcommittee's order and to issue new orders allowing ships at sea to return to their original course, sending ships already loaded on their way, and continuing loadings of ships at berth. Clayton attempted to explain to the Russian Embassy that the cutoff had been a mistake and that it had been corrected, but he cautioned them that the law required review and readjustment of lend-lease after V-E Day, and advised that further discussions would have to be held to work out the details of a new program.[57]

The abrupt stoppage of lend-lease shipments, although quickly corrected, constituted a serious diplomatic blunder. The mere adjustment of lend-lease to the USSR after four years of generous treatment was bound to evoke protests from the Russians. American officials had on occasion warned their Russian counterparts that V-E Day would force reductions in lend-lease, but they had not emphasized the point nor had they adequately prepared the Russians in April and May for changes they knew would soon take place. The sudden, drastic, even rude, stoppage of shipments on May 12—without warning and without consultation—needlessly antagonized the Russians at a critical juncture in Soviet-American relations. It accomplished precisely what Harriman and Stettinius had attempted to avoid, giving the Russians the impression that the United States was attempting to use economic pressure to coerce them into making concessions.

The Russians made no attempt to hide their displeasure. I. A. Eremin, the Acting Chairman of the Soviet Purchasing Commission, expressed great disappointment that he had learned of the changes in policy from New York rather than from Washington. The official response of the Russian government to the State Department's aide mémoire of May 12 noted that the discontinuance of lend-lease deliveries had been "a complete surprise." The most bitter protests came from top Russian officials in Moscow. When Harry Hopkins went to Russia in late May to talk with Stalin personally about the deadlock in Russian-American relations, the Soviet leader made a special point of expressing his irritation

at the way in which the cutback of lend-lease had been handled. He understood that the end of the war in Europe required a reevaluation of the lend-lease operation and conceded that the United States had every right to reduce
shipments to Russia. But he complained bitterly about the
"unfortunate and even brutal" handling of the reduction. It
had severely hampered Soviet economic planning and terminated in a "scornful and abrupt" way an agreement made in
good faith between two allies. He warned Hopkins that if
the lend-lease cutback was "designed as pressure on the Russians in order to soften them up then it was a fundamental
mistake." If the Soviet Union were approached on a frank
and friendly basis "much could be done," but "reprisals in
any form would bring about the exact opposite effect." [58]

Hopkins, who had not attended the meetings in April at
which the new lend-lease policy had been formed, attempted
to persuade Stalin that the drastic action of May 12 did not
represent a decision of policy but had resulted from a "technical misunderstanding" by one government agency. He reaffirmed American intentions to provide full support for Soviet Far Eastern operations, and concluded by emphasizing
that there had been no attempt "or desire on the part of the
United States to use it [lend-lease] as a pressure weapon."
He observed that it would be a "great tragedy" if the "greatest achievement in cooperation" between the two nations
should end on an "unsatisfactory note." [59]

Hopkins' explanation did not satisfy the Russians. Several
weeks later, Mikoyan expressed to Harriman his regrets that
the United States had not given the USSR advance warning
of the reduction in lend-lease shipments and had not tried to
work out ahead of time an arrangement on the volume of
shipments after V-E Day. He rejected Harriman's lame attempts to defend his government, pointing out quite correctly that American authorities had requested and had been
considering Russian requirements for a fifth protocol. "The
Soviet Government could not understand how the United
States would decide to stop shipments without attempting to
reach an agreement on the matter. During the war both

sides had always been successful in reaching agreements because there was good will on both sides." Harriman could not convince Mikoyan of the correctness of his government's position, and the lend-lease cutback continued to be an irritant. Even as late as the Potsdam Conference in July, Stalin would protest to Truman the handling of lend-lease at V-E Day.[60]

Top American officials admitted then and later that they had committed a serious mistake in drastically cutting back aid to Russia. Harriman and Clayton recognized the error immediately, and attempted to do what they could to repair the damage. Stettinius later referred to the action of May 12 as an "untimely and incredible step." In his memoirs, President Truman agreed that his order had been executed in an "unfortunate" manner and had "stirred up a hornets' nest" in the Soviet Union. "The Russians complained about our unfriendly attitude. We had unwittingly given Stalin a point of contention which he would undoubtedly bring up every chance he had."[61]

Truman denied any intention of coercing the Russians. He argued that, with the war in Europe ended, the administration could no longer justify to Congress continued large-scale shipments of lend-lease. His order had applied to the British and French, as well as the Russians, and the British were "hardest hit." Still, he conceded, the reductions should have been instituted gradually in such a way that it would not have appeared as though "somebody had been deliberately snubbed."[62]

Recent revisionist writers on the origins of the Cold War have rejected Truman's defense of his actions, however, arguing that the administration was applying direct economic pressure on the Russians to force them to make concessions on Eastern Europe. Gar Alperovitz avers that the abrupt termination of aid was part of a "strategy of an immediate showdown" aimed at "reducing or eliminating Soviet influence in Europe." Barton J. Bernstein contends that the administration was using its economic power to achieve diplomatic ends, and that Grew, "presumably acting with the

President's approval, had even contrived to guarantee that curtailment would be a dramatic shock." [63]

Neither Truman's account nor the revisionist interpretation offers a satisfactory explanation for the complex events that took place at V-E Day. The revisionists either play down or ignore altogether the importance of domestic pressures in the decision to cut back assistance to the USSR. In fact, the President would have been taking a serious political risk if he had defied the mandate of Congress to restrict lend-lease to the essential military needs of the allies. Some major adjustments in policy and in the volume of shipments had to be made if he was to avoid alienating the congressional support upon which he depended for the enactment of his postwar programs. As the Washington *Post* observed, the reduction of lend-lease was an "inevitable consequence of the end of the European war." Failure to modify the Russian aid program would have subjected the FEA to "well-deserved criticism." [64]

Truman's apologia is also misleading, however, in that it overlooks the influence of diplomatic considerations. Revisionists have correctly noted a relationship between the crisis in Soviet-American relations and the handling of lend-lease. In late April, 1945, the Truman administration carried forward to a conclusion the reevaluation of American aid policy proposed by Standley as early as 1942 and pressed relentlessly by Harriman since the beginning of 1944. Termination of unconditional aid, while necessary to satisfy Congress, also signified a fundamental change in attitudes and policy toward the USSR. Truman and his advisers were determined to show the Russians that the United States was not weak and irresolute and to put them on notice that they could not challenge American interests with impunity. They abandoned the protocol system to allow the use of lend-lease as a diplomatic weapon.

Nevertheless, the revisionist argument oversimplifies the complex relationship between lend-lease and American aims in Eastern Europe and distorts the sophisticated strategy developed by Harriman. The ambassador was not attempting to apply immediate pressure on the Soviet Union to make concessions on political issues. On the contrary, he wished to avoid any action that would produce a premature showdown or come as a "dramatic shock." He wanted the changes made in lend-lease as unobtrusively as possible and "without any hint of relationship with the Polish or other political problems with the Soviet Union" in order to execute the plan he hoped would resolve the impasse over Poland and bring the San Francisco Conference to a successful conclusion. Thus FEA's over-zealous execution of the May 11 directive had just the opposite effect he intended.

Poor planning and bureaucratic confusion account in large part for the blunder. Franklin Roosevelt's failure to establish clearly defined policies for lend-lease after V-E Day and to prepare the Russians for the changes that had to be made left his successor in a most difficult position. Harriman had taken the lead in lend-lease policy-making after his return from Moscow in April, but at the critical May 10 meeting he did not spell out precisely how the changes should be made and he did not make clear to those responsible for implementing policy the necessity of caution. President Truman was ultimately responsible for both the shaping and execution of policy. But his failure to examine carefully and think through the implications of the May 11 directive gave considerable latitude to lesser officials. Thus the Acting Secretary of State and the Foreign Economic Administrator were left in control of events. Neither Grew nor Crowley was aware of the delicate relationship between lend-lease and the crisis at San Francisco. Both men were arch-conservatives who had no desire to conciliate the Russians. Crowley was also imbued with a narrow concept of executive authority and was obsessed with a determination to cut back lend-lease as much as possible.

The result—the sudden cancellation of shipments on May 12—contributed to the widening rift between the allies. It did not noticeably alter the Russian stance on Poland which was already set by the requirements of Soviet foreign policy, nor did it prevent the arrangement in late May of at least a temporary solution to the Polish problem. But it did needlessly provoke the Russians. When combined with Truman's dressing down of Molotov on April 23, it aroused deep and not altogether false suspicions in the Kremlin that Truman was abandoning Roosevelt's policies. And it gave Stalin a splendid opportunity, which he exploited to the fullest, to accuse the United States of violating its agreements and acting in bad faith.

Chapter 8

WITHOUT "FANFARE" OR "REGRET"

THE END OF LEND-LEASE TO RUSSIA

HARRIMAN HAD PROPOSED AN ABANDONMENT OF

the unconditional aid policy at V-E Day primarily to allow a more flexible handling of lend-lease to the USSR and to make possible its use as an instrument of diplomacy. During May and June, 1945, he persisted in trying to relate lend-lease shipments to political goals. In preparation for the direct approach to Stalin on the Polish deadlock, he developed a broad and liberal interpretation of the May 11 memorandum tó govern future assistance to Russia, and when talks with the Soviet leader produced an acceptable compromise he advocated a generous response to the Soviet Union's additional requests for lend-lease in the war against Japan.

Harriman's attempts to base the volume of shipments on Soviet willingness to cooperate in the solution of political problems evoked an unenthusiastic reaction in Washington. Throughout the summer of 1945, the Truman administration was most sensitive to the rising mood of retrenchment in the United States and to Congress' continuing insistence that lend-lease must be restricted to a minimum. The military and civilian officials responsible for handling lend-lease were not inclined to respond generously to Soviet requests for aid, and neither the Joint Chiefs of Staff nor the State Department would provide compelling strategic or diplomatic arguments to offset domestic political limitations. Thus from V-E Day to V-J Day the volume of shipments to Russia gradually declined, and the sudden end of the war against Japan in August brought the immediate termination of all lend-lease programs.

Sometime in the period between late April and V-E Day, President Truman retreated a step from the initial aggressiveness and rigidity he had displayed toward the Russians and especially toward Molotov. He may have been influenced, as Gar Alperovitz has suggested, by the knowledge that the atomic bomb might soon give the United States a powerful, perhaps irresistible, weapon to employ against the USSR. He may have been moved by complaints in the American press that the United States was not doing all it could to establish friendly relations with the Soviet Union.[1]

Most likely, Truman's change of tactics reflects the growing influence of more moderate advisers. Between April 27 and May 13, the President conferred frequently with both Joseph Davies and Harry Hopkins, the two Roosevelt aides who had been the most consistent and influential advocates of a conciliatory policy toward Russia. Truman appears to have been impressed by their arguments. He admitted to Davies that he too was deeply concerned by the progressive deterioration in Soviet-American relations, and he even conceded some inner misgivings about his earlier "toughness." He listened "intently" to Davies' suggestions that he give the Russians the "benefit of the doubt, treat them with tolerance, and try to understand their point of view." He agreed with the former ambassador's warning that the State Department was "conditioned" in hostility toward the USSR, and he indicated that this would change. Davies left the White House on April 30 convinced that the President was "honestly trying to see both sides and to do the one thing that is right."[2]

Both Davies and Hopkins impressed upon Truman the dangers of aligning American policy too closely with Churchill and further arousing Soviet suspicions that the Western allies were "ganging up" on them. Both stressed the importance of personal contact with Stalin in resolving the Polish and other problems. Without consulting the State Department, the President sounded out the two men on their willingness to undertake a mission to Moscow preparatory to a big three meeting. Although desperately ill, Hopkins agreed to go, and when Harriman returned from San Francisco on May 10 his proposal to make a new initiative to Stalin on the Polish question merged with the upcoming Hopkins visit to Russia.[3]

Thus in the interim between V-E Day and the completion of the Hopkins mission in early June, Truman adopted a more cautious and restrained approach toward the Russians. Apprehensive for the success of the San Francisco Conference, hopeful that the Polish crisis might yet be settled by negotiation, still anxious to fulfill Roosevelt's dreams of postwar cooperation with the Soviet Union, he cast aside the tough rhetoric he had employed earlier and carefully disassociated himself from the increasingly hard line advocated by Churchill. Truman did not play a direct role in handling aid to Russia after V-E Day, but the policies developed within the administration reflected his moderation.[4]

In a series of meetings between May 12 and May 15, Harriman took the lead in establishing the broadest possible interpretation of the President's May 12 directive on post-V-E Day lend-lease to the USSR. The ambassador was apparently anxious to repair the damage done by the drastic cutback of aid at V-E Day. He may have wished to create a climate conducive to the success of Hopkins' mission. He probably recognized that if the directive was interpreted rigidly lend-lease could not be converted into an effective instrument of dipolmacy.

Whatever the reason, Harriman insisted that the United States should carry out in full the commitments already made to support Soviet Far Eastern operations. The May 12 directive provided that after V-E Day the United States would be obligated to ship only those supplies included in Annex III to the fourth protocol (a list of items the Russians had requested specifically for use in the Far East) and equipment to complete industrial plants already partially delivered. On May 12, the protocol subcommittee had stopped further loading and shipment of supplies not included in these categories. In reversing the subcommittee's orders, Harriman and Clayton had allowed the dispatch of ships already loaded and had allowed ships at berth to receive their full cargo and proceed to the Soviet Union. To fulfill the provisions of the President's directive, however, they had ordered that no additional ships should be loaded in Atlantic ports until the cargo had been screened and items intended for Europe separated from those intended for the Far East.[5]

At a meeting of the full Protocol Committee on May 15, Crowley had attempted to apply the same screening procedure to West Coast ports, arguing that about 15 percent of the tonnage scheduled for shipment during May and June consisted of regular protocol items not included in Annex III. Harriman demanded a more flexible policy, however, allowing all ships scheduled to depart from the West Coast to sail on the premise that the route was *prima facie* evidence that the cargo was to be used in the war against Japan.

Harriman also fought Crowley's attempts to change the May 12 ruling on industrial equipment. The Foreign Economic Administrator argued that Congress now demanded drastic restrictions on aid to Russia, and that it would be illegal and "silly" to furnish on lend-lease supplies necessary to complete industrial plants under construction since these plants would not be operational before the end of the war against Japan. Up to this point, he maintained, the United States had been "pretty fair" in approving questionable Russian orders for industrial equipment; from now on it should "stick strictly to the rules of the game." Harriman countered that stopping the flow of industrial goods could hold back Soviet production, and if the amount of money involved was not too large the materiel should go ahead. Again he won his point, the May 15 meeting agreeing to stand by the original directive.[6]

The ambassador's liberal interpretation of the May 12 memorandum softened appreciably the immediate impact of the changes in lend-lease policy. Ironically, because shipments from the West Coast made up a large part of the tonnage scheduled for May, deliveries to the USSR totaled more than 768,000 tons, the largest volume exported in any single month during the war. Shipments in June fell off to 329,000 tons. But the United States still completed most of its original commitments to support Soviet Far Eastern operations, and the tonnage furnished from July 1, 1944, to June 30, 1945, exceeded fourth protocol schedules by 10 percent.[7]

Shortly after V-E Day, the administration also invited the Russians to submit additional requests for the war against Japan, and Harriman again urged the establishment of a reasonable procedure for handling them. The May 12 directive had stated that future Russian requirements would be approved only if they were supported by information justifying need. At the meeting on May 15, however, the ambassador recalled that it had taken the British more than a year to learn how to back up a request and advised that there was little time to teach the Russians. Often, he observed, Soviet supply officials did not have the type of information needed, and when they did they shared it only with the greatest reluctance. The United States should be firm in asking for justification, Harriman concluded, but it should not make it an absolute prerequisite for approval. Any information obtained from the Russians could be supplemented by the recommendations of the Military Mission in Moscow and by information possessed by officials in Washington.[8]

As a direct result of the Hopkins-Stalin talks in late May and early June, Harriman urged further concessions to the Russians. The discussions ranged over the entire array of issues dividing the two nations, but in the opening sessions Stalin made a special point of complaining about the manner in which lend-lease had been cut back. The action had alarmed the Soviet Union, he protested, and had conveyed

the distinct impression that the United States had "perceptibly cooled once it became obvious that Germany was defeated." At that point, Harriman, who had returned to Moscow before Hopkins' arrival, attempted to smooth the path
for subsequent discussions by proposing that he, Molotov,
and Mikoyan might discuss lend-lease problems at greater
length.[9]

The ambassador subsequently conferred with the Russian
officials on May 29 and again on June 11. At their first meeting, Mikoyan presented a detailed list of Soviet requirements
for the second half of 1945, requesting 1,000,000 tons of supplies originally included in the fourth protocol but not delivered as a result of the V-E Day reduction and an
additional 570,000 tons of new items for use in the Far
East.[10]

In both sessions, the Russians placed special emphasis on
their need for the undelivered fourth protocol supplies, especially the $300,000,000 worth of industrial equipment
originally designed to be financed under the abortive 3 (c)
agreement. They argued forcefully that Annex III had not
been intended to meet all of their demands for the war
against Japan but would only supplement the protocol. The
undelivered industrial equipment was vital to their economic planning for the war against Japan. The unilateral
American decision to cancel shipment of this equipment
would hamper their military operations.

Harriman vigorously defended American actions, recalling
that Acheson had repeatedly warned Soviet officials that industrial equipment could not be shipped after V-E Day in
the absence of an agreement on finance. "If the present situation was not satisfactory to the Soviet Union," the ambassador argued, "it was the Soviet Union's own doing." Mikoyan
conceded that the Russians had been given vague notice that
V-E Day would affect the supply program. But he also
pointed out that the United States had invited the USSR to
submit requests for a fifth protocol, thus suggesting that it
did not plan to curtail shipments after the end of the war
against Germany. He had assumed that the credit negotia-

tions had not been terminated, but had only lapsed temporarily. And he protested vigorously that shipment of industrial equipment had been canceled without prior notice and the Russians had not been given the opportunity to make alternative arrangements for financing them. Harriman expressed regret for the *misunderstanding,* and the series of talks concluded in "good humor" on June 11 after becoming "somewhat strained." [11]

Although he would not admit American responsibility for the lend-lease impasse in his talks with Molotov and Mikoyan, the ambassador seems to have appreciated the legitimacy of some of their complaints. In addition, the cordial atmosphere established during the Hopkins-Stalin talks encouraged him to look favorably upon the Russians' new requests for lend-lease. The discussions, aptly characterized by William L. Neumann as the "fullest, frankest, and possibly the friendliest Russo-American exchange to take place before the Cold War mood settled down over both capitals," had by early June begun to produce important results. Without sacrificing his ultimate control over events in Poland, Stalin had made concessions, allowing the participation of Poles outside the Warsaw government in consultations to form a new government and agreeing to assign them certain ministries. At the same time, the Russian leader, as a result of Hopkins' intercession, withdrew his original insistence upon a veto to prevent the United Nations Security Council from discussing an issue involving one of its members. [12]

Truman and his advisers recognized that a satisfactory solution to the Polish issue still depended upon the good faith of the Russian government, but they accepted the Hopkins-Stalin compromise as the best that could be achieved and they were relieved that at long last the Polish problem might be eliminated as a major issue. American officials were elated by Stalin's concession on the veto since it removed the last major obstacle to a successful conclusion of the work of the San Francisco Conference. The Hopkins-Stalin discussions thus revived hopes that a successful ending might yet be written to the story of the wartime alliance. "The mood in the White House became briefly blithe," Herbert Feis has written, and even Under Secretary Grew admitted that the picture was brighter than it had been for months.[13]

Encouraged by the accomplishments of the Hopkins mission and eager to nurture the growth of compromise and conciliation, both Harriman and General Deane urged officials in Washington to react favorably to the new Soviet requests for lend-lease. Deane accepted Mikoyan's assertion that part of the fourth protocol supplies had been intended for use in the Far East. After carefully studying the new lists, the general concluded that most of the supplies would contribute to operations against Japan, and he recommended their shipment even though the Russians had not provided detailed justification. "We definitely believe," he cabled the War Department on June 8, "that it is to the United States' interest to make certain that our support is timely and effective even at the risk of supplying the Soviet Union some items over and above the needs which could be fully justified." [14]

Harriman vigorously backed Deane's recommendations and added new ones of his own. He advised the State Department that Mikoyan had been most "reasonable" in their discussions, and he encouraged them to try to resolve some of the lend-lease problems that had developed after V-E Day. Specifically, he proposed that the Russians not be required to pay cash for industrial equipment unshipped at the end of the European war, but that some form of credit arrangement be worked out to finance these items. In addition, he encouraged the opening of negotiations for a new 3 (c) agreement to cover lend-lease supplies not delivered at V-J Day.[15]

The climate in the United States was not favorable to Harriman's proposals. During May and June, domestic pressures for retrenchment mounted. Despite official insistence that the nation must remain mobilized for war, the spirit of reconversion gained strength. Small numbers of troops were already beginning to return home from Europe. Broadway again glittered. The government dropped the midnight curfew, the ban on horseracing, and restrictions against use of the beaches, and it authorized the resumption of whiskey production for one month. Businessmen and consumers impatiently demanded the relaxation of government controls on the economy and the production of more items for civilian use, and in mid-May Director of War Mobilization and Reconversion Fred Vinson reported that the pressures had become so "heavy" that he had to meet "at least some of the demands." Shortly afterwards, the War Production Board announced the revocation of seventy-three orders prohibiting or limiting the manufacture of civilian goods. Supply officials already confronted severe shortages in steel, textiles, and foodstuffs, and the concessions to business, when combined with the strains on supplies and shipping resulting from the redeployment of troops from Europe to the Pacific, made it more and more difficult to secure priorities for the production of items for lend-lease.[16]

At the same time, congressmen insisted upon the curtailment of government expenditures and the reduction of taxes and forced the administration to exercise the greatest care in handling its aid programs. When Acting Secretary of State Grew had revealed on May 14 that lend-lease shipments were continuing to Russia and to other European nations that had not declared war on Japan, a group of Republican Senators accused the President of a "breach of faith with Congress." Senator Styles Bridges of New Hampshire reminded his colleagues that both the Senate and the House would have written major changes into the Lend-Lease Act in the spring had they not trusted Crowley's pledges that aid would be limited to military uses. Bridges, Taft, and Harlan J. Bushfield of South Dakota all protested that shipments to the USSR, France, and the Netherlands violated these promises. Off the floor of the Senate, Taft complained that most of the supplies being sent these nations were really for "rehabilitation purposes," and he, along with the other senators, expressed deep resentment at the administration's "constant attempt to stretch lend-lease beyond its original purpose."[17]

Several weeks later, House Republicans repeated the same charges. In a letter to President Truman (subsequently released to the press), the five members of the House Foreign Affairs Committee who had sponsored the February amendment to the Lend-Lease Act expressed their grave concern that the administration was abusing the authority granted in the act, and warned that any attempt to provide postwar aid to the allies through the lend-lease program would have "disastrous consequences." [18]

The Republican protests deeply concerned Truman and his advisers. During May and June, the new administration faced a stern test in Congress. Conscious of the need for congressional support, the President went out of his way to conciliate leaders of both parties. While his agents engaged in "frenzied lobbying" on the Hill (the words of Dean Acheson, one of the lobbyists) Truman invited Taft and former President Herbert Hoover to visit with him in the White House, and encouraged Democrat Kenneth McKellar of Tennessee, the powerful chairman of the Senate Committee on Appropriations, to sit in on cabinet meetings.[19]

Recognizing the importance Congress attached to lend-lease, the administration shaped its post-V-E Day programs with the greatest caution. Responding to the criticisms of House Republicans, the FEA announced that it would not implement the 3 (c) agreements already concluded with France, Belgium, and the Netherlands. The army drastically reduced munitions shipments to Great Britian, and Crowley cut back the 1945 allocations for British non-munitions more than one third. By the end of May, British supply officials in Washington were warning London that a "wave of economy" had swept over the American capital, and on May 28 Churchill cabled to Truman an urgent appeal for aid, protesting that the supply "machine has come to a standstill." [20]

Because the Soviet Union had not yet declared war on Japan, the administration handled the Russian aid program with especial care. Oscar Cox and Leo Crowley agreed in mid-May that future press releases should emphasize aid to Britain to divert attention from the Soviet program. Truman readily assented to Budget Director Harold Smith's proposal that funds for the USSR be "hidden" along with funds for France, Belgium, and the Netherlands in a contingency fund in the 1945 budget. The Russian figure was "extremely important," the President remarked, and if it "stood out" it might "provoke a lot of argument in Congress." The administration allocated only $936,000,000 for Russia, and FEA officials expressed some reservations whether Congress, "in its present mood," would leave in that full amount.[21]

The budget had just been submitted to Congress when the Deane-Harriman recommendations reached Washington, and administration officials were understandably reluctant to act expeditiously. After two weeks Harriman had still received no reply, and with the compromises on Poland and the UN voting formula completed, he became most concerned with the delay. On June 21, he dispatched an urgent, personal message to Hopkins imploring him to use his influence to secure "immediate action" on the Russian requests.[22]

Harriman's appeal was of little effect. Upon returning from the talks with Stalin, the feeble Hopkins removed himself from active involvement in government. The Protocol Committee approved the Harriman-Deane proposals. But without Hopkins' influence, the small, informal body that had controlled Soviet aid policies under Roosevelt became little more than an implementing organ whose sole function was to put into effect policies established elsewhere. With the termination of the protocol system in May, responsibility for developing lend-lease policies for the USSR passed to Crowley's FEA and to the Joint Chiefs of Staff, both of whom took a highly nationalistic and narrowly legalistic approach toward all foreign requests for assistance.[23]

Crowley paid no heed to the recommendations of Harriman and the Protocol Committee, instead continuing his crusade to limit all lend-lease shipments to the absolute minimum. The Foreign Economic Administrator firmly rejected the Soviet request for shipment of fourth protocol industrial equipment held back at V-E Day. For years, he argued, the United States had given the USSR everything it had re-

quested, including over $1 billion worth of industrial sup-
plies. Now that the war in Europe had ended, Russian production facilities should be adequate to meet most of the
nation's essential needs, and the United States should supply
only those items that could be shown to be necessary for actual field operations against Japan. The shipment of anything else would contribute to Russian reconstruction and
would be "contrary to the spirit of the Lend-Lease Act." [24]
Crowley also rejected Harriman's proposal to arrange credits
to finance the industrial equipment that could not be justified as essential for military use in the Far East. If the Russians wanted this equipment, they would have to pay cash
for it; otherwise it would be diverted to other uses.[25] Crowley and his aides were less than energetic in procuring supplies for programs that had been approved. Within the Foreign Economic Administration, General York complained to
Hopkins in early July, there was a "marked dragging of
feet." [26]

The State Department backed the Foreign Economic Administrator. Acting Secretary Grew tersely summed up the
department's attitude toward aid to Russia in a report to
Stettinius on May 31: "We are going to give very little without strings attached and we will use such shipments for our
own ends and not just for Russian ends." The success of the
Hopkins mission and the imminent completion of the San
Francisco Conference apparently did nothing to modify this
view. Grew endorsed Crowley's stand on industrial equipment. He also advised Harriman that negotiations would not
be reopened on a 3 (c) agreement as long as the USSR was
not actively engaged in the war against Japan.[27]

Admiral William D. Leahy, who as the President's personal chief of staff served as a chairman of the Joint Chiefs,
took the lead in the formulation of policies for military lend-
lease, and like Crowley, he was generally unsympathetic to
allied requests for aid. A veteran of over forty years' service
in the U. S. Navy, an austere and secretive individual with a
passion for anonymity and a penchant for bluntness, the admiral was a staunch nationalist who equally distrusted the

British and Russians. While Chief of Naval Operations, he had been compelled to apologize to the Soviet embassy for his public remark that the Russian people were "virtually slaves" to the communist party organization. In the summer of 1945, he was a persistent critic of Churchill, whom he accused of being more concerned with advancing British interests than with preserving the peace, and of Stalin, whom he privately described (according to Joseph Davies) as both a "liar and a crook."[28]

Leahy saw nothing to gain by liberally supplying the allies, and like most of the American military he found good reason to avoid doing anything that would strengthen them militarily. Alarmed that some individuals within the administration were "desirous of disbursing great sums of lend-lease money on projects that could have no bearing whatever on the prosecution of that part of the war which still remained," the admiral, in collaboration with Crowley, worked vigorously in June and July of 1945 to restrict lend-lease as much as possible.[29]

Neither Leahy nor his colleagues on the Joint Chiefs of Staff could find compelling strategic or political grounds for generous support to Soviet Far Eastern operations. Indeed, by mid-June, Leahy and Admiral Ernest King, the Chief of Naval Operations, harbored fears that the Russians might use intervention in the war against Japan to strengthen their position in Manchuria and elsewhere on the Asian mainland. Revised estimates of Japan's capacity to resist, plus the near completion of the atomic bomb, afforded some hope that the war might be ended before the USSR could intervene. In the event this did not occur, American military planners were confident by mid-June that the mere shock effect of a Soviet declaration of war would be enough to compel Japan to surrender.[30]

In short, although military planning for the war against Japan was still shrouded in uncertainties, the importance of the Soviet Union had been downgraded considerably. The military went ahead drafting contingency plans for an invasion of the Japanese home islands, but they agreed that Russian participation in the invasion would not be required. A Soviet declaration of war might still be desirable, but in Admiral King's words, it was not "indispensable." The cost of defeating Japan might be greater, but King, Leahy, and Arnold concurred that the United States could "go it alone" if necessary. Top administration officials had long agreed that the Russians would enter the war to advance their own interests, regardless of what the United States did or failed to do. Thus there was no need, King advised the President on June 18 for the United States to "beg them" to intervene, and Leahy opposed even encouraging them.[31]

While President Truman was on the West Coast attending the closing sessions of the San Francisco Conference, the J. C. S. handed down a most restrictive decision on the Soviet requests for lend-lease. The Russians had formulated, and Harriman and Deane had endorsed, a supply program to cover the entire period from June to December, 1945. The Joint Chiefs, determined to limit aid to Russia, approved for shipment only those supplies on the list that could be procured and loaded aboard ship before August 31, 1945. Additional requisitions would be accepted for planning only.[32]

The administration took an equally rigid position on lend-lease to Britain. Acheson and Will Clayton of the State Department and Vinson, who had replaced Morgenthau as Secretary of the Treasury in May, viewed Churchill's appeal with considerable sympathy, and urged that aid to Britain could be justified as contributing to the maintenance of stability in occupied Europe. But at a conference on July 2, Leahy and Crowley advised the "lend-lease enthusiasts" that shipment of any supplies not essential for operations in the Far East would be a "plain violation of the letter and spirit of the Lend-Lease Act." When the President returned to Washington, they secured from him a directive limiting further shipment of lend-lease munitions to Britain to those requirements deemed essential by the J. C. S. Thus Crowley and the Joint Chiefs, who shared a dislike for and distrust of the Russians, who could see no good reason to provide substantial aid to the USSR or to the other allies, and who were determined to stick to the letter of the Lend-Lease Act, rejected all proposals to use lend-lease for anything but essential military operations.[33]

Some U.S. officials anticipated that the Big Three conference at Potsdam in July might lead to a reopening of discussions on assistance to the USSR. General Deane expected the Soviet Chiefs of Staff to bring with them another request for the items turned down earlier. General York, betraying a touch of the zeal for aid to Russia which had long characterized the Protocol Committee, expressed hope that the meeting might clear up once and for all the confused status of lend-lease to the Soviet Union. "We must emerge from this conference with a re-vitalized directive which will require all procurement agencies to cease procrastinating and move ahead on providing aid for Russia," he advised Hopkins in early July.[34]

But nothing occurred at Potsdam to alter the lend-lease policies established in June. The Russians did not raise the matter themselves, and no American official, during or after the conference, challenged the existing policy. Harriman was preoccupied with other matters and seems to have lost interest. The sessions in Germany only reinforced Leahy's already profound distrust of Stalin and the Soviet Union. Truman continued to take a middle path between Leahy and Davies. The President developed a certain respect and liking for Stalin, and he still cherished hopes that the United States and the USSR might be able to work together. On the other hand, the conference did not resolve any of the issues dividing the two allies, and the protracted and inconclusive discussions seem to have confirmed Truman's belief that Soviet-American cooperation could best be achieved by standing firm on principle and resisting Russian demands rather than by generosity and conciliation. The successful testing of the atomic bomb while the conference was in session probably encouraged the President's belief that he was dealing with the Russians from a position of strength.

The experience of Great Britain suggests that a proposal to reconsider policies for aid to Russia, had it been made,

would certainly have been rejected. During the second week
of the Potsdam Conference, Churchill appealed directly to
Truman for help, warning that British munitions stocks had
been reduced to the "vanishing point." The President sym-
pathized, but stood firmly by the J. C. S. policy, advising the
Prime Minister that he must "abide strictly by the law." He
refused even to permit the use of lend-lease to equip British
occupation forces in Europe.[35]

The policies established by Crowley and the Joint Chiefs
in June remained in effect throughout the summer of 1945
and brought further cutbacks in the Russian aid program.
Shipments to the USSR during July increased slightly over
June (to 408,000 tons), but still amounted to only about half
the tonnage in May. More important, both the army and the
FEA planned sharp reductions for the future. Of the 570,000
tons of new items requested by the Russians in May, the
War Department approved only 185,000 tons, one half of the
total to be shipped during July and the remainder later if
the military situation required it. By August 2 the FEA had
diverted to other supply programs over $37,000,000 worth of
industrial equipment originally scheduled for delivery to the
Soviet Union.[36]

At the same time, the State Department and FEA began to
take action against Russian retransfers of lend-lease supplies
to third countries. Since mid-1944, American officials had
protested to the Russians without satisfaction, and the problem became acute in early 1945 when reports reached Washington of increased Soviet aid to the Lublin government in
Poland and the Tito faction in Yugoslavia. The State Department studied the retransfer issue in May in conjunction
with the general reevaluation of Soviet aid policies, and in
June Grew advised Harriman that future Russian retransfers
made without consulting the United States would be considered as evidence that the Soviet Union no longer needed the
item transferred and shipments of that particular item would
be halted. The FEA first implemented the new policy in
July. When it was learned that the Russians had agreed to
sell Poland 3,000 tons of tobacco, supply officials immedi-

ately canceled a Soviet request for the shipment of over four million tons of tobacco under lend-lease.[37]

Then, in the first two weeks of August, a rapid sequence of events suddenly ended the war against Japan and brought the termination of the lend-lease program. On August 6 an American aircraft dropped the first atomic bomb on the Japanese city of Hiroshima. Two days later, the Soviet Union declared war on Japan, and on August 9, as the Red Army drove into Manchuria, a second nuclear bomb leveled the city of Nagasaki. At 7:30 on the morning of August 10, American monitors picked up a broadcast over Radio Tokyo indicating the desire of the Japanese government to surrender.

At the first signs of Japan's capitulation, officials within the Truman administration began preparations to liquidate lend-lease. On August 10, Crowley advised the heads of each branch of FEA to begin a review of their requisitions to be ready to cancel those not needed after V-J Day. The following day, the Foreign Economic Administrator called a special staff meeting. Advising his aides that he did not know when V-J Day would come, he proposed to them nevertheless general guidelines to be followed when the announcement was made. Lend-lease munitions should be shipped after the Japanese surrender only upon authorization of the Joint Chiefs of Staff. Vessels loaded at V-J Day should be dispatched, but no further loading should take place. Colonel William McChesney Martin, the former "boy wonder" of Wall Street and president of the New York Stock Exchange who had replaced General York as executive officer of the Protocol Committee in late July, subsequently issued a directive to all departments and agencies applying these principles to the Soviet aid program.[38]

Early in the evening of August 14, Washington learned that the Japanese had accepted the allies' surrender terms. President Truman made clear that the official proclamation of V-J Day would await Japan's formal signature of the documents, but the certainty that the war had ended quickened moves to halt the flow of lend-lease supplies. On August 15, Crowley announced at a press conference that he would act

"immediately" to "adjust" lend-lease operations to a "realistic" basis. He observed that it would be only "fair" to continue small shipments for a brief period to those nations
helping to supply American forces stationed in Europe, but
he made clear that there was "little justification" for other
programs (including the Russian) and he promised to terminate them "as rapidly as possible." The following day, Martin advised the Soviet Purchasing Commission that upon the
official notice of V-J Day, loading of ships would be stopped
and no further ships would be berthed for loading. Only
those ships that had been loaded and passed port clearance
would be allowed to sail.[39]

On the morning of August 17 Leahy, Crowley, Vinson,
and John Snyder, the new Director of War Mobilization and
Reconversion, met at the White House to discuss the future
of lend-lease. Of those present, only Vinson urged the continuation of shipments—to help preserve stability and to
prevent the spread of communism in Europe. Leahy and
Crowley pressed vigorously for the immediate termination of
all programs, and although a final decision was not reached
at the conference, the admiral left the White House convinced that the President would follow the course he had advised.[40]

Leahy's assessment was correct, for later in the same day
the President approved a memorandum drafted in FEA ordering a rapid liquidation of lend-lease. "In order that the
best faith may be observed toward Congress and the Administration protect itself against any charges of misuse of Congressional authorization," the directive provided that upon
the cessation of hostilities against Japan no new contracts
would be made for lend-lease supplies unless approved by
the Joint Chiefs of Staff. Countries with 3 (c) agreements
could accept goods under contract and awaiting shipment;
countries without them could take over such "pipeline" supplies and pay for them under terms approved by the United
States.[41]

Recalling the confusion that had surrounded the handling
of lend-lease after V-E Day and the ill will that had been

provoked by it, numerous officials in the week from August
12 to August 19 issued warnings for caution and moderation
in liquidating the lend-lease program. General Spalding advised Hazard that the administration should move "less vigorously" in terminating aid to Russia because of the "great
stir" in Moscow following the May reductions. Oscar Cox
urged Crowley that the United States should consult closely
with foreign governments well in advance of the stoppage of
shipments and should try to work out with them mutually
satisfactory arrangements to finance supplies in the "pipeline." State Department officials cautioned the secretary that
a coordinated position must be established among all departments and agencies before action was taken.[42]

In its haste to end the lend-lease program, however, the
administration ignored these sound precautions. Again there
was confusion among the various agencies. Again the United
States acted without consulting representatives of allied governments. Again American abruptness stirred up considerable antagonism among the allies.

The Protocol Committee halted loading of Soviet vessels
even before the President had issued a statement of policy.
Anticipating an imminent American decision on lend-lease,
Soviet supply officials had on August 16 hastily dispatched
five partially loaded ships. Early in the morning of August
17 Martin advised FEA that the Russians would probably
continue to try to get to sea every possible item before the
United States began unloading ships and repossessing supplies, and indicated that he saw no alternative but to stop
loadings immediately. The appropriate orders were issued,
and by nine o'clock all loading had been halted.[43]

Crowley canceled these orders at mid-morning, advising
Martin that shipments should continue until V-J Day. After
talking with the President, however, and learning that V-J
Day would be postponed until early September, the Foreign
Economic Administrator, apparently with Truman's ap-
proval, reinstated the orders to begin stopping shipments to
Russia at once. To minimize confusion and congestion in
ports, cargo needed to complete ships at berth would be

loaded. But by mid-afternoon, August 17, all other loading had been halted.[44]

The termination of shipments to the Soviet Union antedated by several days a final decision on policy for aid to other lend-lease nations. On August 20, the Foreign Economic Administration notified representatives of allied governments that all lend-lease programs would be stopped immediately, and the following day the Army cut off further shipment of lend-lease munitions. But when the British, especially hard hit by the abruptness and decisiveness of the action, protested bitterly, the administration agreed to relax the original order, permitting continued shipment of non-munitions and the use of lend-lease funds to cover shipping costs until the official declaration of V-J Day.[45]

The Russians immediately complained to FEA that they were being treated unfairly, and Crowley subsequently agreed to a modification of the August 17 order permitting Soviet vessels to resume loading of non-munitions and allowing repairs on Soviet freighters under lend-lease until V-J Day. On September 2, the day after the Japanese had signed the document of surrender aboard the USS *Missouri,* the administration finally ended all lend-lease shipments. Five partially loaded Soviet vessels were given sufficient additional cargo to attain stability; a sixth was half loaded and permitted to sail. Two Russian ships remained on West Coast ports for repairs. As the wartime aid program came to an unceremonious end, the New York *Times* reported, there was "neither fanfare over its accomplishments nor official regret at its passing." [46]

The termination of lend-lease at V-J Day had a severe impact on those allied nations which since 1941 had depended to at least some degree on American supplies. The abrupt, unilateral manner in which the decision was made and executed accorded poorly with the spirit of international cooperation to which the United States was committed and aroused considerable hostility in several allied capitals.[47]

At the time and later, President Truman defended his

actions on the grounds that lend-lease was exclusively an instrument of war and therefore had to be terminated once hostilities ceased. Recent revisionist historians have rejected Truman's explanation, arguing that it was only a pretext for a deliberate and calculated act of political pressure. The administration, they contend, cut off the wartime aid program completely and abruptly to force the allies, both Britain and Russia, to seek other forms of assistance which the United States could make conditional on major political and economic concessions.[48]

The termination of the Soviet aid program several days in advance of other programs provoked some speculation at the time that the administration was attempting to apply pressure to the Russians. John Hazard of FEA remarked shortly after the Japanese surrender that, although a number of reasons might be advanced to justify the early stoppage of shipments to the USSR, the action had been taken "deliberately" and was "probably" part of a "general squeeze" on the Russians. Hazard's surmise may have been correct, but there is no other evidence to support it. And the decision within several days to restore Russian aid to an equal basis with other nations suggests that the administration, although certainly eager to end lend-lease as soon as possible, was not attempting to use it as a political instrument.[49]

The revisionist argument implies that lend-lease could and should have been extended after the war, and in doing so it grossly exaggerates the Truman administration's freedom of action. In fact, throughout the war the aid program was regarded as a temporary, emergency measure whose sole function was to support allied military operations. At least a brief continuation of lend-lease might have been justified on the grounds that it was necessary for postwar recovery and stability. Aside from a handful of economists and journalists, however, no individuals or pressure groups publicly took such a position. On the contrary, from late 1943 on, business leaders, foreign traders, and some farm organizations vocally insisted that it must be liquidated and trade restored to commercial channels as soon as possible. Both Democratic and

Republican congressmen, concerned with the enormity of wartime expenditures and the rising national debt, shared this view. "The doctrine that clearing up the mess is an integral part of the whole war, and therefore, 'necessary to the defence of the United States,'" *The* (London) *Economist* ruefully observed, "has never had much appeal on the other side of the Atlantic." [50]

Neither the Roosevelt administration nor the Truman administration had challenged this position. In 1942 and 1943, some of Roosevelt's aides had proposed amending the Lend-Lease Act to convert it into an instrument for relief and reconstruction, but the President had given them no encouragement and in 1943 he had privately rejected their suggestion. The act was renewed in 1944 on the assumption that it was intended for war use only and was not to be used, directly or indirectly, for reconstruction. As early as November, 1944, Roosevelt issued public, explicit promises that the aid program would not continue past the end of the war. Democratic leaders in Congress had voiced strong approval of Roosevelt's pledges, and Republicans, doubtful of his sincerity, had in the spring of 1945 amended the act to insure that the authority was not misused.

In August, 1945, therefore, it was a foregone conclusion in the administration, Congress, and the country that lend-lease would be ended as soon as the war was over, and every available index of public opinion demonstrates overwhelming support for Truman's actions. A *Fortune* poll taken in December, 1945, reported that 67.8 percent of those questioned approved the stoppage of lend-lease shipments, and only 19 percent thought the program should have been continued for an additional year. Correspondence in the Truman papers and FEA files runs heavily in favor of the administration. Of thirty-four newspapers examined, twenty-eight approved the President's actions without qualification; four defended the decision but felt that the administration should have implemented it more tactfully; only two opposed termination of lend-lease, one of them because it felt the United States had thrown away a powerful bargaining weapon. When the British protested the end of lend-lease, Democratic and Republican congressmen, liberals and conservatives, quickly came to Truman's defense. Sol Bloom, chairman of the House Foreign Affairs Committee, found the British reaction "unreasonable" especially since the "Act made it perfectly clear what was going to happen." Representative William Colmer of Mississippi spoke for many in Congress when he remarked: "We all naturally assumed that Lend-Lease would cease on V-Day." The Truman administration saw no alternative but to terminate assistance to the allies, and given the state of public and congressional opinion there was none.[51]

Some of the President's top advisers would later admit that the cutoff had been poorly handled. Truman's press secretary, Charley Ross, observed late in 1945 that it had been too abrupt—"The job had to be done, but it should have been done with better manners." Ross attributed the mistake to the fact that the top men in the administration were trying to do too much and did not have time for reflection. Dean Acheson agreed with Ross's assessment, and blamed the failure on "thoroughly bad advice from supposedly responsible officials."[52]

In the case of Russia, however, Truman and his aides seem to have acted with little reluctance and no misgivings. Since 1941, the United States had given the Soviet Union more than $10 billion in assistance. Most American officials felt that the Soviet government had shown little gratitude for the aid rendered, and they were certain that their help had done little to advance Soviet-American friendship. Truman later conceded that the cutoff of aid to Britain had been the greatest mistake of his presidency, but he seems to have ended lend-lease to the USSR without regrets.

Chapter 9

"TO HELP OUR FRIENDS"

AID TO RUSSIA AND THE ORIGINS OF THE COLD WAR

IN THE MONTHS AFTER V-J DAY, THE COLD WAR BEGAN TO TAKE FORM. Soviet-American differences, muted during the years of common dependence, came out into the open once the victory had been secured and the two allies set about the task of shaping the postwar world. Initial attempts to resolve postwar problems ended in deadlock, reinforcing old fears and suspicions on both sides and generating intense conflict and hostility. By early 1946, the leaders of each nation were indulging in heated verbal assaults on the other; within the next year they had begun to take positive steps to combat the adversary; by 1948 they were rapidly building up two antagonistic power blocs.

American policy on aid to Russia provides an accurate gauge to the rise of Soviet-American conflict and the onset of the Cold War. Long before V-J Day, U. S. officials had lost their enthusiasm for postwar assistance to the USSR and had abandoned any illusions that such aid would smooth postwar cooperation with the Russians. But in the first three months after the war, the United States provided the Soviet Union more than $650 million for relief and reconstruction, in part to maintain the appearance of allied cooperation, in part to secure immediate advantages. As conflict with the USSR mounted in the autumn of 1945, however, the Truman administration became increasingly reluctant to furnish additional assistance. It delayed for months before opening formal negotiations on postwar credits, and when it did act, in March, 1946, it attached sweeping political and economic conditions to its offer. The Russians refused even to negotiate on the terms set forth by the United States, and by September, 1946, American policy advanced one step further. Convinced by this time that Soviet expansionism represented a grave threat to America's strategic and economic interests throughout the world, U.S. policy makers had determined, as Secretary of State James F. Byrnes put it, "to help our friends in every way and refrain from assisting those who . . . are opposing the principles for which we stand." [1] The acceptance of this policy in Washington precluded any further aid to the USSR and insured that henceforth the bulk of American economic assistance would go to those nations willing to take a stand against communism.

American attitudes toward the Soviet Union, although hardening, were not rigidly fixed by the end of World War II. Soviet policies in Eastern Europe had begun to dampen the wartime optimism about cooperation with Russia. Representatives of Eastern European ethnic groups and leaders of the American Catholic Church protested Russian policies with increasing bitterness, and growing numbers of Americans began to fear that the Soviet leadership, wartime pretenses to the contrary, had never abandoned its goal of world revolution. To a large majority, however, the end of the war and the opportunity to return to normal took precedence over events in Eastern Europe. To many thoughtful persons, moreover, the creation of the United Nations and the explosion of the first atomic bomb underscored the urgency of maintaining Russian-American cooperation. A *Fortune* poll taken in the late summer of 1945 revealed that Americans were increasingly critical of the USSR, but were still "ready to go at least halfway toward active friendly relations." [2]

American policy toward the Soviet Union reflected some of these same currents. Most U. S. officials recognized, as a State Department document frankly conceded, that Eastern Europe was "in fact a Soviet sphere of influence." Throughout the summer of 1945, the department protested that the USSR had established "an almost airtight economic blackout in the entire area east of the Stettin-Trieste line," and complained bitterly about Soviet seizures of American-owned property in the region and about the bilateral trade treaties imposed upon the Eastern European nations by the Russians. But the rising official concern about Eastern Europe did not lead to forceful action. At Potsdam, the United States had deferred recognition of the governments of Bulgaria, Rumania, and Hungary, but refused—at least for the time being—to do anything else. Byrnes, who replaced Stettinius as Secretary of State at the conclusion of the San Francisco Conference, seemed to believe that the absence of popular concern about Eastern Europe rendered a strong response impracticable, and he may have felt that American possession of the atomic bomb would compel the Russians to make concessions. The inclination of both Byrnes and Truman in August, 1945, was to go slow and await the opening of the Foreign Ministers' Conference scheduled for London in September.[3]

In this uncertain atmosphere, American officials, although not eager to furnish the Russians with generous economic assistance, were still not firmly set against helping them. Postwar aid offered certain practical advantages, both economic and political, and seemed to afford the United States some leverage in dealing with the USSR. At this time, moreover, some Americans were inclined to be sympathetic and conciliatory toward the Russians, and others felt that it was still important to maintain at least a semblance of cooperation. Thus when the Russians, aware by late July that they could no longer count upon lend-lease to meet even a small portion of their needs, began to search for alternatives, American officials gave their proposals serious consideration.

Even before V-J Day, Soviet officials presented the United

Nations Relief and Rehabilitation Administration with a request for $700 million in supplies. They argued that they
needed the aid because lend-lease and credit negotiations
with the United States had failed, and the specific items they
requested bore a close resemblance to lend-lease contracts
canceled after V-E Day. Their proposal, formally submitted
to the meeting of the UNRRA Council in London in early
August, surprised both U. S. and UNRRA officials and confronted them with a dilemma. UNRRA had been established in November, 1943, to provide emergency relief
supplies—food, clothing, medicine—and restore essential
services in those liberated nations which lacked sufficient
foreign exchange to take care of their own needs. Under its
American Director-General, Herbert H. Lehman, UNRRA
had gone into operation in late 1944, and in the ensuing
year had provided over 1,250,000 tons of supplies in Greece,
Poland, and Yugoslavia. But Lehman advised the council in
August that this volume had not been adequate to take care
of the minimal relief needs of liberated Europe, and he fore-
cast that the liberation of China and increased demands in
Europe would enormously raise requirements in the year to
come.[4]

Within a year after its birth, UNRRA faced a financial
crisis. Most member nations had not met their original
promise to furnish 1 percent of their national income in
fiscal year 1943—the United States had made available only
$793 million of a total commitment of $1.35 billion—and by
August the international relief agency's funds were exhausted. Lehman predicted that an additional $1.5 billion
would be required for operations in 1946, and warned members of the American delegation to the council meeting that
"without further funds in the amount of at least 1 percent
from the chief contributing countries, we not only would be
unable to undertake additional responsibility, but could not
carry out our existing programs much beyond the early
months of 1946."[5]

The Russian request would raise by one half the financial
demands on UNRRA, and Lehman doubted that the addi-

tional money could be found. The British had already indicated that their own economic crisis would prevent them from making a substantial contribution to relief, and Americans questioned whether Congress would appropriate enough funds to take care of the increased demands. The House and Senate had approved the original appropriation with the understanding that nothing more would be asked of them. In addition, by the summer of 1945, UNRRA had attracted vocal political opposition. Congressmen returned from visits to Europe with tales of scandalous waste and inefficiency in UNRRA operations and demanded a full investigation. As Soviet-American conflict mounted, congressmen and some government officials charged that the Russians were undermining the purposes of UNRRA by distributing supplies only to those people who supported the communist-dominated governments in Poland and Yugoslavia.[6]

Before the council meeting opened, the Truman administration had agreed that the United States should join with other nations in contributing another 1 percent appropriation to UNRRA, and the State Department had received assurances from congressional leaders that a modest request would be approved. But both Lehman and the American delegation doubted that Congress would accept an appropriation large enough to meet the additional needs, and feared that a request including funds for the USSR might threaten the future existence of UNRRA. The American columnist Marquis Childs observed in August that the Russian petition posed the "64 dollar question the UNRRA Council will have to try to answer."[7]

In theory, UNRRA was an international organization created to distribute relief on a non-political basis. In practice, however, the United States, which provided the bulk of UNRRA funds (70 percent in 1944 and 1945), and most of its top officials, exercised a powerful voice in its operations. Despite the internationalism of Lehman and his associates, UNRRA could not be kept separate from U. S. foreign policy. Thus, shortly after the opening of the council meeting, Will Clayton, Assistant Secretary of State for Economic Affairs and head of the American delegation to the London conference, solicited from Washington an "urgent expression" of the State Department's position on the Soviet request for assistance.[8]

The department, which had already taken a firm stand against continued generous shipments of lend-lease and liberal credit terms, advanced a number of arguments against endorsing the $700 million. Acting Secretary Grew advised Clayton that UNRRA had been designed to provide essential imports to those nations that had no other means of obtaining them, and that the USSR, which had a strong foreign exchange position, was receiving reparations from former Axis nations, and could secure credits from the Export-Import Bank, did not fit into that category. Grew doubted that Congress would appropriate funds to meet the Soviet request, and urged Clayton to persuade the Russians to withdraw it lest the entire UNRRA program be jeopardized.[9]

From Moscow, W. Averell Harriman expressed even more vigorous opposition. The ambassador flatly denied the urgency of Russia's need, recalling that the USSR had received substantial volumes of lend-lease supplies throughout the summer and pointing out that she would have sufficient food to sustain her people on at least a minimum diet through 1946. Large numbers of Red Army troops were living off the land in Germany and other occupied nations, and in general, Harriman concluded, "Russia's situation cannot be compared with the difficult position of countries which were completely occupied by the Germans."[10]

Despite the opposition of Harriman and the State Department, the American delegation in London recognized that an outright rejection might have profound implications for Soviet-American relations and for UNRRA. Some members of the delegation found the arguments against aid for the USSR quite unconvincing. Russia had suffered as much devastation as any other nation during the war, and its standard of living was among the lowest in Europe. The Soviet case for UNRRA aid differed from that of China, Poland, or Yugoslavia "only in degree." In granting relief assistance, moreover, UNRRA had never given primary consideration to the applicant's foreign exchange position or ability to procure credits from the United States.[11]

The delegation also perceived that denial of the Russian request could place the United States in an awkward position. Canadian delegates had warned that their Parliament would be unlikely to appropriate additional funds for UNRRA if assistance was not given to the USSR. More important, the Russians had made clear that if their own proposal was not approved they would fight an American resolution to undertake a large UNRRA program in Italy. This program had been formulated at least in part to pacify congressmen with large Catholic or Italian-American constituencies, and the Soviet threats convinced Clayton that if their own demands were not met they might attempt to disrupt UNRRA or at least block the Italian aid program which would in turn make congressional support of the appropriation more difficult.[12]

Clayton also saw an opportunity to extract limited concessions from the Russians in return for UNRRA assistance. Under the original charter, officials of the international agency had no authority to control or even oversee the distribution of supplies within national boundaries. As noted, some Americans had vigorously protested the distribution of supplies in areas occupied by the Red Army, and the American delegation had submitted to the council a resolution giving to UNRRA missions the authority to observe distribution of relief supplies in liberated areas.

Thus the Assistant Secretary of State, working with Britain and Canada in the council, arranged a compromise with the Soviet delegation. The USSR agreed to withdraw its request for $700 million, to approve the proposal for UNRRA aid to Italy, and to accept the council resolution allowing missions to observe relief operations. The United States in return promised to recommend acceptance of a request to be submitted by the two "independent" Soviet Republics, Byelorussia and the Ukraine, for $250 million in UNRRA assistance.[13]

Harriman expressed unqualified displeasure with the compromise. He continued to argue that the USSR had other sources of assistance and did not need aid from UNRRA. The extension of such aid would make it easier for the Soviet leadership to maintain "an enormous military establishment." And he insisted once again that "our overall relations with the Soviet Union" should be given "full weight" in reaching decisions on economic assistance. "Having observed carefully the effect on the Soviet Government of our generous lend-lease policy over the past 4 years," he warned, "I have not found that we have obtained any benefit in goodwill on the part of the Soviet Government in connection with actions which affect our interests." Now that the war is over, the United States should deal with the Russians on a "realistic reciprocal basis." Such a policy was "understood and respected by the Soviet Government and is more apt to obtain reasonably satisfactory results." [14]

Over Harriman's heated opposition, Clayton and the State Department went through with the arrangement. One could legitimately question the independence of the Soviet republics, but only the most hardened critic of the USSR could doubt their need for assistance. It has been estimated that 50 percent of the war damage suffered by the Soviet Union took place in the Ukraine. Soviet scorched-earth tactics and the destruction wreaked by retreating Nazi armies combined to devastate a rich and fertile area that had once fed much of the nation and provided a large portion of its mineral resources. Alexander Werth, who flew over the region shortly after its liberation, found its villages "nothing but a heap of rubble" and its fields "unplanted and empty." Byelorussia lay on the path between Berlin and Moscow, and had been a center of heavy fighting throughout the war. The Germans murdered an estimated million people during the occupation, and those who survived returned to a virtual "desert zone." [15]

Even the State Department, which had originally questioned Russia's need, came around to Clayton's position. Dean Acheson, who replaced Grew as Under Secretary in mid-August, advised Harriman that, although the USSR had substantial gold holdings and a "great power of recuperation," she had made "greater physical sacrifice, suffered more devastation, and lowered her already low standard of living below that of any *repeat any* European nations." [16]

Acheson also informed Harriman that the publicity already given the Russian request for UNRRA aid would have made a "flat turn-down politically very difficult," and that the compromise worked out by Clayton satisfied a number of immediate needs. It would not require additional appropriations from UNRRA nations or force a reduction in other programs, and the Russians had made important concessions in return. "We thus felt," Acheson concluded, "that the whole UNRRA negotiation with the Russians had been quite successful and that the entire results of the Council meeting had been rather better than we had hoped for." [17]

Soviet-American agreement on the terms of a 3 (c) credit to finance lend-lease supplies still in the "pipeline" suggests along with the UNRRA discussions that in the weeks immediately following V-J Day U. S. aid policy was still flexible and governed by expediency. On August 20, shortly after the termination of lend-lease, the FEA invited the Soviet Purchasing Commission to indicate its wish to buy lend-lease supplies already manufactured and awaiting shipment and to open negotiations on the terms of payment. The Russian government, obviously eager to secure those items which had originally been ordered for reconstruction, responded rapidly. Within a week, the Purchasing Commission submitted a request for $400 million worth of material in the "pipeline," including industrial equipment, locomotives, rails, spare parts for vehicles, and footstuffs. The volume and type of supplies closely resembled those of the original 3 (c) agreement, but this time the Russians seemed more concerned with getting the equipment than with driving a good bargain, their proposed credit terms paralleling exactly the final terms offered by the United States in September, 1944.[18]

Nor was the United States in a mood to haggle. Most of

the items requested by the Russians had been manufactured especially for them, and could not be consumed at home or sold elsewhere. With large stocks of surplus lend-lease on hand in the United States and across the globe, the FEA was eager to dispose of as much as it could as quickly as possible. The United States quickly accepted the terms proposed by the Russians, and by October 15 the two nations had signed a 3 (c) "pipeline" agreement for approximately $400 million.[19]

The State Department also facilitated delivery of this material to the USSR. Because of the worldwide shortage of vessels at V-J Day (and perhaps to atone in some measure for the abrupt stoppage of lend-lease), the United States had in August authorized a sixty day extension of lend-lease shipping. The 3 (c) shipments to Russia did not begin until after the original sixty-day period had ended, and because the Russians had received "less favorable consideration in this regard than other countries . . ." the State Department on October 31 agreed to furnish them lend-lease shipping for two months. Thus both the UNRRA and the 3 (c) agreements indicate that the United States, even after the end of the war, was willing to consider seriously Russian requests for aid and to treat them on an equal basis with those of the other allies.[20]

American handling of postwar credits for the USSR, on the other hand, reveals a growing caution and firmness in U. S. policy. Anglo-American negotiations for a postwar loan began shortly after V-J Day and were concluded by December, 1945. Soviet-American negotiations did not even get underway in 1945, in large part because American officials felt no inclination to press for their opening.

Indeed, since the beginning of 1945, the United States had evinced the greatest caution on postwar aid to Russia. Alarmed by developments in Eastern Europe, the State Department had urged that credits be withheld until Soviet-American relations improved. Roosevelt had refused to make any commitment on Molotov's January request for a $6 billion credit until he had talked with Stalin at Yalta, and after his return from the Crimea he took no action on the matter. The State Department did not begin to formulate a concrete response to Molotov's note until mid-April, and its initial thoughts reveal the direction of American policy. The office of Financial and Development Policy proposed that any credits extended the USSR should be handled through the Export-Import Bank and that legislation should be secured to make possible the opening of negotiations "shortly after the conclusion of the San Francisco Conference, if political conditions are favorable. . . ." The terms departed drastically from Molotov's request. Instead of $6 billion, OFD recommended a credit of only $1 billion, and it rejected as too low the interest rate of 2½ percent proposed by the Russians.[21]

At their May 30 meeting on lend-lease, Molotov pointedly reminded Harriman that the United States had not answered his note of January 3, and the ambassador, agreeing that "some reply or explanation is due the Soviet Govt," immediately asked for guidance from Washington. Acting Secretary Grew responded within several days, informing Harriman that he had proposed to the President legislation to expand the lending authority of the Export-Import Bank to $3.5 billion, with about $1 billion to be set aside for the USSR if "events so warrant." The ambassador subsequently told Molotov that the United States was actively seeking legislation to make credits possible, but that negotiations could not begin until it had been secured.[22]

The administration got the authority in August with little difficulty. A bill was introduced in the House in mid-July, and although it did not include specific provision for credits to the Soviet Union, Crowley advised congressional committees that the government planned to offer the Russians between $700 million and $1 billion. Neither the bill nor the indication that Russia would receive aid under it attracted much opposition. Even Senator Taft agreed that $1 billion was a "fair amount" to finance trade with the Soviet Union. The House passed the legislation quickly and by a large majority, and easily rejected an anti-Soviet amendment proposed by Representative Everett M. Dirksen of Illinois that would have denied credits to any nation guilty of violating the Atlantic Charter. The Senate approved the House bill by voice vote, and President Truman signed it into law on August 4.[23]

Harriman then informed the Soviet government that credits were available and invited them to submit a request. As with the "pipeline" credit, they responded quickly. On August 28, General Leonid Rudenko of the Russian Purchasing Commission presented to Crowley a proposal for a $1 billion credit on the same terms as the 3 (c) credit, an amortization period of thirty years and an interest rate of 2⅜ percent. Crowley indicated that the interest rate must conform to the standard Export-Import figure of 3 percent, but advised Rudenko that he would pass the note on to the bank.[24]

Within the next few weeks, various U. S. agencies and officials gave careful study to a number of proposed Export-Import Bank loans, including the $1 billion loan for the USSR. On September 12, the Board of Trustees of the bank approved "in principle" $1 billion for Russian reconstruction. Several days later, the National Advisory Council on International Monetary and Financial Problems, a cabinet-level committee established in August to coordinate foreign lending policies and programs, recommended that negotiations with the Russians should "go forward." Acheson and Crowley subsequently met with the President, and on September 21 secured his approval of the opening of negotiations with the USSR.[25]

At this point, however, the loan was held up pending the approval of the State Department. The department had long since determined that reconstruction loans should be used to extract political and economic concessions from recipient nations, and in September officials in the Eastern European Division and the economic offices began "preparatory" studies to establish the conditions that might be attached to any credits extended the Russians. Before leaving for the London Conference of Foreign Ministers in early September, Secretary Byrnes had emphasized to Crowley the importance of relating the lending program of the Export-Import Bank to the broader foreign policy objectives of the United States. Crowley assured Byrnes that his wishes would be respected, and the National Advisory Council agreed at a meeting on September 27 that negotiations with the Soviet Union would not proceed until the Secretary of State had been consulted.[26]

This decision left the initiative with the State Department, but during the next four months it took no action on the Russian loan. Clayton and his aides in the economic offices of the department were completely preoccupied with the Anglo-American financial negotiations which opened in Washington on September 12 and were not finished until the first week of December. Some officials in the department were apparently not aware, moreover, that the Russians had actually submitted a formal request for $1 billion, interpreting the Crowley-Rudenko discussions of August 28 as merely "preliminary discussions" which bound the United States to do nothing. This misunderstanding might have been cleared up by Crowley or by the Export-Import Bank. But the Foreign Economic Administrator retired to private life on October 15, 1945, the same day his emergency wartime agency was liquidated. The bank was reorganized after Crowley's resignation. His successor as Chairman of the Board, William McChesney Martin, was not appointed until late November and did not take office until January, 1946.[27]

There were other reasons for Washington's inaction in the fall and early winter of 1945. The Russians themselves did not raise the matter of credits again after presenting the request. From a tactical standpoint, they may have wished to avoid creating the impression they were too eager for an American loan—they had consistently taken the position that they were accepting orders for supplies to help the United States ease its postwar economic problems. Most likely, they had their eyes on the British-American discussions and awaited their outcome to get a better idea of what they might expect from the United States. Whatever the explanation, Russian officials did not press their American counterparts for action on the $1 billion. This passivity was quite uncharacteristic of Soviet behavior. During the war, they had applied vigorous and constant pressure to get what they wanted. American officials were conditioned by this experience, Willis Armstrong of FEA has recalled, to deal "only with the things about which they screamed the loudest," and when they were not "needling, all of us figured they weren't interested in what they had originally asked for." [28]

In the absence of Soviet pressure, there was little incentive to take the initiative. Public attitudes toward postwar aid for the USSR had cooled considerably since the first discussions had taken place in 1944. A public opinion poll taken shortly after V-J Day indicated that 60 percent of those questioned disapproved a $6 billion loan for Russia and only 27 percent approved. As late as January, 1945, *Fortune* had expressed the general enthusiasm of American business interests for postwar credits to Russia, but by summer it had shifted to disapproval. Soviet policies in Eastern Europe, the editors observed, had "frittered away Russia's enormous store of good will in this country," and until the "profound political difficulties" between the two nations were resolved "Russian credits should remain in abeyance." [29]

More important, the failure of the London Foreign Ministers Conference in September opened wide the fissure in Soviet-American relations and aroused considerable resentment against the Russians within the Truman administration. After the American delegation rejected draft treaties prepared by the USSR for Hungary, Rumania, and Bulgaria, Molotov angrily denounced American interference in Eastern Europe and accused the United States of supporting elements unfriendly to the Soviet Union. When the Soviet Foreign Minister then demanded a greater role for the USSR in the occupation of Japan and insisted that France and China be excluded from subsequent peace discussions, Secretary of State Byrnes refused to go along. The conference broke up without accomplishing anything, and tensions between the former allies increased considerably. "Relations between the two great Allied powers . . . are unquestionably cooler at this juncture than at any period since the Yalta Conference," New York *Times* correspondent C. L. Sulzberger reported from London in early October.[30]

Byrnes returned to Washington incensed with Molotov's performance. He told Stettinius that the United States faced a "new Russia, totally different than the Russia we dealt with a year ago. As long as they needed us in the War and we were giving them supplies we had a satisfactory relationship but now that the War was over they were taking an aggressive attitude and stand on political and territorial questions that was indefensible." He informed Joseph Davies that the Russians had been "insufferable" and that he had regretted taking it. In his memoirs, he recalled that after London he had determined to make no further concessions to the Russians. As "far as I was concerned, Christmas was over. . . . Instead of issuing more I.O.U.'s, I wanted to collect some we held." Byrnes' angry mood extended throughout much of the administration. Secretary of the Navy James Forrestal pressed Truman to speak out forcibly against the Russians, and in a belligerent Navy Day address on October 27, the President did emphasize America's military might and proclaimed his intention not to recognize any government imposed on a nation without its consent.[31]

The administration's dissatisfaction with the Russians explains in part its unwillingness to take the initiative in credit negotiations in the fall of 1945. In late October, Byrnes emphatically denied a National Association of Manufacturers report that the United States was blocking all credits to the USSR until a "satisfactory diplomatic understanding had been achieved," and told reporters that the United States would consider a Russian request for aid on the same basis as one from any other nation. But the Secretary's statement was something less than candid. An American diplomat who had participated in the London meeting advised Sulzberger that no credits should be extended "by Washington to Moscow until diplomatic harmony is more evident." A U. S. credit official also denied the NAM report as "not wholly true," but he conceded that there were "good diplomatic reasons for the State Department to want to 'make haste slowly' with regard to Soviet credits. . . ." The issue was not dead—Clayton advised Secretary of the Treasury Fred Vinson in early November that "Consideration is being given to the possibility of financial assistance to the USSR along special lines not unlike that which may be extended to the United Kingdom." But Clayton also informed Harriman later in the month that the State Department had "been pursuing a policy of not encouraging active discussions and at present the matter is dormant." [32]

While the State Department "made haste slowly," the issue of credits to the USSR continued to attract attention in the press and other public forums. In mid-November, Secretary of Commerce Henry A. Wallace and Edward Carter, president of the American Society for Russian Relief, delivered widely publicized speeches calling for generous postwar aid to the Soviet Union. The conclusion of Anglo-American negotiations for a $3.75 billion loan in late November naturally raised questions about possible assistance to the USSR. Eleanor Roosevelt privately advised President Truman that if the United States wished to promote world cooperation it must grant roughly equal loans to Britain and Russia. Even a hardened critic of the USSR like Senator Vandenberg conceded that the British loan created a dilemma for the United States. "It seems to me," Vandenberg confided to John Foster Dulles, "if we grant a loan to England and then deny one to Russia (if she asks for it as she undoubtedly will) we have thereby made further cooperation among the 'Big Three' practically impossible (which incidentally, would be the end of UNO)." And the Michigan senator admitted to a columnist that it seemed more important to him to cement "this more formidable foreign tie [Russia] than with a weakened Britain." [33]

This renewed interest in a loan to Russia evoked a confused and contradictory response from the administration. When asked by reporters on December 7 whether he had any plans for opening negotiations on the $6 billion loan requested by the Russians, the President denied that such a request had been made. If so, he observed, "it has never been officially given to me. They have never asked me for a $6 billion loan since I have been President." Although literally correct, Truman's statement implied that the Russians had never requested aid. Officials in the lower echelons of the State Department were shocked, and immediately began searching the files to locate the Soviet note of August 28 requesting the $1 billion credit.[34]

When Secretary of the Treasury Vinson corrected the President's statement on January 16, informing reporters that the Russians had requested substantial credits from the United States some months before, the State Department felt compelled to issue an explanation. Spokesmen indicated that Vinson must have been referring to a message received from Harriman in January, 1945, reporting a request for postwar assistance. The Soviet government had been informed that no funds were available; but in August they had been invited to submit a formal request. Since that time, the statement concluded, the only approach had been an "informal discussion" between the former chairman of the Export-Import Bank (Crowley) and Soviet supply officials.[35]

The State Department's "explanation" quieted public discussion of the issue temporarily, and throughout the remainder of January and into the first week of February the department continued to delay further action on credits. Emilio Collado, one of Clayton's top aides, urged continued inaction, and as late as February 5 Byrnes informed William McChesney Martin of the Export-Import Bank that he was not prepared to act.[36]

Within several days, the secretary suddenly reversed himself, abruptly ending the policy of delay and directing that discussions on credits should be initiated as soon as possible. On February 21, the State Department responded officially to the Soviet request of August 28, proposing immediate opening of formal negotiations on a $1 billion Export-Import credit and related questions.[37]

The State Department announced on March 1 that it had invited the Russians to begin credit negotiations, and at the same time issued an explanation for the administration's earlier confusing statements and for the decision to act. Without any apologies, department spokesmen revealed that the Soviet request of August 28, 1945—which, they said, was not really a formal request because the Russians did not use the standard forms and procedures required by the Export-Import Bank—had been misplaced in the transfer of records from the Foreign Economic Administration. The document had turned up only recently and a "prompt and cordial" reply had been dispatched to the USSR at once. Fault for the error, an additional release explained, lay with a snarled and tangled bureaucracy, in which numerous agencies worked on the same problem at the same time without keeping each other informed and with "substantial confusion as the net result." [38]

Contemporary observers accepted the State Department's explanation—although some sharply criticized what the New York *Herald-Tribune* labeled an "inexcusable blunder"—but the most recent student of the loan question has been less generous. Thomas G. Paterson charges that the explanation was "false and bizarre," and raises the question: "Did the United States, because it needed a public excuse for not having pursued the loan with the Soviet Union from August to February, feign administrative clumsiness and incompetence?"

It is difficult to understand why a government agency—indeed an administration—would feel compelled to admit publicly to its own incompetence, but the department's story appears to have been substantially correct. The end of the war and the liquidation of emergency wartime agencies did create enormous confusion within the bureaucracy. Crowley had not informed top State Department officials or his successor at the Export-Import Bank of the contents of the note. The State Department was aware of the Crowley-Rudenko discussions, but regarded them simply as informal, preliminary talks, and because of the tension in Soviet-American relations in late 1945 felt no urge to press them further. But when the Truman and Vinson statements again called attention to the Russian loan, officials began to investigate more closely the events of August, and William McChesney Martin even telephoned Crowley to find out what had happened. Crowley insisted that General Rudenko's request had been quite informal and that the issue was dead. It seems entirely possible, however, that someone in the State Department located Rudenko's note in the voluminous files left by the FEA, and that the top officials in the department decided that it required an answer.[39]

Discovery of the "lost" request provides only a partial explanation, however, for the State Department's February decision to reverse its policy of inaction on credits to Russia. By late January, the Russians, who had been conspicuously silent on the issue throughout the fall and early winter, began to show a revived interest in American aid for reconstruction. According to Herbert Feis, Stalin mentioned the matter to Harriman when the ambassador paid a call at the Kremlin on January 23. Clayton informed the National Advisory Council on February 7 that the State Department had received inquiries from Russian officials regarding the status of their request of August 28, 1945, and William McChesney Martin reported conversations in which Soviet officials indicated that they expected terms as favorable as those offered the British.[40]

The administration's need to build congressional support for the British loan also required that it clarify the long-confused status of the Russian loan negotiations. When President Truman urged Congress in late January to approve the $3.75 billion loan to Britain with dispatch, many administration officials privately expressed doubts that his plea would be followed. Domestic problems occupied center stage in early 1946, and Congress was not in a mood for spending, especially for foreign aid. One of the principal arguments against the British loan was that it would set a precedent for large loans to the other allies, and Senator Theodore Bilbo of Mississippi, already leading a filibuster against establishment of a permanent Fair Employment Practices Commission, immediately threatened to filibuster against the loan as well. Counting himself a staunch friend of the British, Bilbo protested that he was "tired of seeing Uncle Sam as Santa Claus." As soon as the loan proposal reached Capitol Hill, congressmen of both parties demanded to know what other foreign loans the administration had under consideration.[41]

The Russian loan presented an especially complicated political problem. For months, rumors had circulated in Washington that the United States was considering postwar aid to Russia ranging anywhere from $1 billion to $6 billion, and the administration's vague and contradictory statements had only added to the uncertainty. Senator Vandenberg pointed out that Congress in its present mood was not likely to approve a loan for the USSR, but he also observed that if the United States granted a loan to Britain but denied one to the Russians it would be placed in an awkward position. The administration recognized that some congressmen might attempt to use the British loan to force action on aid to Russia; it also perceived that those who opposed the British loan could use the possibility of a Russian loan to defeat it.

"The pressing problem," Emilio Collado advised Byrnes on February 4, is "how to handle possible credits to the Soviets in the British loan hearings in Congress." Anticipating this problem, Clayton had already advised the National Advisory Council that it should present to the President and to Congress a full report on its entire lending program. Following this lead, Byrnes determined in the first week of February to clear up the status of the Russian loan. In a speech to the Foreign Policy Association on February 11, he pointed out that Britain's urgent need for aid and her unique position in world trade rendered the British loan a special case that would not set precedents for other loans. Any other requests for foreign aid could be handled through the Export-Import Bank, for which funds had already been appropriated. On March 1, four days before the Senate Banking and Currency Committee opened hearings on the Anglo-American Financial Agreement, the

State Department publicly announced that the Russians had been invited to open formal negotiations on a $1 billion credit.[42]

The decision to take the initiative in credit negotiations also reflects pressures from within the Truman administration for a closer coordination of foreign aid with political and economic objectives. Harriman had been pressing for such coordination for months, and again in December, 1945, he objected strenuously to the ambivalence and confusion in American policies. The United States had been protesting Soviet economic policies in the liberated nations of Eastern Europe, he argued, but it had not backed up these protests with action, and indeed had granted the Russians substantial UNRRA and 3 (c) assistance with no strings attached. "From Moscow," he concluded, "it would appear that piecemeal dealing with these economic subjects can not lead to satisfactory results. Since Soviet political policy appears to be influenced by economic objectives it would seem that we should give at this time greater attention to the concerting of our economic policy with our political policy. . . ."[43]

A Soviet request of January, 1946, for the purchase of additional American surplus property on credit focused attention on the question again. Although Byrnes and Acheson approved the unconditional sale of up to $100 million in surplus property on 3 (c) terms, Harriman again insisted that the United States must tell the Russians that their request would not be considered "until an understanding had been reached regarding the manner in which outstanding economic questions between the two countries are to be adjusted." [44]

Elbridge Durbrow, chief of the State Department's Eastern European Division, agreed with Harriman. "Despite our many protests and requests for coordinated action regarding the economic blackout in Eastern Europe and other related questions," Durbrow advised Acheson, "the Soviet government has consistently refused to accept any of our views on this point." Economic aid afforded the "only real lever" possessed by the United States "to bring about any semblance of economic and political stability in Eastern Europe," and the United States had substantially weakened its hand by granting UNRRA and 3 (c) assistance.[45]

Acheson doubted that the sale of surplus property provided the United States much bargaining power, but he agreed with Harriman's "general analysis" of Russian-American economic relations. Within the State Department, moreover, there was agreement by early February that further delay on credit negotiations offered no advantage to the United States. The tactic of holding back on credits until diplomatic relations improved had not worked, and Harriman had remarked some months before that the evasiveness in U. S. policy might have "added to our misunderstandings and increased the Soviets' recent tendency to take unilateral action." The Russians, still convinced that a postwar depression would force the United States to grant credits on favorable terms, had shown no inclination to adjust their foreign policy in order to secure American assistance. Important negotiations were scheduled for March and April on possible Soviet entry into the International Monetary Fund and the World Bank and on a final lend-lease settlement, and the State Department determined to hold out immediately a concrete prospect of aid for reconstruction as an inducement to the USSR to reach agreement on other problems. On February 8, Byrnes authorized a note inviting the Russians to open credit negotiations, and within the next week his aides hurriedly began framing plans for a Soviet-American conference on a broad range of economic and political issues.[46]

The decision to initiate credit negotiations also paralleled the formulation of what President Truman called the "get tough policy." The breach in Russian-American relations had widened still further following the London Conference. Soviet occupation policies in Korea, Manchuria, and Iran angered and deeply disturbed Truman and many of his advisers, strengthening their suspicions of the global proportions of Soviet ambitions and hardening their opposition to further concessions. When Byrnes agreed at the Moscow Conference in December to endorse recognition of the governments of Rumania and Bulgaria, the reaction in Washington was sharp. Admiral Leahy denounced the Moscow communique as an "appeasement document which gives to the Soviet everything they want and preserves to America nothing." Truman, especially annoyed at Byrnes' independence, privately complained that he was tired of "babying the Soviets." Unless they were faced with an "iron fist and strong language," the President warned, "another war is in the making. Only one language do they understand—'how many divisions have you?' " [47]

As with some of his earlier outbursts against the Russians, Truman did not move immediately to translate these sentiments into action. But events in January and February reinforced his administration's hostility toward the USSR. Conflicts in Manchuria and Iran exploded into full-blown crises. Revelations of Soviet atomic espionage in Canada and presumably the United States as well heightened suspicions and anxieties. Stalin's militant election speech of February 9, 1946, referring in ominous tones to the implacable hostility between communism and capitalism and calling for a massive expansion of heavy industry, appeared to be a direct challenge and threat to the United States. *Time* magazine said what many in official Washington were thinking: the United States now confronted a "world-wide Russian power drive." [48]

On February 20, Truman confided to Leahy his "sharp disapproval" of recent "appeasement" of the Soviet Union, and stated his conviction that the administration must take a "strong attitude without delay." One week later, Senator Vandenberg, expressing a rising Republican dissatisfaction with the administration's foreign policy, raised the fundamental question "What is Russia up to now?" and demanded that the United States speak "as plainly upon all occasions as Russia does" and "just as vigorously" sustain "its own purposes and ideals upon all occasions as Russia does." The next day Secretary of State Byrnes fell into line. In a forceful speech to the Overseas Correspondents Club in New York, he indicated that the United States would not hesitate to use force to defend its own interests and security and to "preserve the peace of the world." [49]

As both contemporary observers and historians have noted, February and March, 1946, marked a significant turning point in American attitudes toward Russia. Up to this point, Professor John Gaddis has observed, the United States considered the Soviet Union as an ally; afterward she was regarded as a "potential enemy." Truman and most of his advisers agreed that America's past willingness to compromise had only encouraged the Russians to be more aggressive, and that henceforth they must stand up for the principles in which they believed and use their power to enforce these principles. An easing of tensions would come only after the Soviet government abandoned its own expansionist designs.[50]

The conditions proposed to the Russians for the opening of credit negotiations reflected the administration's new toughness. Since 1941, the United States had extended substantial lend-lease aid and agreed to UNRRA and 3 (c) credits without demanding major concessions in return. But the State Department note of February 21, 1946, made clear that credits were only "one among a number of outstanding economic questions the settlement of which is necessary to provide a sound basis for the mutually beneficial development of economic relations between the United States and the U.S.S.R." The discussions should also consider claims against the Soviet government for seizure of American property in the liberated nations; arrangements to protect the patents and copyrights of American inventors and writers; a greater voice for the United States (under the terms of the Declaration of Liberated Europe) in assisting the peoples of Eastern Europe to "solve by democratic means their pressing economic problems"; freedom of navigation on rivers of international concern (especially the Danube); civil aviation matters of mutual interest to both nations; a comprehensive treaty of friendship, commerce, and navigation; and a final settlement of lend-lease obligations. In a still broader vein, the note called for discussion of "methods for giving effect to the terms of Article VII" of the Soviet-American Lend-Lease Agreement, which provided for cooperative efforts to eliminate trade barriers, and for talks on other "economic questions, the settlement of which in the opinion of either government, would be conducive to the attainment of the general aims of the negotiations as herein proposed." [51]

The conditions attached to the credit negotiations had broad endorsement from business interests and Republican and Democratic congressmen, many of whom had been demanding protection for American property rights and freedom of trade with Eastern Europe as the price for any aid extended the USSR. More important, the State Department's agenda for negotiations embraced a set of ideas accepted by most business and political leaders as the proper bases for America's postwar foreign economic policy. Many Americans agreed that peace and prosperity in the postwar era depended upon an expanding international trade and that this could best be achieved be eliminating discrimination and removing artificial trade barriers. Exclusive trading blocs and bilateral, discriminatory trade treaties impeded the flow of trade and the attainment of prosperity, bred suspicion and conflict, and threatened world peace. The United States must therefore use its influence to promote equality of opportunity in trade and investment, unrestricted access to raw materials, and freedom of the seas. American loan policy, an official statement pronounced in March, 1946, "is directed toward the creation of an international economic environment permitting a large volume of trade among all nations" and is "predicated on the view that a productive and peaceful world must be free from warring economic blocs and from barriers which obstruct the free flow of international trade and productive capital." [52]

Since 1941, the United States had attempted to incorporate these principles into international agreements. American diplomats had applied persistent pressure to commit the United Kingdom to multilateralism and non-discrimination, and in the Anglo-American Financial Agreement of 1945 had finally extracted binding pledges from the beleaguered

British. Up to February, 1946, Americans had dealt much more gently with the Soviet Union. Recognizing that Soviet state trading practices did not lend themselves to multilateralism, State and Treasury Department officials, especially in the Roosevelt years, had tactfully encouraged the Russians to join in discussions on international trade and to enter the Bretton Woods organizations, but they had refused to apply any pressure. By early 1946, however, many administration officials regarded Soviet economic and political practices in Eastern Europe as a threat to trade and investments and to the broader economic principles to which they were committed, and in the loan negotiations they determined to confront this threat.[53]

Even though it satisfied domestic political needs and fitted the requirements of America's postwar foreign economic policy, the attempt to secure sweeping economic concessions from the Russians in return for credits was both unrealistic and futile. Soviet planning aimed for self-sufficiency, and Russian leaders were not interested in expanding trade along American lines or anxious to sacrifice the leverage that trade provided them over the nations along their periphery. The United States sought greater access to the Soviet Union and the nations under its control, but in the immediate postwar period the USSR was moving in the opposite direction. "Not even during the purge period of 1934–1939," Adam Ulam has written, "had there been such a frantic attempt to isolate Russian life from any foreign influence and contacts." [54]

The Russians were especially reluctant to permit expanded American influence in Eastern Europe, a region considered vital to their security. Soviet writers denounced American insistence upon fulfillment of the Declaration on Liberated Europe as a thinly veiled move to "undermine the still unfirmly cemented democratic regimes" in Eastern Europe; internationalization of the Danube as an attempt to "turn back the wheel of history" to the "Balkanization policy" pursued by the imperialist powers in the nineteenth century; equal opportunity and the open door as the slogans of

British and American "monopoly trusts," a "quasi liberal guise" to take advantage of the "temporary enfeeblement of the vanquished countries in order to deprive them of economic independence." [55]

In view of the strongly held convictions on both sides, the credit negotiations as proposed by the United States had little chance of success. The Russians agreed to consider only a settlement of lend-lease accounts, general problems related to Article VII, and a treaty of commerce and friendship. While expressing a guarded readiness to "discuss the other questions enumerated in your note," the Soviet government did not consider it "expedient" to connect these with credit negotiations.[56]

State Department officials deemed the Russian response "entirely unsatisfactory." Not eager at this point to break off negotiations, however, they agreed to limited concessions, expressing a willingness to separate discussions of civil aviation and navigation of international waterways from the credit negotiations. This was as far as they would go, and as the New York *Times* predicted, the terms were still too "rugged" for the Russians to accept. Insisting that there was no direct relation between the "several sets of problems," Soviet officials indicated that they would agree only to "exchange in a preliminary fashion opinions on these questions." [57]

By May, 1946 the United States was no more willing to budge from its position than the USSR. Soviet agreement to withdraw from Iran after the steady application of American pressure probably confirmed in the minds of most officials in the Truman administration the wisdom of the "get tough" policy. Byrnes continued to pursue a hard line at the opening session of the Paris Peace Conference in April, and when it produced deadlock on every issue, Vandenberg publicly suggested that the American delegation might return home. Back in Washington during a recess in the proceedings, the Michigan senator introduced a resolution tying future loans to fulfillment of the provisions of the Yalta and Potsdam agreements. Byrnes and Vandenberg, an informed columnist commented, "quite obviously are determined that there is going to be no more American signing on the dotted line of measures favorable to Russia until the Russians show a greater inclination to respond in kind." [58]

Cold War divisions substantially cooled what little enthusiasm remained within the administration for aid to Russia. Reports that the USSR had extended assistance to Poland on very generous terms raised doubts about its need for credits and the advisability of granting them. And as the British loan debate dragged on in Congress, defenders of the measure increasingly justified it on grounds that it would strengthen a nation whose support was essential to counter the Russian threat. House Majority Leader John McCormack of Massachusetts posed the issue directly: the United States must give effective aid to friendly nations or leave them "no alternative but to be subjected to the sphere of influence of Moscow." [59]

During this same period, the United States replaced Britain as the target of Russian verbal assaults. "Soviet propaganda is at the present time attacking the United States with an unremitting ferocity which not only equals but in certain respects exceeds the severity of its previous campaign against the British," the American Embassy cabled from Moscow in July. Russian writers singled out U. S. economic policies for special abuse. *New Times* headlined a story on the British loan under the sarcastic title "American generosity," and noted that the harsh conditions attached to the loan by the United States had brought forth no rejoicing in Great Britain. Soviet commentators denounced U. S. aid policy as a "starvation strategy," warning that the Americans were using food supplies, promises of loans, and credit negotiations as a "means of exercising political pressure with the purpose of imposing an alien will on the peoples of Europe." The rhetoric and actions of both sides make clear that by the middle of May the United States and the Soviet Union had reached an impasse on the issue of credits without even agreeing on an agenda for negotiations.[60]

At about the same time, the Truman administration took action which eliminated any possibility of a loan for Russia in the immediate future and which suggests a distinct shift in the priorities of American aid policy. The Export-Import Bank had only a little more than $1 billion available for use, and in April France had asked for credits of $500 million. The State Department placed great importance on approval of the request. The French economy was chaotic, the political situation unstable, and elections were set for June which appeared likely to strengthen the position of the Communists. To turn down or sharply reduce the request for credits, Ambassador Jefferson Caffery warned from Paris, would "pull out one of the last props of substance and of hope from those in France who want to see France remain an independent and democratic country." Clayton agreed with Caffery that a decision against a "substantial" loan to France would be a "catastrophe," and recommended that the figure be upped to $650 million. England and France provided the "Key to the whole Western European situation," and it was "urgent" to act at once to prevent a collapse. The National Advisory Council in early May approved the proposal for a $650 million loan to France. Negotiations were concluded quickly, and the deal was completed on May 28.[61]

The French loan exhausted most of the funds of the Export-Import Bank and rendered credits to the USSR a "practical political impossibility." It had been recognized from the outset that approval of the French request would leave insufficient funds for the Soviet Union, but the small likelihood of successful negotiations with the Russians and the urgency attached to aid to France made this a matter of less consequence. The National Advisory Council had drafted a proposal to ask Congress for an additional $1.25 million for the Export-Import Bank. But the State Department feared that such a request would probably be regarded as authorization for a loan to the USSR, and might therefore jeopardize passage of the British loan. According to one official, two alternatives were left: "to take advantage that the Soviet reply of May 17th gives to break off gracefully loan negotiations with the Soviet Union; to postpone the $1 1/4 billion request for additional lending power until we have a clearer picture of the likelihood of successful negotiations with the USSR." [62]

The administration pursued both alternatives simultaneously. The State Department sent a third note to the Soviet Embassy on June 13 but it did not retreat from the conditions set in the previous note, and American officials admitted publicly that the Russians would not accept the terms. After consulting with Democratic leaders and determining that it would be inadvisable to request additional funds from Congress, President Truman made clear that no further legislation would be introduced. This foreclosed any chance of a loan for Russia before 1947.[63]

Alarmed by the steady deterioration of Soviet-American relations, Secretary of Commerce Henry A. Wallace attempted in July to revive prospects of a loan for the USSR as one means of healing the rupture in the wartime alliance. Since the beginning of the war, Wallace had been a persistent and eloquent advocate of Soviet-American accord, and in a twelve-page letter to President Truman on July 23 he set forth his objections to the administration's policies and his proposed alternatives. Wallace argued that history had left the Russian people with ample grounds for "fear, suspicions and distrust," and observed that the present Soviet leaders saw themselves "fighting for their existence in a hostile world." America's postwar policies—the maintenance of substantial military forces; the quest for bases across the globe; the refusal to share atomic secrets; the vocal resistance to Soviet efforts to obtain warm water ports and "friendly" neighboring states; the reluctance to extend economic assistance on generous terms—had reinforced Russian fears and confirmed suspicions that the capitalist nations aimed at their destruction.

Wallace therefore argued that the principal objective of American policy should be to "allay reasonable Russian grounds for fear, suspicions and distrust." The administration should be prepared to "agree to reasonable Russian guarantees of security," and should "make every effort to head off the atomic bomb race." The Secretary conceded that economic problems were "not as critical as others," but contended that successful negotiations on economic issues might "help considerably to bridge the chasm that separates us." Criticizing the Truman administration's stance in the loan discussions, Wallace argued that the United States should offer the Russians a loan on "economic and commercial grounds" without demanding that they "agree in advance to a series of what are to them difficult and somewhat unrelated political and economic concessions." Generous aid for Russian reconstruction could help to promote a mutually advantageous trade between the two nations and might establish an "atmosphere of mutual trust and confidence" that would promote the resolution of other problems.[64]

Truman politely acknowledged the letter, but paid no attention to the recommendations. He viewed Wallace's specific proposals as tantamount to surrender, and subsequent events reinforced his determination to deal firmly and forcefully with the Russians. In August, the USSR applied intensive diplomatic pressure upon Turkey for revision of the Montreux Convention governing use of the Turkish Straits, and launched a furious propaganda assault against the government of Greece, which was attempting with British assistance to put down a communist-supported insurgency. During the same period, the Yugoslav government shot down two unarmed U. S. transport planes. The cabinet met in a crisis atmosphere on August 15. The State, War, and Navy Departments warned Truman that these latest developments were all part of a Soviet drive for domination of the Balkans and Eastern Mediterranean, and advised that they should be "resisted at all costs." The President agreed, remarking that the United States "might as well find out whether the Russians were bent on world domination now as in fifteen years."[65]

In the next few weeks, the administration dispatched firm notes to the USSR on the Greek and Turkish problems, expanded its naval forces in the Mediterranean, and strengthened air and army units in Northern Italy along the Yugoslav border. When Wallace delivered a much publicized speech at Madison Square Garden on September 12, criticizing the "get tough" policy and advocating acceptance of the Soviet sphere of influence in Eastern Europe, the President demanded his resignation from the cabinet.[66]

Throughout the autumn of 1946, Wallace continued to advocate a large, generous, and "nonpolitical" loan to the USSR, and in late October, Stalin indicated to an American newsman that he was still interested in securing assistance from the United States. By this time, however, the Truman administration was moving beyond the "get tough" policy. Less than a week after Wallace's resignation, special counsel Clark Clifford presented Truman with a detailed document on "American Relations with the Soviet Union" that outlined the policy of containment. The memorandum set forth in a clear, comprehensive manner an interpretation of Russian behavior that had already gained wide acceptance in the administration. It argued that the Soviet leaders, driven on by a "haunting sense of insecurity" and by an ideology that promised the "ultimate destruction of capitalist states," had committed themselves irrevocably to a policy of expansionism. Despairing of cooperation with the USSR, the study proposed that the United States must "seek to prevent additional aggression," must "resist vigorously and successfully any efforts of the U.S.S.R. to expand into areas vital to American security," and must be prepared to "join with the British and other Western countries in an attempt to build a world of our own which will pursue its own objectives. . . ."

It stressed that the United States must develop an arsenal capable of resisting Russian expansion. But it added that "military support in case of attack is a last *resort;* a more effective barrier to communism is strong economic support. Trade agreements, loans, and technical missions strengthen our ties with friendly nations and are effective demonstrations that capitalism is at least the equal of communism." All nations "not now in the Soviet sphere should be given generous economic assistance and political support in their opposition to Soviet penetration." [67]

Clifford's proposals did not exclude altogether the

possibility of aid to the Soviet Union. Economic assistance might be extended and trade encouraged "provided the results are beneficial to our interests and do not simply strengthen the Soviet program." But the principles set forth in the statement made further aid to Russia quite unlikely. Secretary Byrnes had reached much the same conclusions independently. His cable from Paris, advocating that the United States should "help its friends in every way and refrain from assisting those who . . . are opposing the principles for which we stand," reached Washington on September 24, the same day Clifford presented his study to the President, and it received immediate and vigorous support from the War and Navy Departments. Thus by the end of September, 1946, the Truman administration had reoriented its foreign aid policy, abandoning any further pretense of treating all nations on an equal basis and concentrating its program on those outside the Soviet sphere.[68]

American officials began immediately to put these ideas into effect. The State Department did not even consider a new initiative to break the deadlock on credit negotiations with the USSR, and it allowed discussions on the $100 million surplus property credit to lapse. Angered by Czech support of the Soviet position at the Paris Peace Conference, Byrnes instructed his subordinates to hold back the unused portion of a surplus property credit and to suspend Czechoslovakia's application for a $50 million Export-Import loan.[69]

In November, the administration rid itself of UNRRA, which many officials had long regarded as a political and diplomatic liability. The London Council meeting in August, 1945 had agreed that UNRRA should wind up its operations by the end of 1946, but the world food crisis of 1945–1946 made plain that relief needs would increase rather than diminish in 1947, and UNRRA officials, supported by humanitarian groups in the United States, pressed for an extension of the agency's existence. Truman and his advisers were unsympathetic to these appeals. Congress had approved UNRRA appropriations in December, 1945, and

July, 1946, only after prolonged and sometimes stormy debates, and the Republican victory in the congressional elections of 1946 insured that a request for additional UNRRA funds would meet powerful opposition. The State Department was itself reluctant to continue furnishing economic assistance to nations whose policies it disapproved through an international agency over which it could exert only limited control, and the Yugoslav attacks on American aircraft in August produced widespread demands for termination of UNRRA shipments to all communist governments. Secretary Byrnes therefore told a Senate committee in November that UNRRA would end as scheduled, and advised that if additional relief assistance were provided it would be done by the United States "unilaterally." In succeeding weeks the administration began to draw up a new relief program, concentrating its assistance in areas where the United States had "special responsibilities and interests." [70]

Six months before the Truman Doctrine, the United States had begun to convert its economic aid program into an instrument of containment. The President's dramatic speech of March 12, 1947, calling for $400,000,000 in economic and military assistance to Greece and Turkey and for a broader commitment to support "free peoples who are resisting attempted subjugation by armed minorities or by outside pressure" brought that policy before the public and represented the next step in its implementation.

The adoption of this distinctly anti-communist line ended any possibility of further aid to the USSR. When the State Department began framing the Marshall Plan in the summer of 1947 to rescue Europe from a complete economic collapse, it did avoid the strong ideological overtones of the Truman Doctrine and even left the door open for Russian participation. But the administration adopted this position on the likelihood that the Russians would reject the American offer and in order to place upon them ultimate responsibility for the division of Europe. American officials were not disappointed, therefore, when Molotov in July, 1947, angrily rebuffed the Marshall proposal for European reconstruction.[71]

As Adam Ulam has observed, the beginning of the Marshall Plan "constitutes a watershed in the Cold War." From this point on, both sides became "frozen in mutual unfriendliness" and moved more vigorously to defend their own interests against the adversary. During the remainder of 1947, the United States concentrated on implementing the aid programs for Greece and Turkey, on completing plans for European recovery, and on selling these plans to Congress. The USSR exerted a heavy hand to prevent Poland and Czechoslovakia from joining the Marshall Plan, and hurriedly designed its own "Molotov Plan" for aid to Eastern Europe.[72]

After the summer of 1947, no U. S. official seriously considered postwar aid for the Soviet Union, and the administration, under intense pressure from Congress, terminated the agreements negotiated with the USSR shortly after V-J Day. UNRRA shipments to the Ukraine and Byelorussia had already ceased in the spring of 1947 with both programs over 99 percent completed. But the 3 (c) agreement of October 15, 1945, was never fulfilled. As early as February, 1946, Republicans in Congress had attempted to cut off lend-lease pipeline shipments to Russia, and in June, with Democratic support, they attached a rider to an appropriations bill that required cutoff of 3 (c) deliveries after December 31. The Russians quickly took title to the equipment available for shipment and rushed freighters to the United States to carry it away before the deadline. But delays in the production of supplies and their transportation to portside left some $20 million worth of equipment still unshipped at the end of the year.[73]

The administration made a half-hearted attempt to execute the agreement in early 1947. Dean Acheson pressed Congress to appropriate sufficient funds to complete deliveries, arguing that contracts had been made in good faith with the Russians and with American businessmen and warning that if they were not carried out the equipment would have to be sold as surplus property at a substantial loss. By this time, however, the legislators were not concerned with the sanctity of contracts or with business arguments. Critics stressed that the aid sent since V-J Day had helped to keep "Russia on a war footing" and made it easier for her to "build vast new arsenals of aggression for imperialism." Congressmen pointed out that it was absurd to sustain shipments to the Russians while they "continued kicking us in the shins." During the debate on the Truman Doctrine, Republicans emphasized the obvious contradiction in the administration's wish to ship industrial equipment to the USSR at the same time it was pressing Congress to enact an aid program to stop communist expansion.[74]

Led by Senator Vandenberg and by Styles Bridges, the firmly anti-communist chairman of the Senate Appropriations Committee, the Republican 80th Congress refused to appropriate funds to complete the 3 (c) agreements. The last pipeline shipments (of supplies to which the Russians had taken title before December 31, 1946) left American ports in the early summer of 1947. Later in the year, supply officials put up for sale as surplus property the remaining $20 million worth of equipment originally procured for the Soviet Union.[75]

The volume of assistance provided the USSR by the United States during the immediate postwar period compares quite unfavorably with that given the other major allies; it was considerably less than the Russians desired and felt they had a right to expect, and it played only an insignificant part in the rehabilitation of the war-devastated Soviet economy. Recent critics of U. S. postwar foreign policy have argued, therefore, that the American refusal to extend generous aid to Russia aroused deep and long-standing fears among the Soviet leaders, put them on the defensive, and left them no alternative but to extract severe reparations from the former Axis nations and to impose more rigorous restrictions on their own people and the peoples of Eastern Europe. Those historians who have assigned to the United States primary responsibility for the origins of the Cold War have singled out American policy on postwar aid as a principal source of conflict between the two nations. Even some historians highly critical of "revisionism" have suggested that greater "liberality with aid might . . . have offered United States policy makers a chance to dissipate quarrels." [76]

The Truman administration's handling of the postwar loan did intensify Russia's growing suspicion of the United States. On several occasions, Stalin protested to both Harriman and his successor, Walter Bedell Smith, against the long delay in the response to Molotov's request of January, 1945, for a $6 billion loan. Andrei Gromyko informed an American businessman in 1948 that Stalin's suspicions of the United States, first aroused by the abrupt cutback of lend-lease at V-E Day, "froze into a weary distrust" when the State Department revealed that the Soviet Union's application for a $1 billion loan had been lost. The department's attempt in the spring of 1946 to extract maximum concessions in return for only a small loan probably reinforced and strengthened these fears and suspicions.[77]

It is indeed difficult to defend American policy in the months after V-J Day. The Truman administration was understandably cautious on credits, but the mishandling of Rudenko's request for $1 billion was clumsy and unnecessarily offensive, and the bargaining position adopted by the United States betrayed a considerable naiveté. The UNRRA negotiations indicate that the Russians were willing to give a modest *quid pro quo* in return for economic aid, but the American attempt to make the $1 billion credit conditional on sweeping economic and political concessions rested on a gross exaggeration of American economic power and on an underestimation of Russian pride and sensitivity to alien influences. By assuming this position, the United States carelessly threw away whatever chance it had to use economic assistance to secure limited gains from the Russians.

On the other hand, it seems extremely doubtful that $1 billion or even $6 billion would have altered Russian policies significantly or established a basis for cordial postwar relations. Nations do not, as a rule, repay economic aid in good will, and the Russians, with their own brand of self-righteousness, felt that they were fully entitled to anything given them. In any event, they would have argued, the

United States would not have given them help unless it served a selfish American interest. By easing the Russians' reconstruction problems, American aid might have made it possible for them to deal more liberally with the former Axis nations and the other nations in their sphere of influence, but this is difficult to prove. In the absence of a broader Soviet-American agreement on postwar problems, economic assistance could not have accomplished much, and the wide divergence of attitudes and objectives rendered such an agreement impossible. The most that can be said with certainty is that American policy on aid for Russian reconstruction secured no advantage for the United States and that it aggravated the tensions that had already developed.

Chapter 10

CONCLUSION

AMERICAN AID TO RUSSIA ENDED BY THE MIDDLE of 1947, but the unresolved economic issues left over from this time have remained a source of contention in the relations between the two nations. Negotiations on a lend-lease settlement, initiated in that same year after months of haggling, quickly reached an impasse. The discussions were revived periodically during the 1950s and 1960s, but no progress could be made. Not until October, 1972, would the two nations finally reach agreement on the terms of the lend-lease obligation.[1]

The question of wartime and postwar aid to the USSR has also aroused heated controversy among historians. By 1948, Russian and American writers were angrily debating the role of lend-lease in the victory over the Axis. American revisionists of the 1940s and 1950s accused Roosevelt of appeasing the Russians by extending them lavish assistance without attaching any political strings, thereby facilitating their drive for postwar domination of Europe. Revisionists of the 1960s and 1970s, on the other hand, regard American attempts to force an exhausted Soviet Union to conform with their own postwar designs by the ruthless application of economic pressure as a principal source of Cold War conflict. A study of this subject, therefore, demands answers to the following questions: for what purposes and in what manner did the United States employ its economic assistance to the USSR during the years from 1941 to 1946 and what effect did its policies have on Soviet-American relations?

The most significant point is that the Roosevelt administration—and, indeed, the Truman administration—always regarded lend-lease to the Soviet Union as primarily an instrument of war and only secondarily (if at all) as a means of promoting the postwar objectives of the United States. Franklin D. Roosevelt conceived lend-lease as a means of countering the German threat—H. R. 1776 was entitled a bill to "promote the defense of the United States"—and he implemented it thereafter with the overriding purpose of speeding the defeat of the enemy.

In handling lend-lease to Russia, Roosevelt always gave top priority to strategic concerns. He extended aid to the Soviet Union in 1941 and continued it on a large scale throughout the war to sustain Russian defenses against the German invasion and later to expedite the Soviet counteroffensive across Europe. He regarded economic assistance as a principal means of holding together the uneasy alliance until the common threat could be removed. He appreciated the broad gulf that had developed between the USSR and the western nations since 1917 and the profound suspiciousness with which Russian leaders looked upon the outside world. Vividly recalling Russia's exit from the war in 1917 and the Molotov-Ribbentrop Pact of 1939, he feared that if the United States did not provide timely assistance to the Russians, Stalin might be tempted to conclude a separate peace with Hitler. Unable until 1944 to launch the second front the Russians so desperately wanted, the President relied primarily on lend-lease to demonstrate to them his concern for their plight and his commitment to the cause.

The men responsible for U. S. wartime diplomacy did not,

as an earlier generation of writers contended, ignore postwar problems in their concentration on winning the war. Recent studies have demonstrated conclusively that officials in the State Department and other agencies devoted a considerable amount of time to postwar planning and that they developed a coherent set of war aims. They were anxious to avoid a repetition of the mistakes of the interwar period. Recalling the long years of depression in the 1930s, they sought to promote postwar stability and prosperity. Above all, they wished to protect the next generation from the horrors of war they had known. To advance these goals, they worked for a peace based on the principles of the Atlantic Charter —self-determination for all peoples; the freeing of trade from restrictive and discriminatory barriers; the establishment of an international organization to preserve the peace —principles that squared with traditional American ideals and with tangible vital interests.[2]

Many officials recognized that the USSR might pose an obstacle to the fulfillment of these objectives, and they also perceived that lend-lease could be used as a political instrument to promote Russian-American agreement after the war had ended. Views on such problems are seldom monolithic, and during the war there were two schools of thought on how economic assistance might best be used for political gain.

Former ambassador Bullitt, ambassadors Steinhardt, Standley, and Harriman, and General Deane, all of whom had served in Moscow and had experienced first-hand the frustrations of dealing with Soviet officials, shared a generally pessimistic view of Russian-American cooperation and advocated the importance of toughness. From personal experience, they concluded that the Soviet leaders did not share American ideals, values, or aspirations for the postwar period. Rather they were tough, sometimes cynical realists, who would pursue their own aims relentlessly and would respect opposition only when it was backed by power.

These Americans did not despair altogether of accommodation, but they felt it could be achieved only if the United

States demonstrated a firm commitment to the principles in which it believed and used the instruments available to it to force Soviet compliance. Thus they advocated that economic assistance should be conditioned on the receipt of a *quid pro quo*. The Russians, they argued, could not be dealt with on any other basis. They would not understand or appreciate American generosity; they would not repay American aid in good will. Only if the United States required military, political, or economic concessions in return for its help could it be sure to protect its own interests and establish the mutual respect and reciprocity that was essential for postwar collaboration between the two nations.

Other Americans, notably Joseph E. Davies, General James H. Burns, and Harry Hopkins, advanced directly opposite arguments. These men admitted that the Russians were difficult to get along with, that they were abnormally suspicious, and that their postwar aims clashed with those of the United States. But they were generally sympathetic toward the Soviet Union, arguing that its extreme concern about security derived from a history of costly invasions and from the open hostility capitalist nations had displayed toward it since the revolution. They speculated that if the Russians were treated generously, they might respond in kind. Liberal assistance, given in a spirit of real friendship and without crude efforts to attach conditions, would indicate to them that Americans could be trusted and would establish a firm basis for postwar collaboration.

In deciding the issue between these two groups, Roosevelt consistently sided with Davies, Burns, and Hopkins. He extended aid to the USSR without condition, established unique procedures to handle that aid, required his subordinates to be patient with Russian officials, and rejected all proposals to use lend-lease as a bargaining lever. He may have shared the view that a generous, friendly policy would contribute to postwar amity, and he certainly hoped that it would promote wartime cooperation. But he was more concerned with immediate strategic necessities. His principal purpose was to furnish maximum assistance to the Soviet

Union and to build an effective alliance against Hitler, and he recognized that attempting to extract a *quid pro quo* from the Russians would only complicate the attainment of these immediate objectives.

Many writers have charged Roosevelt with ignoring long-range political calculations in his obsession with winning the war, and his handling of lend-lease has been cited as a case in point. Yet when the matter is considered in all its dimensions, the President's reasoning appears to have been sound. Those who advocated the use of lend-lease as an instrument of pressure exaggerated its strength. Roosevelt correctly perceived that to require the Russians to make political concessions in 1941 would have been pointless; agreements negotiated under duress in that year would have been of no value when the war ended. Standley's proposal to require closer military collaboration in return for aid was advanced at a time when the United States was far behind in its supply commitments, the second front was still on the planning boards, and the Russians were dissatisfied and angry. Such a proposal held out risks greater than any possible gains that might have been secured.

Harriman and Deane suggested changes in lend-lease policy during a period when victory was near and the outlines of postwar conflict were already becoming apparent. But they too overestimated the capacity of economic assistance to influence Soviet actions. The "firm but friendly *quid pro quo* approach" might have brought forth from the Russians some limited military or political concessions, but it would not have compelled them to conform to American standards of behavior in international relations. To protect the USSR against a future invasion, Stalin had set as the preeminent goal of his foreign policy the establishment of a buffer zone in Eastern Europe, and he would not have deviated from it for any amount of economic assistance. Had Roosevelt followed Harriman's advice, it would probably have aroused the Soviet leader's already profound anxieties and might have led him to press toward his objectives all the more rapidly and ruthlessly.

Critics of unconditional aid correctly noted that it afforded little protection against waste or misuse of supplies. Since the Russians did not allow regular observers at the front, it has been difficult to determine with precision how effectively they used lend-lease or to what extent they took advantage of American liberality. Some vital supplies deteriorated awaiting shipment to Russia during the most severe period of the shipping crisis in 1942 and 1943. Soviet abuse of the marine diesel engines provides one blatant and costly example of the dangers of unconditional aid, and an American official who visited Russian industrial plants in 1944 later commented that the Russians had "unbelievably mistreated" some expensive pieces of oil refinery equipment furnished on lend-lease. The United States continued to deliver large quantities of aircraft long after the Russians had established air superiority over the Germans and at a time when the planes might have been employed more effectively in other theaters. It is also clear, although it is impossible to determine the extent of the practice, that the USSR used American supplies to advance its own prestige and interests in neighboring countries such as Iran and Poland.[3]

It seems likely, however, that those who have criticized the policy have exaggerated its cost to the United States. Waste and inefficiency are inevitable in total war, and the Russians probably had more than their share, especially in the first years of the conflict. But those Americans who visited the front and toured war industries, even such critics as Harriman, came away generally impressed with the effective use to which American supplies were being put. Harriman and Deane discovered little evidence to prove that equipment was going into stockpiles. Even in 1944 and 1945, limitations on shipping compelled the Russians to give top priority to those items they needed most, thus minimizing their ability to put aside supplies for future use and to transfer them to other nations. The limited waste and misuse that did occur did not severely hamper operations in other theaters, and in the long run was of small importance compared with Russia's contribution to victory over Germany.[4]

It has also been argued that Roosevelt's handling of lend-lease enormously increased the Soviet Union's military power and enabled it to "swallow up much of Eastern and Central Europe." Undeniably, American aid strengthened Russia both militarily and industrially, and American trucks speeded the passage of the Red Army across Europe. "Just imagine how we would have advanced from Stalingrad to Berlin without them," the former Soviet premier Nikita Khrushchev has remarked. Yet, given the conditions under which the war was fought, it is difficult to see how this result could have been avoided. The United States could not have restricted its assistance to the USSR without risking a slow-down in Russian operations or a break in the alliance. The cost in either case would have been excessive. Victory would have been delayed, American deaths and casualties would have increased to unacceptable proportions, and there is no way of proving that from the standpoint of American interests the end result would have been more satisfactory. Indeed, it could have been worse.[5]

The unconditional aid policy did not achieve all that its advocates hoped. Those Presidential advisers who predicted that generous assistance to the USSR would break down old suspicions and earn for the United States good will that might be cashed in after the war misjudged the Russians and vastly overestimated the power of foreign aid. It was naive to expect that $10 billion—or even more—could alter Russia's centuries-old tradition of distrust of foreigners or soothe the personal paranoia of a man such as Joseph Stalin. The statements of Russian officials make clear that they valued U. S. help. But they recognized correctly that the United States would not have assisted them had it not served an American interest. And they felt, with some justification, that they had more than repaid the price of lend-lease by their own sacrifices and their contribution to the defeat of Germany. In any event, gratitude is a transient commodity in international relations. As Samuel P. Huntington has recently observed, expressions of appreciation from the recipients of foreign aid usually approximate the "classic expression of the ward heeler to the political boss: 'But what have you done for me lately?' " It was natural, especially after the United States began to challenge Soviet moves in Eastern Europe, that the Russian leaders should quickly and conveniently forget the help they had received through lend-lease.[6]

Roosevelt's policies may also have contributed to later Russian-American conflict by raising hopes that could not be realized. His no-strings-attached dispensation of assistance and his efforts to meet every Russian request may not have encouraged the notion that the United States was an easy mark, but they did create certain expectations that the President himself could not possibly fulfill. The Russians apparently concluded that lend-lease would be continued indefinitely on the same basis and in substantial quantities and that the United States would provide generous aid for Russian reconstruction. Roosevelt may have intended to do this, but if so he had not properly prepared the groundwork at home. Precisely because the American people and Congress always looked upon lend-lease as essentially a military weapon to be discarded when the war was over, there were inherent limitations to its use. The President's own statements to Congress did not discourage these notions, stressing that lend-lease was exclusively an instrument of war, that it would be reduced as the urgency of military need declined, and that it would be terminated when the war ended. But Roosevelt did not make this clear to the Russians, and his actions left a broad gap between the expectations raised in Moscow and those at home. It would have taken the most accomplished diplomatist and skillful politician to bridge that gap.

Still, on balance, Roosevelt's handling of lend-lease was generally wise and realistic and contributed immeasurably to the major goals set for it. Those writers who have charged the President with appeasing Russia and ignoring long-range political objectives have minimized the difficulties in holding the alliance together and have taken Allied victory for granted. Triumph over the Axis was by no means certain in 1942 and 1943. The President may have taken too seriously the dangers of a separate peace between Russia and Germany, but the possibility existed and he would have been foolhardy to have ignored it. By 1944 the United States and Britain might have been able to win the war without Russian help, but it would have taken much longer and the cost in lives and money would have been enormous. The American people demanded that the war be won as quickly and inexpensively as possible, and to accomplish that it was essential for Russia to remain in the war and to conduct her campaigns as effectively as possible.

Lend-lease did much to bring about that result. The more than $10 billion worth of equipment and supplies sent to the Soviet Union did represent only a small percentage of Russian production—best estimates set the figure at 10 or 11 percent. But such figures are misleading at best. In some cases, raw materials or machinery helped to expand Russian productivity. Arms, industrial equipment, raw materials, and food filled critical gaps in Russian output and allowed Soviet industry to concentrate on production of items for which it was best suited. Railroad and automotive equipment facilitated the delivery of all types of supplies to the battle fronts. Lend-lease probably did not decide the outcome of the war in Russia, but the wartime statements of Soviet leaders make clear that it helped to make the nation and the Red Army a much more potent fighting force.[7]

The unconditional aid policy was an essential ingredient in this formula of success. It assured maximum shipments when aid to Russia faced serious, seemingly insuperable obstacles. If it did not overcome Russia's suspicions of the West, it did minimize Soviet-American tension and helped to hold the alliance together during a period of great stress. Roosevelt's refusal to use lend-lease as a bargaining weapon and his generally benevolent and liberal policies on economic assistance, were, to be sure, motivated by expediency and self-interest. Nevertheless, his handling of lend-lease offers a convincing refutation to those recent revisionists who have conjured up an image of the United States aggressively using its economic power to shape the world in its own image. Quite the contrary, it suggests how far the President was willing to go to establish a workable relationship with the Russians in war and peace and reveals some of the practical limitations that hindered the realization of this goal.

The revisionists of the 1960s and 1970s have correctly noted that Roosevelt's successor, Harry S. Truman, initiated significant changes in lend-lease policy. Within a month after taking office, the new President abandoned unconditional aid and in the weeks that followed he sharply reduced the volume of shipments to the USSR. They have also argued, again correctly, that these changes stemmed from a growing distrust of the Russians and were designed to influence Soviet policy in Europe. Truman was much less sympathetic to Stalin's security concerns than Roosevelt, and he regarded the Soviet leader's policies in Eastern Europe as immoral and a threat to America's aims for the postwar world. He intended the cutback in aid to indicate to the Kremlin U. S. displeasure with its actions and to make clear that the USSR could not defy American wishes with impunity.

But to stop there is to provide only an incomplete and distorted picture of the circumstances under which Truman acted. "Generosity, even though serving a common purpose and joint interest, is hard to sustain," Herbert Feis has written. "When tension comes between those who give and those who receive, the giver is apt to yield to the impulse to end the giving as soon as it is feasible to do so." By the spring of 1945, the basic conflict in postwar objectives had come into the open. The Russians' adamant refusal to accept American interpretations of the Yalta agreement on Poland and the Declaration on Liberated Europe, as well as their occupation policies in Eastern Europe, had aroused deep concern in Washington. The American urge to assist the USSR waned proportionally. At the same time, the imminent end of the war in Europe removed the most compelling rationale for aid to Russia and reduced still further the pressures for continued generosity.[8]

In any event, domestic pressures made it impossible for

Truman to continue the unconditional aid policy and very difficult for him to sustain large volumes of shipments to the Soviet Union after V-E Day. Powerful interest groups and congressmen of both parties had long made clear their unwillingness to sanction the use of lend-lease for anything but essential military purposes, and in April of 1945 Congress had written this principle into law. The Soviet role in the war against Japan was necessarily less important than its part in the European war, and it would have been very difficult to justify shipments on a comparable scale. In addition, Truman's newness in office, his seemingly formidable problems in securing congressional approval of Roosevelt's postwar designs, his recent service in the Senate, all made him especially sensitive to congressional attitudes toward lend-lease.

Indeed, partly because of these domestic limitations and as a result of bureaucratic confusion and administrative bungling, the Truman administration was unable to employ lend-lease as a diplomatic weapon in the manner conceived by Harriman, the architect of the new policy. The ambassador designed post-V-E Day policy to make possible the use of lend-lease as an instrument of diplomacy. But strategies, however well developed, are sometimes faulty in execution. The implementation of the V-E Day cutback, a product of the anti-Russian leanings and political inhibitions of two of Truman's advisers and of the President's own inexperience, conflicted with Harriman's immediate desire to forestall harsh action against the USSR. And despite the ambassador's persistent efforts after V-E Day, continued domestic pressures, the growing disinclination of U. S. officials to look kindly upon the Soviet Union, and the declining strategic importance of Russia in the war against Japan forced continued reductions in aid and the rapid termination of lend-lease at V-J Day. Truman's policies undoubtedly reflected a growing suspicion of the USSR, but the administration did not employ lend-lease systematically to achieve its foreign policy objectives.

American handling of lend-lease between V-E Day and V-J Day did nonetheless contribute to the rise of Soviet-Ameri-

can tension in the summer of 1945. The abrupt cutback, executed with no warning, disrupted Russian planning for the
last stages of the war and the initial period of reconstruction.
Coming as it did during a period of political crisis, it was
naturally interpreted in Moscow as an attempt at economic
coercion. The manner in which the new administration
acted contrasted so blatantly with Roosevelt's conduct of
lend-lease diplomacy that it could not but have aroused Russian suspicions of the new President. Stalin exaggerated in
citing the lend-lease reduction as the first American action to
raise doubts about the possibility of postwar cooperation.
One suspects that he always had profound doubts, and the
conflict over Poland in March and April must stand as more
significant than Truman's handling of economic assistance.
Still, lend-lease reinforced these fears and misgivings.

If lend-lease was conceived and implemented mainly as an
instrument of war, aid for Russian reconstruction was regarded by U. S. officials from the very beginning as a potentially powerful weapon of foreign policy. But, here again,
they disagreed on how it could be employed most effectively.
Along with Henry Morgenthau and Henry Wallace, that
group which had viewed lend-lease as a means of demonstrating friendship generally looked upon postwar credits the
same way: generous American assistance would ease Russia's
task of reconstruction, soften her outlook toward the rest of
the world, and create bonds that would encourage the continuation of wartime cooperation. Others, among whom
Harriman was again the most consistent and forceful advocate, emphasized that postwar loans or credits offered the
United States its strongest lever to promote foreign policy
objectives. Exhausted from the war, the Russians would have
to depend upon U. S. aid to reconstruct their economy. The
United States could therefore demand in return significant
political and economic concessions that would promote its
own interests and bring Soviet policies in line with its own
goals.

Support for the Harriman position grew substantially in
late 1944 and early 1945. The conflict over Poland and East-

ern Europe brought a growing realization that the Russians did not intend to comply with American principles, convincing many that some form of pressure should be used. Some officials in the State Department and in other agencies felt it necessary to dispel the Russians' apparent illusion that they could defy American interests without fear of reprisal. Although Roosevelt had persistently refused to permit the use of lend-lease as an instrument of diplomacy, his unwillingness to commit himself on a postwar loan for Russia and his agreement to halt negotiations on the 3 (c) agreement suggest that he too was leaning in the direction of Harriman's arguments in the last months of his life.

At least from early 1945 on, the United States attempted to exploit the apparent advantage offered by postwar assistance, but both the Roosevelt and Truman administrations employed the weapon erratically and ineffectively, securing no tangible gain and only contributing to the rise of tension with their adversary. Harriman had warned that if the United States was to secure maximum benefit from the aid given Russia, it must come forward with a specific plan before the war ended. Soviet purchasing was based on long-range plans, and the Russians would want to know what they could expect to get well in advance of the actual date of transaction. An early offer of aid would help to sustain the cooperative spirit of the war, whereas delay would only enhance Soviet suspicions. Harriman might also have noted that the earlier negotiations were begun, the greater the possibility of securing concessions. Had the U. S. acted in 1944 or even in 1945, when Russian diplomacy retained some flexibility (in method if not in ultimate objective) and before divisions on postwar problems had hardened, some concessions on trade or political problems might have been secured.

Roosevelt did not follow Harriman's sound advice, however, refusing to take decisive action in 1944 or even in 1945. After raising Russian hopes in 1943 by informal discussions, he did not press Congress to secure the authority necessary to make possible credits for the USSR, and for over a year he responded to Russian overtures with nothing more than vague statements expressing America's desire to help. Roosevelt's hesitance was in part motivated by domestic political considerations. Especially in the election year 1944 he was reluctant to raise an issue he felt was potentially divisive.

Even after the election was over, however, the President did not place postwar aid high on his list of legislative priorities or make more concrete overtures to the USSR. His caution, at this point, most likely derived from calculations of diplomatic tactics. In 1945, those Americans (Harriman excepted) who wished to use economic assistance to influence Soviet foreign policy apparently felt that if they held back from definite commitments, at the same time protesting Russian actions more vigorously, the Soviet leaders would get the idea that they must adjust to American demands if they wished to receive help. Assuming that Russia's weakness and need would make it dependent on U. S. aid, they concluded that in time Stalin would have no choice but to come around.

As with lend-lease, U. S. officials overestimated the potential bargaining power of credits. The Soviet leaders wanted American supplies, especially heavy equipment and machine tools, which they considered superior to their own products and those of other nations, and which would facilitate and speed up their industrial recovery. But they were not dependent upon these supplies; reconstruction might take longer, but it could be accomplished without U. S. help. Indeed, as Alexander Werth has suggested, Soviet officials probably felt certain "ideological and political inhibitions" about an American loan, fearing that "excessive financial dependence on the United States might well go counter to their own security considerations." Stalin and his top advisers must have agreed, especially at the end of the war and with tension with the west on the rise, that American aid was not worth concessions that could weaken their defenses. Under no circumstances would they have bargained away their influence in Eastern Europe for credits. Instead of adjusting their foreign policy, they simply waited, confident that once the inevitable depression hit the United States, American leaders would have no choice but to come through with a substantial and generous loan.[9]

Throughout 1945, therefore, each side worked under illusions about the behavior of the other, and as long as these persisted, no serious discussions could take place. In inviting the Russians to open formal negotiations in February, 1946, the Truman administration seems to have abandoned its earlier hopes that they would alter their behavior in order to secure U. S. assistance. But the conditions it attempted to connect with discussions on a loan insured that talks would never get started. The mere suggestion of major economic and political concessions in Eastern Europe in the tense atmosphere of early 1946 made Soviet rejection probable if not inevitable. Preliminary exchanges on the issue continued into the fall of the year, but by the time they had become obviously deadlocked and futile, the entire question of aid for Russian reconstruction was an anachronistic holdover from an earlier era of hope and promise.

Along with the abrupt termination of lend-lease, American handling of postwar aid contributed to the rise of Soviet-American hostility in the first year after the end of World War II. The evasive and ambiguous replies to Soviet overtures, the long delay before making a formal offer, the lost request, the conditions connected to the loan negotiations could not have been better calculated to strengthen the already profound Russian suspicions of American intentions. When combined with the loud protests about Soviet actions in Eastern Europe and with the American position on atomic energy, U. S. economic policies confirmed Russian fears of the hostility of American leaders. The American decision to concentrate economic assistance programs on the containment of communism sharpened divisions, and contributed to the increasing aggressiveness of Stalin after 1947.

It cannot be proven, however, that continuation of lend-lease after V-J day, the provision of transitional assistance, and a postwar loan would have altered the course of Russian-American relations. It is naive to assume that postwar American generosity would have evoked deep gratitude and good will in the Soviet Union. The experience of lend-lease in fact suggests that postwar aid, by itself, would not have done much to allay Soviet suspicions. Economic aid could have acted as a healing force only if accompanied by an American willingness to accept, at least tacitly, predominant Soviet influence in Eastern Europe. The wisdom of such a course has much to commend it in retrospect, but history and experience had not prepared American leaders to act in this fashion. American policies on economic issues in 1945 and 1946 reflected and in large part derived from the clash in postwar objectives. While they admittedly contributed to the rising tensions between the two former allies, they were as much a result as a cause of the Cold War.

Despite the shortsightedness of U. S. policy in 1945 and 1946, the story of American aid to Russia constitutes one of the most noteworthy chapters in the history of American diplomacy. Lend-lease was not what Churchill once called it in a flight of hyperbole—"the most unsordid act in the history of any nation." It was an act of calculated self-interest and Americans were ever conscious of the advantages that might be secured from it. But it was a vast improvement over the methods of finance used in World War I, and as employed by Franklin D. Roosevelt it contributed mightily to the success of the Grand Alliance. It did more than any other single act to cement the fragile ties between the Soviet Union and the United States and to promote a spirit of cooperation and harmony in the relations between these two nations. That it did not make possible attainment of the ultimate goal, a lasting peace, reflects the depth of the issues that divided the two allies and the inherent limitations of foreign aid itself, not the spirit in which lend-lease was handled.

Appendix

LEND-LEASE SETTLEMENT NEGOTIATIONS, 1946-1972

FORMAL NEGOTIATIONS ON A LEND-LEASE SETTLEMENT FInally got under way in 1947 after more than a year of preliminary haggling. As Roosevelt had implied when lendlease had been proposed, the United States sought no compensation for equipment consumed or destroyed in the war, and in fact requested nothing for military supplies still operational at the end of the conflict. The Truman administration asked payment only for civilian supplies—locomotives, trucks, machine tools, and other industrial equipment—in stock in the USSR at V-J Day. The Russians refused American requests for an inventory of the volume of these items. U. S. officials estimated their value at $2.6 billion, but in 1948 agreed to settle for $1.3 billion.

The United States assumed that its offer was a generous one—the USSR had been furnished supplies estimated at more than $10 billion and was being asked to pay for less than 10 percent and that for items still of significant value to the Russian economy. From the very beginning of the negotiations, however, the Soviet government took a different position. The Russians were quite obviously annoyed that any compensation had been requested. "Why it is like asking us to pay for saving your life after we have been severely wounded in the process," one writer commented. "What are a few thousand trucks and planes compared with the blood of 7,000,000 Russians?" was a typical reaction according to Drew Middleton of the New York *Times*. Soviet negotiators also charged that the United States had exaggerated the value of the civilian supplies in their possession. Nevertheless, in 1948 the USSR offered to pay $170 million.[1]

Despite subsequent moves toward a compromise, the two nations could not agree upon a mutually acceptable figure. In 1951, the Soviet Union raised its offer to $240 million. The United States reduced its claim to $800 million and indicated that it was prepared to go still further if the Russians would make another offer. Soviet negotiators then went up to $300 million, but in January, 1952, Secretary of State Dean Acheson rejected this as "far from fair and reasonable compensation" and demanded that the Russians agree to reasonable terms or submit the dispute to international arbitration. The Soviet government refused, and the financial talks reached an impasse.[2]

Discussions on the financial settlement were exacerbated by sharp differences over the disposition of a large number of lend-lease vessels in the possession of the Soviet Union at the end of the war. The United States had turned over to its ally ninety-six merchant ships, most of which were used on the Pacific run to Vladivostok, and an additional 615 naval vessels, including twenty-seven frigates, three icebreakers, and 585 small craft (submarine chasers, torpedo boats, etc.). At the beginning of the negotiations, the United States maintained a "pressing" need for the icebreakers, frigates, and 186 of the small craft and requested their immediate return. At the same time, it expressed a willingness to sell the merchant vessels and those military craft that were declared surplus property.[3]

After months of prodding, the USSR returned the frigates, icebreakers, and nine freighters, but negotiations on the other ships got nowhere. The Russians agreed to buy the freighters and some of the small craft, but the two nations could not agree on the terms of sale. Exasperated with the delay, the United States in 1951 withdrew its offer to sell and demanded the immediate return of all the ships, claiming that it needed them for its own use. The USSR responded angrily, accusing the Truman administration of acting illegally and in bad faith by withdrawing its previous offer and charging that the United States could not need the ships when it was liberally giving and selling similar types to its allies throughout the world.[4]

By 1951, the lend-lease negotiations were hopelessly stalemated, and the positions assumed by both nations reflected the enormous rise in hostility that accompanied the intensification of the Cold War and the outbreak of hot war in Korea. The New York *Times* observed that the Russians' refusal to return the lend-lease ships was "in the familiar tradition of Soviet insolence in diplomatic negotiations," accused the USSR of making no "real effort" to reach a financial settlement despite the generous terms offered by the United States, and warned that the Russians were using "some of these very lend-lease goods . . . supplied them to repel aggression to prepare and support aggression of their own."[5]

Pravda responded in kind, charging that the United States was "inflating the value of the supplies for which it asked payment and was trying to impose more severe terms on the USSR—which had borne the "main weight of the struggle against the Hitlerite invaders"—than those offered Britain. The Americans were acting like "usurers and not like wartime allies," and were "piling up one artificial obstacle after another in order to hamper the successful conclusion of the negotiations." "Such tactics," it concluded, were "dictated by the aggressive policy of the American ruling circles, which stop at nothing in their striving to aggravate further the relations between the Soviet Union and the United States. . . ."[6]

The wrangle over lend-lease ships produced equally heated exchanges. The Soviet press claimed that the ships the United States demanded returned were "extremely dilapidated" and "not fit for sailing," and a Russian ship captain, interviewed in Singapore, said that the vessels ought to be returned because they were "no good anyway." American observers contended, on the other hand, that the Liberty Ships comprised a "significant portion" of the Soviet merchant fleet and the naval vessels represented an "important portion" of the USSR's "not-too-considerable navy." "Little wonder," the New York *Times* remarked, that the "Kremlin does not wish to give them up." [7]

The extent of mutual hostility was clearly revealed, in the form of comic opera, when the Soviet Union returned the frigate *Milwaukee* to Lewes, Delaware, in 1949. Soviet seamen insisted upon a "unique ceremony" to avoid the usual courtesy of saluting the U. S. flag, leaving the ship immediately after the Soviet ensign was hauled down. American sailors who subsequently boarded the ship promptly informed reporters that the Red Navy had left the *Milwaukee* in a "total state of neglect," adding that they had found an "overpowering stench" below decks and had encountered evidence of rats everywhere.[8]

Following the death of Stalin in March, 1953, the new Soviet regime assumed a more conciliatory tone in the lend-lease negotiations, and by 1956 some progress had been made in resolving the dispute over the ships. Between 1954 and 1956, the Russians returned 127 small craft and destroyed another ninety under the eyes of American observers. At the same time, Soviet officials claimed that an additional 146 naval craft had already been scrapped or lost in the war and that another 171 were inoperable. If these figures are accurate, the USSR after 1956 still held fifty-one small craft and eighty-seven merchant vessels for which no settlement has been made. Ironically, five of the lend-lease freighters were used by the Soviet Union to carry supplies to Cuba during the buildup that immediately preceded the missile crisis of October, 1962.[9]

A growing Soviet desire for expanded trade with the United States led to one serious attempt in 1959–1960 to settle the lend-lease financial obligation. At their Camp David meeting in September, 1959, Nikita Khrushchev stressed to Dwight D. Eisenhower his earnest wish that the United States restore to the USSR the most-favored-nation status withdrawn by Congress in 1951 and remove other legal obstacles to trade with Russia. Eisenhower made clear that trade concessions would require the approval of Congress, and that a "fair" settlement of lend-lease would be most helpful in this regard. The Soviet premier accordingly agreed to resume talks in early 1960.[10]

But the discussions, which opened in Washington in January, were no more successful than previous efforts. American negotiators contended that the talks should deal exclusively with lend-lease, a point they said had been understood at Camp David. Soviet diplomats adamantly insisted, on the other hand, that a settlement of lend-lease must be accompanied by a trade agreement, including the extension of most-favored-nation status and long-term credits. After three meetings, the negotiations reached an impasse, and the United States indicated that it would resume discussions only when the USSR agreed to treat lend-lease as a "separate and independent issue." [11]

There the matter remained until early 1972, when the two nations once again agreed to resume negotiations. By this time, each of them had strong incentives to remove this long-standing irritant in their relations. Increasingly concerned with the Chinese threat, the Soviet government was anxious to patch up its relations with the United States. It also looked upon trade with the U. S. as a possible means of ameliorating economic difficulties within the USSR, and was particularly eager to expand exports to pay for imports of American food products and sophisticated technological equipment. The administration of Richard M. Nixon was also attempting to improve relations with the Soviet Union, partly in hopes that its influence might be brought to bear for a settlement in Vietnam, and American businessmen and government officials hoped that expanded trade with Russia would help solve the nation's economic problems.

A new round of negotiations thus opened in April, 1972, and continued intermittently throughout the summer, occupying a prominent place in President Nixon's much publicized summit talks in Moscow. Despite the strong inducements for agreement, the lend-lease issue turned out to be one of the most difficult issues confronting Russian and American negotiators. The Nixon administration, much like that of Eisenhower before it, looked upon lend-lease as a "barometer" for future trade relations, and insisted that a "good settlement" must be reached before it would approach Congress to remove discrimination against Russian imports and barriers against credits. The Soviet government still was reluctant to make major concessions. "It is lousy of the Americans to ask us to pay that debt when we lost 20 million people in that war," a Russian spokesman complained.[12]

Nevertheless, after more than six months of discussions, the White House on October 18, 1972, announced the signing of a broad package deal combining a lend-lease settlement with a trade agreement. To resolve the lend-lease obligation, the Soviet Union consented to pay a sum of $722 million, including principal and interest, by July 1, 2001. In return, the Nixon administration pledged to grant the USSR Export-Import credits in an unspecified amount and to seek from Congress the authority to extend most-favored-nation treatment to Russian imports. After more than twenty-five years of wrangling, the two nations appeared to have laid to rest an old and extremely difficult impediment to better relations.[13]

NOTES

INTRODUCTION

1. For representative American expressions of
the possible impact of lend-lease on Soviet-American relations, see broadcast by Gabriel Heatter,
September 28, 1943, in "Lend-Lease News Digest,"
September 29, 1943, Edward R. Stettinius, Jr.
Manuscripts, University of Virginia Library, and
Edward R. Stettinius, Jr., *Lend-Lease: Weapon for
Victory*, pp. 211–12; for representative Russian
comment, see Department of State, *Foreign Relations of the United States—Diplomatic Papers,
1944,* Vol. IV: *Europe,* pp. 884–85.

2. Robert A. Divine (ed.), *Causes and Consequences of World War II,* p. 3.

3. *Trud,* quoted in New York *Times,* February
26, 1948; Nikolai A. Voznesensky, *The Economy
of the USSR During World War II,* pp. 43–44;
for American comment on the Voznesensky book,

see New York *Times,* September 23, 1948, and review by Alexander Gerschenkron in *The American Economic Review,* XXXVIII (September, 1948), 649–57; for further Russian comment on lend-lease, see New York *Times,* December 12, 1949, and A. Alexeyev, "Lend-Lease— Weapon of Aggressive American Imperialism," *The Current Digest of the Soviet Press,* III (September 8, 1951), 8–10; Soviet historians' revisions of the history of World War II are analyzed in Matthew P. Gallagher, *The Soviet History of World War II: Myths, Memories, and Realities.*

4. Thomas A. Bailey, *America Faces Russia: Russian-American Relations from Early Times to Our Day,* pp. 291–92.

5. John T. Flynn, *The Roosevelt Myth,* p. 356.

6. George N. Crocker, *Roosevelt's Road to Russia,* pp. 4, 62–65, 162–63, 263–64.

7. George Racey Jordan, *From Major Jordan's Diaries.*

8. Bailey, *America Faces Russia,* pp. 295–96.

9. George F. Kennan, *American Diplomacy, 1900–1950,* p. 75.

10. Robert Huhn Jones, *The Roads to Russia: United States Lend-Lease to the Soviet Union,* p. 269.

11. Convenient summaries of the revisionist viewpoint can be found in Christopher Lasch, "The Cold War, Revisited and Re-visioned," New York *Times Magazine* (January 14, 1968), pp. 26ff, and Walter Lafeber, "War: Cold," *Cornell Alumni News* (October, 1968), pp. 24–29. One of the earliest critiques of revisionism is Arthur Schlesinger, Jr., "Origins of the Cold War," *Foreign Affairs,* XLVI (October, 1967), 22–52. The best recent critiques are Charles S. Maier, "Revisionism and the Interpretation of Cold War Origins," *Perspectives in American History,* IV (1970), 313–47, and John L. Gaddis, "A Revisionist Monolith: American Foreign Policy and the Origins of the Cold War," paper delivered at the Annual Convention of the American Historical Association, Boston, December 29, 1970.

12. The moderate position is stated in Gar Alperovitz, *Atomic Diplomacy: Hiroshima and Potsdam;* the radical in Gabriel Kolko, *The Politics of War: The World and United States Foreign Policy, 1943–1945.*

13. See, for example, Alperovitz, *Atomic Diplomacy,* pp. 19–40, 223–24, Kolko, *Politics of War,* pp. 337–39, 397–98, Lloyd C. Gardner, *Architects of Illusion: Men and Ideas in American Foreign Policy, 1941–1949,* pp. 61–62, 128–130, and Thomas G. Paterson, "The Abortive Loan to Russia and the Origins of the Cold War," *Journal of American History,* LVI (June, 1969), 89–92.

14. Schlesinger, "Origins of the Cold War," pp. 44–45; Maier, "Revisionism," pp. 340–41.

1. THE DECISION TO AID RUSSIA:
JUNE—NOVEMBER, 1941

1. Winston S. Churchill, *The Grand Alliance*, p. 372.

2. The abandonment of neutrality is discussed in Robert A. Divine, *The Illusion of Neutrality* and *The Reluctant Belligerent*, and in William L. Langer and S. Everett Gleason, *The Challenge to Isolation* and *The Undeclared War*.

3. Warren F. Kimball's monograph, *The Most Unsordid Act: Lend-Lease, 1939–1941*, analyzes in detail the origins of the lend-lease idea.

4. Franklin D. Roosevelt, "Aid to the Democracies," *Vital Speeches*, VII (April 1, 1941), 355. Kimball, *Unsordid Act*, pp. 151–94, covers the lend-lease debate. The isolationist position is discussed in Wayne Cole, *America First: The Battle Against Intervention*, pp. 35–50, and Mark Chadwin, *The Hawks of World War II*, pp. 151–58, deals with the interventionists.

5. "Dollars and Pounds," *The Economist*, CXL (March 15, 1941), 321; New York *Times*, March 12, 1941; Arthur Vandenberg, *The Private Papers of Senator Vandenberg*, ed. by Arthur Vandenberg, Jr., p. 10.

6. America First, *Washington News Letter* (March 12, 1941).

7. See the polls in Hadley Cantril (ed.), *Public Opinion, 1935–1946*, pp. 411 and 975.

8. Robert A. Divine, *Roosevelt and World War II*, p. 43.

9. New York *Times*, June 30, 1941.

10. Quoted in Raymond Dawson, *The Decision To Aid Russia: Foreign Policy and Domestic Politics*, pp. 82–83, 102.

11. Richmond *Times-Dispatch*, June 23, 1941; Dawson, *Decision To Aid Russia*, pp. 69–79.

12. Washington *Post*, June 28, 1941. For an excellent statement of the interventionist dilemma, see John Sorrells (Executive Editor, Scripps-Howard newspaper syndicate) to Raymond Clapper, June 26, 1941, Raymond Clapper Manuscripts, Library of Congress.

13. Cantril, *Public Opinion*, p. 1102; Dawson, *Decision To Aid Russia*, pp. 96–101.

14. Quoted in Robert E. Sherwood, *Roosevelt and Hopkins: An Intimate History*, pp. 303–4.

15. On Davies, see "Ambassador Davies," *Fortune*, XVI (October, 1937), 94–98; *Newsweek*, VIII (November 28, 1936), 17–18; "Joseph E. Davies," *Current Biography, 1942*, pp. 177–80. For Davies' account of his ambassadorship in the USSR, see Joseph E. Davies, *Mission to Moscow*. His activities in the summer of 1941 can be followed

in Davies' Diary, July 7, 9, 16, 1941, and Davies to Harry Hopkins, July 18, 1941, Joseph E. Davies Manuscripts, Library of Congress.

16. James MacGregor Burns, *Roosevelt: The Soldier of Freedom*, p. 103; verbatim transcript of press conference, June 24, 1941, Franklin D. Roosevelt Manuscripts, Franklin D. Roosevelt Library.

17. Dawson, *Decision To Aid Russia*, p. 122; memorandum of conversation by Sumner Welles, June 30, 1941, *Foreign Relations of the United States—Diplomatic Papers, 1941*, I, 779–80.

18. Memorandum of conversation by Welles, July 10, 1941, *ibid.*, pp. 788–89.

19. Dawson, *Decision To Aid Russia*, pp. 163–66.

20. *Ibid.*, pp. 169–71; Roosevelt to Jesse H. Jones, July 31, 1941, Jesse H. Jones Manuscripts, Library of Congress.

21. Felix Belair, "Harry L. Hopkins: Lender and Spender," *Life*, XI (September 22, 1941), 89–99; Sherwood, *Roosevelt and Hopkins*, pp. 1–8, 202–203, 211–12.

22. Sherwood, *Roosevelt and Hopkins*, pp. 4, 318. Ivan Maisky, the Soviet ambassador in London in 1941, argues in his *Memoirs of a Soviet Ambassador*, pp. 181–82, that he originally suggested to Hopkins the idea of a trip to Moscow.

23. Sherwood, *Roosevelt and Hopkins*, p. 328.

24. Stalin revealed his underlying pessimism in a statement to Hopkins that he would "welcome . . . American troops on any part of the Russian front under the complete command of the American Army." Sherwood, *Roosevelt and Hopkins*, p. 343. Isaac Deutscher, in *Stalin: A Political Biography*, pp. 464–65, considers this "one of the most revealing statements attributed to Stalin by the memoirists of the Second World War," and concludes that the words were uttered in a "mood of flagging confidence, perhaps of despair." Adam Ulam in *Expansion and Coexistence: The History of Soviet Foreign Policy, 1917–1967*, pp. 319–20, concurs. That a "regime so deeply suspicious of any contact with the West, so intent on preserving its people from any exposure to foreigners should beg" for American and British soldiers to fight on its soil, Ulam writes, is "convincing proof" that in 1941 "all other aspects of the war were pushed aside, and only one, the imperative need of stopping the Germans, remained."

25. Henry L. Stimson Diary, May 23, 1941, Henry L. Stimson Manuscripts, Yale University Library; New York *Times*, July 21–24, 1941; *Time*, XXXVIII (July 21, 1941), 32–33, (July 28, 1941), 29, (August 4, 1941), 31–32.

26. Emory S. Land to Roosevelt, April 11, 1941, Roosevelt MSS, President's Personal File 7492; Stimson Diary, August 1, 1941, Stimson MSS; John M. Blum, *From the Morgenthau Diaries: Years of Urgency, 1938–1941*, p. 263.

27. Blum, *Years of Urgency*, p. 264; Stimson Diary, August 1, 1941, Stimson MSS.

28. Blum, *Years of Urgency*, p. 264; Wayne Coy, "Get Things Moving—FDR," *The New Republic*, CXIV (April 15, 1946), 546–47. FDR's memo to Coy is printed in Elliot Roosevelt (ed.), *FDR: His Personal Letters, 1928–1945*, II, 1195–96.

29. George Fort Milton record of interview with Wayne Coy, May 29, 1943, Records of the Foreign Economic Administration (USSR Branch), Washington National Records Center, Box 89. John D. Biggers to Coy, August 12, 1941, G. H. Pinsett to Coy, August 7, 1941, Coy to Oumansky, August 12, 1941, Wayne Coy Manuscripts, Roosevelt Library, Box 15.

30. Richard M. Leighton and Robert W. Coakley, *Global Logistics and Strategy, 1940–1943*, pp. 97–98; Forrest Pogue, *George C. Marshall: Ordeal and Hope, 1939–1942*, pp. 73–74.

31. Roosevelt to Stimson, August 30, 1941, *FR, 1941*, I, 826–27; Marvin D. Bernstein and Francis L. Loewenheim, "Aid to Russia: The First Year," in Harold Stein (ed.), *American Civil-Military Decisions: A Book of Case Studies*, p. 116.

32. "W. Averell Harriman," *Current Biography, 1941*, pp. 366–67; Sherwood, *Roosevelt and Hopkins*, pp. 110–11. For two sympathetic appraisals of Harriman based on wartime associations, see George F. Kennan, *Memoirs, 1925–1950*, pp. 231–34, and John R. Deane, *The Strange Alliance*, p. 3. Harriman has recently recalled that Roosevelt selected him for the mission because "he knew that I could work with Beaverbrook—not always easy—and then, too, that I clearly understood his own objectives." W. Averell Harriman, *America and Russia in a Changing World*, p. 14.

33. Bernstein and Loewenheim, "Aid to Russia," pp. 112–14.

34. *Ibid.*, p. 116.

35. William H. Standley to Harriman, October 8, 1941, William H. Standley Manuscripts, University of Southern California Library; Harriman, *America and Russia*, pp. 15–17.

36. Sherwood, *Roosevelt and Hopkins*, p. 391.

37. Bernstein and Loewenheim, "Aid to Russia," pp. 118–19.

38. Memorandum of conversation by Hull, September 4, 1941, *FR, 1941*, I, 827; Blum, *Years of Urgency*, p. 267.

39. Cantril, *Public Opinion*, pp. 1102, 1162; Dawson, *Decision To Aid Russia*, p. 224; New York *Times*, September 18, 1941.

40. Cantril, *Public Opinion*, p. 411; memorandum of conversation by Hull, September 11, 1941, *FR, 1941*, I, 832–33.

41. Blum, *Years of Urgency*, pp. 268–70; Roosevelt to Jones, September 11, 1941, Jones MSS; John N. Hazard Day Journal, September 26, 1941, FEA Records (USSR Branch), Box 139; Edward R.

Stettinius, Jr., memorandum of conversation with Hopkins, September 25, 1941, Stettinius MSS.

42. Dawson, Decision To Aid Russia, p. 226; Stettinius notes on meeting with FDR and Congressional leaders, October 1, 1941, Stettinius MSS.

43. Stettinius notes on meeting with congressional leaders, October 13, 1941, Stettinius MSS.

44. Dawson, Decision To Aid Russia, pp. 274–84.

45. Harriman to Roosevelt, October 29, 1941, FR, 1941, I, 851.

46. Alexander Werth, Russia at War, 1941–1945, pp. 225–42.

47. Blum, Years of Urgency, pp. 270–71, for the framing of the special lend-lease agreement. The Roosevelt-Stalin exchange is in FR, 1941, I, 851–52. Russia's eagerness to get the lend-lease agreement through is revealed by the uncharacteristic rapidity with which Soviet diplomats accepted the obligation required of all lend-lease recipients to pay for American patents used in the manufacture of equipment transferred. John Hazard took the document to the Soviet Embassy on the afternoon of November 7, and the chargé, Andrei Gromyko, after inquiring whether the British had signed it, immediately put his signature on it. "I never knew whether the Soviet Foreign Office had anticipated this document and instructed him to sign it," Hazard has recalled, "or whether he courageously stuck his neck out." Hazard to author, March 4, 1972.

48. Dawson, Decision To Aid Russia, pp. 284–89; "Playing the Red," Saturday Evening Post, CCXIV (November 8, 1941), 26; Chicago Tribune, November 8, 1941; Philadelphia Dispatch, December 7, 1941.

49. Time, XXXVIII (December 1, 1941), 25; "The Fortune Survey," Fortune, XXIV (October, 1941), 105–6. The survey showed that 39.7 percent thought the Russian government as bad or worse than the German, 32 percent thought it only slightly better, and only 8.5 percent thought it much better. The Woodrum statement is from Congressional Record, 77 Cong., 1 Sess., 1941, p. 7763.

50. Dawson, Decision To Aid Russia, p. 287.

2. THE UNCONDITIONAL AID POLICY, SEPTEMBER–DECEMBER, 1941

1. Memorandum by Edward Page, October 3, 1940, FR, 1940, III, 229–230. For Russian-American relations during the 1930s, see Robert Paul Browder, The Origins of Soviet-American Diplomacy, and Donald Bishop, The Roosevelt-Litvinov Agreements.

2. Herbert Feis, Churchill—Roosevelt—Stalin: The War They Waged and the Peace They Sought, p. 7; Dawson, Decision To Aid Russia, pp. 14–19, 59–60.

3. Hull to Steinhardt, June 14, 1941, *FR, 1941*, I, 757–58.

4. Steinhardt to Hull, June 17, 1941, *ibid.*, pp. 764–66.

5. *FR, The Soviet Union, 1933–1939*, p. 294; William C. Bullitt, "How We Won the War and Lost the Peace," *Life*, XXV (August 30, 1948), 83 ff. For Bullitt's changing views toward the USSR see Beatrice Farnsworth, *William C. Bullitt and the Soviet Union*.

6. Bullitt, "How We Won the War," p. 94.

7. George N. Crocker, *Roosevelt's Road to Russia*, pp. 4, 62–65, 162–63, 263–64, and John T. Flynn, *The Roosevelt Myth*, p. 356, contain the most severe attacks on the unconditional aid policy. Thomas A. Bailey criticizes it with more restraint in *America Faces Russia*, pp. 294–96.

8. *Newsweek*, XVIII (October 20, 1941), 23; Werth, *Russia at War*, pp. 189–97, 202–12; Harrison E. Salisbury, *The 900 Days*, pp. 291–97, 368–87.

9. Werth, *Russia at War*, pp. 310–28; Salisbury, *The 900 Days*, pp. 371–87.

10. Werth, *Russia at War*, pp. 213–24; Deutscher, *Stalin*, p. 470.

11. Davies to Hopkins, July 18, 1941, Davies Diary, October 28, 1941, Davies MSS; Sherwood, *Roosevelt and Hopkins*, p. 391; Harriman to Roosevelt, October 3, 1941, Harry L. Hopkins Manuscripts, Roosevelt Library, Box 303.

12. Langer and Gleason, *Undeclared War*, pp. 568–70, 732–36.

13. *Ibid.*, pp. 737–41.

14. Problems in the early administration of lend-lease are discussed in Sherwood, *Roosevelt and Hopkins*, pp. 280–88, 376–77, and Leighton and Coakley, *Global Logistics and Strategy, 1940–1943*, p. 78. See also Richmond *Times-Dispatch*, September 17, 1941; Robert P. Patterson to Stimson, September 17, 1941, Robert P. Patterson Manuscripts, Library of Congress.

15. Roy F. Harrod, *The Life of John Maynard Keynes*, p. 515; *Time*, XXVIII (September 29, 1941), 12; Clapper to John Sorrells, September 17, 1941, Clapper MSS.

16. Stettinius, *Lend-Lease*, pp. 105–6.

17. New York *Times*, September 21, 1941; Stettinius Lend-Lease Scrapbook, Stettinius MSS.

18. H. Duncan Hall and C. C. Wrigley, *Studies of Overseas Supply*, p. 132; Leighton and Coakley, *Global Logistics and Strategy, 1940–1943*, pp. 81–82; Patterson to Stettinius, November 18, 1941, Patterson MSS; Stettinius to Roosevelt, December 1, 1941, Stettinius MSS; Stimson Diary, November 18, 1941, Stimson MSS.

19. Dean Acheson, *Present at the Creation*, p. 34; Edwin A. Locke oral history interview, Harry S. Truman Library; Stettinius notes on conversation with Hopkins, October 3, 1941, Stettinius MSS; John N. Hazard, "Negotiating under Lend-Lease," in Raymond Dennett and

Joseph E. Johnson, *Negotiating with the Russians,* pp. 36–38; Richard C. Lukas, *Eagles East,* pp. 24–27.

20. Hazard, "Negotiating under Lend-Lease," pp. 33–34; Stimson Diary, November 24, 1941, Stimson MSS.

21. Dean Albertson, *Roosevelt's Farmer,* p. 267; personal interview with John N. Hazard, December 30, 1968; Willis C. Armstrong letter to author, July 8, 1971; Cordell Hull, *The Memoirs of Cordell Hull,* I, 743; Stimson Diary, August 5, 1941, Stimson MSS.

22. Hazard, "Negotiating under Lend-Lease," pp. 40–41; personal interview with Hazard, December 30, 1968; Lukas, *Eagles East,* p. 63.

23. Bullitt, "How We Won the War," pp. 91–92; Hull to Prentiss M. Brown, September 29, 1941, quoted in Bishop, *Roosevelt-Litvinov Agreements,* p. 174; William H. Standley and Arthur A. Ageton, *Admiral Ambassador to Russia,* p. 63.

24. Stettinius to Donald Nelson, November 4, 1941, and Stettinius to Stimson, December 3, 1941, Stettinius MSS.

25. Harriman to Hopkins and Roosevelt, September 28, 1941, Hopkins MSS, Box 304; Harold Macmillan, *The Blast of War, 1939–1945,* p. 100.

26. Bernstein and Loewenheim, "Aid to Russia," pp. 127–29; Hazard letter to author, March 4, 1972.

27. Personal interview with Hazard, December 30, 1968; S. P. Spalding to Lukashev, November 5, 1941, FEA Records (USSR Branch), Box 107; memorandum of conversation by Page, November 15, 1941, *FR, 1941,* I, 860–61; OLLA, Soviet Supply Section, "Report on Operations, November 1–15, 1941," Stettinius MSS; Stettinius transcript of conversation with Harriman, November 7, 1941, Stettinius MSS.

28. New York *Times,* April 12, 1942; "New Chief for Ordnance," *Time,* XXXIX (April 13, 1942), 68; Sherwood, *Roosevelt and Hopkins,* pp. 160–61. In November, 1941, the administration considered appointing Burns ambassador to the USSR because of the importance of supply matters in relations between the two nations. Roosevelt later changed his mind, however, apparently because he considered Burns too valuable to be spared for service outside Washington. Hull to Steinhardt, November 5, 1941, *FR, 1941,* I, 852–53.

29. Demaree Bess, "The General Called the Turn," *Saturday Evening Post,* CCXIV (August 29, 1942), 12, 101–2.

30. Sherwood, *Roosevelt and Hopkins,* p. 395; Pogue, *Marshall: Ordeal and Hope,* p. 75.

31. Bernstein and Loewenheim, "Aid to Russia," pp. 126–27.

32. Personal interview with Hazard, December 30, 1968.

33. OLLA, Soviet Supply Section, "Report on Operations, November 1–15, 1941," Stettinius MSS.

34. New York *Times,* September 27, 28, 1941; *Time,* XXXVIII

(September 29, 1941), 32; Leighton and Coakley, *Global Logistics and Strategy, 1940–1943*, pp. 58–59.

35. Leighton and Coakley, *Global Logistics and Strategy, 1940–1943*, pp. 113–14; Coordinator of Information, "Report on Supply Routes from the US to the Russo-German War Zone," December 22, 1941, Stettinius MSS; B. B. Schofield, *The Russian Convoys*, pp. 27–40.

36. T. H. Vail Motter, *The Persian Corridor and Aid to Russia*, pp. 3–27; Stettinius, *Lend-Lease*, pp. 213–16.

37. Minutes of meeting, OLLA Senior Staff, November 13, 1941, OLLA, Soviet Supply Section, "Report on Operations, November 1–15, 1941," Burns to Land, November 18, 1941, Stettinius MSS.

38. Memorandum of conversation by Loy Henderson, November 19, 1941, *FR, 1941*, I, 862; Embassy of the USSR to OLLA, November 22, 1941, Stettinius MSS.

39. Stettinius memorandum of conversation with Burns, November 26, 1941, Stettinius cable to Harriman, November 24, 1941, Land to Stettinius, November 27, 1941, Stettinius to Land, November 27, 1941, Stettinius MSS; Sherwood, *Roosevelt and Hopkins*, pp. 398–99.

40. Stettinius notes on meeting with Hopkins, November 28, 1941, Stettinius memorandum to Burns, December 2, 1941, Stettinius MSS; New York *Times*, December 3, 4, 1941.

41. Stettinius to Hull, December 11, 1941, John J. McCloy to Stettinius, December 10, 1941, Stettinius MSS; Leighton and Coakley, *Global Logistics and Strategy, 1940–1943*, p. 143.

42. Stettinius memoranda of conversations with Burns, December 2, 1941, and with Dean Acheson, December 27, 1941, Stettinius MSS; Department of State, *Report on War Aid Furnished by the United States to the U.S.S.R.;* Isador Lubin to Hopkins, January 7, 1942, Hopkins MSS; Leighton and Coakley, *Global Logistics and Strategy, 1940–1943*, p. 115.

43. The P-40 shipments are discussed in detail in Lukas, *Eagles East*, pp. 69–79. See also chargé in the Soviet Union to Hull, February 3, 1942, *FR, 1942*, III, 688–89.

44. Werth, *Russia at War*, pp. 251–57.

3. PEARL HARBOR TO STALINGRAD

1. Quoted in Henry F. Pringle, "The Production and Delivery of Supplies in World War II," (unpublished manuscript prepared for the Secretary of War, 1946), p. 55, copy in Patterson MSS.

2. Quoted in Lukas, *Eagles East*, p. 58.

3. McCloy to Stettinius, December 10, 1941, memorandum of conversation, Stettinius and General Moore, December 12, 1941, Stettinius

notes on meeting with Hopkins, December 10, 1941, Stettinius MSS: Leighton and Coakley, *Global Logistics and Strategy, 1940,–1943*, p. 552.

4. Memorandum by Churchill, December 16, 1941, *FR, The Conferences at Washington and Casablanca*, p. 22.

5. Stettinius memorandum of conversation with General Rutherford, December 11, 1941, Spalding to Stettinius, December 28, 1941, Stettinius MSS; Roosevelt to department and agency heads, December 28, 1941, *FR, 1941*, I, 865.

6. Record of meeting at White House, January 12, 1942, *FR, Washington and Casablanca*, pp. 185–91.

7. Leighton and Coakley, *Global Logistics and Strategy, 1940–1943*, pp. 247–52.

8. *Ibid.*, pp. 252–53.

9. Stettinius memorandum of conversation with Burns, December 29, 1941, Stettinius MSS.

10. Faymonville to Spalding, January 13, 1942, 861.24/796, Department of State Records, Record Group 59, National Archives; Faymonville to Spalding, January 14, 1942, 861.24/799, Department of State Records.

11. Stettinius to Roosevelt, January 16, 1942, Stettinius MSS; Roosevelt to Land, January 16, 1942, Hopkins MSS; Hopkins to Faymonville, January 21, 1942, 861.24/796, Department of State Records.

12. Repin to Roosevelt, February 16, 1942, Stettinius MSS.

13. Stettinius to Hopkins, February 21, 1942, Stettinius MSS; John Morton Blum, *From the Morgenthau Diaries: Years of War, 1941–1945*, p. 81.

14. Stettinius memorandum of conversation with Batt, February 16, 1942, Stettinius to Morgenthau, February 25, 1942, Stettinius MSS.

15. Blum, *Years of War*, p. 81; Ferdinand Eberstadt to General Lucius Clay, March 9, 1942, quoted in Robert G. Albion, *Forrestal and the Navy*, p. 105; Lukas, *Eagles East*, pp. 62–68; Stimson Diary, April 25, 1942, McCloy to Stimson, February 12, 1942, Stimson MSS.

16. Stettinius memorandum of conversation with Thomas McCabe, February 17, 1942, Stettinius MSS; Blum, *Years of War*, p. 83.

17. Hopkins to Harriman, March 4, 1942, Hopkins MSS; Stettinius to Harriman, March 4, 1942, Stettinius MSS; Hazard, "Negotiating under Lend-Lease," p. 36.

18. Hopkins to Roosevelt, February 26, 1942, Roosevelt MSS, Confidential File: "Lend-Lease," and Roosevelt to Sumner Welles, February 26, 1942, *ibid.* Stettinius to William H. Standley, February 28, 1942, minutes of meeting, OLLA Executive Staff, February 18, 1942, Stettinius to McCloy, February 24, 1942, Stettinius MSS; Blum, *Years of War*, p. 82.

19. The problem is conveniently summarized in Gaddis Smith, *American Diplomacy During the Second World War*, pp. 39–42; Hull's

views are expressed in a cable to John G. Winant, December 5, 1941, *FR, 1941*, I, 194–95.

20. Welles memorandum of conversation, March 30, 1942, *FR, 1942*, III, 536–37.

21. *Ibid.*, pp. 536–37, 540, 542; Hull to Roosevelt, February 4, 1942, *ibid.*, 504–5.

22. Wickard Diary, March 28–29, 1942, quoted in Albertson, *Roosevelt's Farmer*, p. 267.

23. Roosevelt to Stettinius, March 17, 1942, Stettinius MSS; Roosevelt to Land, March 17, 1942, Hopkins MSS, Box 306. In his own hand FDR wrote at the bottom of the letter to Land: "This is a directive from the Commander-in-Chief." The Hopkins statement is quoted in Leighton and Coakley, *Global Logistics and Strategy, 1940–1943*, p. 556.

24. Sherwood, *Roosevelt and Hopkins*, p. 490; A. Russell Buchanan, *The United States and World War II*, I, 80–104, 214–16.

25. For domestic pressures, see Burns, *Soldier of Freedom*, pp. 210–12; Roosevelt's letter to MacArthur is quoted in Maurice Matloff and Edwin M. Snell, *Strategic Planning for Coalition Warfare, 1941–1942*, p. 214; Clapper notes on briefing by Hopkins, May 18, 1942, Clapper MSS, Box 23.

26. Leighton and Coakley, *Global Logistics and Strategy, 1940–1943*, pp. 552–56.

27. Feis, *Churchill—Roosevelt—Stalin*, pp. 60–61; Smith, *American Diplomacy*, pp. 44–45, and Lloyd C. Gardner, *Economic Aspects of New Deal Diplomacy*, pp. 299–300, argue that the invitation to send Molotov to Washington involved at least an implied *quid pro quo*. Divine, *Roosevelt and World War II*, pp. 87–91, expresses a dissenting view.

28. Werth, *Russia at War*, pp. 365–409.

29. Churchill, *Hinge of Fate*, p. 258.

30. McCabe to Roosevelt, May 21, 1942, Roosevelt MSS, Confidential File: "Lend-Lease."

31. Sherwood, *Roosevelt and Hopkins*, p. 570.

32. *Ibid.*, pp. 575–76; Hopkins memorandum to Roosevelt, June 9, 1942, Roosevelt MSS, President's Secretary's File: "Russia."

33. Sherwood, *Roosevelt and Hopkins*, pp. 574–75.

34. *Ibid.*, pp. 577–78; Davies Diary, May 29, 1942, Davies MSS.

35. Sherwood, *Roosevelt and Hopkins*, pp. 589–91, 602–12.

36. Churchill, *Hinge of Fate*, pp. 262–70; Schofield, *Russian Convoys*, pp. 81–111; David Irving, *The Destruction of Convoy PQ. 17*.

37. Churchill, *Hinge of Fate*, pp. 266–67.

38. Hazard to Stettinius, September 16, 1942, Stettinius MSS; Leighton and Coakley, *Global Logistics and Strategy, 1940–1943*, pp. 558–60; Department of State, *Report on War Aid*, p. 2.

39. Hazard memorandum to Stettinius, September 16, 1942, Stettinius MSS.

40. Werth, *Russia at War*, pp. 400–9.

41. Davies Diary, July 20, 1942, Davies MSS; Standley to Hull, July 22, 1942, *FR, 1942*, III, 612–14; Standley and Ageton, *Admiral Ambassador*, p. 243; Churchill, *Hinge of Fate*, pp. 270–71.

42. Standley to Hull, April 24, 1942, *FR, 1942*, III, 545–48; Churchill, *Hinge of Fate*, p. 270; Faymonville to McCabe, May 7, 1942, *FR, 1942*, III, 701–2.

43. Sherwood, *Roosevelt and Hopkins*, pp. 617–20.

44. Roosevelt to Churchill, July 29, 1942, quoted in Churchill, *Hinge of Fate*, pp. 271–72; memorandum by Roosevelt, July 23, 1942, *FR, 1942*, III, 715; Roosevelt to Stalin, August 19, 1942, *ibid.*, p. 626.

45. Faymonville to Stettinius, September 28, 1942, *FR, 1942*, III, 725–26; Clapper notes on briefing by Gardner Cowles, October 21, 1942, Clapper MSS.

46. Werth, *Russia at War*, pp. 484–87; First Secretary of the U. S. Embassy, Moscow, to Secretary of State, October 6, 1942, *FR, 1942*, III, 461; Churchill, *Hinge of Fate*, p. 580.

47. Roosevelt to Churchill, October 27, 1942, quoted in Sherwood, *Roosevelt and Hopkins*, p. 641.

48. Roosevelt memorandum to department and agency heads, October 2, 1942, Roosevelt MSS; Motter, *Persian Corridor*, pp. 207–8; Lewis Douglas to Hopkins, March 30, 1943, Hopkins MSS, Box 306. After extended discussions it was decided that the Bering route was impractical.

49. Roosevelt to Jeffers, October 13, 1942, Roosevelt MSS, Confidential File: "Lend-Lease." The background of the tire plant project is discussed in Deane, *Strange Alliance*, pp. 100–1.

50. Hazard memorandum to Stettinius, September 16, 1942, Stettinius MSS; Frederick Reinhardt memorandum of conversation, September 19, 1942, *FR, 1942*, III, 722–23.

51. Stalin to Roosevelt, October 7, 1942, Ministry of Foreign Affairs of the U.S.S.R., *Correspondence between the Chairman of the Council of Ministers of the U.S.S.R. and the Presidents of the U.S.A. and the Prime Ministers of Great Britain during the Great Patriotic War of 1941–1945*, II, 35.

52. The problem of aircraft allocations during 1942 is covered in detail in Lukas, *Eagles East*, pp. 109–24. For specific recommendations on Stalin's requests, see Hopkins to Marshall, October 10, 1942, Henry A. Arnold Manuscripts, Library of Congress, Box 129, and Marshall to Roosevelt, October 10, 1942, *ibid.*; also Roosevelt to Stalin, January 9, 1943, *FR, 1943*, III, 740–41, and Hopkins to Arnold, February 2, 1943, Arnold MSS, Box 129.

53. In a cable to Stalin, October 16, 1942, printed in *Stalin Correspondence*, II, 37–38, Roosevelt promised to send to the USSR each

month between eight and ten thousand trucks, 15,000 tons of fresh meat, 10,000 tons of canned meat, and 12,000 tons of lard, and to send two million tons of wheat before June 30, 1943. For Persian Gulf and Alsib problems see Leighton and Coakley, *Global Logistics and Strategy, 1940–1943*, pp. 577–78, and Jones, *Roads to Russia*, pp. 158–60.

54. Admiral Akulin report to OLLA, October 29, 1942, Stettinius MSS; Faymonville to Stettinius, November 5, 1942, *FR, 1942*, III, 741–42.

55. Hazard memorandum to Stettinius, September 16, 1942, Stettinius MSS; Leighton and Coakley, *Global Logistics and Strategy, 1940–1943*, p. 586.

56. Minutes of meeting, OLLA Executive Staff, March 29, 1943, Stettinius MSS; Deane, *Strange Alliance*, pp. 100–1. For the demise of VELVET, see Lukas, *Eagles East*, pp. 153–63.

57. Hazard memorandum to Stettinius, October 7, 1942, Stettinius MSS.

58. Stettinius notes on meeting with Hopkins, October 14, 1942, and Roosevelt to Stettinius, October 30, 1942, Stettinius MSS.

59. Minutes of meeting, President's Soviet Protocol Committee, November 25, 1942, Stettinius MSS; Leighton and Coakley, *Global Logistics and Strategy, 1940–1943*, p. 586.

60. Stettinius, *Lend-Lease*, pp. 209–11; Hazard memorandum to Oscar Cox, February 13, 1943, Stettinius MSS.

61. Hazard to Cox, February 13, 1943, Stettinius MSS; Werth, *Russia at War*, pp. 622–28.

4. ADMIRAL STANDLEY AND UNCONDITIONAL AID

1. The fullest descriptions of Standley's press conference are in Standley and Ageton, *Admiral Ambassador*, pp. 331–49, and in Quentin Reynolds, *The Curtain Rises*, pp. 86–89.

2. *Ibid.*

3. Quentin Reynolds, "Diplomat on the Spot," *Colliers*, CXII (July 24, 1943), 13; "William H. Standley," *Current Biography, 1942*, pp. 797–99.

4. For Standley's appointment, see Standley and Ageton, *Admiral Ambassador*, pp. 92–93, and Sherwood, *Roosevelt and Hopkins*, p. 496.

5. Standley and Ageton, *Admiral Ambassador, passim.;* Standley to Father O'Donohue, May 14, 1942, to Llewellyn Thompson, May 29, 1942, to Sumner Welles, September 2, 1942, Standley MSS.

6. Standley and Ageton, *Admiral Ambassador*, pp. 182–94; Standley to Hull, July 5, 1942, *FR, 1942*, III, 606.

7. Reynolds, "Diplomat on the Spot," p. 13; Standley and Ageton, *Admiral Ambassador*, p. 195.

8. *Ibid.*, pp. 235–47.

9. *Ibid.*, pp. 293–95.
10. *Ibid.*, p. 308.
11. Davies Diary, October 16, 29, 1942, Davies MSS; minutes of meeting, Protocol Committee, November 25, 1942, Stettinius MSS.
12. Sherwood, *Roosevelt and Hopkins*, p. 643. For background on the Burns memorandum and a similar expression of views see Davies Diary, October 29, 1942, Davies MSS.
13. Leighton and Coakley, *Global Logistics and Strategy, 1940–1943*, p. 587.
14. *FR, Washington and Casablanca*, pp. 593, 623–24, 633, 709.
15. *Ibid.*, pp. 783–84, 805.
16. Minutes of meeting, Protocol Committee, February 23, 1943, Stettinius to Harriman, March 3, 1943, Stettinius MSS; Leighton and Coakley, *Global Logistics and Strategy, 1940–1943*, pp. 589–90; Schofield, *Russian Convoys*, pp. 162–66.
17. Sherwood, *Roosevelt and Hopkins*, pp. 704–5; Davies Diary, February 23, March 9, 1943, Davies MSS.
18. Jones, *Roads to Russia*, pp. 244–45, includes a survey of Russian press comment in 1942 and 1943.
19. Standley and Ageton, *Admiral Ambassador*, pp. 331–33.
20. Cantril, *Public Opinion*, p. 411; Richmond *Times-Dispatch*, January 29, 1943; Tom Wenner to Cox, January 25, 1943, Stettinius MSS.
21. *Wall Street Journal*, July 20, 1942; also *U. S. News*, XIII (August 14, 1942), 16–17; "A Cure for Complacency," *Nation*, CLV (September 26, 1942), 253–54; "Willkie Speaks Out," *The New Republic*, CVII (October 19, 1942), 483; I. F. Stone, "Capital Thoughts on a Second Front," *Nation*, CLV (October 3, 1942), 288.
22. *The Economist*, CXLIV (January 2, 1943), 12; Richmond *Times-Dispatch*, January 7, 1943; Arthur Krock in New York *Times*, January 10, 1943; Drew Pearson in Washington *Post*, January 21, 1943; *U. S. News*, XIV (January 15, 1943), 14.
23. Stettinius notes on meeting with Roosevelt, December 10, 1942, Stettinius MSS; Vice-President Henry A. Wallace expressed similar views in a statement to reporters on December 27, 1942, recorded by Raymond Clapper and in Clapper MSS; Standley and Ageton, *Admiral Ambassador*, p. 333, for State Department's request to the ambassador.
24. Standley and Ageton, *Admiral Ambassador*, pp. 332–33, 340–41.
25. *Ibid.*, p. 341.
26. Chicago *Tribune*, March 9, 1943; New York *Journal-American*, March 9, 1943; *PM*, March 9, 1943.
27. Stettinius to Hopkins, March 9, 1943; Stettinius MSS; *Congressional Record*, 78 Cong., 1 Sess., pp. 1821–23; John Vorys to Stanley High, March 9, 1943, John M. Vorys Manuscripts, Ohio State Historical Society.
28. *FR, 1943*, III, 628–29; Stettinius to Hopkins, March 9, 1943, Stettinius MSS; *Congressional Record*, 78 Cong., 1 Sess., pp. 1700–1.

29. *Congressional Record*, 78 Cong., 1 Sess., p. 1851.

30. "Truth or Diplomacy," *Catholic World*, CLVII (April, 1943), 1–9.

31. Jerome S. Bruner, *Mandate from the People*, pp. 105–25; Paul Willen, "Who 'Collaborated' with Russia," *Antioch Review*, XIV (September, 1954), 264–66; "Hand Is Out to Russia," *Fortune*, XXVII (June, 1943), 22–25.

32. Johnson quoted in Willen, "Who 'Collaborated,' " p. 274; for a summary of press reaction see *U. S. News*, XIV (March 19, 1943), 24.

33. Clapper notes on briefing by Welles, March 10, 1943, Clapper MSS; Davies Diary, March 9, 13, 14, 1943, Davies MSS; Hopkins memorandum, March 10, 1943, Hopkins MSS, Box 321.

34. Werth, *Russia at War*, p. 628; Davies Diary, March 10, October 2, 1943, Davies MSS; *War and the Working Class* quoted in New York *Times*, September 10, 1943.

35. *FR, 1943*, III, 629–30; Standley and Ageton, *Admiral Ambassador*, pp. 347–48.

36. Standley to Loy Henderson, n.d., Standley MSS; Standley to Hull, March 11, 1943, *FR, 1943*, III, 636–38.

37. Sherwood, *Roosevelt and Hopkins*, p. 733; Davies Journal, May 13, 1945, Davies MSS.

38. Standley to Roosevelt and Hull, March 10, 1943, *FR, 1943*, III, 509–11.

39. Churchill, *Hinge of Fate*, pp. 752–53; Leighton and Coakley, *Global Logistics and Strategy, 1940–1943*, pp. 590–92.

40. Ulam, *Expansion and Coexistence*, p. 339.

41. Stalin to Churchill, March 15, 1943, in Churchill, *Hinge of Fate*, pp. 750–51; Stalin to Churchill, April 2, 1943, *ibid.*, p. 755.

42. Hull to Standley, March 18, 1943, *FR, 1943*, III, 514; Standley and Ageton, *Admiral Ambassador*, pp. 357–58.

43. Harriman to Hopkins, March 14, 1943, in Sherwood, *Roosevelt and Hopkins*, p. 706.

44. Harriman to Hopkins, February 22, 1943, Hopkins MSS, Box 306; Harriman to Stettinius, April 16, 1943, Stettinius MSS.

45. Knollenberg to Stettinius, June 25, 1943, Stettinius notes for talk with Hopkins, June 29, 1943, Stettinius MSS.

46. Quoted in Maurice Matloff, *Strategic Planning for Coalition Warfare, 1943–1944*, p. 282.

47. H. C. L. Miller to Arthur Van Buskirk, December 7, 1943, Stettinius MSS.

48. Deane, *Strange Alliance*, pp. 48–49. For similar British experiences see Sir Gifford Martel, *The Russian Outlook*, pp. 167–69. The Russians provided exceptional treatment for General Burns. During his visit to Russia in the spring of 1943, he was told that he could "see anything, go anywhere." Burns report to OLLA Executive Staff, June 28, 1943, Stettinius MSS.

49. Patterson to Hopkins, April 17, 1943, ABC 400.3295 Russia (19 Apr 1942), Sec. 3, Records of the Operations Division, War Department General Staff, World War Records Section, National Archives, Alexandria, Virginia.

50. For the policy change on shipment of industrial equipment, see Stettinius to General Charles M. Wesson, April 22, 1943, and Stettinius to Roosevelt, June 11, 1943, Stettinius MSS. For the Protocol Committee's opposition to the British proposal for bases in North Russia, see Spalding to Hopkins, May 15 and 24, 1943, Records of the President's Soviet Protocol Committee, Roosevelt Library, Box 18. Spalding's memorandum to the Joint Chiefs of Staff, May 15, 1943, Protocol Committee Records, Box 18, expresses the committee's opposition to Patterson's proposals.

51. Reynolds, *Curtain Rises,* pp. 80–85, and Standley and Ageton, *Admiral Ambassador,* pp. 371–72.

52. Standley to Hull, May 22, 1943, *FR, 1943,* III, 651–52.

53. Burns report to Executive Staff, OLLA, June 28, 1943, Stettinius MSS.

54. Draft memorandum for the Secretaries of War and Navy, *ca.* May 28, 1943, Hopkins MSS, Box 306.

55. For the embassy conflict and its resolution, see Standley and Ageton, *Admiral Ambassador, passim;* Davies Diary, May 24, June 3, September 24–25, 1943, Davies MSS; New York *Times,* October 19, November 18, 1943; "The First Thirty Years," *Time,* XLII (November 29, 1943), 65–66. Deane, *Strange Alliance,* pp. 10–12, discusses the origins and objectives of the military mission. Conflicting reasons were given for the recall of Faymonville. Raymond Clapper speculated that the army brought him back because he "wouldn't double as a G-2 man." Roosevelt intimated in a background briefing for reporters that he was too friendly with the Russians. See Clapper notes, October 20, November 11, 1943, Clapper MSS.

56. Forrest Davis, "Roosevelt's World Blueprint," *Saturday Evening Post,* CCXV (April 10, 1943), 21–22, 109–10; Feis, *Churchill—Roosevelt—Stalin,* pp. 119–25. The Davis article was based on a confidential interview with FDR in December, 1942.

57. Leighton and Coakley, *Global Logistics and Strategy, 1940–1943,* p. 596.

58. Werth, *Russia at War,* pp. 585–678.

59. *Ibid.,* pp. 669–71, 674; Standley to Hull, June 12, 1943, *FR, 1943,* III, 544–45.

60. Werth, *Russia at War,* pp. 679, 727.

61. Stalin to Roosevelt, June 11, 1943, *Stalin Correspondence,* II, 70, and Stalin to Churchill, June 19, 1943, *ibid.,* I, 136–38. Sherwood's comments are in *Roosevelt and Hopkins,* p. 734.

62. For Standley's decision to resign, see his undated memorandum,

ca. May, 1943, in Standley MSS. His letter of resignation, dated May 3, 1943, is in *FR, 1943*, III, 521.

63. Reynolds, *The Curtain Rises*, pp. 85–86; Walter Kerr, *The Russian Army*, p. 236; Russell's speech is excerpted in the New York *Times*, October 29, 1943.

64. Kerr, *Russian Army*, p. 236; New York *Times*, October 12, 1943.

65. Deane, *Strange Alliance*, p. 49.

66. Roosevelt's statement to reporters is recorded in Raymond Clapper's notes on White House briefing, September 15, 1943, Clapper MSS.

5. HARRIMAN AND DEANE

1. Werth, *Russia at War*, pp. 679–87.

2. For general discussions of the Teheran Conference, see Smith, *American Diplomacy during the Second World War*, pp. 74–79, and William L. Neumann, *After Victory: Churchill, Roosevelt, Stalin and the Making of the Peace*, pp. 115–25.

3. On war production, see Buchanan, *United States and World War II*, I, 134–41; for shipping, Samuel Eliot Morison, *The Two Ocean War*, pp. 244–46, 366–82, and Robert W. Coakley and Richard M. Leighton, *Global Logistics and Strategy, 1943–1945*, pp. 352–53, 366–68, 552–53.

4. New York *Times*, April 28, 29, September 16, 1943; John Greeley, "Iran in Wartime," *National Geographic*, LXXXIV (August, 1943), 131–59; Coakley and Leighton, *Global Logistics and Strategy, 1943–1945*, p. 676.

5. Coakley and Leighton, *Global Logistics and Strategy, 1943–1945*, p. 678; Lewis Douglas and Emory S. Land to Roosevelt, July 10, 1944, Roosevelt MSS, Confidential File: "Lend-Lease;" Department of State, *Report on War Aid*, p. 4.

6. Harriman to Hull, June 30, 1944, *FR, 1944*, IV, 973; Harvey Klemmer, "Lend-Lease and the Russian Victory," *National Geographic*, LXXXVIII (October, 1945), 499–512.

7. Stettinius, *Lend-Lease*, p. 210; Sidney P. Spalding, Diary of Trip to the Russian Front, July 20, 1944, FEA Records (USSR Branch), Box 88; Werth, *Russia at War*, p. 624.

8. Henry Cassidy, *Moscow Dateline*, p. 137; Edgar Snow to Standley, n.d., Standley MSS; Martel, *Russian Outlook*, p. 81; Leighton Rogers, "Russians Like Our Planes," *Harpers*, XLXXXIX (September, 1944), 314–16.

9. Deane, *Strange Alliance*, pp. 93–94; Spalding Diary, July 20, 1944, FEA Records (USSR Branch), Box 88; Klemmer, "Lend-Lease," pp. 499–512; Werth, *Russia at War*, p. 625; Alan Clark, *Barbarossa: The*

Russian-German Conflict, 1941–1945, p. 372; minutes of meeting, Protocol Committee, May 10, 1944, Protocol Committee Records, Box 5, Albert Seaton, *The Russo-German War, 1941–1945*, pp. 352, 421, 588–590, estimates that about half the trucks in use on the Russian front came from the United States and attributes to them primary responsibility for the mobility that made possible the great success of the Red Army in 1944.

10. Werth, *Russia at War*, p. 627; Ralph Parker in New York *Times*, March 18, 1944; Spalding Diary, July 21, 1944, FEA Records (USSR Branch), Box 88; Deane, *Strange Alliance*, p. 36; New York *Times*, April 22, 1944; minutes of meeting, Protocol Committee, May 10, 1944, Protocol Committee Records, Box 5.

11. Edgar Snow, *People on Our Side*, p. 138; New York *Times*, March 18, 1944; Jones, *Roads to Russia*, pp. 246–47; New York *Times*, January 19, 1944.

12. Frederick Barghoorn, *The Soviet Image of the United States*, pp. 58–59.

13. New York *Times*, November 18, 1943; *FR, Cairo and Teheran*, p. 585; New York *Times*, April 21, 1944; Chargé in the USSR to Secretary of State, May 1, 1944, *FR, 1944*, IV, 864; New York *Times*, June 4, 1944.

14. Harriman to Hull, June 13, 1944, *FR, 1944*, IV, 885; New York *Times*, June 12, 1944.

15. For the army's changing policies on lend-lease, see Coakley and Leighton, *Global Logistics and Strategy, 1943–1945*, pp. 637–44; International Division, Army Service Forces, "Lend-Lease as of September 30, 1945," (unpublished MS in the Office of Chief of Military History), I, 240–47, 260–62.

16. New York *Times*, March 3, 1944; for representative comment from business and foreign trade interests, see Edna Lonigan, "Lend-Lease—A Tool for Planners," *Barrons*, XXIV (March 20, 1944), 3; "The Editor Thinks Out Loud," *American Exporter*, XXXII (February, 1943), 23; and "Private Enterprise," *American Exporter*, XXXIII (December, 1943), 34. Samplings of press attacks on lend-lease may be found in Washington *Times-Herald*, May 17, 1943, and Chicago *Tribune*, July 19, 1943. For complaints about domestic shortages, see *Investor's Reader* (Merrill, Lynch, Pierce, Fenner, and Smith), March 8, 1944. Butler's comments are in "Lend-Lease for War Only?," *Nation's Business*, XXXI (May, 1943), 34, 36, 94–95.

17. The five senators were Russell, James M. Mead, New York Democrat, Albert B. Chandler, Kentucky Democrat, Owen Brewster, Maine Republican, and Henry Cabot Lodge, Massachusetts Republican. Joining them in the debate against the administration were Democrats Allan Ellender of Louisiana, Kenneth McKellar of Tennessee, Robert Reynolds of North Carolina, and Republicans Gerald Nye of North

Dakota and Hugh Butler of Nebraska. Democrats Harry Truman of
Missouri and Millard Tydings of Maryland offered occasional support.
See New York *Times,* October 8, 13, 14, 28, 29, 1943; New York *Sun,*
October 12, 1943; R. Owen Brewster, "Don't Blame the British—
Blame Us!," *Colliers,* CXII (December 25, 1943), 21.

18. Roosevelt to Victor Sholis, October 15, 1943, *FDR—Personal
Letters,* II, 1455; Clapper notes on briefing, October 20, 1943, Clapper
MSS.

19. Robert A. Divine, *Second Chance: The Triumph of Internationalism During World War II,* pp. 93–94, 107–8, 141–55.

20. New York *Times,* October 14, November 11, 1943; Oscar Cox to
Hopkins, October 16, 1943, Oscar S. Cox Manuscripts, Roosevelt Library.

21. For congressional praise of Stettinius, see statements by Representative John Taber in *Congressional Record,* 77 Cong., 1 Sess., p.
7924, by Representative John Vorys in *ibid.,* 78 Cong., 1 Sess., p. 1652;
also Cox to Hopkins, February 2, 1943, Stettinius MSS, and Arthur
Krock column, New York *Times,* March 12, 1943. For the Wallace-
Jones feud and its resolution, see James F. Byrnes, *All in One Lifetime,* pp. 193–97. The executive order creating FEA is in Roseman,
Public Papers, XII, 406–9.

22. On Crowley, see especially Laurence Eklund, "Adviser to Presidents," Milwaukee *Journal,* August 17–27, 1969, John MacCormac,
"Diplomat of Global Economics," New York *Times Magazine* (November 7, 1943), p. 14, and John O'Donnell, "Capitol Stuff" column, September 27, 1943, Acheson, *Present at the Creation,* pp. 46–47. Crowley's appointment was widely regarded as a triumph for conservatives
and as an indication of Roosevelt's pre-election shift to the right. See
especially Marquis Childs columns, St. Louis *Post-Dispatch,* December
29, 30, 31, 1943.

23. For the changes in lend-lease policy in 1943 and 1944, see Hall
and Wrigley, *Overseas Supply,* pp. 120–21, Coakley and Leighton,
Global Logistics and Strategy, 1943–1945, pp. 627–60, and George C.
Herring, Jr., "Experiment in Foreign Aid; Lend-Lease, 1941–1945,"
(unpublished Ph.D. dissertation, 1965), pp. 200–16.

24. Army Service Forces, *International Aid Statistics, World War II,*
pp. 32, 40.

25. An Office of War Information poll taken in August, 1943,
reached the revealing conclusion that a majority of Americans felt the
Russians had made sufficient contribution to the war and should be
under no obligation to repay the United States for lend-lease while the
same majority felt the British should be required to pay. See minutes
of meeting, OLLA Executive Staff, August 30, 1943, Stettinius MSS.

26. Stettinius, *Lend-Lease,* pp. 211–12.

27. For concern about Russian orders of industrial equipment, see

Stettinius to Oscar Cox, April 8, 1943, minutes of meeting, OLLA Executive Staff, April 19, 1943, and Harriman to Stettinius, April 16, 1943, Stettinius MSS. On July 16, 1943, Hull reported to Hopkins evidence that the Russians were selling American supplies to Iran and warned that this posed obvious political dangers to the administration. In reply, Hopkins urged caution, warning that the "effect of our overall relations with Russia must be considered before the question is further agitated." Hull to Hopkins, July 16, 1943, and Hopkins to Hull, August 10, 1943, Hopkins MSS, Box 306. Additional evidence of Soviet retransfers is reported in Stettinius to Acheson, December 27, 1943, and Stettinius to Hull, February 22, 1944, Stettinius MSS.

28. Deane, *Strange Alliance*, pp. 10–12; New York *Times*, November 18, 1943.

29. On Spalding, see *ibid.*, pp. 91–92; Deane's initial attitudes are recalled in John R. Deane, "Negotiating on Military Assistance," in Dennett and Johnson, *Negotiating with the Russians*, p. 5.

30. Deane, *Strange Alliance*, p. 96.

31. *Ibid.*, p. 97.

32. Harriman to Hopkins, January 15, 1944, *FR, 1944*, IV, 1039.

33. The military's reaction to Deane's cable is discussed in Coakley and Leighton, *Global Logistics and Strategy, 1943–1945*, p. 686. Knox's proposal is summarized in draft memorandum for the Secretary of the Navy, ca. February, 1944, Department of State Records, FW 861.24/1758 PS/CH.

34. Lubin memorandum for Roosevelt, January 19, 1944, Hopkins MSS, Box 323; Lubin memorandum for Roosevelt, February 21, 1944, Roosevelt MSS, Confidential File: "Lend-Lease;" MF memorandum for Admiral Leahy, January 20, 1944, OPD Records, ABC 400.3295 Russia (19 Apr 42), Sec. 3; York memorandum to Leahy, January 21, 1944, Protocol Committee Records, Box 14.

35. Lubin to Roosevelt, January 19, 1944, Hopkins MSS, Box 323; York to Leahy, January 21, 1944, Protocol Committee Records, Box 14.

36. Protocol Committee to Harriman, February 25, 1944, *FR, 1944*, IV, 1055–56; Roosevelt to Knox, March 6, 1944, Roosevelt MSS, Confidential File: "Lend-Lease."

37. Harriman to Protocol Committee, March 2, 1944, *FR, 1944*, IV, 1057–58.

38. Protocol Committee to Harriman, March 16, 1944, *ibid.*, pp. 1062–63.

39. Kennan, *Memoirs*, p. 195.

40. Deane, *Strange Alliance*, pp. 46–86, 107–61. "Every effort to collaborate," Deane later recalled, "was a negotiation which had to be bargained out."

41. For background on the Polish problem, see Feis, *Churchill—Roosevelt—Stalin*, pp. 287–302, 373–79. Harriman's views of early July

are in his cable to the President and Secretary of State, July 5, 1944, *FR, 1944,* III, 1424.

42. Kennan, *Memoirs,* p. 211; Harriman to Roosevelt, August 15, 1944, *FR, 1944,* III, 1376.

43. Kennan, *Memoirs,* p. 267.

44. Harriman to Hopkins, September 10, 1944, *FR, 1944,* IV, 988–90.

45. *Ibid.;* Harriman to Hull, September 20, 1944, *ibid.,* pp. 992–98.

46. *Ibid.*

47. Harriman to Hopkins, September 3, 1944, *ibid.,* p. 1130.

48. Harriman to Roosevelt and Hull, September 29, 1944, *ibid.,* pp. 1001–2.

49. Arnold to Hopkins, September 30, 1944, Arnold MSS, Box 43.

50. Feis, *Churchill—Roosevelt—Stalin,* p. 405; Hopkins to Arnold, October 16, 1944, Arnold MSS, Box 43.

51. Deane, *Strange Alliance,* pp. 240–251.

52. H. Freeman Matthews to Hull, October 16, 1944, *FR, 1944,* IV, 1016–17; Feis, *Churchill—Roosevelt—Stalin,* p. 467.

53. Minutes of meeting, Protocol Committee, November 10, 1944, Protocol Committee Records, Box 5.

54. Deane, *Strange Alliance,* p. 250.

55. *Ibid.,* pp. 84–86.

56. Acheson to Stettinius, January 11, 1945, Stettinius MSS.

57. For Harriman's reports, see minutes of meetings, Protocol Committee, May 10, November 10, 1944, Protocol Committee Records, Box 5.

58. Roosevelt to Secretary of State, January 5, 1945, *FR, 1945,* V, 944; Protocol Committee to Harriman, March 3, 1945, *ibid.,* 650.

59. Protocol Committee to Harriman, March 3, 1945, *ibid.*

6. AID FOR RUSSIAN RECONSTRUCTION

1. For early discussions on aid for reconstruction, see Acheson, *Present at the Creation,* pp. 64–72. Divine, *Second Chance,* pp. 64–81, deals with the roles of Wallace and Welles in 1942.

2. The draft amendment to the Lend-Lease Act is included in Stettinius memorandum to Hopkins, June 24, 1942, and in minutes of meeting, OLLA Executive Staff, November 9, 1942, Stettinius MSS. For the UNRRA decisions, see Acheson, *Present at the Creation,* pp. 70–72, and Divine, *Second Chance,* pp. 117–19, 156–57. In a conference with Stettinius on October 12, 1943, Roosevelt stated definitely that lend-lease must end with the war. See Stettinius memorandum to Acheson, October 12, 1943, Stettinius MSS.

3. Acheson, *Present at the Creation,* pp. 68–69; Postwar Programs

Committee, Department of State, Document No. 19, February 17, 1944, Stettinius MSS.

4. See "The Editor Thinks Out Loud," *American Exporter*, XXXIII (February, 1943), 23, and "Private Enterprise," *American Exporter*, XXXIII (December, 1943), 34; statement of the Los Angeles Chamber of Commerce quoted in Charles Burton Marshall, "The Lend-Lease Operation," *The Annals of the American Academy of Political and Social Science*, CCXXV (January, 1943), 188; a poll of businessmen conducted by *Modern Industry* in early 1944 showed that 78.4 percent favored ending lend-lease with the war. See "Readers Vote To End Lend-Lease with War," *Modern Industry*, VII (March 15, 1944), 10. Conservative reaction to the Wallace and Welles speeches is discussed generally in Divine, *Second Chance*, pp. 78–79. Vandenberg's statement on UNRRA is quoted in Acheson, *Present at the Creation*, pp. 71–72.

5. Memorandum, "U.S. Proposal on Cooperation in Rehabilitation of War Damage in the Soviet Union," *FR, 1943*, I, 739; Maxwell M. Hamilton notes on Nelson conversation with Stalin, October 16, 1943, *FR, 1943*, III, 713–15; Charles Bohlen memorandum of Harriman-Mikoyan conversation, November 5, 1943, *ibid.*, pp. 781–85; Harriman to Hopkins, January 7, 1944, FEA Records, Administrator's File, Box 819.

6. Sherwood, *Roosevelt and Hopkins*, p. 643.

7. William A. Williams, *The Tragedy of American Diplomacy*, pp. 232–37; see also Gardner, *Economic Aspects of New Deal Diplomacy*.

8. Memorandum by Elbridge Durbrow, November 29, 1943, *FR, 1943*, III, 722–23.

9. Currie memorandum to Hopkins, December 31, 1943, Hopkins MSS, Box 310; White to Morgenthau, March 7, 1944, Harry Dexter White Manuscripts, Firestone Library, Princeton University; Blum, *Years of War*, p. 304; Hamilton notes on Nelson conversation with Molotov, October 12, 1943, *FR, 1943*, III, 710–12.

10. Hamilton notes on Nelson conversations with Stalin and Molotov, *FR, 1943*, III, 710–16; Harriman to Hull, November, 1943, *ibid.*, pp. 788–89; *War and the Working Class*, quoted in New York *Times*, February 20, 1944.

11. Harriman to Hull and Stettinius, February 1, 1944, *FR, 1944*, IV, 1041–42; Durbrow memorandum, November 29, 1943, *FR, 1943*, III, 722–23; Currie to Hopkins, December 31, 1943, Hopkins MSS, Box 310; Blum, *Years of War*, p. 304.

12. Hull to Harriman, February 8, 1944, *FR, 1944*, IV, 1047.

13. *Ibid.*

14. Cox memorandum to Crowley, January 26, 1944, Cox memorandum to Currie, March 6, 1944, FEA Records, Administrator's File, Box 767.

15. Cox to Harriman, March 22, 1944, Cox MSS, explains the origins and intent of the 3 (c) proposal.

16. Cox to Crowley, January 26, 1944, FEA Records, Administrator's File, Box 767.

17. Draft memorandum for the President, May 16, 1944, Henry Morgenthau Diaries, vol. 732, p. 97, Henry Morgenthau Manuscripts, Roosevelt Library.

18. Harriman to Hopkins, February 9, 1944, *FR, 1944*, IV, 1048–51; Harriman to Hopkins, February 13, 1944, *ibid.*, pp. 1052–53; Harriman to Hull and Stettinius, February 14, 1944, *ibid.*, pp. 1054–55.

19. Harriman to Hull, February 20, 1944, *ibid.*, pp. 944–45; Harriman to Hull, March 13, 1944, *ibid.*, p. 951.

20. Harriman to Hull, February 14, 1944, *ibid.*, pp. 1054–55.

21. *Ibid.*

22. Burns, *Soldier of Freedom*, pp. 426–37.

23. Vandenberg to Acheson, February 19, 1944, quoted in Milton O. Gustafson, "Congress and Foreign Aid: The First Phase, UNRRA, 1943–1947," (unpublished Ph.D. dissertation), p. 116.

24. For the 1944 debate on lend-lease, see *Congressional Record*, 78 Cong., 2 Sess., pp. 3510–19, 3541–47, 3553–89, 4044, 4093–97. For comment on the debate, see *The Economist*, CXLIV (April 1, 1944), 428; Louisville *Courier-Journal*, April 21, 1944; Krock in New York *Times*, April 20, 1944.

25. Stettinius to Harriman, March 7, 1944, *FR, 1944*, IV, 1060–62; Stettinius Calendar Notes, July 31, 1944, Stettinius MSS; Cox Diary, January 5, 1945, Cox MSS.

26. Aide mémoire, Department of State to Embassy of the USSR, May 24, 1944, *FR, 1944*, IV, 1087–94.

27. Acheson, *Present at the Creation*, p. 85.

28. Stettinius to Harriman, August 2, 1944, *FR, 1944*, IV, 1108–10 and Stettinius to Harriman, August 5, 1944, *ibid.*, pp. 1111–13.

29. Acheson, *Present at the Creation*, p. 85; Hull to Harriman, August 17, 1944, *FR, 1944*, IV, 1115–19; Hull to Harriman, August 22, 1944, *ibid.*, pp. 1119–21; Hull to Harriman, August 29, 1944, *ibid.*, pp. 1123–26.

30. John Hazard memorandum to C. M. Wesson, August 12, 1944, *FR, 1944*, IV, 1114–15; Hull to Harriman, August 17, 1944, *ibid.*, pp. 1115–18; Hazard memorandum to S. P. Spalding, August 26, 1944, FEA Records (USSR Branch), Box 84.

31. Hazard to Wesson, August 12, 1944, *FR, 1944*, IV, 1114–15.

32. For the Treasury Department's recommendations, see Blum, *Years of War*, p. 304; Harriman to Hull, August 30, 1944, *FR, 1944*, IV, 1128; Acheson, *Present at the Creation*, p. 86.

33. Hull to Harriman, September 16, 1944, *FR, 1944*, IV, 1135–45;

Durbrow memorandum to Matthews, September 25, 1944, *ibid.*, pp. 1148–49.

34. Harriman to Stettinius, January 4, 1945, *FR, 1945*, V, 942–43; Harriman to Stettinius, January 6, 1945, *ibid.*, pp. 945–47.

35. For Morgenthau's activities in 1940 and 1941, see Blum, *Years of Urgency*, pp. 129–32, 255–74. His 1944 comment on Russia is quoted in Blum, *Years of War*, p. 262.

36. Morgenthau's negotiations with the Russians at Bretton Woods are covered in detail in Blum, *Years of War*, pp. 252–76; his comment to Roosevelt is in *ibid.*, pp. 277–78.

37. Morgenthau to Roosevelt, January 1, 1945, *FR, 1945*, V, 937–38; Morgenthau to Roosevelt, January 10, 1945, *ibid.*, pp. 948–49; Morgenthau Diary, January 9, 1945, vol. 808, pp. 198–203, Morgenthau MSS.

38. For Morgenthau's activities at Quebec and the cabinet conflict that followed, see Blum, *Years of War*, pp. 327–90.

39. Divine, *Second Chance*, pp. 258–60, Lloyd C. Gardner, *Architects of Illusion: Men and Ideas in American Foreign Policy, 1941–1949*, pp. 46–47, and John L. Gaddis, "The United States and the Origins of the Cold War" (unpublished Ph.D. dissertation), pp. 28–35, discuss generally the American reaction to the events of late 1944 and early 1945. Also *Time*, XLV (January 8, 1945), 13, and Hadley Cantril to Cox, December 29, 1944, Stettinius MSS, reporting data from recent polls.

40. Stettinius Calendar Notes, December 18, 1944, and notes on conversation with Archbishops Spellman, Mooney, and Stritch, December 13, 1944, Stettinius MSS. For protests from Congressmen to the State Department, Stettinius Calendar Notes, December 13, 18, 22, 1944, January 5, 1945, Stettinius MSS. The B2H2 threat is noted in Gaddis, "United States and the Cold War," pp. 29–30. Also Allen Drury, *A Senate Journal, 1943-1945*, pp. 332-34.

41. Joseph C. Grew memorandum to Roosevelt, January 12, 1945, Stettinius MSS; *NAM News*, XI (November 4, 1944), 7; for congressional protests against use of lend-lease in Greece and Eastern Europe, Stettinius Calendar Notes, December 15, 22, 1944, January 2, 1945, Stettinius MSS; for press comment, New York *Journal-American*, January 12, 1945, citing article in *The Pilot*, official organ of the archdiocese of Boston, and Washington *Post*, January 3, 1945.

42. Vandenberg to Harvey Goldman, June 7, 1944, and to Allen Shoenfield, July 3, 1944, Arthur H. Vandenberg Manuscripts, Clements Library, University of Michigan.

43. *Congressional Record,* 78 Cong., 2 Sess., p. 4097.

44. See statement by Kenneth McKellar, *ibid.*, p. 4044; Vandenberg to Shoenfield, July 3, 1944, Vandenberg MSS; Robert A. Taft, "Government Guarantee of Private Investments Abroad," *Vital Speeches*, XI (August 1, 1945), 634–38.

45. For the Quebec agreement and its aftermath, see George C. Herring, Jr., "The United States and British Bankruptcy: Responsibilities Deferred," *Political Science Quarterly*, LXXXVI (June, 1971), 260–80; for the President's pledges to limit lend-lease to military use, see *Seventeenth Report to Congress on Lend-Lease Operations*, November, 1944, pp. 7–8, and New York *Times*, January 7, 1945. Roosevelt's recommendations for repeal of the Johnson Act and expansion of the Export-Import Bank are in Rosenman, *Public Papers*, XIII, 477–78, 553.

46. For the State Department's concern about Soviet activities in Rumania, see Stettinius to Kennan, November 3, 1944, *FR, 1944*, IV, 253. Roosevelt's reaction to Stalin's recognition of the Lublin regime is expressed in his cable to Stalin, December 30, 1944, *FR, 1944*, III, 1444. Harriman appraises Russian objectives and tactics in Eastern Europe in a cable to Stettinius, January 10, 1945, copy in FEA Records, Administrator's File, Box 819.

47. Crowley to Stettinius, January 13, 1945, *FR, Yalta*, pp. 316–17; Clayton to Stettinius, January 20, 1945, *FR, 1945*, V, 964–65; Grew to Harriman, January 26, 1945, *ibid.*, p. 967.

48. Harriman to Stettinius, January 6, 1945, *FR, Yalta*, pp. 313–15; Stimson to Roosevelt, January 3, 1945, *ibid.*, p. 447; minutes of meeting, Secretaries of State, War, Navy, January 9, 1945, Stettinius MSS; Clayton to Stettinius, January 20, 1945, *FR, Yalta*, pp. 318–21; Grew to Harriman, January 26, 1945, *ibid.*, pp. 321–23.

49. Morgenthau Diary, January 10, 1945, vol. 808, p. 310, Morgenthau MSS; Stettinius Calendar Notes, January 10, 1945, Stettinius MSS.

50. Blum, *Years of War*, pp. 305–6.

51. Stettinius Calendar Notes, January 19, 1945, Stettinius MSS; Stettinius notes on conversation with Roosevelt, December 29, 1944, Stettinius MSS.

52. Blum, *Years of War*, p. 306; Grew to Chargé in the Soviet Union, January 26, 1945, *FR, 1945*, V, 969–70.

53. For general discussions of Yalta, see John L. Snell, *The Meaning of Yalta*, Neumann, *Making the Peace*, pp. 126–60, and Feis, *Churchill—Roosevelt—Stalin*, pp. 489–558.

54. Smith, *American Diplomacy*, pp. 152–53.

55. Harriman to Stettinius, April 3, 1945, *FR, 1945*, V, 197, and April 6, 1945, *ibid.*, pp. 821–24.

56. Transcript of telephone conversation, Stettinius and Stimson, March 16, 1945, Stettinius MSS.

57. Waldo Heinrichs, *American Ambassador: Joseph C. Grew and the Development of the United States Diplomatic Tradition*, pp. 159, 217–18, 223.

58. Oral communication by Acting Secretary of State to the Ambassador of the Soviet Union, March 3, 1945, *FR, 1945*, V, 985–87.

59. Vandenberg to James V. Oxtoley, November 15, 1944, Vanden-

berg MSS; reports that lend-lease might be used for reconstruction are in *NAM News*, XI (August 5, 1944), 3, New York *Times*, August 6, November 1, 1944, January 10, 26, March 1, 1945. For publication of the French agreement and Congressional reaction, see New York *Times*, February 28, March 1, 3, 4, 1945.

60. House, *Hearings Before the Committee on Foreign Affairs, House of Representatives, on H. R. 2013, A Bill to Extend for One Year the Provision of an Act to Promote the Defense of the United States, March 11, 1941*, 79 Cong., 1 Sess., pp. 49, 53, 139, 141, 162; for private assurances by administration officials, see Charles Taft memorandum to Acheson, February 28, 1945, Department of State Records, 800.24/2-2845; Cox memorandum to Byrnes, March 12, 1945, Cox MSS; Crowley to Vandenberg, April 8, 1945, Cox MSS.

61. Vorys' motives are reported in New York *Times*, March 3, 1945, and stated in a letter to Geoffrey Parsons, March 16, 1945, Vorys MSS. Cox explains the agreement with Republicans in a letter to Byrnes, March 12, 1945, Cox MSS. Arthur Krock commented in New York *Times*, March 14, 1945, that without the amendment extension of lend-lease might have been defeated or delayed indefinitely.

62. Stettinius to Harriman, March 16, 1945, *FR, 1945*, V, 988; memorandum, Grew and Crowley to Roosevelt, March 23, 1945, *ibid.*, p. 991; aide mémoire, Department of State to Embassy of the USSR, March 24, 1945, *ibid.*, pp. 991–93.

63. Eklund, "Adviser to Presidents," Milwaukee *Journal*, August 19, 1969.

64. Harriman to Stettinius, April 11, 1945, *FR, 1945*, V, 996.

65. Davies Journal, March 4, 1945, Davies MSS.

66. New York *Times*, April 3, 1945.

7. THE END OF UNCONDITIONAL AID

1. New York *Times*, May 8, 10, 1945; Kennan, *Memoirs*, pp. 240–42.

2. Herbert Feis, *Between War and Peace: The Potsdam Conference*, pp. 20–21.

3. E. A. Krauss, "Lend-Lease and Postwar Foreign Trade," *Magazine of Wall Street*, LXXIV (April 15, 1944), 14–15, 48–49; "The Coming Battle on Lend-Lease," *Business Week* (November 18, 1944), pp. 15–17; "The Editor Thinks Out Loud," *American Exporter*, CXXXV (December, 1944), 43. The U. S. Chamber of Commerce report is in New York *Times*, November 20, 1944. Resolutions of the National Foreign Trade Council are reported in *American Exporter*, CXXXVI (January, 1945), 104. The National Grange convention is reported in New York *Times*, November 23, 1944.

4. Special Report of the Truman Committee, "Outline of Problems of Reconversion from War Production," November 5, 1943; *Congressional Record*, 78 Cong., 2 Sess., p. 4097.

5. Coakley and Leighton, *Global Logistics and Strategy, 1943–1945*, pp. 656, 688.

6. *Ibid.*, pp. 657–61.

7. Minutes of meeting, Protocol Committee, August 7, 1944, Protocol Committee Records, Box 5; ID, ASF, "Lend-Lease as of September 30, 1945," II, 1040–49; Wesson to Crowley, September 11, 1944, FEA Records, Administrator's File, Box 819.

8. Roosevelt memorandum to department heads, September 9, 1944, *FR, 1944*, III, 57.

9. Currie memorandum, January 29, 1945, Roosevelt MSS, President's Secretary's File: "Crimea Conference."

10. For expressions of concern about this problem, see Wesson to York, April 14, 1945, Protocol Committee Records, Box 17.

11. Coakley and Leighton, *Global Logistics and Strategy, 1943–1945*, pp. 688–90; President to Secretary of State, January 5, 1945, *FR, 1945*, V, 944.

12. Coakley and Leighton, *Global Logistics and Strategy, 1943–1945*, p. 663.

13. *Ibid.;* Patterson to Roosevelt, March 24, 1945, copy in ID, ASF, "Lend-Lease Documentary Supplement," IX; Roosevelt memorandum to Fred Vinson, April 4, 1945, Roosevelt MSS, Confidential File: "Lend-Lease," indicates, however, that the War Department's request to begin planning for post-V-E Day lend-lease had been approved.

14. Burns, *Soldier of Freedom*, pp. 593–94; Drury, *Senate Journal*, pp. 378–409.

15. *Congressional Record*, 79 Cong., 1 Sess., pp. 3198–3202.

16. *Ibid.*, pp. 3218–22.

17. *Ibid.*, pp. 3232–46; Drury, *Senate Journal*, p. 409.

18. *Congressional Record*, 79 Cong., 1 Sess., p. 3246.

19. Notes on Executive Policy meeting, FEA, March 22, 1945, FEA Records, Box 3174; Crowley to Truman, July 6, 1945, FEA Records, Administrator's File, Box 794.

20. Crowley to the editor, *Life*, XXIX (November 14, 1955), 30.

21. Notes on Executive Policy meetings, FEA, March 1, June 7, 1945, FEA Records, Box 3174.

22. Notes on Executive Policy meetings, FEA, March 1, 22, 1945, FEA Records, Box 3174; minutes of meeting, Secretary's Staff Committee, May 9, 1945, Stettinius MSS.

23. York memorandum to Hopkins, April 26, 1945, Protocol Committee Records, Box 17; Deane to Marshall, April 24, 1945, OPD Records, ABC 400.3295 Russia (19 Apr 42), Sec. 3.

24. George A. Lincoln to the Chief of Staff, May 11, 1945, OPD Records, ABC 400.3295 Russia (19 Apr 42), Sec. 3.

25. Acheson, *Present at the Creation*, pp. 106–9.

26. Harold Smith Diary, April 26, 1945, Harold Smith Manuscripts, Roosevelt Library.

27. Coakley and Leighton, *Global Logistics and Strategy, 1943–1945*, p. 664.

28. Department of State, *Report on War Aid*, p. 15; Coakley and Leighton, *Global Logistics and Strategy, 1943–1945*, p. 694.

29. Harriman to Secretary of State, April 3, 1945, *FR, 1945*, V, 197.

30. Harriman to Secretary of State, April 6, 1945, *ibid.*, pp. 821–24.

31. Cabell Phillips, *The Truman Presidency*, p. 79; Stettinius to Harriman, April 14, 1945, *FR, 1945*, V, 212–13.

32. Memorandum of conversation by Bohlen, April 20, 1945, *FR, 1945*, V, 231–34; minutes of meeting, Secretary's Staff Committee, April 20, 1945, *ibid.*, pp. 839–42; minutes of meeting, Secretary's Staff Committee, April 21, 1945, *ibid.*, pp. 842–46.

33. *Ibid.*

34. *Ibid.*

35. For the State Department memorandum, see Harry S. Truman, *Memoirs*, I, 15; Heinrichs, *American Ambassador*, p. 374.

36. Samuel Lubell, *The Future of American Politics*, pp. 11–12.

37. Memorandum of conversation by Bohlen, April 20, 1945, *FR, 1945*, V, 231–34.

38. The April 23 meeting is recorded in Truman, *Memoirs*, I, 77–78; also William Leahy Diary, April 23, 1945, William Leahy Manuscripts, Library of Congress; memorandum by Bohlen of meeting at the White House, April 23, 1945, *FR, 1945*, V, 252–55.

39. *Ibid.*

40. Davies Journal, April 30, 1945, Davies MSS; Truman's meeting with Molotov is described in Truman, *Memoirs*, I, 82, and in more restrained language in Bohlen's memorandum of conversation, April 23, 1945, *FR, 1945*, V, 256–58.

41. Minutes of meeting, Secretary's Staff Committee, April 21, 1945, *FR, 1945*, V, 843–45.

42. *Ibid.;* for background on the Rumanian oil dispute and Harriman's proposals to use lend-lease to indicate American displeasure, see Harriman to Secretary of State, February 21, 1945, *FR, 1945*, V, 649–50.

43. Minutes of meeting, Secretary's Staff Committee, April 20, 1945, *ibid.*, p. 842.

44. Harriman to Secretary of State, April 4, 1945, *ibid.*, pp. 817–20.

45. Minutes of meeting, Secretary's Staff Committee, April 21, 1945, *ibid.*, pp. 844–46; Deane to Marshall, April 24, 1945, OPD Records, ABC 400.3295 Russia (19 Apr 42), Sec. 3; York to Hopkins, April 26,

1945, enclosing draft memorandum for the President dated April 24, 1945, Protocol Committee Records, Box 17.

46. Memorandum of conversation by Bohlen, April 20, 1945, *FR, 1945*, V, 232–34; minutes of meeting, Secretary's Staff Committee, April 20, 1945, *ibid.*, p. 842.

47. Divine, *Second Chance*, p. 290–93.

48. Memorandum of conversation by Bohlen, May 9, 1945, *FR, 1945*, V, 291–92.

49. Notes on Stettinius-Harriman meeting, May 9, 1945, Stettinius MSS; Stettinius to Grew, May 9, 1945, *FR, 1945*, V, 998.

50. Transcript of telephone conversation, Stettinius and Truman, May 10, 1945, Stettinius MSS; the May 10 meeting is recorded in minutes of meeting, Secretary's Staff Committee, May 11, 1945, Stettinius MSS, and Lincoln to Marshall, May 11, 1945, and memorandum by Lincoln, May 11, 1945, OPD Records, ABC 400.3295 Russia (19 Apr 42), Sec. 3.

51. Grew and Crowley memorandum for the President, May 11, 1945, *FR, 1945*, V, 999–1000.

52. *Ibid.;* Lincoln to John Hull, May 13, 1945, and Lincoln memorandum for the record, May 14, 1945, OPD Records, ABC 400.3295 Russia (19 Apr 42), Sec. 3.

53. Minutes of meeting, Secretary's Staff Committee, May 11, 1945, Stettinius MSS; Stimson Diary, May 11, 1945, Stimson MSS.

54. Memorandum of conversation, Grew and Crowley, May 11, 1945, Joseph C. Grew Manuscripts, Houghton Library, Harvard University; Truman, *Memoirs*, I, 228; Acting Secretary of State to Chargé of the Soviet Union, May 12, 1945, *FR, 1945*, V, 1000–1.

55. Minutes of meeting, Protocol Subcommittee on Shipping, May 12, 1945, Records of the Army Service Forces, Director of Matériel File, General Correspondence, Gen. Edgerton's Lend-Lease File, USSR Folder, Box 5. See also John Hazard Journal, May 12, 1945, John N. Hazard Manuscripts (in possession of Mr. Hazard, New York). The subcommittee's instructions are in Hutchings' cable to War Shipping Administration, Naples, May 12, 1945, Protocol Committee Records, Box 17.

56. Hazard Journal, May 14, 1945, Hazard MSS; memorandum of conversation, Grew and Chargé of the USSR, May 12, 1945, Department of State Records, 861.24/5-1245.

57. Hazard Journal, May 12, 1945, Hazard MSS; minutes of meeting, Secretary's Staff Committee, May 14, 1945, Stettinius MSS; transcript of telephone conversation, Gen. Hull and Gen. York, May 12, 1945, OPD Records, ABC 400.3295 Russia (19 Apr 42), Sec. 3.

58. For Eremin's complaints, see Hazard Journal, May 14, 1945, Hazard MSS; the official Russian response is in Chargé of the USSR to Acting Secretary of State, May 16, 1945, *FR, 1945*, V, 1003. Stalin's protests are in Sherwood, *Roosevelt and Hopkins*, pp. 894–96.

59. Sherwood, *Roosevelt and Hopkins*, p. 896.

60. Memorandum of conversation, Harriman and Mikoyan, June 11, 1945, *FR, 1945*, V, 1018–21.

61. Edward R. Stettinius, Jr., *Roosevelt and the Russians*, p. 318; Truman, *Memoirs*, I, 227–28.

62. Truman, *Memoirs*, I, 228–29.

63. Gar Alperovitz, *Atomic Diplomacy*, pp. 19–40; Barton J. Bernstein, "American Foreign Policy and the Origins of the Cold War," in Bernstein (ed), *Politics and Policies of the Truman Administration*, pp. 27–28. See also Kolko, *Politics of War*, pp. 397–98, and Gardner, *Architects of Illusion*, p. 66.

64. Washington *Post*, May 15, 1945. Also transcript of radio broadcast by Raymond Gram Swing, May 14, 1945, Raymond Gram Swing Manuscripts, Library of Congress.

8. THE END OF LEND-LEASE TO RUSSIA

1. Alperovitz, *Atomic Diplomacy*, pp. 54–71; Gaddis, "Origins of the Cold War," p. 60.

2. Truman, *Memoirs*, I, 110, 257–59; Sherwood, *Roosevelt and Hopkins*, p. 883; Davies Diary, April 27, 1945, Davies Journal, April 30, May 13, 1945, Davies MSS.

3. *Ibid.*

4. Feis, *Between War and Peace*, pp. 76–85. In a conversation with Stettinius on May 23, Truman expressed "great confidence" that Hopkins would be able to "straighten things out with Stalin" and that the Hopkins mission would "unravel a great many things." Stettinius Calendar Notes, May 23, 1945, Stettinius MSS.

5. Minutes of meeting, Protocol Committee, May 15, 1945, Protocol Committee Records, Box 5.

6. Crowley to I. A. Eremin, May 18, 1945, FEA Records, Administrator's File, Box 819; notes on meeting, Protocol Committee, May 15, 1945, Protocol Committee Records, Box 5.

7. USSR Branch, FEA, "Weekly News Letter No. 183," May 26, 1945, FEA Records, Administrator's File, Box 818; Department of State, *Report on War Aid*, pp. 6, 15.

8. Minutes of meeting, Protocol Committee, May 15, 1945, Protocol Committee Records, Box 5.

9. Sherwood, *Roosevelt and Hopkins*, pp. 894–96.

10. Harriman to Grew, May 30, 1945, *FR, 1945*, V, 1008–9.

11. Memorandum of conversation, Harriman and Mikoyan, June 11, 1945, *ibid.*, pp. 1018–21.

12. Neumann, *After Victory*, p. 165; Feis, *Between War and Peace*, pp. 102–11, 117–22.

13. *Ibid.*, pp. 122–23.

14. Deane to Protocol Committee, June 8, 1945, *FR*, *1945*, V, 1012–14.

15. Harriman to Protocol Committee, June 11, 1945, *ibid.*, pp. 1016–18, Harriman to Grew, June 12, 1945, *ibid.*, pp. 1025–26.

16. For the growth of the spirit of reconversion, see "Half-War, Half-Peace," *Time*, XLV (June 4, 1945), 19, and "One War To Go," *Fortune*, XXXI (June, 1945), 281–82; Vinson's reports of business pressures are recorded in Leahy Diary, May 15, 1945, Leahy MSS; for general summaries of the supply problem in the summer of 1945, see Civilian Production Administration, *Industrial Mobilization for War*, I, 860; for difficulties in procuring supplies for lend-lease, see Hazard Journal, June and July, 1945, *passim*, FEA Records (USSR Branch).

17. *Congressional Record*, 79 Cong., 1 Sess., pp. 4689–4700; Washington *Post*, May 18, 1945.

18. Reps. Chiperfield, Vorys, Mundt, Jonkman, and Smith, to Truman, May 31, 1945, copy in Vorys MSS.

19. Grew's reaction to the senators' charges is in minutes of meeting, Secretary's Staff Committee, May 18, 1945, Stettinius MSS; Truman's reaction to the letter from the Republican representatives is in *Memoirs*, I, 231–32; Acheson, *Present at the Creation*, p. 107, and Drury, *Senate Journal*, pp. 430–60, convey the administration's concern about Congress and its efforts to conciliate leaders of both parties.

20. Washington *Post*, June 5, 1945; Coakley and Leighton, *Global Logistics and Strategy, 1943–1945*, p. 664; minutes of meeting, Secretary's Staff Committee, May 9, 1945, Stettinius MSS; H. Duncan Hall, *North American Supply*, pp. 454–55; the Churchill cable is quoted in Truman, *Memoirs*, I, 230–31.

21. Cox Diary, May 12, 1945, Cox memorandum to Crowley, May 14, 1945, Cox MSS; Hazard to Spalding, June 6, 1945, FEA Records (USSR Branch), Box 87; Smith Diary, May 21, 1945, Smith MSS.

22. Harriman to Hopkins, June 21, 1945, *FR*, *1945*, V, 1026.

23. For the Protocol Committee's approval of the Deane-Harriman proposals, see Lincoln to Assistant Secretary of War, June 19, 1945, OPD Records, ABC 400.3295 Russia (19 Apr 42), Sec. 3.

24. European Division, Department of State, "Summary of Current Foreign Developments," June 4, 1945, Stettinius MSS; JDB memorandum to Lincoln, June 9, 1945, OPD Records, ABC 400.3295 Russia (19 Apr 42), Sec. 3; Crowley to Secretary of State, June 12, 1945, *FR*, *1945*, V, 1023–25; Acting Secretary of State to Harriman, June 23, 1945, *ibid.*, pp. 1026–27.

25. Crowley to Secretary of State, June 12, 1945, *FR*, *1945*, V, 1023–25.

26. York to Hopkins, July 11, 1945, Protocol Committee Records, Box 17.

27. European Division, Department of State, "Summary of Current Foreign Developments," May 31, 1945, Stettinius MSS; Grew to Harriman, June 23, 1945, *FR, 1945*, V, 1026–27.

28. On Leahy, see Delbert Clark, "Sailor, Diplomat, Strategist," New York *Times Magazine*, (November 29, 1942), p. 6; Nauticus, "The President's Admiral," *New Republic*, CVII (November 9, 1942), 605–7; *Time*, XLV (May 28, 1945), 14–15. Leahy's anti-Soviet speech and subsequent apology are reported in New York *Times*, July 1, 1937. His attitudes toward Britain and Russia in 1945 are noted in Feis, *Between War and Peace*, pp. 82–83, 126, and in Davies Diary, August 1, 1945, Davies MSS.

29. Leahy, *I Was There*, p. 377; Leahy Diary, June 29, July 2, 1945, Leahy MSS.

30. Alperovitz, *Atomic Diplomacy*, pp. 106–16.

31. See especially minutes of meeting at the White House, June 18, 1945, *FR, Conference of Berlin*, I, 903–10.

32. Grew to Chargé of the Soviet Union, June 27, 1945, *FR, 1945*, V, 1028–29.

33. For the deliberations on Churchill's appeal, see minutes of meeting, Secretary's Staff Committee, May 31, 1945, and European Division, Department of State, "Summary of Current Foreign Developments," June 7, 1945, Stettinius MSS; ID, ASF, "Lend-Lease as of September 30, 1945," I, 308–10; Crowley's and Leahy's opposition is recorded in Leahy, *I Was There*, pp. 370, 372–73, 376–77, and Leahy Diary June 29, July 2, 1945, Leahy MSS; the President's directive of July 5 is in *FR, Conference of Berlin*, I, 818.

34. York to Hopkins, July 11, 1945, Protocol Committee Records, Box 17.

35. *FR, Conference of Berlin*, II, 1186–87.

36. USSR Branch, FEA, "Status of the Soviet Aid Program as of July 31, 1945," FEA Records; Secretary of War to President, August 11, 1945, OPD Records, OPD 400.3295 Russia SPLIM 031.1.

37. Grew to Harriman, June 9, 1945, *FR, 1945*, V, 1014–15; Wesson to M. S. Stepanov, July 25, 1945, FEA Records, Administrator's File, Box 818.

38. Hazard Diary, August 10, 11, 1945, Hazard MSS; memorandum by W. M. Martin, n.d., copy in Cox MSS.

39. New York *Times*, August 16, 1945; for background on Crowley's press conference and further evidence of his determination to end lend-lease as quickly as possible, see Oral History Interview with Roger Tubby (Director of Information, FEA), Truman Library. Martin to Rudenko, August 16, 1945, FEA Records (USSR Branch), Box 89; Hazard Diary, August 16, 1945, Hazard MSS.

40. Leahy Diary, August 17, 1945, Leahy MSS.

41. Memorandum attached to memorandum from Frank Fetter to

Acheson, August 27, 1945, Department of State Records, 800.24/2745; the JCS directive is in *FR, 1945*, VII, 558–59.

42. Hazard Journal, August 10, 1945, FEA Records (USSR Branch), Box 89; Cox Diary, August 19, 1945, Cox MSS; J. A. Maxwell memorandum, August 17, 1945, Department of State Records, 800.24/8–1745.

43. Hazard Journal, August 17, 1945, FEA Records (USSR Branch), Box 139.

44. Hazard to Col. Morgan Sibbett, August 17, 1945, FEA Records (USSR Branch), Box 153.

45. New York *Times*, August 24, 1945.

46. Memorandum by Willis C. Armstrong, August 25, 1945, FEA Records (USSR Branch), Box 153; USSR Branch, FEA, "Weekly News Letter No. 197," September 1, 1945, FEA Records (USSR Branch), Box 86; USSR Branch, FEA, "Weekly News Letter No. 198." September 8, 1945, FEA Records (USSR Branch), Box 153; New York *Times*, August 23, 1945.

47. For the British reaction, see especially Richard C. Gardner, *Sterling-Dollar Diplomacy*, pp. 184–87.

48. Truman's defense is in *Memoirs*, I, 475–76; for the revisionist critique see Alperovitz, *Atomic Diplomacy*, pp. 223–24, and Kolko, *Politics of War*, p. 500.

49. Memorandum by Assistant Chief of the Division of Lend-Lease and Surplus War Property, August 21, 1945, *FR, 1945*, V, 1032–33.

50. *The Economist*, CXLIX (August 18, 1945), 224, 230.

51. Cantril, *Public Opinion*, p. 415; of sixty-seven letters in the FEA files, fifty-eight approved the administration's actions. See Herbert Willet to Crowley, September 7, 1945, FEA Records, Box 794. Correspondence in the Truman Manuscripts, Official File: "Lend-Lease," runs about two to one in favor of the decision. The survey of press opinion is based on a large collection of clippings in FEA files. The Bloom and Colmer statements are quoted in Gardner, *Sterling-Dollar Diplomacy*, p. 185.

52. Charles Ross to Arthur Krock, October 17, 1945, Charles Ross Manuscripts, Truman Library; Acheson, *Present at the Creation*, p. 122.

9. AID TO RUSSIA AND THE ORIGINS OF
THE COLD WAR

1. Byrnes to Clayton, September 24, 1946, *FR, 1946*, VII, 223.

2. For general discussions of American attitudes toward the USSR in the late summer of 1945, see Gaddis, "United States and the Origins of the Cold War," pp. 75, 108–10, and "U. S. Opinion of Russia, "*Fortune*, XXXII (September, 1945), 233–34. For comment on the atomic

bomb and Soviet-American cooperation, see Marquis Childs, Washington *Post*, August 8, 1945, and Barnet Nover, Washington *Post*, August 9, 1945.

3. For representative State Department protests, see *FR, Conference of Berlin*, I, 359, and Durbrow to Matthews, May 30, 1945, *FR, 1945*, V, 852–53. Herbert Feis, *From Trust to Terror*, pp. 44–54, summarizes official attitudes after V-J Day.

4. The Soviet request is reported in Roy F. Hendrickson to Clayton, July 30, 1945, *FR, 1945*, II, 1001. Gustafson, "Congress and Foreign Aid," pp. 1–140, Allan Nevins, *Herbert H. Lehman and His Era*, pp. 221–70, and George Woodbridge *et al, UNRRA: The History of the United Nations Relief and Rehabilitation Administration*, I, 1–43, discuss the founding and early operations of UNRRA.

5. Nevins, *Lehman*, pp. 266–67; Childs in Washington *Post*, August 3, 1945.

6. Gustafson, "Congress and Foreign Aid," pp. 140–70.

7. Grew to Kirk, July 17, 1945, *FR, 1945*, II, 993; Clayton to Byrnes, Grew, and Acheson, August 6, 1945, *ibid.*, pp. 1003–4; Nevins, *Lehman*, p. 267; Childs, Washington *Post*, August 3, 1945.

8. Clayton to Byrnes, Grew, and Acheson, August 6, 1945, *FR, 1945*, II, 1003–4.

9. Grew to Clayton, August 7, 1945, *ibid.*, pp. 1005–6.

10. Harriman to Byrnes, August 9, 1945, *ibid.*, p. 1008.

11. Clayton to Byrnes, August 6, 1945, *ibid.*, p. 1004.

12. John G. Winant to Byrnes, September 5, 1945, *ibid.*, p. 1025; Acheson to Harriman, September 8, 1945, *ibid.*, pp. 1025–27.

13. *Ibid.*

14. Harriman to Grew, August 29, 1945, *ibid.*, pp. 1022–24.

15. Woodbridge, *UNRRA*, II, 232; Werth, *Russia at War*, pp. 784–85, 863–64, 1004–6.

16. Acheson to Harriman, September 8, 1945, *FR, 1945*, II, 1025–26.

17. *Ibid.*

18. Byrnes to Harriman, August 20, 1945, *FR, 1945*, V, 1031–32; Rudenko to Crowley, August 28, 1945, *ibid.*, pp. 1034–35.

19. Crowley to Rudenko, October 15, 1945, *ibid.*, p. 1043; for the 3 (c) negotiations, see Crowley to Rudenko, September 4, 24, October 3, 1945, FEA Records, Administrator's File, Box 819.

20. Clayton to Land, October 31, 1945, *FR, 1945*, V, 1046.

21. Memorandum by Collado, April 19, 1945, *ibid.*, pp. 997–98.

22. Harriman to Grew, May 30, 1945, *ibid.*, pp. 1008–9; Grew to Harriman, June 2, 1945, *ibid.*, 1011–12; Department of State, "Summary of Current Foreign Developments," June 13, 1945, Stettinius MSS.

23. New York *Times*, July 12, 18, 21, August 5, 1945.

24. Minutes of meeting, FEA and Russian Purchasing Commission, August 28, 1945, FEA Records, Administrator's File, Box 819; Rudenko

to Crowley, August 28, 1945, *FR, 1945*, V, 1034–36; Crowley to Harriman, August 31, 1945, *ibid.*, pp. 1036–37.

25. Crowley to National Advisory Council, September 12, 1945, *FR, 1946*, I, 1403–4; Vinson to Truman, undated (ca. September 1945), *ibid.*, 1407–8; minutes of meeting, National Advisory Council, September 27, 1945, *ibid.*, 1409–10.

26. Memorandum of conversation, Hooker and Flory, September 24, 1945, Department of State Records, 861.51/9-2445; Byrnes to Crowley, undated, *FR, 1946*, I, 1402–3; Crowley to Byrnes, September 11, 1945, FEA Records, Administrator's File, Box 850; minutes of meeting, National Advisory Council, September 27, 1945, *FR, 1946*, I, 1409–10.

27. Significantly, the National Advisory Council and the President in September approved a loan of $1 billion to Russia "in principle" and did not refer specifically to the August 28 note. For references to the August 28 meeting as a "preliminary" discussion, see Clayton to Harriman, November 30, 1945, *FR, 1945*, V, 1048 and New York *Times*, January 18, 1946. At a meeting of the National Advisory Council on January 29, 1946, Marriner Eccles of the Federal Reserve Board commented that the Russians had never presented a "formal application" for a loan. See *FR, 1946*, I, 1417. Apparently even William McChesney Martin was not informed of the Soviet note for in early February he had to call Crowley to learn the details of the Soviet request. Hazard Diary, February 8, 1946, Hazard Papers.

28. Willis C. Armstrong to author, July 8, 1971.

29. Cantril, *Public Opinion*, pp. 213–14; *Fortune*, XXXII (July, 1945), 110.

30. For the London Conference, see Gardner, *Architects of Illusion*, pp. 89–98, Gaddis, "United States and the Origins of the Cold War," pp. 73–4, and Sulzberger, New York *Times*, October 8, 1945.

31. Stettinius Calendar Notes, September 28, 1945, Stettinius MSS; Davies Journal, October 9, 1945, Davies MSS; James F. Byrnes, *Speaking Frankly*, pp. 104–5; Walter Millis (ed.), *The Forrestal Diaries*, pp. 101–2; Truman's Navy Day address is printed in Walter Lafeber, *The Origins of the Cold War, 1941–1947*, pp. 69–72. Despite the belligerent tone of this speech, Truman still appears at this date to have been optimistic about the future of Soviet-American relations. On October 22, he conceded to Stettinius that the end of the war had brought "real problems" between the two nations, but he had "every hope that we could work them out amicably if we gave ourselves time." Stettinius Calendar Notes, October 22, 1945, Stettinius MSS.

32. Byrnes's statement is quoted in Paterson, "Abortive Loan," p. 84; Sulzberger, New York *Times*, October 8, 24, 1945; Clayton to Vinson, November 7, 1945, Department of State Records, William Clayton Reading File, Lot 148, Box 13590.

33. New York *Times*, November 13, 19, 1945; Eleanor Roosevelt to Truman, November 20, 1945, cited in Gardner, *Architects of Illusion*,

p. 129; Vandenberg to John Foster Dulles, December 19, 1945, Esther Tufty column, December 17, 1945, Vandenberg MSS.

34. Transcript of press conference, December 7, 1945, *Public Papers of the Presidents: Harry S. Truman, 1945*, p. 527; John Hazard Journal, December 10, 1945, FEA Records (USSR Branch), Box 139.

35. New York *Times*, January 17, 18, 1946.

36. Memorandum by Collado, February 4, 1946, *FR, 1946*, VI, 823–24; Hazard Journal, February 5, 1946, FEA Records (USSR Branch), Box 139.

37. Hazard Journal, February 8, 1946, FEA Records (USSR Branch), Box 139; Secretary of State to Chargé of the Soviet Union, February 21, 1946, *FR, 1946*, VI, 828–29.

38. New York *Times*, March 2, 3, 1946.

39. New York *Herald-Tribune*, March 3, 1946; Paterson, "Abortive Loan," p. 86; Hazard Diary, February 1, 5, 1946, Hazard MSS.

40. Feis, *Trust to Terror*, p. 73; minutes of meeting, National Advisory Council, February 7, 1946, *FR, 1946*, I, 1421; minutes of meeting, National Advisory Council, January 29, 1946, *ibid.*, 1418.

41. Gardner, *Sterling-Dollar Diplomacy*, pp. 237–38; New York *Times*, February 1, 8, 1946.

42. Vandenberg to Dulles, December 19, 1945, Vandenberg MSS; *Christian Science Monitor*, January 19, 1946; Collado memorandum, February 4, 1946, *FR, 1946*, VI, 823–24; minutes of meeting, National Advisory Council, January 29, 1946, *FR, 1946*, I, 1417; New York *Times*, February 12, March 3, 1946.

43. Harriman to Byrnes, December 11, 1945, *FR, 1945*, V, 1049.

44. Harriman to Byrnes, January 19, 1946, *FR, 1946*, VI, 820.

45. Durbrow to Acheson, January 21, 1946, *ibid.*, pp. 820–21.

46. Acheson to Byrnes, January 22, 1946, *ibid.*, p. 822; Harriman memorandum, November 14, 1945, quoted in Paterson, "Abortive Loan," p. 85; Durbrow memorandum, January 21, 1946, *FR, 1946*, VI, pp. 820–21; Collado memorandum, February 4, 1946, *ibid.*, pp. 823–24.

47. Leahy Diary, December 28, 29, 1945, January 1, 1946, Leahy MSS; Truman, *Memoirs*, I, 552.

48. The best discussion of the origins and meaning of the "get tough" policy is in Gaddis, "United States and the Origins of the Cold War," pp. 212–55.

49. Leahy Diary, February 20, 1946, Leahy MSS; Gaddis, "United States and the Origins of the Cold War," pp. 245–46; New York *Times*, March 1, 1946.

50. Gaddis, "United States and the Origins of the Cold War," pp. 245–46.

51. Secretary of State to Chargé of the Soviet Union, February 21, 1946, *FR, 1946*, VI, 828–29.

52. For business attitudes toward postwar aid for the USSR, see New York *Times*, November 13, 1945, January 31, 1946, Herbert Bratter, "Preview of That Loan to Russia," *Nation's Business*, XXXIV (March, 1946), 60–66. A poll of businessmen taken by *Modern Industry* in the summer of 1946 indicated that 82.8 percent opposed a loan to the USSR and only 17.2 percent favored it. See "Landslide Vote Buries Russian Loan," *Modern Industry*, XII (August 15, 1946), 134. For representative statements by Republican and Democratic congressmen, see New York *Times*, February 10, March 9, 16, 1946, Paterson, "Abortive Loan," pp. 84–85, and Gaddis, "United States and the Origins of the Cold War," p. 163. American foreign economic policy is discussed in Gardner, *Architects of Illusion*, and in Thomas G. Paterson, "The Quest for Peace and Prosperity: International Trade, Communism, and the Marshall Plan," in Bernstein, *Politics and Policies*, pp. 78–105. The best official statement of the relationship between loans and U. S. foreign economic policy is *Foreign Loan Policy of the United States*, House Doc. No. 489, 79 Cong., 2 Sess., March 1, 1946.

53. For American policies toward Britain during and immediately after the war, see Gardner, *Sterling-Dollar Diplomacy*, pp. 1–223, Gardner, *Architects of Illusion*, especially pp. 113–38, and Kolko, *Politics of War*, pp. 242–313.

54. Ulam, *Expansion and Coexistence*, pp. 401–2.

55. For representative Soviet comment on the issues raised by the United States in the loan discussions, see I. Taigin, "Development Democracy in the East European Countries," *New Times*, X (May 15, 1946), 7–9; Z. Lipatov, "The Balkans, Old and New," *New Times*, XII (June 15, 1946), 9–11; N. Sergeyeva, "Different Attitudes Toward the Vanquished Countries," *New Times*, XVII (September 1, 1946), 3–7. Also V. M. Molotov, speech of October 10, 1946, in *Problems of Foreign Policy, Speeches and Statements, April, 1945–November, 1948*, pp. 210–16.

56. Chargé of the Soviet Union to Secretary of State, March 15, 1946, *FR, 1946*, VI, 829–30.

57. Hazard Journal, March 18, 1946, FEA Records (USSR Branch), Box 139; Secretary of State to Chargé of the Soviet Union, April 18, 1946, *FR, 1946*, VI, 834–36; New York *Times*, April 21, 1946; Chargé of the Soviet Union to Secretary of State, May 17, 1946, *FR, 1946*, VI, 841–42.

58. For the Paris Peace Conference, see Gardner, *Architects of Illusion*, pp. 105–7; John C. Campbell, *The United States in World Affairs, 1945–1947*, pp. 118–25; on the Vandenberg resolution, Jay C. Hayden column, May 24, 1946, clipping in Vandenberg MSS.

59. New York *Times*, June 23, 1946; *Congressional Record*, 79 Cong., 2 Sess., p. 8824.

60. Walter Bedell Smith to Byrnes, July 18, 1946, *FR, 1946*, VI,

768; "American Generosity," *New Times,* XII (June 15, 1946), 14, and "Starvation Strategy," *New Times,* XI (June 1, 1946), 19.

61. For full documentation on the French loan, see *FR, 1946,* V, 413–42.

62. For the relationship between the French and Russian loans, see minutes of meeting, National Advisory Council, April 25, 1946, *FR, 1946,* I, 1430–31, and minutes of meeting, National Advisory Council, May 6, 1946, *ibid.,* 1432–33. George F. Luthringer to Clayton, May 23, 1946, *FR, 1946,* VI, 842–43.

63. New York *Times,* June 16, 1946; Secretary of State to Embassy of the Soviet Union, June 13, 1946, *FR, 1946,* VI, 844–46; *Public Papers: Harry S. Truman, 1946,* p. 351; *FR, 1946,* I, 1435–36.

64. Alonzo L. Hamby, "Henry A. Wallace, the Liberals, and Soviet-American Relations," *Review of Politics,* XXX (April, 1968), 153–69. Wallace's letter to Truman was later printed in Henry A. Wallace, "The Path to Peace with Russia," *New Republic,* CXV (September 30, 1946), 401–6.

65. Truman recalls his reaction to the Wallace letter in *Memoirs,* I, 556–57; for the crisis of mid-August, see especially Acheson, *Present at the Creation,* pp. 194–96, Millis, *Forrestal Diaries,* pp. 191–93.

66. Acheson, *Present at the Creation,* p. 195; on Wallace's dismissal from the cabinet, see Truman, *Memoirs,* I, 557–59.

67. The Clifford memorandum is printed in full in Arthur Krock, *Memoirs: Sixty Years on the Firing Line,* pp. 225–31, 421–82.

68. Krock, *Memoirs,* pp. 230–31; Byrnes to Clayton, September 24, 1946, *FR, 1946,* VII, 223; Forrestal Diary, September 25, 1946, Millis, *Forrestal Diaries,* p. 210.

69. Byrnes to Clayton, August 30, 1946, *FR, 1946,* VI, 216–17; Clayton to Laurence Steinhardt, September 28, 1946, *ibid.,* pp. 228–29.

70. Gustafson, "Congress and Foreign Aid," pp. 181–283, discusses the end of UNRRA; *FR, 1946,* VI, 930–68, contains extensive documentation on US reaction to the downing of American aircraft and demands to stop UNRRA shipments to Yugoslavia; Byrnes's statement is quoted in Campbell, *The United States in World Affairs, 1945–1947,* p. 335.

71. For the question of Russian participation in the Marshall Plan, see Joseph M. Jones, *The Fifteen Weeks,* pp. 251–55, Kennan, *Memoirs,* pp. 342–43, and Acheson, *Present at the Creation,* pp. 234–35.

72. Ulam, *Expansion and Coexistence,* p. 437.

73. New York *Times,* February 7, 10, 17, 23, 1947.

74. For representative protests against continued shipment of equipment to the USSR, see statement of Matthew Woll, vice-president of the American Federation of Labor, in New York *Times,* December 4, 1946; "Our Assistance to the Soviet Bloc," *U. S. News,* XXI (Septem-

ber 6, 1946), 15–16; and statements by Republican congressmen reported in New York *Times,* December 28, 1946, February 10, 17, April 19, 1947.

75. New York *Times,* April 20, 1947.

76. The USSR received $249,017,300 of the $250,000,000 originally scheduled for shipment under the UNRRA agreement and $244,000,000 worth of pipeline supplies; the United Kingdom received $4,400,000,000 in credits from V-J Day to the end of 1946, France received $1,950,000,000, the Netherlands $493,000,000, and Italy and Belgium $205,000,000 each. Paterson, "Abortive Loan," pp. 89–92, and Gardner, *Architects of Illusion,* pp. 317–18, are "revisionist" critiques; Maier, "Revisionism and the Cold War," while critical of revisionism, argues that more generous U. S. loan policies might have eased postwar tensions.

77. For Stalin's complaints, see Walter Bedell Smith, *My Three Years in Moscow,* p. 222; Gromyko's statement is in "Stalin's Price for Peace," *United Nations World,* III (August, 1949), 7–9; for Soviet comment on the American position on credits, see statement by Alexander S. Panyushkin, Russian ambassador to the United States, in New York *Times,* January 26, 1948.

NOTES TO CONCLUSION

1. For a discussion of the lend-lease settlement negotiations, 1947–1972, see Appendix.

2. Kolko, *Politics of War,* provides the fullest account of American postwar planning with heavy stress on the economic side. John L. Gaddis, "The Past as Prologue: Franklin D. Roosevelt and the American Vision of the Postwar World," emphasizes the importance of the World War I experience in shaping America's war aims.

3. For Russian mistreatment of oil refinery equipment, see Edwin A. Locke, oral history interview, Truman Library. On aircraft allocations, see Lukas, *Eagles East.*

4. Minutes of meetings, Protocol Committee, May 10, November 10, 1944, Protocol Committee Records, Box 5.

5. Jones, *Roads to Russia,* p. 269, argues that lend-lease made possible Soviet conquest of Eastern Europe. The Khrushchev quote is from "Khrushchev Remembers," p. 68. The American dilemma created by the need for Soviet advance in Europe and fears of Soviet political control over Eastern Europe is cogently discussed in Stephen E. Ambrose, *Rise to Globalism,* pp. 77–78.

6. Samuel P. Huntington, "Foreign Aid for What and for Whom," *Foreign Policy,* I (Winter, 1970–1971), 178.

7. Jones, *Roads to Russia,* pp. 215–39, contains a full and gener-

ally convincing analysis of the value of lend-lease to the Soviet war effort. See also Seaton, *Russo-German War*, pp. 588–90.

8. Feis, *Between War and Peace*, p. 26.

9. Werth, *Russia at War*, pp. 937–38. Stalin's biographer, Isaac Deutscher, argues in much the same vein that "Stalin must, anyhow, have been reluctant to bring his country to that position of relative dependence in which any debtor inevitably finds himself vis-à-vis his creditor." Deutscher, *Stalin*, p. 551.

APPENDIX

1. New York *Times*, December 26, 1946; *Thirty-Second Report to Congress on Lend-Lease Operations* (1951), pp. 5–6.

2. U. S. Note, January 7, 1952, *Department of State Bulletin*, XXVI (January 21, 1952), 86–87; New York *Times*, August 24, 1951, January 10, 1952; *Thirty-Second Report to Congress on Lend-Lease Operations* (1951), pp. 5–6.

3. Secretary of State to Chargé of the Soviet Union, July 26, 1946, *FR, 1946*, VI, 852; U. S. Note, January 7, 1952, *Department of State Bulletin*, XXVI (January 21, 1952), 86–87; *Thirty-Fifth Report to Congress on Lend-Lease Operations* (1954), p. 7.

4. New York *Times*, August 22, 1951, January 10, 1952; Soviet Note, August 21, 1951, *Department of State Bulletin*, XXVI (January 21, 1952), 87–88.

5. New York *Times*, January 30, March 23, 1951.

6. *Pravda*, February 7, 1951, in *Current Digest of the Soviet Press*, III (March 10, 1951), 21–23.

7. *Pravda*, February 7, 1951, in *Current Digest of the Soviet Press*, III (March 10, 1951), 21; New York *Times*, February 14, March 23, 1951.

8. New York *Times*, March 17, 1949.

9. For the return and destruction of lend-lease ships, see New York *Times*, March 27, 1954, April 22, May 28, 1955, March 27, July 3, 1956, and *Thirty-Eighth Report to Congress on Lend-Lease Operations* (1958), pp. 10–15. For the use of Liberty Ships in the Cuban buildup, see New York *Times*, September 29, 1962.

10. *Department of State Bulletin*, XLI (October 19, 1959), 545–48.

11. *Forty-Second Report to Congress on Lend-Lease Operations* (1960), pp. 8–9.

12. New York *Times*, February 18, March 23, April 14, 1972; Louisville *Courier-Journal*, May 27, June 18, August 1, 1972.

13. Louisville *Courier-Journal*, October 19, 1972.

BIBLIOGRAPHY

I. MANUSCRIPTS

A. U. S. GOVERNMENT RECORDS

Department of State. Decimal File, 1941–1945. Record Group 59, National Archives, Washington, D. C.

Department of State. William Clayton Reading File. Lot 148. Box 13590. Department of State, Washington, D. C.

Foreign Economic Administration. Records, 1943–1945. Record Group 169, National Archives, Washington, D.C.

Foreign Economic Administration. Records of the USSR Branch, 1943–1945. Washington National Records Center, Suitland, Maryland.

Office of Lend-Lease Administration. Records, 1941–1943. Record Group 169, National Archives, Washington, D. C.

President's Soviet Protocol Committee. Records,

1941–1945. Franklin D. Roosevelt Library, Hyde Park, New York.
U. S. Army. International Division, Army Service Forces. Records, 1941–1945. Military Records Section, National Archives, Washington, D. C.
U. S. Army. Operations Division, War Department General Staff. Records, 1941–1945. World War II Records, National Archives, Alexandria, Virginia.

B. MANUSCRIPT COLLECTIONS

Arnold, Henry H. Manuscript Division, Library of Congress, Washington, D. C.
Clapper, Raymond. Manuscript Division, Library of Congress, Washington, D. C.
Cox, Oscar S. Franklin D. Roosevelt Library, Hyde Park, New York.
Coy, Wayne. Franklin D. Roosevelt Library, Hyde Park, New York.
Davies, Joseph E. Manuscript Division, Library of Congress, Washington, D. C.
Grew, Joseph C. Houghton Library, Harvard University, Cambridge, Massachusetts.
Hazard, John N. In possession of Mr. Hazard, New York, New York.
Hopkins, Harry L. Franklin D. Roosevelt Library, Hyde Park, New York.
Hull, Cordell. Manuscript Division, Library of Congress, Washington, D. C.
Jones, Jesse. Manuscript Division, Library of Congress, Washington, D.C.
Leahy, William D. Manuscript Division, Library of Congress, Washington, D. C.
Morgenthau, Henry. Franklin D. Roosevelt Library, Hyde Park, New York.
Patterson, Robert P. Manuscript Division, Library of Congress, Washington, D. C.
Roosevelt, Franklin D. Franklin D. Roosevelt Library, Hyde Park, New York.
Ross, Charles. Harry S. Truman Library, Independence, Missouri.
Smith, Harold D. Franklin D. Roosevelt Library, Hyde Park, New York.
Standley, William H. University of Southern California Library, Los Angeles.
Stettinius, Edward R., Jr. University of Virginia Library, Charlottesville, Virginia.
Stimson, Henry L. Yale University Library, New Haven, Connecticut.
Swing, Raymond Gram. Manuscript Division, Library of Congress, Washington, D. C.
Truman, Harry S. Harry S. Truman Library, Independence, Missouri.

Vandenberg, Arthur H. William L. Clements Library, University of Michigan, Ann Arbor, Michigan.
Vorys, John. Manuscript Division, Ohio State Historical Society, Columbus, Ohio.
White, Harry D. Firestone Library, Princeton University, Princeton, New Jersey.

C. INTERVIEWS, ORAL HISTORY, LETTERS
Armstrong, Willis C. Letter to Author, July 8, 1971.
Hazard, John N. Personal Interview, New York, December 30, 1968.
Locke, Edwin A. Oral History Interview, Harry S. Truman Library.
Tubby, Roger. Oral History Interview, Harry S. Truman Library.

II. UNPUBLISHED STUDIES

A. OFFICIAL HISTORIES
International Division, Army Service Forces. "Lend-Lease as of September 30, 1945." 2 vols. Office of the Chief of Military History, Washington, D. C.
International Division, Army Service Forces. "Lend-Lease Documentary Supplement." 10 vols. Office of the Chief of Military History, Washington, D. C.
Office of Lend-Lease Administration and Foreign Economic Administration. "Lend-Lease History." Records of the Foreign Economic Administration, National Archives, Washington, D. C.

B. UNPUBLISHED MANUSCRIPTS
Gaddis, John Lewis. "The United States and the Origins of the Cold War." Unpublished Ph.D. dissertation, Department of History, University of Texas, 1968.
Gustafson, Milton O. "Congress and Foreign Aid: The First Phase, UNRRA, 1943–1947." Unpublished Ph.D. dissertation, Department of History, University of Nebraska, 1966.
Hamby, Alonzo L. "Harry S. Truman and American Liberalism, 1945–1952." Unpublished manuscript in possession of the author.
Herring, George C., Jr. "Experiment in Foreign Aid: Lend-Lease, 1941–1945." Unpublished Ph.D. dissertation, Department of History, University of Virginia, 1965.
Lukas, Richard C. "Air Force Aspects of American Aid to the Soviet Union: The Crucial Years, 1941–1942." Unpublished Ph.D. dissertation, Florida State University, 1963.

III. PUBLIC DOCUMENTS

U. S. *Congressional Record*. 77th through 79th Congresses.

U. S. Department of State. *Foreign Relations of the United States*. Vols. for 1941 through 1946.

U. S. Department of State. *Report on War Aid Furnished by the United States to the U. S. S. R.* 1945.

U. S. Department of State. *Soviet Supply Protocols*. n.d.

U. S. Department of War. *International Aid Statistics, World War II*. 1946.

U. S. House of Representatives, Committee on Foreign Affairs, *Hearings on H. R. 2013, A Bill To Extend for One Year the Provisions of an Act To Promote the Defense of the United States, March 11, 1941*. 79th Cong., 1st Sess., 1945.

U. S. National Advisory Council on International Financial and Monetary Problems. *Foreign Loan Policy of the United States*. 1946.

U. S. President. *Reports to Congress on Lend-Lease Operations*. 1941–1961.

U. S. Senate, Committee on Foreign Relations. *Hearings on H. R. 2013, An Act To Extend for One Year the Provisions of an Act To Promote the Defense of the United States, March 11, 1941*. 1945.

IV. NEWSPAPERS

Chicago *Tribune*
Christian Science Monitor
Louisville *Courier-Journal*
New York *Herald-Tribune*
New York *Journal-American*
New York *Times*
Philadelphia *Dispatch*
Richmond *Times-Dispatch*
St. Louis *Post-Dispatch*
Wall Street Journal
Washington *Post*
Washington *Times-Herald*

V. BOOKS

A. OFFICIAL HISTORIES

Civilian Production Administration, *Industrial Mobilization for War: History of the War Production Board and Predecessor Agencies. Vol.*

I: Program and Administration. Washington: Government Printing Office, 1947.

Coakley, Robert W. and Richard M. Leighton. *Global Logistics and Strategy, 1943–1945.* A vol. in *U. S. Army in World War II: The War Department.* Washington: Office of the Chief of Military History, 1969.

Hall, H. Duncan. *North American Supply.* United Kingdom Civil Series. London: Her Majesty's Stationery Office, 1955.

Hall, H. Duncan and C. C. Wrigley. *Studies of Overseas Supply.* United Kingdom Civil Series. London: Her Majesty's Stationery Office, 1956.

Leighton, Richard M., and Robert W. Coakley. *Global Logistics and Strategy, 1940–1943.* A vol. in *U. S. Army in World War II: The War Department.* Washington: Office of the Chief of Military History, 1955.

Matloff, Maurice. *Strategic Planning for Coalition Warfare, 1943–1944.* A vol. in *U. S. Army in World War II: The War Department.* Washington: Office of the Chief of Military History, 1959.

Morison, Samuel E. *The Two Ocean War.* Boston: Little, Brown, and Co., 1963.

Motter, T. H. Vail. *The Persian Corridor and Aid to Russia.* A vol. in *U. S. Army in World War II: The Middle East Theater.* Washington: Office of the Chief of Military History, 1952.

Voznesensky, Nikolai. *The Economy of the USSR During World War II.* Washington: Public Affairs Press, 1948.

Woodbridge, George, *et al. UNRRA: The History of the United Nations Relief and Rehabilitation Administration.* 3 vols. New York: Columbia University Press, 1950.

B. PUBLISHED CORRESPONDENCE, SPEECHES, AND PAPERS

Molotov, V. M. *Problems of Foreign Policy: Speeches and Statements, April 1945–November 1948.* Moscow, 1949.

Roosevelt, Franklin D. *F. D. R.: His Personal Letters, 1928–1945.* Edited by Elliott Roosevelt. 3 vols. New York: Duell, Sloan and Pearce, 1950.

Truman, Harry S. *Public Papers of the Presidents of the United States: Harry S. Truman, 1945–1947.* 3 vols. Washington: Government Printing Office, 1961–63.

USSR, Ministry of Foreign Affairs. *Correspondence Between the Chairman of the Council of Ministers of the USSR and the Presidents of the USA and the Prime Ministers of Great Britain During the Great Patriotic War of 1941–1945.* Moscow, 1957.

C. MEMOIRS, DIARIES, AUTOBIOGRAPHIES

Acheson, Dean G. *Present at the Creation: My Years in the State Department.* New York: Norton, 1969.

Blum, John M. *From the Morgenthau Diaries: Years of Urgency, 1938–1941.* Boston: Houghton-Mifflin, 1965.

——— *From the Morgenthau Diaries: Years of War, 1941–1945.* Boston: Houghton-Mifflin, 1967.

Byrnes, James F. *All in One Lifetime.* New York: Harper & Row, 1958.

——— *Speaking Frankly.* New York: Harper & Row, 1947.

Churchill, Winston S. *The Second World War.* 6 vols. Boston: Houghton-Mifflin, 1948–53.

Davies, Joseph E. *Mission to Moscow.* New York: Simon & Schuster, 1941.

Deane, John R. *The Strange Alliance: The Story of Our Efforts at Wartime Cooperation with Russia.* New York: Viking Press, 1947.

Drury, Allen. *A Senate Journal, 1943–1945.* New York: McGraw-Hill, 1963.

Harriman, W. Averell. *America and Russia in a Changing World.* New York: Doubleday, 1971.

Hull, Cordell. *The Memoirs of Cordell Hull.* 2 vols. New York: Macmillan, 1948.

Jones, Joseph M. *The Fifteen Weeks: An Inside Account of the Genesis of the Marshall Plan.* New York: Viking Press, 1955.

Jordan, George Racey. *From Major Jordan's Diaries.* New York: Harcourt, Brace, 1952.

Kennan, George F. *Memoirs, 1925–1950.* Boston: Little Brown, 1967.

Krock, Arthur. *Memoirs: Sixty Years on the Firing Line.* New York: Funk and Wagnalls, 1968.

Leahy, William D. *I Was There: The Personal Story of the Chief of Staff to Presidents Roosevelt and Truman Based on His Notes and Diaries Made at the Time.* New York: Whittlesey House, 1950.

Macmillan, Harold. *The Blast of War, 1939–1945.* New York: Harper & Row, 1968.

Maisky, Ivan, *Memoirs of a Soviet Ambassador.* New York: Scribners, 1968.

Martel, Sir Gifford. *The Russian Outlook.* London, 1947.

Millis, Walter (ed.). *The Forrestal Diaries.* New York: Viking Press, 1951.

Rosenman, Samuel I. *Working with Roosevelt.* New York: Harper, 1952.

Sherwood, Robert E. *Roosevelt and Hopkins: An Intimate History.* New York: Harper, 1948.

Smith, Walter Bedell. *My Three Years in Moscow.* Philadelphia: Lippincott, 1949.

Standley, William H., and Arthur A. Ageton. *Admiral Ambassador to Russia.* Chicago: Regnery, 1955.

Stettinius, Edward R., Jr. *Lend-Lease: Weapon for Victory.* New York: Macmillan, 1944.
—— *Roosevelt and the Russians.* New York: Macmillan, 1949.
Truman, Harry S. *Memoirs by Harry S. Truman.* 2 vols. Garden City: Doubleday, 1955.

D. BIOGRAPHIES

Albertson, Dean. *Roosevelt's Farmer: Claude R. Wickard in the New Deal.* New York: Columbia University Press, 1961.
Albion, Robert G. *Forrestal and the Navy.* New York: Columbia University Press, 1962.
Burns, James MacGregor. *Roosevelt: The Soldier of Freedom.* New York: Harcourt Brace Jovanovich, 1970.
Daniels, Jonathan. *The Man of Independence.* Philadelphia: Lippincott, 1950.
Deutscher, Isaac. *Stalin: A Political Biography.* Vintage edition. New York: Alfred A. Knopf, 1960.
Farnsworth, Beatrice. *William C. Bullitt and the Soviet Union.* Bloomington: University of Indiana Press, 1967.
Harrod, Roy F. *The Life of John Maynard Keynes.* London: Macmillan, 1951.
Heinrichs, Waldo. *American Ambassador: Joseph C. Grew and the Development of the United States Diplomatic Tradition.* Boston: Little Brown, 1966.
Nevins, Allan. *Herbert H. Lehman and His Era.* New York: Charles Scribners, 1963.
Phillips, Cabell. *The Truman Presidency.* Pelican edition. Baltimore: Penguin Books, 1969.
Pogue, Forrest C. *George C. Marshall: Ordeal and Hope, 1939–1942.* New York: Viking Press, 1966.

E. GENERAL

Alperovitz, Gar. *Atomic Diplomacy: Hiroshima and Potsdam. The Use of the Atomic Bomb and the American Confrontation with Soviet Power.* Vintage Edition. New York: Random House, Knopf, 1965.
Bailey, Thomas A. *America Faces Russia: Russian-American Relations from Early Times to Our Day.* Ithaca: Cornell University Press, 1950.
Barghoorn, Frederick. *The Soviet Image of the United States: A Study in Distortion.* New York: Harcourt Brace, 1950.
Bernstein, Barton J. (ed.). *Politics and Policies of the Truman Administration.* Chicago: Quadrangle, 1970.
Bishop, Donald. *The Roosevelt-Litvinov Agreements.* Syracuse: Syracuse University Press, 1965.

Browder, Robert Paul. *The Origins of Soviet-American Diplomacy.* Princeton: Princeton University Press, 1953.

Bruner, Jerome S. *Mandate from the People.* New York: Duell, Sloan and Pearce, 1944.

Buchanan, A. Russell. *The United States and World War II.* 2 vols. New York: Harper & Row, 1964.

Campbell, John C. *The United States in World Affairs, 1945–1947.* New York: Harper, 1947.

Cantril, Hadley (ed.). *Public Opinion, 1935–1946.* Princeton: Princeton University Press, 1951.

Cassidy, Henry. *Moscow Dateline, 1941–1943.* Boston: Houghton Mifflin, 1943.

Chadwin, Mark. *The Hawks of World War II.* Chapel Hill: University of North Carolina Press, 1968.

Clark, Alan. *Barbarossa: The Russian-German Conflict, 1941–1945.* New York: Morrow, 1965.

Cole, Wayne S. *America First: The Battle Against Intervention.* Madison: University of Wisconsin Press, 1953.

Crocker, George N. *Roosevelt's Road to Russia.* Chicago: Regnery, 1959.

Dawson, Raymond. *The Decision To Aid Russia, 1941: Foreign Policy and Domestic Politics.* Chapel Hill: University of North Carolina Press, 1959.

Dennett, Raymond, and Joseph Johnson (eds.). *Negotiating with the Russians.* Boston: World Peace Foundation, 1951.

Divine, Robert A. *Causes and Consequences of World War II.* Chicago: Quadrangle, 1969.

———— *The Illusion of Neutrality.* Chicago: University of Chicago Press, 1962.

———— *The Reluctant Belligerent.* New York: John Wiley, 1965.

———— *Roosevelt and World War II.* Baltimore: The Johns Hopkins Press, 1969.

———— *Second Chance: The Triumph of Internationalism in America During World War II.* New York: Atheneum, 1967.

Feis, Herbert. *Between War and Peace: The Potsdam Conference.* Princeton: Princeton University Press, 1960.

———— *Churchill—Roosevelt—Stalin: The War They Waged and the Peace They Sought.* Princeton: Princeton University Press, 1957.

———— *From Trust to Terror: The Onset of the Cold War, 1945–1950.* New York: Norton, 1970.

Flynn, John T. *The Roosevelt Myth.* New York: Devin-Adair, 1948.

Gallagher, Matthew P. *The Soviet History of World War II: Myths, Memories, and Realities.* New York: Praeger, 1963.

Gardner, Lloyd C. *Architects of Illusion: Men and Ideas in American Foreign Policy, 1941–1949.* Chicago: Quadrangle, 1970.

———— *Economic Aspects of New Deal Diplomacy*. Madison: University of Wisconsin Press, 1964.

Gardner, Richard C. *Sterling-Dollar Diplomacy: The Origins and the Prospects of Our International Economic Order*. New York: McGraw-Hill, 1969.

Herz, Martin. *Beginnings of the Cold War*. Bloomington: University of Indiana Press, 1966.

Irving, David. *The Destruction of Convoy PQ 17*. New York: Simon & Schuster, 1968.

Jones, Robert H. *The Roads to Russia: United States Lend-Lease to the Soviet Union*. Norman: University of Oklahoma Press, 1969.

Kerr, Walter. *The Russian Army: Its Men, Its Leaders, and Its Battles*. New York: Knopf, 1944.

Kimball, Warren F. *The Most Unsordid Act: Lend-Lease, 1939–1941*. Baltimore: The Johns Hopkins Press, 1969.

Kolko, Gabriel. *The Politics of War: The World and United States Foreign Policy, 1943–1945*. New York: Knopf, 1969.

Lubell, Samuel. *The Future of American Politics*. 2d rev. ed., New York: Doubleday Anchor Books, 1956.

Lukas, Richard C. *Eagles East: The Army Air Force and the Soviet Union, 1941–1945*. Tallahassee: Florida State University Press, 1970.

McNeill, William Hardy. *America, Britain, and Russia: Their Cooperation and Conflict, 1941–1946*. London: Oxford University Press, 1953.

Neumann, William L. *After Victory: Churchill, Roosevelt, Stalin and the Making of the Peace*. New York: Harper, 1967.

Reynolds, Quentin. *The Curtain Rises*. New York: Random House, 1944.

Salisbury, Harrison. *The 900 Days: The Siege of Leningrad*. New York: Harper & Row, 1969.

Schofield, B. B. *The Russian Convoys*. New York: Ballantine Books, 1967.

Seaton, Albert. *The Russo-German War, 1941–1945*. New York: Praeger, 1971.

Smith, Gaddis. *American Diplomacy During the Second World War*. New York: John Wiley, 1965.

Snell, John L. *The Meaning of Yalta*. Baton Rouge: Louisiana State University Press, 1956.

Snow, Edgar. *People on Our Side*. New York: Random House, 1944.

Ulam, Adam. *Expansion and Coexistence: The History of Soviet Foreign Policy, 1917–1967*. New York: Praeger, 1968.

Werth, Alexander. *Russia at War, 1941–1945*. New York: Dutton, 1964.

Westerfield, H. Bradford. *Foreign Policy and Party Politics: Pearl Harbor to Korea*. New Haven: Yale University Press, 1955.

Williams, William A. *The Tragedy of American Diplomacy.* Delta Edition. New York: Dell Publishing Co., 1962.

Young, Roland. *Congressional Politics in the Second World War.* New York: Columbia University Press, 1956.

VI. ARTICLES

Alexeyev, A. "Lend-Lease—Weapon of Aggressive American Imperialism," *The Current Digest of the Soviet Press,* III (September 8, 1951), 8–10.

"Ambassador Davies," *Fortune,* XVI (October, 1937), 94–98.

"American Generosity," *New Times,* XII (June 15, 1946), 14.

Belair, Felix. "Harry L. Hopkins: Lender and Spender," *Life,* XI (September 22, 1941), 89–99.

Bernstein, Marvin D., and Francis L. Loewenheim. "Aid to Russia: The First Year," in Harold Stein (ed.). *American Civil-Military Decisions: A Book of Case Studies* (Birmingham, 1963), 97–152.

Bess, Demaree. "The General Called the Turn," *Saturday Evening Post,* CCXIV (August 29, 1942), 12, 101–2.

Bratter, Herbert. "Preview of That Loan to Russia," *Nation's Business,* XXXIV (March, 1946), 60–66.

Brewster, Owen. "Don't Blame the British—Blame Us!" *Collier's,* CXII (December 25, 1943), 21, 68, 70.

Bullitt, William C. "How We Won the War and Lost the Peace," *Life,* XXV (August 30, 1948), 83–97.

Butler, Hugh. "Lend-Lease for War Only?", *Nation's Business,* XXXI (May, 1943), 34, 36, 94–95.

Clark, Delbert. "Sailor, Diplomat, Strategist," New York *Times Magazine* (November 29, 1942), 6.

Coy, Wayne. "Get Things Moving—FDR," *The New Republic,* CXIV (April 15, 1946), 546–47.

"A Cure for Complacency," *Nation,* CLV (September 26, 1942), 253–54.

Davis, Forrest. "Roosevelt's World Blueprint," *Saturday Evening Post,* CCXV (April 10, 1943), 20–21, 109–10.

"Does America's Best Chance of Prosperity Lie in Helping Other Countries After the War?" *Free World,* IX (June, 1945), 74–75.

"Dollars and Pounds," *The Economist,* CXL (March 15, 1941), 321.

"The Editor Thinks Out Loud," *American Exporter,* XXXII (February, 1943), 43.

Eklund, Lawrence. "Adviser to Presidents (Leo T. Crowley)," Milwaukee *Journal,* August 17–27, 1969.

"The First Thirty Years," *Time,* XLII (November 29, 1943), 65–66.

"The Fortune Survey," *Fortune,* XXIV (October, 1941), 105–6.

Greeley, John. "Iran in Wartime," *National Geographic,* LXXXIV (August, 1943), 131–59.

"Half-War, Half-Peace," *Time,* XLV (June 4, 1945), 19.

Hamby, Alonzo L. "Henry A. Wallace, The Liberals, and Soviet-American Relations," *Review of Politics,* XXX (April, 1968), 153–69.

"Hand Is Out to Russia," *Fortune,* XXVII (June, 1943), 22–25.

Herring, George C., Jr. "Lend-Lease to Russia and the Origins of the Cold War, 1944–1945," *Journal of American History,* LVI (June, 1969), 93–114.

———— "The United States and British Bankruptcy, 1944–1945: Responsibilities Deferred," *Political Science Quarterly,* LXXXVI (June, 1971), 260–80.

"Joseph E. Davies," *Current Biography, 1942,* pp. 177–80.

Klemmer, Harvey. "Lend-Lease and the Russian Victory," *National Geographic,* LXXXVIII (October, 1945), 499–512.

Krauss, E. A. "Lend-Lease and Postwar Foreign Trade," *Magazine of Wall Street,* LXXIV (April 15, 1944), 14–15, 48–49.

"Khrushchev Remembers, Part II," *Life,* LXIX (December 4, 1970), 48–68.

Lafeber, Walter. "War: Cold," *Cornell Alumni News* (October, 1968), pp. 24–29.

"Landslide Vote Buries Russian Loan," *Modern Industry,* XII (August 15, 1946), 134.

Lasch, Christopher. "The Cold War, Revisited and Re-Visioned," New York *Times Magazine* (January 14, 1968), pp. 26 ff.

"Lend-Lease—A Tool for Planners," *Barrons,* XXIV (March 20, 1944), 3.

Lipatov, Z. "The Balkans, Old and New," *New Times,* XII (June 15, 1946), 9–11.

Lukas, Richard C. "The Velvet Project: Hope and Frustration," *Military Affairs,* XXVIII (Winter, 1964), 145–62.

MacCormac, John. "Diplomat of Global Economics," New York *Times Magazine,* (November 7, 1943), pp. 14–15.

Maier, Charles S. "Revisionism and the Interpretation of Cold War Origins," *Perspectives in American History,* IV (1970), 313–47.

Marshall, Charles Burton. "The Lend-Lease Operation," *The Annals of the American Academy of Political and Social Sciences,* CCXXV (January, 1943), 183–89.

Nauticus, "The President's Admiral," *New Republic,* CVII (November 9, 1942), 605–7.

"New Chief for Ordnance," *Time,* XXXIX (April 13, 1942), 68.

"One War To Go," *Fortune,* XXXI (June, 1945), 281–82.

Paterson, Thomas G. "The Abortive Loan to Russia and the Origins of the Cold War, 1943–1946," *Journal of American History,* LVI (June, 1969), 70–92.

"Postwar Lend-Lease and Jobs: Results of Free World's American Opinion Poll," *Free World*, X (August, 1945), 62–64.

"Private Enterprise," *American Exporter*, XXXIII (December, 1943), 34.

"Readers Vote To End Lend-Lease With the War," *Modern Industry*, VII (March 15, 1945), 10.

Reynolds, Quentin. "Diplomat on the Spot," *Collier's*, CXII (July 24, 1943), 134.

Rogers, Leighton. "Russians Like Our Planes," *Harper's*, CLXXXIX (September, 1944), 314–16.

Roosevelt, Franklin D. "Aid to the Democracies," *Vital Speeches*, VII (April 1, 1941), 355.

Schlesinger, Arthur M., Jr. "Origins of the Cold War," *Foreign Affairs*, XLVI (October 1967), 22–52.

Sergeyeva, N. "Different Attitudes Toward the Vanquished Countries," *New Times*, XVII (September 1, 1946), 3–7.

"Stalin's Price for Peace," *United Nations World*, III (August, 1949), 7–9.

"Starvation Strategy," *New Times*, XI (June 1, 1946), 19.

Stone, I. F. "Capital Thoughts on a Second Front," *Nation*, CLV (October 3, 1942), 288.

Taft, Robert A. "Government Guarantee of Private Investment Abroad," *Vital Speeches*, XI (August 1, 1945), 634–38.

Taigin, I. "Development Democracy in the East European Countries," *New Times*, X (May 15, 1946), 7–9.

"Truth or Diplomacy," *Catholic World*, CLVII (April, 1943), 1–9.

"U. S. Opinion on Russia," *Fortune*, XXXII (September, 1945), 233–34.

Wallace, Henry A. "The Path to Peace with Russia," *New Republic*, CXV (September 30, 1946), 400–6.

"W. Averell Harriman," *Current Biography, 1941*, pp. 366–67.

Willen, Paul. "Who 'Collaborated' with Russia?" *Antioch Review*, XIV (September, 1954), 259–83.

"William H. Standley," *Current Biography, 1942*, pp. 797–99.

"Willkie Speaks Out," *New Republic*, CVII (October 19, 1942), 483.

INDEX